ON THE NATURE OF ORGANIZATIONS

OTHER BOOKS BY PETER M. BLAU

The Dynamics of Bureaucracy
Bureaucracy in Modern Society
Formal Organizations (with Richard Scott)
Exchange and Power in Social Life
The American Occupational Structure (with Otis D. Duncan)
The Structure of Organizations (with Richard Schoenherr)
The Organization of Academic Work

On the Nature of Organizations

PETER M. BLAU

A WILEY-INTERSCIENCE PUBLICATION

JOHN WILEY & SONS

New York • London • Sydney • Toronto

Library of Congress Cataloging in Publication Data

Blau, Peter Michael.
   On the nature of organizations.

   "A Wiley-Interscience publication."
   1.   Organization.   2.   Organizational research.
   3.   Bureaucracy.   I.   Title.

HM131.B592   301.18′32   74–7392
ISBN 0–471–08037–3

Printed in the United States of America

10 9 8 7 6 5 4

To

Judith R. Blau

Acknowledgments

Permission to reprint the following papers is gratefully acknowledged:

Chapter 1. "The Study of Formal Organization," Chapter 5 (pp. 54–65), *American Sociology: Perspectives, Problems, Methods*, edited by Talcott Parsons, © 1968 by Basic Books, Inc., Publishers, New York.

Chapter 2. "Critical Remarks on Weber's Theory of Authority," *The American Political Science Review* 57, No. 2, June 1963, 305–316; reprinted by permission of *The American Political Science Review*.

Chapter 3. "Formal Organization: Dimensions of Analysis," *The American Journal of Sociology* 63, No. 1, July 1957, 58–69; copyright 1957 by the University of Chicago.

Chapter 4. "Structural Effects," *American Sociological Review* 25, No. 2, April 1960, 178–193; reprinted by permission of the American Sociological Association.

Chapter 5 and pp. 5—8. "The Research Process in the Study of the Dynamics of Bureaucracy," Chapter 2 (pp. 18–22, 24–32, 33–36), *Sociologists at Work: Essays in the Craft of Social Research*, edited by Philip E. Hammond, copyright © 1964 by Basic Books, Inc., Publishers, New York.

Chapter 6. "The Comparative Study of Organizations," *Industrial and Labor Relations Review* 18, No. 3, April 1965, 323–338; copyright © 1965 by Cornell University. All rights reserved.

Chapter 7. "Co-Operation and Competition in a Bureaucracy," *The American Journal of Sociology* 59, No. 6, May 1954, 530–536; copyright 1954 by the University of Chicago.

Chapter 8. "Statistical Records of Performance," Chapter 3 (pp. 36–49), *The Dynamics of Bureaucracy* (revised edition), 1963; copyright 1955 by the University of Chicago.

110142

Chapter 9. "Consultation Among Colleagues," Chapter 7 (pp. 121–123, 126–127, 142–143), *The Dynamics of Bureaucracy* (revised edition), 1963; copyright 1955 by the University of Chicago.

Chapter 10. "Orientation Toward Clients in a Public Welfare Agency," *Administrative Science Quarterly* **5**, No. 3, December 1960, 341–361; © 1960 by the Graduate School of Business and Public Administration, Cornell University.

Chapter 11. "A Theory of Social Integration," *The American Journal of Sociology* **65**, No. 6, May 1960, 545–556; copyright 1960 by the University of Chicago.

Chapter 12. "Interaction: Social Exchange," *International Encyclopedia of the Social Sciences* **7**, 1968, 452–458; copyright © 1968 by Crowell Collier and Macmillan, Inc.

Chapter 13. With Wolf V. Heydebrand and Robert E. Stauffer, "The Structure of Small Bureaucracies," *American Sociological Review* **31**, No. 2, April 1966, 179–191; reprinted by permission of the American Sociological Association.

Chapter 14. "The Hierarchy of Authority in Organizations," *The American Journal of Sociology* **73**, No. 4, January 1968, 453–467; copyright 1968 by the University of Chicago.

Chapter 15. "The Comparative Study of American Universities and Colleges," Chapter 2 (pp. 33–34); "Variables and Simple Correlations for Individual Faculty Members," Appendix D (pp. 297–298); "Orientations to Academic Work and Institution," Chapter 5 (pp. 110–120, 124–128, 130), *The Organization of Academic Work*, 1973; copyright © 1973, John Wiley & Sons, Inc., Publishers, New York.

Chapter 16. "Contexts of Organizations," Chapter 8 (pp. 206–207, 211–214, 215–216, 218–220, 221–227) and Chapter 6 (pp. 151–152), *The Structure of Organizations* (with Richard A. Schoenherr), 1971; copyright © 1971 by Basic Books, Inc., Publishers, New York.

Chapter 17. "A Formal Theory of Differentiation in Organizations," *American Sociological Review* **35**, No. 2, April 1970, 201–218; reprinted by permission of the American Sociological Association.

Chapter 18. "Interdependence and Hierarchy in Organizations," *Social Science Research* **1**, No. 1, April 1972; copyright © 1972 by Seminar Press, Inc.

PETER M. BLAU

New York, New York
June 1974

Contents

Introduction

The papers collected in this book deal with theory and research that seeks to clarify the nature of formal organizations. My approach to the study of organizations, and to sociological inquiry generally, has changed in the course of the two decades during which these pieces were written. This change is reflected in the difference in theoretical focus between the papers in Part Two and those in Part Three, a difference that is explicated in the discussions of various conceptual and methodological approaches to the study of organizations in several chapters of Part One. Despite this change, there is some underlying continuity in my theoretical orientation; at least, I think so.

Contrasting Theoretical Approaches

My sociological objective throughout has been to contribute to a better understanding of the social structure of interrelated positions that characterize all collectivities, from small groups to entire societies, including, naturally, formal organizations. This conception of social structure in terms of differentiated positions and social relations between their incumbents is narrower and less abstract than the one prevalent in much sociological theorizing in terms of common values, social institutions, or functional systems. Although I did not explicitly formulate it earlier, this view of social structure has been implicit in most of my work, and it provides a continuing thread in the face of changes in theoretical emphasis and methodological framework. Such an interest in social structure involves studying the external constraints the social relations in a group exert upon its members, as exemplified by the analysis of structural effects in Chapters 4 and 15. It also involves investigating the processes of social interaction in which interpersonal relations find expression and which manifest the patterns of social relations characterizing group structures, as exemplified by the discussions of cooperation, competition, consultation, integration, and exchange in Part Two. And it involves concern with the interrelations of the characteristics of social structures themselves, as exemplified by the discussions of the relationships of organizational size, division of labor, hierarchical and functional differentiation, and administrative apparatus in Part Three.

The study of the social processes that occur *in* organizations and the study of the structure of interdependent attributes *of* organizations are complementary. Only the former can tell us about informal relations and practices and convey a vivid impression of the social experience of being a member of a complex bureaucracy. Only the latter can tell us which conditions in organizations tend to occur together and thus provide the basis for explaining why organizations differ, for instance, why some have tall and others squat hierarchical structures, or what conditions in organizations produce differences in the size of their administrative apparatus. In short, either type of study makes contributions to our knowledge about organizations that the other does not make and, indeed, cannot make. The systematic analysis of informal processes in organizations and that of the formal structures of organizations, though the knowledge they furnish are complementary, are incompatible and cannot be carried out together, because they require entirely different theoretical frameworks and consequently different methods of inquiry. If one is concerned with clarifying the subtle sociopsychological processes that underlie social integration and differentiation of informal status in work groups, one cannot simultaneously be concerned with the complex interrelations of the various characteristics of organizations, and systematic analysis of these interrelations precludes diverting attention recurrently to the underlying processes. The two entail different theoretical foci, conceptual schemes, and research methods.

Over the years, the focus of my theoretical interest shifted from seeking to gain insight into the sociopsychological processes that govern the informal relations in work groups of organizations to trying to discover the principles that can explain the structure of organizations on the basis of the relationships between organizational characteristics. What prompted this shift? My earliest research was stimulated by Weber's theoretical analysis of bureaucracy, and it entailed case studies of work groups in two government bureaus. The field work in particular work groups centered my attention on the informal relations and daily practices I observed, but Weber's conceptual scheme led me recurrently to infer how bureaucratic conditions affect these informal processes and patterns. An illustration is the analysis in Chapter 7 of statistical records of performance, a bureaucratic procedure that influences the work of individuals and their interpersonal relations by making differences in performance visible. But such analysis is a very indirect way of applying Weber's scheme to empirical data. It is essentially an inquiry into the nature of work groups, not into the nature of bureaucratic organization, which requires tracing the complex interdependence of various traits of organizations, as Weber did. Only empirical data about many organizations make it possible to dissect the relationships between various organizational characteristics and thus to test and refine Weber's theory of these relationships.

At first sight, conducting research on many organizations seems to be an impossible task, because even the study of a few work groups in one organization takes months. As I reread Weber's discussion again and again, however, I came to realize that most of the factors he analyzed do not require information obtained through painstaking observation of day-to-day operations, but merely data that can be collected on short visits to organizations, because Weber is concerned with the formal characteristics of organizations, such as their size, the division of labor among official positions, the hierarchy of authority, and the written rules. This makes it feasible for an empirical study to obtain data on sufficient numbers of organizations to ascertain which of their characteristics tend to occur together, for instance, whether increasing organizational size is accompanied by various bureaucratic attributes, as Weber implies. Thus, a shift in my theoretical focus led to a change in the research methods I employed, for the information needed to infer theoretical explanations of why organizations have certain characteristics depends on quantitative comparisons of many organizations and is not available in intensive case studies of social processes in one or two.

These contrasting approaches to organizational inquiry are discussed in greater detail in Part One, following an introduction to the study of formal organization in Chapter 1 and a conceptual critique of Weber's analysis in Chapter 2. Several theoretical foci in the analysis of organizational life are distinguished, with special emphasis on the two represented in this book. The last two chapters comment on the different research methods appropriate for the two theoretical foci, respectively—the case study and the comparative study of organizations. This is not the same as the difference between qualitative and quantitative procedures. Case studies may utilize quantitative procedures to analyze social processes, and comparative studies may confine themselves to qualitative comparisons of organizations (though my comparative research employs quantitative procedures), which is why I refer to the comparative rather than the quantitative method of organization research. Whereas conceptual and methodological papers have been put into Part One regardless of when they were written, the chapters in Parts Two and Three are, with few exceptions,[1] in chronological order.

Informal processes in bureaucratic work groups are analyzed in Part Two. The endeavor is to achieve theoretical insights into the sociopsychological processes that govern social relations and work practices in groups operating under bureaucratic conditions. The topics examined include the conditions in organizations that foster competition or cooperation, the significance of unofficial consultation among colleagues, the influence that social support from co-workers has on treatment of clients, and the processes of social exchange that engender both social integration and status differentiation in groups. The first four chapters present case studies of work groups in government bureaus of various kinds, and the last two are devoted to the theoretical analysis of processes of social integration and social exchange in groups generally.

In Part Three, the formal structure of organizations is analyzed on the basis of quantitative data. Each empirical study is confined to organizations of a single type, lest differences among types confound the dissection of the relationships between structural features, but some papers compare the research findings on several types. Since my initial interest was in government bureaucracy, three of the six types on which data are presented are different kinds of government bureaus; the other three are academic institutions, department stores, and hospitals. Main topics under consideration are the relationship of size and structural differentiation, the effects of both on the administrative component, the significance of professional qualifications for decentralized authority, the influence of automation on the shape of the structure, the conditions that effect manpower economies, and the structural effects of colleague groups on the orientations of their members. As most factors analyzed, though not all, are formal characteristics of organizations, and informal practices are not taken into account, the objection is sometimes raised that the actual conditions in organizations are ignored. But whatever the informal relations and practices of its members, the fundamental structure of an organization is defined by its formally instituted char-

[1] Chapter 12 (Part Two) was written later than some of the papers in Part Three, though the book it summarizes was written before any of them. Chapter 15 was published after the last two chapters, and Chapter 16 was published after one of them, but I put the two theoretical chapters about organizational structure at the end of Part Three, just as the two theoretical chapters about group processes are at the end of Part Two.

acteristics—by its different departments, specialized positions, administrative levels, distribution of authority, and span of control of supervisors, for example. Other formal characteristics, such as automation and rules, affect an organization's structure, and so does the external environment, as illustrated in Chapter 16. Research results are discussed in the first four chapters of Part Three, and a general theory of differentiation in organizations is advanced in the last two. My conception of theorizing has undergone alteration with the change in my theoretical focus. The theoretical objective here is not so much to suggest imaginative insights as to construct a rigorous system of related propositions in which lower-order generalizations supported by empirical evidence are deducible from higher-order theoretical assumptions.

The two contrasting approaches outlined are brought into stark relief by comparing the theoretical analysis in the last two chapters of Part Two (Chapters 11 and 12) with that in the last two chapters of Part Three (Chapters 17 and 18). The difference can also be vividly seen when the two approaches are applied to research on the same organization, which is apparent if the case study of one employment office in Chapters 7 and 8 is contrasted with the comparative study of 1,201 such offices in Chapters 16 and 17. Still another juxtaposition that may illustrate this difference in approach is that of my two favorite papers (for whatever an author's judgment of his own work is worth), Chapter 9, which analyzes consultation among colleagues, and Chapter 17, which formulates the theory of organizational differentiation.

Notes on the Development of Ideas

I shall now try to illustrate how my sociological ideas slowly emerged in these two types of studies, first tracing the development of the conception of consultation as social exchange, which is discussed in Chapter 9, and then reconstructing the steps that led to the formulation of the theory of differentiation in organizations, which is presented in Chapter 17.[2] The first of these two autobiographical accounts of a sociologist at work has been published previously;[3] the second has not.

Consultation among Colleagues. The case study of work groups in a federal agency in which I discovered the pattern of unofficial consultation involved direct observation in the field for several months and interviewing. A major

[2] It might be preferable to read this section after having read Chapters 9 and 17.

[3] Phillip E. Hammond (ed.), *Sociologists at Work* (New York: Basic Books, 1964), pp. 34–36 (slightly revised).

problem I wanted to study was how informal relations among colleagues in a bureaucracy influence the performance of duties. As I explored this problem while preparing the research design before starting the field work, I specified the hypothesis that officials who have frequent informal contacts (for example, who regularly lunch together) tend to ask one another for information they need rather than some other official whom they might be officially expected to ask. Here I seem to have predicted the existence of the consultation pattern I later observed, but what I predicted was actually only a small element of what I was to find. I had in mind simple requests for information and did not anticipate at all the extensive practice that prevailed among agents of giving advice on complex problems. Nor did I realize the important implications of the consultation pattern for the group structure.

During my period of orientation in the federal agency, I asked a supervisor whether agents sometimes cooperated with each other. I did not yet know the operating procedures well and wanted to find out whether their duties sometimes required agents to work together on a case. The supervisor's answer, however, was not in terms of what I had had in mind. He said: "They are not permitted to consult other agents. If they have a problem, they must take it up with me." Unexpectedly, I had obtained my first clue to the unofficial practice of consulting colleagues.

At the very beginning of the intensive observation in Department Y, I could not fail to notice that agents frequently discussed problems of their cases with other agents and asked their advice. I was impressed right away by the significance of this pattern. Here was an officially prohibited practice that clearly had important implications for official operations, providing the kind of link between informal work group and bureaucratic operations in which I was primarily interested. Besides, this practice offered an opportunity for analyzing an aspect of the content of the informal relations among officials, which would supplement the analysis I had already planned of the quantitative form of their social interaction. Exactly one week after I had entered Department Y, I started a tally of all the consultations I could observe, recording on a matrix which agent asked which colleague for advice. Two weeks later, when I went over my procedure schedule, I noted that I should ask in the interview sociometric and other questions about consultation as well as continue the record of consultations in the office.

A section on consultation was included in the preliminary analysis I did near the end of the period of field observation. In brief outline, I pointed out that agents who needed advice on difficult problems were put under cross pressure by the requirement to consult only the supervisor and their reluctance to reveal their difficulties to him lest it affect his evaluation of them. The unofficial practice of consulting colleagues that resulted from this cross pressure served to cement the informal relations in the work group. I suggested also that the social esteem for the consultant strengthened his position among colleagues and that one dysfunction of the pattern might be that it weakens the esteem for and position of the supervisor. This discussion of consultation was the central topic of my first report to the Social Science Research Council, which I prepared around this time.

The skeleton of the final analysis of the consultation pattern can already be discerned in this early exploration. Numerous specific elements were still to be added, of course. For example, there yet were no data on the actual network of consultation nor any discussion of the tendency to consult not only experts but often colleagues whose competence is not superior to one's own. Most important, however, was the fact that the two crucial insights for an understanding of this pattern were still missing: the principle that the informal institution of unofficial consultation improves performance even when no advice is obtained, and the conception of consultation as an exchange process.

The interviews furnished clues for these insights. Several agents explained that they often discussed their cases with colleagues not in order to ask advice but because they wanted to share an interesting experience or have an opportunity to think out loud. At first, I interpreted these statements as defensive reactions through which agents wanted to convince me that they really did not need advice as often as I had seen them discuss problems with colleagues. The fact that the most expert agent in the department made such a statement, however, was not compatible with this interpretation. As I tried to think of a better one, the expression "thinking out loud" gave me the idea of what I called consultation in disguise. Analyzing a problem in the presence of a fellow expert can be considered consultation in disguise, since the nonverbal communications from listener to speaker indicate to the latter whether he is on the right track and thus serve the same function as explicit requests for confirmation of one's judgment. Talking out loud reduces the anxiety engendered by difficult problems and thereby improves the ability to solve them.

This interpretation of a special case of consultation suggested a principle for explaining consultations in general. The experience of being able to obtain advice from colleagues tends to relieve anxiety over decision-making, and the experience of being consulted by colleagues tends to increase self confidence. Through these two processes, the pattern of consultation improves the ability of agents to make correct decisions on their own without consulting anyone. (I would have liked to obtain empirical evidence to confirm this conclusion, but only an experiment or a panel study could furnish the data necessary for this purpose. Although the data do show, for instance, that the agents most often consulted were the most expert decision-makers, this was, of course, largely due to the fact that experts were particularly attractive consultants. Whether it was also true that being consulted often improved decision-making ability, as hypothesized, could be ascertained only by observing changes in competence over an extended period of time.)

The interview responses indicated that agents enjoyed being consulted, and the explanation one agent volunteered, "It's flattering, I suppose," gave me the idea of conceptualizing consultations as an exchange of value. By asking a colleague for help with solving problems, an agent implicitly paid his respect to the other's superior competence in exchange for the advice he received. When I first had this crucial insight in my initial comments on the interviews, it was crudely formulated and embedded in a discussion that required much subsequent refinement; it later became the cornerstone of the analysis of consultation.

Two important implications of this principle were perceived only later in the course of the intensive analysis of my data. Taking a hint from Whyte's discussion of the relationship between incurring obligations and the status hierarchy in a gang,[4] I came to realize that the process of consultation may be the basic mechanism through which informal status became differentiated among agents. Some agents acquired superior status in the group in exchange for helping others with their work, just as the gang leader's status entailed doing more favors for the other members than they did for him. Expert knowledge was necessary but not sufficient for achieving high status among colleagues. Those agents who possessed expert knowledge but did not freely give advice to others did not achieve high standing in the group.

Another implication of the concept of exchange was that the marginal principle of economics might be applied to the analysis of social processes. As experts were increasingly consulted, the value (utility) of the respect implicit in being asked once more for advice declined, and the value of the cost in time of giving another piece of advice increased. This could explain why popular consultants, although they enjoyed giving advice, did not like it when others consulted them very frequently. It also explained why agents often consulted partners on their own level of competence rather than superior experts; by doing so with their less serious problems, they did not exhaust the supply of advice that superior experts were willing to give them. Although the application of the marginal principle to social interaction was merely implicit and still quite primitive here, it was later made explicit and refined in the theory of social exchange by Homans and by myself.[5]

[4] William F. Whyte, *Street Corner Society*, rev. ed. (Chicago: University of Chicago Press, 1955).

[5] George C. Homans, "Human Behavior as Exchange," *American Journal of Sociology* 63 (1958), 597–606; George C. Homans, *Social Behavior* (New York: Harcourt, 1961); and Peter M. Blau, *Exchange and Power in Social Life* (New York: Wiley, 1964).

Theory of Differentiation in Organizations. The theory of organizational differentiation was the outgrowth of a long period of gestation that started with the shift in my focus from case studies of bureaucratic work groups to comparative studies of the characteristics of bureaucracies themselves. This new sociological interest led me to establish the Comparative Organization Research Program at the University of Chicago more than a decade ago under a grant, later continued, from the National Science Foundation, which is gratefully acknowledged. Most of the early research entailed studies of government bureaus of various kinds, but attention later turned to other types of organizations. Whereas data on a great variety of organizational characteristics were collected and analyzed, in each study from a substantial number of organizations, my own primary theoretical focus was, and is, on characteristics of the organizational structure in the narrow sense, by which is meant the distribution of employees among positions and subunits, as exemplified by the division of labor, the hierarchy of managerial ranks, the different divisions and sections within them, and the administrative staff. Operational measures in accordance with this conceptual scheme were devised, such as the number of different occupational positions to indicate the division of labor.

The largest study we did in the early period was one of all employment security agencies and their local offices in this country, for which data were collected in personal visits to the agency headquarters in every state in 1966. The analysis of these data, on which Richard A. Schoenherr and Sheila R. Klatzky collaborated with me, revealed that organizational size, as indicated by number of employees, is associated with many organizational characteristics and particularly with the various structural features in which I was most interested. Two earlier studies of different kinds of government bureaus had yielded similar findings. Since I did not consider size to be a concept of sufficient theoretical significance, however, I tried to get rid of its disturbing effects in the analysis of the influences of other conditions on various structural characteristics and of the relationships between these characteristics. Thus, we substituted for the original structural variables—for example, number of occupational positions and of hierarchical levels—their residuals from their regression lines on size, and we also transformed size logarithmically, because it became apparent that its distribution is not normal and many of its relationships with other variables are not monotonic. These two procedures, designed to reveal the correlations between structural features, actually concealed the very research results that I later found of greatest theoretical interest. We abandoned the use of residuals when we realized that regression analysis achieves the same purpose of controlling size to examine the direct links between other variables, manifest in the partial coefficients, without simultaneously hiding the influences of size itself.

We prepared hundreds of tabulations and wrote scores of memos analyzing their results in the course of more than one year. While we were analyzing the data on entire agencies and their headquarters, which occupied most of this time, we looked at so many factors that the relationship between size and various attributes of the formal structure, though the regression procedure we had begun to use made it observable, did not attract much attention. When we started to analyze the data on local offices, on which only limited information was available, I was struck by the fact that the relationships of size with division of labor, number of hierarchical levels, and number of subdivisions assume the same form in these small offices as they do in the large agency headquarters. All these relationships are positive, all are pronounced, and all are nonmonotonic. Moreover, size exhibits a similar relationship with the average span of control of first-line supervisors in local offices, and when we turned to the analysis of headquarters divisions, we found parallel relationships in divisions with diverse functions between their size and the span of control of higher managers as well as first-line supervisors.

Now I could no longer dismiss the size of organizations as a factor of little import for a theoretical understanding of their formal structure. The consistent empirical regularities observed forced me to take organizational size seriously as a substantive independent variable instead of primarily treating it as a control in the analysis of other influences. My interest in size was further stimulated by the discovery that it and its structural correlates have sometimes opposite consequences, for example, for the proportionate size of the administrative staff, the managerial ratio, and the span of control of supervisors. I pulled these findings together by using the concept of structural differentiation to subsume several structural variables—number of divisions and of sections within them, division of labor, number of hierarchical levels. Our substantive concern with size also prompted us to reconsider its logarithmic transformation, which had initially been simply a convenient technique for regression analysis, but which led us now to inquire into the nature of the relationships of size with other variables that required such transformation.

I wrote some memos advancing theoretical conjectures about these research results in the spring of 1968, after one year of data analysis preceded by another year of data collection and processing. (To be sure, the analysis of the data, to which I could only devote a portion of my time, and which was not confined to those pertaining to differentiation, already included limited interpretations of findings, which typically indicated a need for additional tabulations, and these in turn required revising the interpretations.) I suggested that large organizations cope with their broad and complex responsibilities by breaking them up into simpler components, the narrower responsibilities of subunits and individual positions. Hence, large size promotes structural differentiation, but the two have opposite effects on administration. Large organizational size reduces the proportionate size of the administrative component, reflecting an economy of scale in administration, whereas differentiation increases it, reflecting the problems of coordination in complex structures. I also speculated that the economic principle of the eventually declining marginal productivity may be used to explain why the impact of size on structural features declines with increasing size, and I noted that these curvilinear relationships imply that large organizations tend to have larger as well as more numerous subunits than small ones. Although these ideas contain the germs of those in the theory of differentiation, they are not yet formulated as a theoretical system of rigorously interrelated propositions, and they are dispersed in memos discussing a variety of other theoretical themes.

In the meantime, I had become increasingly interested in the principles of deductive theorizing, which give theories a different form from that of my previous theoretical work, and I lectured on these principles in my course on social theory at the University of Chicago. The fact that several variables encompassed by the concept of structural differentiation exhibit consistent empirical relationships with size and with various administrative ratios made it tempting to try to construct a deductive theory of differentiation on the basis of these findings. For this purpose, I searched for the most general propositions that are derivable from the empirical regularities observed and from which a number of other propositions implicit in these regularities can be deduced. I developed such a scheme first for the effects of size on differentiation and their implications, and then for the effects of differentiation on administration and the indirect effects of size implied by them. The causal assumptions are that organizational size is an antecedent and administrative ratios are consequences of differentiation. An important connecting link is provided by the inference that feedback effects of problems of administration created by differentiation dampen the influences of size. The assumption that research on one kind of government agency yields theoretical principles that apply to organizations generally received subsequently some support from empirical data on various other types of organizations, which conform to the theoretical expectations.

Social Structure

As mentioned at the beginning of this Introduction and again in the preceding section, my conception of social structure, which is the focus of my sociological inquiries, is less encompassing than that used by many social scientists. It does not include everything important in social life. Social values and institutions, organizational goals and regulations, and the technology are not part of the social structure in the narrow sense of the term adopted, though they surely are important conditions of social life that influence the social structure and are influenced by it. My view of social structure is essentially similar to those of Radcliffe-Brown and Nadel.[6] Whether dealing with entire societies, formal organizations, or collectivities of any other sort, I refer by social structure to the distributions, along various lines, of people among social positions that influence the role relations among these people. This terse definition requires clarification, and the term *structural parameter* is introduced to explicate it.

A social structure is defined by its parameters. A parameter is any criterion for making social distinctions among people. Age, sex, education, occupation, and socioeconomic status are parameters, provided that people actually make social distinctions along these lines that influence the relations among them. The simplest form of social structure is the distribution of people in accordance with a single parameter. Thus, we speak of the age structure of a population, the kinship structure of a tribe, the power structure of a community, the class structure of a society, and the authority structure of an organization. These are not types of social structures but analytical abstractions, and the elements abstracted by several parameters must be combined to give a meaningful description of social structures. For social structures, with the possible exception of those in small groups, are divided along a number of lines, and in the case of complex societies, a very large number. People belong to ethnic groups, communities, religious denominations, firms or other places of employment, political parties, and groupings along various other lines; they differ in social origin, education, occupation, prestige, power, and in many other respects. Since social structure is defined by the social distinctions people make, it always entails social differentiation. An undifferentiated social structure is a contradiction in terms. Not all forms of differentiation entail status inequalities, however.

Two fundamental types of parameters can be distinguished. First, a nominal parameter divides people into subgroups with distinct boundaries, but there is no inherent rank order among these groups. Sex, religion, racial identification, place of employment, and political community are nominal parameters in society. Nominal parameters of formal organizations are manifest in departments, work groups, and occupational specialties. Second, a graduated parameter distinguishes people on the basis of a criterion of status

---

[6] A. R. Radcliffe-Brown, *Function and Structure in Primitive Society* (Glencoe: Free Press, 1952), pp. 188–203; and S. F. Nadel, *The Theory of Social Structure* (Glencoe: Free Press, 1957).

gradation without delineating distinct boundaries. Prestige, education, income, wealth, and power illustrate graduated parameters. A third type can be generated by combining the characteristics of the other two, which may be called an ordinal parameter, and which divides people into groups that have distinct boundaries and that are ordered in a hierarchy of ranks. Castes and estates exemplify ordinal parameters.

Whereas there are no such inherently ranked groupings in modern society, there are quasi-castes. A nominal parameter that is strongly associated with several graduated parameters produces hierarchical differences in status between groups with relatively little overlap, approximating the hierarchical ranking of groups with no overlap produced by an ordinal parameter. The pronounced associations of racial differences with all kinds of differences in status make races quasi-castes in American society. The structure of formal organizations is governed by a genuine ordinal parameter, not merely an approximation of one, which divides employees into a hierarchy of levels with distinct boundaries and with inherent differences in authority and in rewards. Although administrative rank in an organization is not an ascribed status, it acquires an ascribed ingredient if mobility between ranks is rare, which makes the authority structure of organizations resemble the structure of caste societies.

The assumption is that structural parameters affect interpersonal relations and the social interaction and communication in which these relations find expression. Existing evidence often suffices to satisfy this assumption. For instance, much research has shown that social intercourse between blacks and whites is less frequent and less close than that within each group, or that the role relations between supervisor and subordinates differ from those among subordinates, or that large differences in education inhibit frequent and intimate social contacts. If such evidence does not already exist, the assumption should be empirically tested by ascertaining whether differences in social position are associated with differences in role relations. In the case of nominal parameters, social intercourse within groups is expected to differ, typically by being more prevalent and intimate,[7] than that between groups, and in the case of graduated parameters, such differences are expected to be inversely related to status distance. If these expectations are not met by any indication of interpersonal relations for an attribute the investigator initially assumed to be a parameter, the assumption that it is a structural parameter that serves as a basis for making social distinctions must be abandoned.

---

[7] One of the rare exceptions in which outgroup relations exceed ingroup relations is sex, but only for marriage and sexual relations, not for friendships, which are more frequent among men and among women than between the two sexes.

In short, the defining criterion of structural parameters is their association with processes of social interaction, which provides a nexus in the conceptual scheme between social structure and social processes. However, the intensive analysis of sociopsychological processes is not part of the systematic analysis of social structures; indeed, the two are in my opinion incompatible, as previously noted. The former entails dissecting in great detail interpersonal relations, the reciprocal influences in them, and the meaning they have for participants; the attributes of the broader social structure are viewed as given conditions that affect these sociopsychological processes but that are not themselves under investigation. The latter entails close scrutiny of the complex interdependence of various structural features and of the conditions affecting them. While manifestations of social processes are taken into account to assure that significant aspects of the social structure are being investigated, no attempt is made to analyze the multitude of sociopsychological processes underlying the social structure. The theoretical focus in these two basic kinds of sociological inquiry is so different that seeking to encompass both is unlikely to produce a systematic empirical or theoretical inquiry of either.

Processes of social interaction are at the roots of the social integration within groups and among them in the larger social structure. Since parameters are manifest in barriers to sociable intercourse, they strengthen ingroup integration but at the same time create segregating boundaries between groups, the more so the closer their association with sociable intercourse is. However, virtually all social structures are characterized by multiform differentiation, produced by a number of parameters, which are more or less intersecting. That is, each person belongs to a variety of groups and his or her status can be distinguished along various lines, one for every parameter, and the same persons do not occupy the same positions with respect to all parameters. For instance, Catholics live in different towns, blacks have different occupations, and the income of college graduates varies.

The social integration in complex social structures rests on multiform differentiation. If people who are alike in one respect differ in others, their tendency to associate with persons in their own group or stratum in terms of one parameter inevitably involves that their associates belong to different groups or strata in terms of other parameters. The resulting intergroup social interaction and communication provide the connective tissues that integrate the various parts of the social structure. When one parameter much exceeds the rest in its salience and thus its association with sociable intercourse, it diminishes tendencies to enter into intergroup relations. Great differences in hierarchical status, particularly if status differences in several respects coincide, constitute strong barriers to sociable intercourse. This implies that pronounced and coinciding differences in wealth, prestige, power, and rewards are an impediment to the social integration of complex social structures and, specifically, that the authority structure in large organizations, which tends to entail great and coinciding status differences, is such an impediment. Indeed, I assume this to be the case.

The analysis of social structure—as I conceive it, which is very different from Lévi-Strauss's structural analysis[8]—is concerned with the conditions that affect and the consequences of structural features, including especially how some structural features influence others, that is, their interdependence. The first question is what conditions determine the structural attributes of a society, such as its division of labor. According to Durkheim, a society's division of labor depends on its size and, particularly, on its population density, which intensifies both social interaction and competition in the struggle for existence, thereby facilitating the exchange transactions required for specialized pursuits and providing incentives for mitigating competitive conflicts among persons in the same occupation by diversifying their pursuits.[9] Other important influences on the division of labor are undoubtedly the stage of the technology and the degree of industrialization in a society, because they free manpower from agricultural work, required for providing the means of subsistence, to go into a variety of other occupations. The situation in organizations is different. Although some investigators claim that the technology also exerts much influence in organizations on the administrative structure,[10] others, including myself, find that the influence of the technology on the organizational structure is minor and far overshadowed by the strong impact on it of size.[11]

A second question is what the social consequences of various attributes of social structures are. Durkheim held that the division of labor in society reduces competitive conflict, as just noted, and he attributes its development largely to its having this function. The division of labor may also affect levels of education and skill. Whereas the subdivision of work makes some jobs more routine, it makes other jobs more specialized, requiring greater training, knowledge, and skills. As a matter of fact, the increases in the division of labor that have occurred in American society for many decades have been accompanied by parallel increases in median education. However, whether these parallel trends reflect the influence of the division of labor on education or are the result of the effects of the advancing technology and industrialization on both is a moot question. Within organizations, structural differ-

[8] Claude Lévi-Strauss, *Structural Anthropology* (New York: Basic Books, 1963).

[9] Emile Durkheim, *The Division of Labor in Society* (Glencoe: Free Press, 1947), pp. 256–275.

[10] For example, Joan Woodward, *Industrial Organization* (London: Oxford University Press, 1965).

[11] For example, David J. Hickson *et al.*, "Operations Technology and Organization Structure," *Administrative Science Quarterly* 14 (1969), 378–397.

entiation, by enhancing problems of coordination and communication, enlarges the administrative component.[12] The same may well be true for entire societies. Specifically, the increasing differentiation of societies may expand the proportion of their civil servants and of their labor force in other administrative positions.

A final problem of structural analysis is to dissect the interrelations of various structural features. It must be stressed that reference here is not to the relationships between the underlying variables, the parameters themselves, but to the relationships between the degrees of differentiation in various respects, as indicated by the parameters. These are two completely different kinds of relationships, which are often confused. The one is exemplified by the association between the ethnic affiliation of individuals and their income, while the other refers to the association between the extent of ethnic heterogeneity and the extent of inequality in incomes. Now we are concerned with the latter. It is not meaningful to ask what the relationships between degrees of differentiation in various respects are in a given society. This question only has meaning in a comparative framework, that is, if substantial numbers of societies are compared or substantial numbers of historical periods. The fact that family size is related to socioeconomic status for *individuals* does not tell us whether or how the variances in the two (or other indicators of variation) are related for *societies*, which is what we want to know in structural analysis.

I consider the study of the interrelations of various forms of inequality and heterogeneity, as well as the conditions that produce these structural features and their consequences, to constitute the very core of sociological inquiry. But lacking a comparative framework and structural focus, most sociological research and theory has little bearing on these issues. Social problems of great practical significance could be clarified with a comparative structural approach, which would, for example, seek to explain poverty, not by investigating poor people in one society, but by analyzing the conditions in societies that account for severe income inequalities. Much comparative research to collect and analyze information on differentiation in numerous societies is needed before we can build sociological theories that can explain the structure of societies. A beginning of such structural analysis of the nature of organizations is made in Part Three.

Organizations and Society

Organizations are important elements in the structure of modern societies. Membership in work organizations is a nominal parameter of the structure

---

[12] Only the subdivision of work among organizational components—divisions, sections per division, and levels—has these effects, not that among occupational positions of individuals.

of society, which divides the labor force on the basis of the place where they work into a large number of groups of widely varying size. The relations between organizations and the environment in which they exist are often neglected in organizational inquiries. These relations can be studied from different perspectives. One of these looks at the significance of the conditions in a bureaucracy and its work groups for the orientations of its members to the public; this is illustrated in Chapter 10. Another examines the influences on organizations of their community environment and the broader organizational context in which they are embedded, as exemplified in Chapter 16. A third perspective centers attention on the implications the existence of many large organizations have for the structure of society. Systematic research on this problem would require comparable data on the organizations in and the other structural characteristics of a variety of societies. Only limited comparative data on structural features in numerous societies are available, and none at all to my knowledge on their work organizations. To be sure, theoretical speculations about the impact of bureaucratization on social life abound. Given the absence of systematic information, I can do no more than also offer a few theoretical conjectures concerning the significance of formal organizations for contemporary society, but these deal primarily with concentration of power rather than bureaucratization.

As a starting point, a basic generalization of the theory of differentiated subunits in organizations is applied to the different organizations in societies. The generalization is that with increasing organizational size differentiation into subunits increases at decelerating rates, and it implies, in strict logic, that large organizations have both more and larger subunits, on the average, than small ones. Much empirical evidence supports these implications. Applied to organizations in societies, the expectation is that both the number and the average size of formal organizations increase with the expanding size of a society. Indeed, the population growth in the last century, in our society and others, has apparently been accompanied by a proliferation of organizations, and the average size of work organizations, and probably of others too, has increased during this time, as the number of people working in large organizations has increased and the number working in small places has decreased.

Top executives of large organizations have more power than those of small ones, just as the managers of large departments within an organization exercise more power than those of small ones. There is a difference, however. In organizations, top management has the interest and authority to restrain the competition among departmental managers for budgets to hire more employees and for power,[13] but society's government exerts much less re-

---

[13] Such competition among managers within an organization is illustrated in Melville Dalton, *Men Who Manage* (New York: Wiley, 1959).

straint on the competition among organizations to expand their size and their power, especially in a political system based on a laissez-faire ideology, like ours. The economy of scale and their greater power give large organizations competitive advantages which make it likely that large organizations are more successful than small ones in further enhancing their size and their power. As a result, resources and power become concentrated in huge organizations and consolidate their dominant position in society. Illustrations of these tendencies are mergers of firms, the creation of the Pentagon by combining three federal departments, the growth in staff and power of the White House, and the establishment of conglomerates that absorb many companies.

In theoretical terms, formal organization may be considered to make power liquid and for this reason make it possible for much power to be concentrated in few hands. The economic concept of liquidity refers to the ease with which valuable objects can be exchanged for any others, which also implies that they can be transferred, stored, and accumulated.[14] Money is most liquid, and bonds or stocks are more liquid than real estate. Personal power is restricted in scope by its limited liquidity. To be sure, it can be used to obtain other valuables in a sort of exchange, by employing coercive threats or having charismatic appeal. But the coercive force of an individual is confined to those he can subdue, and the influence of a charismatic leader is confined to those inspired by his charisma. The exchange value of money has a much wider scope. Personal power cannot be readily transferred to other persons or stored to be added to later and accumulated for successors. The difficulty of transferring personal power is reflected in the crisis of succession that typically occurs at the end of an individual's charismatic leadership and in the consequent transformation of charismatic authority centered on a person into bureaucratic authority grounded in an organization, as Weber noted.[15] Formal organization makes power more liquid in two ways.

To maintain an organization requires financial resources to pay employees and purchase equipment and supplies. Financial resources are potential power in liquid form. In an organization, this potential power is translated into actual power. The economic resources utilized to pay wages and salaries make employees dependent on the organization and subject to the directives of its management. The economic dependence of employees is the source of management's authority over them. The larger the financial resources available to pay many employees relatively high wages and salaries, the greater is the power of management. Having many dependent employees

[14] Kenneth E. Boulding, *Economic Analysis*, 3rd ed. (New York: Harper, 1955), pp. 308–313.

[15] Max Weber, *The Theory of Social and Economic Organization* (New York: Oxford University Press, 1947), pp. 363–373.

widen the scope of management's authority, and high incomes make employees more dependent by restricting their equally good alternative opportunities, and thus strengthen management's power over them. Moreover, a large organization with many employees enhances top management's power in the market and in the society at large. The institution of the corporation further increases the power of top executives, particularly in the largest corporations, because it puts at their command far greater financial resources— the investments of a multitude of stockholders—than those they personally own, substantial as the latter often are.

Another source of the liquidity of organizational power is the authority structure. Power in organizations is institutionalized as official authority that is vested in impersonal offices and principles, and the employment contract obligates employees to conform to these principles governing official relations between incumbents of different offices. The chain of command makes power cumulative by giving successive managerial ranks authoritative control over increasingly large numbers of employees. The authority of management is reinforced by impersonal mechanisms of control designed under its direction, such as official written procedures, performance records that influence advancement chances, and the setup of the mechanized or automated equipment. Impersonal authority rooted in offices can be transferred from person to person—from one incumbent of an office to another, and from a superior to subordinates through official delegation of responsibilities. While a manager's influence also depends on personal qualities and relations with subordinates, the pronounced influence of a successful manager who occupies a position for long tends to become institutionalized and expand the authority of the position, thereby strengthening the control its next occupant can exercise. Some indication of this transfer of expanded authority is provided by a study that found that college presidents exercised more authority if their predecessors had been in office for many years, presumably because the latter's successful leadership enhanced the authority of the office of president.[16]

In sum, formal organization makes power relatively liquid by transforming the potential power of financial resources, which are inherently liquid, into actual power over employees dependent on their incomes, and by vesting this power in the form of institutionalized authority in official positions. Since both financial resources and official authority reside in the formal organization and do not belong to its particular members, the powers emanating from them can readily be transferred from existing personnel to new replacements and from one position to another. Indeed, the entire power of an organization may be transferred to enhance that of another, as illustrated

[16] Peter M. Blau, *The Organization of Academic Work* (New York: Wiley, 1973), pp. 181–183.

by mergers of companies and by reorganizations that combine several government departments into one superdepartment. The hierarchy of authority makes it possible for the limited power of many lower managers to be accumulated through the chain of command into much controlling power of top executives. Additional accumulation of power occurs in corporations owing to the investments of large numbers of small stockholders, which give corporation executives far more power than their own financial resources alone would command. Thus, organizational power can be accumulated in very large amounts as well as transferred, which makes it much more liquid than personal power.

Tremendous power is concentrated in the hands of top executives of giant organizations, owing to the liquidity of organizational power. More power than most entire nations have is at the disposal of senior officials of huge conglomerates, of other vast corporations, of the Pentagon, of the White House staff. These men—the term is appropriate, since there are few if any women among them—are not responsible to the electorate, and their interests lie with their organizations, not with the commonweal. The concentration of organizational power in the hands of few men shielded from public surveillance and control poses a serious threat to democracy. Social action is needed to avert this threat, and so is knowledge about both the internal structure of organizations and the structure of societies that is increasingly dominated by organizations. The papers in this book are attempts to contribute to the understanding of organizations, but there is as yet little sociological knowledge that contributes to the systematic understanding of organizations as elements in the power structure of societies.[17]

[17] This book is C.O.R.P. Report No. 18.

PART ONE

Approaches, Concepts, Methods

Introductory Remarks

The six papers in this first part deal with various approaches to the study of formal organizations and examine the conceptual and methodological frameworks employed. Basic concepts are explicated, Weber's theoretical scheme for understanding bureaucracy is summarized, some analytical distinctions are made, and procedures are suggested for the sociological inquiry into the nature of work organizations. The specific subject matter—formally established organizations in which people perform work to achieve designated objectives—can be viewed from different perspectives. Organizations may be investigated from the standpoint of economics, political science, or sociology. But even within the sociological perspective, which is the one in this book, various ways of formulating the problems under investigation can be distinguished. The concern may be to explain the roles of individual members of the organization, or the informal processes of social interaction in work groups, or the interrelated characteristics of the organizations themselves, or the changes that occur within organizations, or the interdependence between organizations and the communities of which they are part. Some papers compare different foci of analysis and discuss their methodological and theoretical implications. A contrast singled out for attention is that between a focus on informal processes in work groups and a focus on the formal structure of the organization as a whole. Different research methods are required for these two approaches—the case study being appropriate for the former, the comparative study of organizations for the latter—and different social theories are generated depending on which one is used. The papers in Part Two and Part Three illustrate these two contrasting foci of organizational analysis.

The first chapter, which was originally a radio lecture, presents an introductory overview of the field. After clarifying the concept of formal organization, Weber's classical theory of bureaucratic organization is outlined, and the concept of informal organization, to which Weber paid scant attention, is introduced. In conclusion, the significance of Weber's comparative framework for organizational analysis is emphasized.

The next essay is a conceptual analysis of Weber's theory of bureaucratic authority, which seeks to refine Weber's scheme. The ideal type, which is Weber's conceptual tool for distinguishing types of authority, is criticized. I endeavor to resolve the paradox that authority *commands* compliance but that this compliance is at the same time *voluntary*, not coerced, by analyzing the conditions and processes that transform other forms of power into authority and the emergence of normative group pressures demanding compliance. It is an interesting observation in the sociology of knowledge that a man rooted in Imperial Germany, like Weber was, failed to draw an explicit distinction in his fundamental typology between democratic and bureaucratic control, both of which are encompassed by his legal type. Such an analytical distinction is suggested.

The third paper is my earliest attempt to classify different approaches to or dimensions in the analysis of work organizations. As a starting point, the distinctive significance for the performance of tasks of three factors is discussed: the structure of work groups, the impersonal constraints exerted by the formal conditions in the organization, and the continual emergence of new problems. From this discussion, three dimensions in the study of organizations are derived (and a fourth, the investigation of the relationships between organizations and their environment, is mentioned in passing). The first refers to the effects of the social structure of work groups on their members, as mediated by processes of social interaction, and a procedure for analytically separating these structural effects from the effects of the characteristics of the individual members of the groups is indicated. The second is the investigation of the relationships between different attributes of organizations, such as their size, division of labor, hierarchy, official regulations, and turnover, in order to ascertain how various combinations of attributes produce the constellation characterizing an organization and affect its operations. The third pertains to the processes of change and development in organizations. This classification scheme has influenced much of my subsequent work, as reflected in this book, although it was later revised, some of the discussion is in need of further clarification, and two of the points made there I would no longer make. It is not true that "the investigation of a large sample of organizations is hardly feasible"; numerous such investigations, several of which are reported on in Part Three, have been carried out since this was written in 1957. Moreover, I no longer think that systematic theories of the structure of organizations should explicitly include variables referring to sociopsychological processes. (Indeed, I reworded the relevant passage slightly for this edition to lessen its difference from my present theoretical position.)

A procedure for analyzing the distinctive effects of group structure, which is one of the dimensions outlined, is described in detail and illustrated in the next chapter. If individuals are influenced by the social conditions that prevail in the groups to which they belong, in accordance with a basic sociological assumption, the question arises how to differentiate the external social constraints exerted by the orientations that prevail in a group on the conduct of individuals from the internal influences of their own orientations on their conduct. The method introduced is designed to isolate these structural effects of group characteristics in empirical analysis. The empirical findings presented for illustrative purposes are weak, however, and the specific statistical procedure employed has shortcomings that have been rightly criticized. These criticisms will be summarized and answered in Chapter 15, where a refined procedure that meets them will be described and applied to empirical data. I think that the method of abstracting structural effects is fundamentally sound, and a number of investigators have used it to reveal the distinctive effects of the group context on conduct and attitudes.[1] At the end of Chapter 4, six types of structural effects are distinguished in terms of two dimensions.

The last two papers in Part One deal with two different research methods—the case study and the comparative study of organizations. Which of the two is adopted depends on the theoretical focus of the inquiry, whether concern is with the informal processes in work groups, as in the studies in Part Two, or with the formal structure of organizations, as in the studies in Part Three. Chapter 5 is an autobiographical discussion of field work in case studies of bureaucratic work groups. I point out the significance of an explicit research design for the field work and of a systematic schedule indicating the observations to be made. The advantage of the case study is that several procedures for collecting data can be utilized in combination, which means that impressionistic observations furnishing new insights can be com-

[1] A good example of research on structural effects, which are called *compositional effects* there, is James A. Davis, *Great Books and Small Groups* (New York: Free Press, 1961). The classification of such effects developed in this book (pp. 1–25) is a refined version of one of the two dimensions of the typology presented in my paper.

plemented with some quantitative data based on systematic observation, interviewing, or official records. I discuss some blunders I made that illustrate problems occurring at the time of initial entry and difficulties posed by the observer's role. In closing I point out why assurances of individual anonymity, even when they are believed, do not overcome the reluctance of respondents to reveal information that may reflect adversely on groups with which they are identified. Selected results of the field work here discussed are analyzed in Chapters 7, 8, and 9.

The comparative approach to the study of formal organizations is the main topic of the sixth paper. Three foci of analysis in inquiries into organizational life are first distinguished, two of which correspond to two of the dimensions discussed in Chapter 3. The reason for the difference is that the new classification scheme is rigorously based on a single criterion. The criterion is whether the units of analysis whose interrelated characteristics are under investigation are the individual members of organizations, the work groups within organizations, or entire organizations. After indicating the contributions case studies can make to organizational analysis and their limitations, attention centers on the comparative method in which entire organizations are the units of analysis and the characteristics of organizations are the variables being analyzed. The importance of quantitative comparisons of many organizations is stressed. I argue that it is quite feasible to collect theoretically relevant data on large numbers of organizations, and subsequent research proved this to be true. The concluding section indicates why I consider this approach to be essential for constructing and refining systematic theory on the nature of formal organization.

1.   *The Study of Formal Organization*

If a number of men have a common aim but each simply proceeds to work toward it as he sees fit in disregard of the rest, they are likely to work at cross purposes. Sooner or later, one of them will probably seek to improve the situation by suggesting, "Let's get organized!"

The effective accomplishment of a common task requires that men organize themselves by establishing procedures for working together. Sometimes they do so informally by coming to implicit agreements concerning how to proceed. But often, particularly when large numbers are involved, men establish explicit procedures for coordinating their activities in the interest of achieving specified objectives, which means that they create a formal organization. They establish a club or a firm, they organize a union or a political party, or they set up a police force or a hospital, and they formulate procedures that govern the relations among the members of the organization and the duties each is expected to perform. Once firmly established, an organization tends to assume an identity of its own which makes it independent of the people who have founded it or of those who constitute its membership. Thus organizations can persist for several generations, not without change

Originally published in 1968.

but without losing their fundamental identity as distinct units, even though at some time none of the original members remain. The United States Army today is the same organization as the United States Army in the World War of 1914–1918, despite the fact that none of its 1918 personnel have remained in it and its structure has undergone basic alterations.

The collective efforts of men may become formally organized either because all of them have some common interests or because a subgroup has furnished inducements to the rest to work in behalf of its interest. Factory workers organize themselves into unions to bargain collectively with management, and management has organized the workers' tasks for the purpose of producing goods marketable for a profit. Unions and factories exemplify formal organizations, as do government bureaus and political parties, armies and hospitals.

The Concept of Formal Organization

Although a wide variety of organizations exists, when we speak of an organization it is generally quite clear what we mean and what we do not mean by this term. We may refer to the American Medical Association as an organization, or to a college fraternity; to the Bureau of Internal Revenue, or to a union; to General Motors, or to a church; to the Daughters of the American Revolution, or to an army. But we would not call a family an organization, nor would we so designate a friendship clique, or a community, or an economic market, or the political institutions of a society. What is the specific and differentiating criterion implicit in our intuitive distinction of organizations from other kinds of social groupings or institutions? It has something to do with how human conduct becomes socially organized, but not—as one might at first suspect—with whether or not social controls order and organize the conduct of individuals, since such social controls operate in both types of circumstances.

There are two basic principles that govern social life, and organizations manifest one of these. Social structures may emerge as the aggregate result of the diverse actions of individuals, each pursuing his own ends, or they may reflect the joint endeavors of individuals pursuing commonly accepted ends. Thus, as individuals and groups in a community compete, enter into exchange relations, and use their resources to exercise power over others, an economic system and a class structure develop which reveal organized patterns of social conduct, even though nobody has explicitly organized the endeavors of individuals. The government of a society or a football team, on the other hand, are social structures deliberately established to achieve certain objectives, and the regularities observable in them reflect the deliberate design. The distinction is essentially the one William Graham Sumner makes between "crescive" and "enacted" institutions. Social systems produced by formally enacted procedures rather than merely emergent forces are organizations. Whereas the distinction is an analytical one, since crescive and enacted forces typically interact in their effects on social systems, it finds expression in concrete entities—the many organizations that can be found in modern societies.

Whenever groups of men associate with one another, social organization develops among them, but not every collectivity has a formal organization. The defining criterion of a formal organization—or an organization, for short—is the existence of procedures for mobilizing and coordinating the efforts of various, usually specialized, subgroups in the pursuit of joint objectives. If all relations among the members of organizations and all their activities were completely predetermined by formal procedures, however, organizations would evidently not pose meaningful problems for scientific inquiry, because everything about them could be ascertained by simply examining the official blueprints and procedure manuals. Actually, the social interaction and activities in organizations never correspond perfectly to official prescriptions, if only because not all prescriptions are compatible, and these departures from the formal blueprint raise problems for empirical study. Paradoxically, therefore, although the defining characteristic of an organization is that a collectivity is formally organized, what makes it of scientific interest is that the developing social structure inevitably does not completely coincide with the preestablished forms.

Organizations generally have an administrative machinery, a specialized administrative staff responsible for maintaining the organization as a going concern and for coordinating the activities of its members. In a large factory, for example, there is not only an industrial work force directly engaged in production, but also an administration composed of executive, supervisory, clerical, and other staff personnel. The term *bureaucracy*, which connotes colloquially red tape and inefficiency, is used in sociology neutrally to refer to these administrative aspects of organizations. The common element in the colloquial and the scientific meaning of the term is that both are indicative of the amount of energy devoted to keeping the organization going rather than achieving its basic objectives. Not all soldiers are actually in combat; not all employees of manufacturing concerns are production workers; not all members of police departments are out "on the beat"; many members of every organization have the administrative task to maintain the organization. But wide variations among organizations exist in the degree of bureaucratization, as indicated by the amount of effort devoted to administrative problems, the proportion of administrative personnel, the hierarchical character of the organization, or the strict enforcement of administrative procedures and rigid compliance with them.

Weber's Theory of Bureaucracy

In his classical theory of bureaucracy, the German sociologist Max Weber outlined the distinctive characteristics of formal organizations that are bureaucratically organized. The most important of these characteristics are:[1]

1. Organizational tasks are distributed among the various positions as official duties. Implied is a clear-cut division of labor among positions which makes possible a high degree of specialization. Specialization in turn promotes expertness among the personnel by narrowing the range of duties of jobs and by enabling the organization to hire employees on the basis of their technical qualifications.

2. The positions or offices are organized into a hierarchical authority structure. In the usual case this hierarchy takes on the shape of a pyramid wherein each official is responsible to the superior above him in the pyramid for his subordinates' decisions and actions as well as his own, and wherein each official has authority over the officials under him. The scope of authority of supervisors over subordinates is clearly circumscribed.

3. A formally established system of rules and regulations governs official decisions and actions. In principle, the operations in such administrative organizations involve the application of these general regulations to particular cases. The regulations ensure the uniformity of operations and, together with the authority structure, make possible the coordination of the various activities. They also provide for continuity in operations regardless of changes of personnel, thus promoting a stability lacking in many other types of groups and collectivities, such as social movements.

4. There is a specialized administrative staff whose task it is to maintain the organization and, in particular, the lines of communication in it. The lowest level of this administrative apparatus consists of the clerical staff responsible for keeping the written records and files of the organization, in which all official decisions and actions are embodied. Whereas the "production" staff contributes directly to the achievement of the organization's objectives, whether this involves producing cars, collecting taxes, fighting wars, or curing patients, the administrative staff contributes to goal achievement only indirectly by keeping the organization itself going.

5. Officials are expected to assume an impersonal orientation in their contacts with clients and with other officials. Clients are to be treated as cases, the officials being expected to disregard all personal considerations and to maintain complete emotional detachment, and subordinates are to be treated in a similarly impersonal fashion. The social distance between

---

[1] Max Weber, *Essays in Sociology* (New York: Oxford University Press, 1946), pp. 196–204, and *The Theory of Social and Economic Organization* (Glencoe: Free Press, 1947), pp. 329–336.

hierarchical levels and that between officials and their clients is intended to foster such formality. Impersonal detachment is designed to prevent the personal feelings of officials from distorting their rational judgment in carrying out their duties.

6. Employment by the organization constitutes a career for officials. Typically an official is a full-time employee and looks forward to a lifelong career in the agency. Employment is based on the technical qualifications of the candidate rather than on political, family, or other connections. Usually such qualifications are tested by examination or by certificates that demonstrate the candidate's educational attainment—college degrees, for example. Such educational qualifications create a certain amount of class homogeneity among officials, since relatively few persons of working-class origin have college degrees, although their number is increasing. Officials are appointed to positions, not elected, and thus are dependent on superiors in the organization rather than on a body of constituents. After a trial period officials gain tenure of position and are protected against arbitrary dismissal. Remuneration is in the form of a salary, and pensions are provided after retirement. Career advancements are "according to seniority or to achievement, or both."[2]

Weber presents an implicit functional analysis of the interdependence between the characteristics of bureaucracy, with rational, efficient administration as the criterion of function. Effective accomplishment of complex administrative tasks on a large scale requires that they be subdivided into specialized responsibilities because a wide range of duties reduces skills, and that qualified experts be appointed to discharge these responsibilities. This pronounced division of labor creates serious problems of coordination, particularly in a large organization. A special administrative staff is needed to maintain channels of communication and coordination, and a strict hierarchy of authority serves to effect the coordination of diverse tasks in the pursuit of organizational objectives by enabling superiors on successive levels to guide, directly or indirectly, the performance of increasingly wider circles of subordinates. But close supervision of all decisions is inefficient and produces strains. The system of official rules is designed to standardize operations and restrict the need for direct supervisory intervention largely to extraordinary cases. Technical training and official rules notwithstanding, however, strong emotions and personal bias would interfere with the ability to make rational decisions. The emphasis on impersonal detachment has the function of precluding the intrusion of such irrational factors into official decisions. Lest the impersonal discipline in the hierarchical bureaucracy

[2] *Ibid.*, p. 334.

alienate its members, secure careers lessen this burden and promote loyalty to the organization.

In brief, the problems created by one condition in the organization stimulate the development of another to meet them. A number of interdependent processes of this kind give rise to the constellation of features characteristic of the typical bureaucracy, as conceptualized by Weber. He held that these features of an administrative organization and, especially, their combination are "capable of attaining the highest degree of efficiency."[3]

Informal Organization

Weber has been criticized for presenting an idealized conception of bureaucracy. His implicit functional scheme addresses itself to the problem of how a given element of the organization contributes to its strength and effective functioning. What is missing is a similar systematic attempt to specify the *dysfunctions* of the various elements[4] and to examine the conflicts that arise between the elements comprising the system. Thus, even if it is true that the hierarchy of authority promotes discipline and makes possible the coordination of activities, does it not also discourage subordinates from accepting responsibility? Or, granted that promotion should be based on objective criteria rather than on personal considerations or family connections, which of the two major criteria is to be selected—seniority or merit? When questions such as these are raised, it is seen that Weber's one-sided concern with the functions of bureaucratic institutions blinds him to some of the most fundamental problems bureaucratization creates.

Another criticism of Weber's analysis that has been advanced is that he is preoccupied with the formally instituted aspects of bureaucracies and ignores the informal relations and unofficial patterns that develop in formal organizations. Selznick has emphasized that the formal structure is only one aspect of the actual social structure and that organizational members interact as persons and not merely in terms of the formal roles they occupy.[5] Many empirical studies of work groups in formal organizations have called attention to the importance of the informal organization that emerges in these work groups and that constitutes a dynamic force in the organization.

[3] *Ibid.*, p. 337.

[4] See Robert K. Merton, *Social Theory and Social Structure*, 3rd ed. (New York: Free Press, 1968), pp. 104–108, who calls attention to the importance of systematically investigating dysfunctions as well as functions.

[5] Philip Selznick, "Foundations of the Theory of Organizations," *American Sociological Review*, 13 (1948), 25–35.

To be sure, Weber realized that actual practice does not follow in every detail the formal blueprint. The new discovery was, however, that these departures from official procedures are not idiosyncratic but become socially organized. The social patterns that are informally organized by the participants themselves complement those formally organized for them by management. Furthermore, the informal organizations that always arise in formal organizations, as Barnard pointed out, are essential for operations.[6]

Simultaneously with Barnard, a research team arrived at the same insight from its study of industrial workers in an electric plant. Roethlisberger and Dickson[7] found that the informal relations in a work group assumed a distinctive structure, with subgroups and status differences, and that informal norms emerged that regulated the performance of workers. Specifically, workers were expected by their fellows neither to produce too fast nor to produce too slowly, and deviations from these group norms were penalized by ridicule, loss of status, and eventually ostracism. In other words, workers informally organized themselves to control output, and an informal status structure complemented this organized social control. The informal organization, therefore, had important implications for production.

Research on human relations in industry proliferated widely after this pioneering study, and a number of case studies of bureaucracies have attempted to apply its insights in order to refine Weber's analysis. Gouldner, for example, shows that managerial succession in an industrial organization promoted bureaucratization, as implied by Weber's theory, because a new manager unfamiliar with informal practices is constrained to rely on official procedures to implement his directives. But such exercise of authority that rests on bureaucratic rules and discipline should be distinguished from professional authority that rests on technical expertness, a distinction Weber failed to make explicit.[8]

The general conclusion that emerges from these case studies of informal organization in bureaucracies is that procedures formally instituted for specific purposes in organizations recurrently create disturbances in other respects and the informal patterns that typically arise to cope with these disruptions often produce a basic reorganization of operations. Whereas the focus on informal practices and relations permitted some refinement of Weber's theory, it also led investigators increasingly away from the study of the fundamental structural features of complex organizations

[6] Chester I. Barnard, *The Functions of the Executive* (Cambridge: Harvard University Press, 1938), pp. 115–123.

[7] Fritz J. Roethlisberger and William J. Dickson, *Management and the Worker* (Cambridge: Harvard University Press, 1939).

[8] Alvin W. Gouldner, *Patterns of Industrial Bureaucracy* (Glencoe: Free Press, 1954).

Recent Research on Administrative Structure

The purpose of a theory of formal organizations is to explain the distinctive features of these complex structures in terms of some general principles; for instance, to explain under what conditions an advanced division of labor develops in organizations, or a separate administrative staff emerges, or an explicit body of rules becomes elaborated. In other words, a theory of organizations cannot take the characteristics of organizations as given but always raises the question of why these characteristics came into existence. The first step in answering this question is to discover which characteristics of organizations tend to occur together, and this requires comparing the characteristics of many different organizations. A basic limitation of the case studies of work groups in organizations is that they have to take the characteristics of the single organization under investigation in each case as given and merely examine how these given characteristics influence informal relations and practices. These case studies, therefore, necessarily neglected the central problem of organization theory—namely, what produces various bureaucratic characteristics—since this problem can only be studied in a comparative framework in which many organizations are contrasted. Weber's analysis is clearly conceived in such a comparative framework in which the characteristics of the organizations themselves are the center of attention. Case studies of organizations do not have this primary focus, but recent research has again adopted such a comparative approach.

A number of empirical studies have investigated whether the proportionate size of the administrative staff is bigger in large organizations than it is in small ones. Since Weber held that large organizations are more bureaucratized than small ones and that the elaboration of the administrative machinery is a bureaucratic characteristic, his analysis implies that the relative size of the administrative component should be directly associated with the size of an organization. Actually, however, studies of industrial concerns, hospitals, and some other organizations found that the proportionate size of the administrative component decreases as the size of organizations increases.[9] It is true that more complex organizations have a larger administrative ratio than simpler ones and that large organizations tend to be complex, but the proportion of staff devoted to administrative tasks nevertheless declines with increasing size. There is an economy of scale which enables larger organizations to get along with a proportionately smaller administrative staff.

At least one aspect of bureaucratization, the elaboration of the administrative apparatus, is not a function of increasing size, contrary to what

[9] For a summary of such studies, see Peter M. Blau and W. Richard Scott, *Formal Organizations* (San Francisco: Chandler, 1962).

Weber implies. Other aspects of bureaucratization, however, appear to be directly related to size, in accordance with Weber's analysis. Thus, one study found a very strong relationship between the size of government agencies and the division of labor in them; the larger an agency, the more subdivided are responsibilities.[10] Subsequent research has shown that other types of organizations exhibit a similar association between size and division of labor. Written rules and procedures also seem to be more prevalent in large organizations than in small ones. Moreover, recent comparative studies corroborate some of Weber's propositions about the functional interdependence between organizational characteristics. For example, although task specialization improves operating economy in government agencies, it makes the organizational structure more complex, and the problems of communication produced by such complexity impede economy. A sizable administrative apparatus, apparently serving the function of coping with these problems of communication, restores operating economy in complex organizations.

Comparative research on organizations promises to contribute most to the refinement of organizational theory by indicating the conditions under which various bureaucratic characteristics tend to arise. Finally, one more illustration from an exploratory study of written rules in different types of organizations may be cited. An important and widely discussed issue is that of the relationship between professionalization and bureaucratization. Weber implies that the two tend to occur together, whereas some of his critics have indicated the fundamental differences between these two methods of rationalizing social action. One might assume, for instance, that professionalization lessens the need for explicit written rules. However, the comparative analysis suggests that this is not necessarily the case. If professional organizations are compared with nonprofessional ones, it seems that professionalization has a standardizing effect on the elaboration of written rules. Specifically, professionalization tends to encourage the development of written rules when few exist, as in small organizations, and to discourage their development only when many exist, as in large organizations. The discharge of professional responsibilities appears to be hampered not only by excessive bureaucratic rules that impinge on discretion but also by rules that are insufficient to create an orderly working environment. The tentative conclusion from this exploratory study,[11] which needs to be confirmed in future research, is that professionalization promotes the development of explicit rules in organiza-

[10] Peter M. Blau et al., "The Structure of Small Bureaucracies," *American Sociological Review* 31 (1966), 179–191. (Included here as Chapter 13.)

[11] Peter M. Blau and Amy W. Orum, "Conditions of Bureaucratic Formalization," in Albert J. Reiss, Jr. (ed.), *Cooley and Sociological Analysis* (Ann Arbor: University of Michigan Press, 1968), pp. 68–86.

tions as long as few exist, but that it impedes the fuller elaboration of rules once many exist already.

Comparisons of many organizations are needed to arrive at conclusions of this type, because only such comparisons can specify which characteristics of organizations generally occur together and what conditions give rise to them. Comparative research promises to contribute most to the advancement of organization theory, since the refinement of the theory Weber outlined requires further specification of the conditions under which organizations develop various constellations of attributes.

2. Critical Remarks on Weber's Theory of Authority

Max Weber has often been criticized for advocating a *wertfrei*, ethically neutral approach in the social sciences and for thereby denying to man, in the words of Leo Strauss, "any science, empirical or rational, any knowledge, scientific or philosophic, of the true value system."[1] On the other hand, Carl Friedrich points out that Weber's "ideal-type analysis led him to introduce value judgments into his discussion of such issues as bureaucracy."[2] There is some justification for both criticisms. Indeed, a characteristic of Weber's work is that it can be and has been subjected to opposite criticisms, not only in this respect but also in others. Historians object to his disregard for the specific historical conditions under which the social phenomena he analyzes have taken place, which sometimes leads him to combine historical events

Originally published in 1963.

[1] Leo Strauss, *Natural Right and History* (Chicago: University of Chicago Press, 1953), p. 41; see also pp. 35–80.

[2] Carl J. Friedrich, "Some Observations on Weber's Analysis of Bureaucracy," in R. K. Merton *et al.* (eds.), *Reader in Bureaucracy* (Glencoe: Free Press, 1952), p. 31.

that occurred centuries apart into a conception of a social system.[3] Sociologists, in contrast, accuse him of being preoccupied with interpreting unique historical constellations, such as Western capitalism, instead of studying recurrent social phenomena which make it possible to develop testable generalizations about social structures. His methodology is attacked as being neo-Kantian,[4] but his concept of *Verstehen* is decried as implying an intuitionist method. While his theories are most frequently cited in contradistinction to those of Marx, they have also been described as basically similar to Marx's.[5]

The fact that Weber's work can be attacked on opposite grounds is due to his position in the development of social thought and, in particular, to his methodological and theoretical orientation. Weber is one of the fathers of modern sociology. His contribution to the development of this new discipline undoubtedly has been more significant than Comte's or Spencer's and nearly as important as—some would say more important than—Durkheim's or Simmel's. Implicitly in his theoretical analyses and explicitly in his methodological writings, he outlined a new approach to the study of social life that helped to differentiate sociology from the other social sciences. He formulated the new approach in contradistinction to various existing alternatives. It was at variance with the idealistic tradition from which Weber himself derived as well as with Marx's materialism; with positivism, utilitarianism, and social Darwinism as well as with the Enlightenment philosophy of natural rights. The task he set for sociology is to interpret historical and social occurrences in terms of the prevailing value orientation that give them their meaning without imposing the investigator's value judgment on them. In short, the substantive aim is a value-free study of value complexes in societies. The methodological aim is a generalizing science of historical phenomena and processes.

One reason, then, why contradictory criticisms advanced against Weber's theory are often both valid is that the new approach he charted is a multiple synthesis which conflicts in some respects with both the various theses and antitheses from which it derived. A more specific reason, as we shall see, is that Weber's method of analysis, notably his ideal-type construct, has limitations that leave his procedure wide open to a variety of criticisms. A final reason is that Weber's substantive theories tend to focus on conflicting social

[3] Notably in his conceptions of religious systems; see Max Weber, *Gesammelte Aufsaetze zur Religionssoziologie*, 3 vols. (Tuebingen: J. C. B. Mohr, 1920–21).

[4] Strauss, *op cit.*, pp. 76–78.

[5] See Karl Loewith, "Max Weber und Karl Marx." *Archiv fur Sozialwissenschaft und Sozialpolitik* 67 (1932), pp. 53–99, 175–214.

forces, which makes them subject to criticism from opposite perspectives; thus his analysis stressed the role of economic interests too little for the Marxist and too much for the idealist.

Despite Weber's great concern with the forces that order and organize social life and integrate social systems (which, however, probably has been exaggerated in Parsons's interpretation of his theories), he did not view social structure as a functionally unified *Gestalt* but as a complex pattern governed by opposing forces and hence in continual flux.[6] His overall conception of reality is perhaps most strongly influenced by Hegel's philosophy, as Bendix suggests.[7] He usually proceeds by developing contrasting social types, only to show that both or all of them can be found in the same empirical situation, creating a dynamic potential for change. Notwithstanding his emphasis on the unrelenting forces of rationalization and bureaucratization, he also calls attention to the intermittent eruption of charismatic leaders and movements, thereby contradicting the linear conception of change his other analysis seems to imply.[8] He is intrigued by the paradoxical consequences of social life. The most famous example is his conclusion that, although Confucianism approves and Puritanism disapproves of the pursuit of material welfare, Confucianism did not but Puritanism did promote the spirit of capitalism. Impatient with the oversimplification necessarily involved in subsuming empirical reality under a few general concepts, he constructed several pairs of concepts to examine the same contrast from slightly different perspectives, such as *wertrational* and *zweckrational*, substantive and formal rationality, charisma and bureaucracy. This dialectical and multi-focused approach makes Weber's analysis rich and full of fascinating insights, but it also makes his theories somewhat unsystematic and open to diverse criticisms.

The purpose of this paper is to examine critically Weber's theory of authority. After briefly summarizing the main concepts and analysis, a methodological criticism of Weber's procedure and some substantive criticisms of this theory will be presented.

[6] See his criticism of functionalism in Max Weber, *The Theory of Social and Economic Organization* (New York: Oxford University Press, 1947), pp. 101–109.

[7] Reinhard Bendix, *Max Weber* (Garden City: Anchor-Doubleday, 1962), pp. 387–388, 490–494.

[8] Bendix focuses upon the nonlinear and dialectical elements in Weber's theory of social change (*op. cit.*, pp. 325–328), whereas Talcott Parsons focuses on Weber's emphasis on progressive rationalization [*The Social System* (Glencoe: Free Press, 1951), pp. 500–502, and Talcott Parsons and Neil Smelser, *Economy and Society* (Glencoe: Free Press, 1956), pp. 291–293].

The Concept of Authority

Power is defined by Weber as a person's ability to impose his will upon others despite resistance.[9] He distinguishes two basic types of power, the domination of others that rests on the ability to influence their interests, and the domination that rests on authority, that is, the power to command and the duty to obey.[10] Weber does not explicitly consider coercive power in his analysis of domination,[11] nor does he deal with such forms of personal influence as persuasion, but it is convenient to clarify his concept of authority by contrasting it with these opposite extremes.

A fundamental criterion of authority is "a certain minimum of voluntary submission."[12] An army commander may impose his will upon the enemy, but he does not have authority over enemy soldiers, only over his own, since only the latter obey his commands because they are duty-bound to do so, while the former merely yield to the coercive force of his superior arms. Since authority entails voluntary compliance with the superior's directives, it obviates the need for coercive force or for sanctions. Resort to either positive incentives or coercive measures by a person in order to influence others is *prima facie* evidence that he does not have authority over them, for if he did their voluntary compliance would serve as an easier method of control over them.

Voluntary obedience is not a sufficient condition for authority, however, since other forms of personal influence also rest on willing compliance. In persuasion, for example, one person permits the influence of another to affect his decisions or actions. Authority is distinguished from persuasion by the fact that people *a priori* suspend their own judgment and accept that of an acknowledged superior without having to be convinced that his is correct. The subordinate in an authority relationship "holds in abeyance his own critical faculties for choosing between alternatives and uses the formal

---

[9] Weber presents slightly different definitions of power (Macht) in two parts of *Wirtschaft und Gesellschaft*, 2 vols. (Tuebingen: J. C. B. Mohr, 1925), which are translated, respectively, in *The Theory* . . ., p. 152, and in *Max Weber on Law in Economy and Society* (Cambridge: Harvard University Press, 1954), p. 323.

[10] The term *Herrschaft* (domination, translated by Parsons as "imperative control") is apparently intended by Weber as a subcategory of power and as a more general concept than authority, but he does not use the term consistently, sometimes including under it the power that rests on constellations of interest, and sometimes confining it to the power of command that rests on the duty to obey; see *Wirtschaft und Gesellschaft*, pp. 603–612, translated in *Max Weber on Law* . . ., Ch. xii.

[11] This criticism is the basis of Amitai Etzioni's typology of power in *A Comparative Analysis of Complex Organizations* (New York: Free Press, 1961), pp. 4–19, esp. p. 14.

[12] Weber, *The Theory* . . ., p. 324.

criterion of the receipt of a command or signal as his basis for choice."[13] In Weber's words, the "ruled" act as if they "had made the content of the (ruler's) command the maxim of their conduct for its own sake."[14]

Authority, then, involves unconditional willing obedience on the part of subordinates. It is not easy, however, to distinguish authority by these criteria from other forms of control. The slaves who blindly obey their master although he does not use a whip, for fear that he may do so, are not very different from the soldiers who obey their commander or the officials who obey their bureaucratic superior, since they too know that the superior may otherwise invoke sanctions to penalize them. But if we consider the slave's obedience to be *voluntary* compliance, then the distinction between this concept and coercion loses all its meaning. Many borderline cases exist, according to Weber, both because the distinction is an analytical one and because coercion or other forms of control often later develop into authority.[15] For this transformation to occur, however, a belief system must emerge that socially legitimates the exercise of control,[16] and this legitimating value system furnishes the final and basic distinguishing criterion of authority. We speak of authority, therefore, if the willing unconditional compliance of a group of people rests upon their shared beliefs that it is legitimate for the superior (person or impersonal agency) to impose his will upon them and that it is illegitimate for them to refuse obedience.

Before turning to the three types of authority Weber differentiates, let us briefly note some problems raised by his central concept. Authority denotes imperative control, from which there is no easy escape, yet a major criterion of it is voluntary compliance. While I may have stressed the voluntary element in authority more than Weber does himself, I have done so deliberately to call attention to the implicit paradox between voluntarism and authoritarian control, since by making it explicit we can hope to clarify it. Weber ignores this paradox, despite his interest in paradoxical phenomena, because his focus on types of legitimacy leads him to take the existence of legitimate authority for granted[17] and never systematically to examine the structural conditions under which it emerges out of other forms of power.

---

[13] Herbert A. Simon, *Administrative Behavior* (New York: Macmillan, 1952), pp. 126–127.

[14] *Max Weber on Law . . .*, p. 328.

[15] *Ibid.*, pp. 325–327.

[16] *The Theory . . .*, p. 325.

[17] Even as sympathetic an interpreter as Bendix notes that Weber takes the existence of traditional and legal authority as given; see *op. cit.*, pp. 386–387. While Bendix adds that Weber traces how legal authority develops from the other two types, even in this case Weber's concern is not with the development of legitimate authority out of other forms of power.

Another problem concerns the specific referent of Weber's concept of authority. When he presents his abstract definitions, he seems to refer to authority in interpersonal relations. In his analysis of empirical situations, on the other hand, he is concerned with political systems or institutions, such as feudalism. Moreover, in his analysis of historical cases where he applies and develops his concepts he sometimes treats them as concrete types and sometimes as analytical elements. Feudalism, for example, can hardly be considered an analytical element that can be found in all kinds of historical situations, but charisma can be, and Weber sometimes, although not always, treats it as an analytical element. To ignore the important methodological difference between these two kinds of concepts confuses the analysis. These difficulties stem from Weber's abstract conception of action[18] and from the particular procedure he employed to derive generalizations about historical reality.

Types of Authority

The distinctive feature of authority is a belief system that defines the exercise of social control as legitimate. Three types of authority are consequently distinguished by Weber on the basis of differences in the legitimating belief systems that validate them.

The first type is authority legitimated by the sanctity of tradition. In "traditional authority" the present social order is viewed as sacred, eternal, and inviolable. The dominant person or group, usually defined by heredity, is thought to have been preordained to rule over the rest. The subjects are bound to the ruler by personal dependence and a tradition of loyalty, and their obedience to him is further reinforced by such cultural beliefs as the divine right of kings. All systems of government prior to the development of the modern state would seem to exemplify traditional authority. Although the ruler's power is limited by the traditions that legitimate it, this restriction is not severe, since some arbitrariness on the part of the ruler is traditionally expected. Generally, traditional authority tends to perpetuate the *status quo* and is ill suited for adaptation to social change; indeed, historical change undermines its very foundation. The spirit of traditional authority is well captured in the phrase, "The king is dead—long live the king."

The values that legitimate "charismatic authority," Weber's second type, define a leader and his mission as being inspired by divine or supernatural powers. The leader, in effect, heads a new social movement, and his followers

---

[18] As noted by Paul F. Lazarsfeld, "A Duality in Max Weber's Writings on Social Action," paper delivered at the meetings of the American Sociological Society, Detroit, 1956.

and disciples are converts to a new cause. There is a sense of being "called" to spread the new gospel, a sense of rejecting the past and heralding the future. Devotion to the leader and the conviction that his pronouncements embody the spirit and ideals of the movement are the source of the group's willing obedience to his commands. Charismatic leaders may appear in almost any area of social life—as religious prophets, political idols, or military heroes. Indeed, an element of charisma is involved whenever a person inspires others to follow his lead. Charismatic authority usually acts as a revolutionary force, inasmuch as it involves rejection of traditional values and a rebellion against the established order, often in reaction to a crisis. There is also an anarchistic streak in charismatic movements, a disdain for routine tasks and problems of organization or administration, since the leader's inspiration and the sacred mission must not be profaned by mundane considerations. For Weber, the innovating spirit of charisma is symbolized by Christ's words, "It is written . . ., but I say unto you. . . ."

The third type, "legal authority," is legitimated by a formalistic belief in the supremacy of the law, whatever its specific content. The assumption is that a body of legal rules has been deliberately established to further the rational pursuit of collective goals. In such a system obedience is owed not to a person—whether traditional chief or charismatic leader—but to a set of impersonal principles. These principles include the requirement to follow directives originating from an office superior to one's own, regardless of who occupies this higher office. All organizations that have been formally established—in contrast to the organizations of social life that have slowly emerged in the course of history or that have spontaneously erupted—illustrate legal authority structures. The prototype is the modern government, which has a monopoly over the legitimate use of physical coercion, and the same principles are reflected in its various executive agencies, such as the army, and also in private corporations, such as a factory. While superiors have authority over subordinates, the former as well as the latter are subject to the authority of the official body of impersonal regulations. Legal authority may be epitomized in the phrase, "A government of laws, not of men."

At one point, Weber outlines these three plus a fourth type of belief that legitimates a social order, namely, "rational belief in an absolute value [which creates the legitimacy] of 'Natural Law.' "[19] This fourth type of legitimate *order*, however, is not included in the subsequent more detailed analysis of legitimate *authority*, while the other three are. Does this imply that Weber considered a *wertrationale* orientation toward natural rights a possible basis of political institutions but not a basis of political authority? He makes no explicit statements to help us answer this question.

[19] *The Theory* . . ., p. 131.

Although his typology of authority involves three main types and not two, it also reveals the Hegelian practice of Weber to refine concepts by juxtaposing opposites; only it entails a more complex combination of contrasts. The traditional authority which maintains the *status quo* is defined by contrast with two dynamic forces that threaten it, the revolutionary ideals advocated by a charismatic leader, and the rational pursuit of ends guided by abstract formal principles in disregard of historical tradition and time-honored convention. The personal submission to a charismatic leader is defined in juxtaposition with two impersonal forces that tend to undermine it in the course of historical developments, the crystallization of the revolutionary movement into a traditional order, and its bureaucratization into a rational formal organization. The formal acceptance of legal principles as authoritative is characterized in contradistinction to two irrational forces which must be overcome for such formal rationality to be realized, the power of tradition, and the power of charisma. Extrapolation from these contrasts yields two important features of each authority system. The power of tradition is neither rational nor strictly personal. (While there are personal elements in traditional authority, analytically traditionalism should be considered an impersonal force.) The power of charisma is dynamic and nonrational. The power of rational law, finally, is impersonal and dynamic.[20]

Weber's extensive analysis of authority structures follows somewhat different directions in the case of each type. His discussion of traditional authority focuses upon differences between subtypes, notably between patrimonialism and feudalism. Although "both types have in common rulers who grant rights in return for military and administrative services,"[21] patrimonialism is an extension of the patriarchal authority of the master over his household to include a group of dependent officials, whereas feudalism originates in a contract between independent knights and an overlord. "If a knight enters the service of a ruler, he remains a free man; he does not become a personal dependent like the patrimonial retainer."[22]

In his analysis of charismatic authority, on the other hand, Weber is not concerned with different subtypes or with historical antecedents but primarily with subsequent developments. He traces in detail the ways in which charisma tends to become routinized in the course of time and to develop into traditional or bureaucratic institutions. The personal significance of the leader makes charismatic structures inherently unstable.

[20] The term *dynamic* is used in the specific sense of "producing social change."

[21] Bendix, *op. cit.*, p. 369.

[22] *Ibid.*, p. 361; see pp. 329–381 for an excellent summary of the contrast between patrimonialism and feudalism, which is based on discussions of Weber that are dispersed in different parts of his writings.

Weber's discussion of legal authority deals both with the historical conditions that led to its development and with its implications for subsequent developments, but there is again a difference in focus. In his treatment of charisma, his concern is with its transformation into *other* systems. In his treatment of legal rationality, however, his concern is with the way in which *this* system increasingly penetrates all institutions and becomes more fully realized throughout society. In short, Weber's theory encompasses only the historical processes that lead from charismatic movements to increasing rationalization and does not include an analysis of the historical conditions and social processes that give rise to charismatic eruptions in the social structure. He has no theory of revolution.

Weber's concept of bureaucracy occupies a central place in his analysis of legal authority, since a bureaucracy is the prototype of a social structure that is formally organized in terms of the principles of legal rationality and authority. The various characteristics of bureaucracy stipulated by Weber are well known: officials are assigned specialized responsibilities; they are appointed to positions on the basis of technical expertness and expected to pursue a lifelong career; offices are organized into a hierarchy of authority and responsibility; operations are governed by a formally established system of rules and regulations; written documents of all official actions are kept; and officials are expected to maintain impersonal detachment in their dealings with clients and subordinates—to name only the most important ones. Weber indicates the interdependence between these organizational attributes, and he stresses that this combination of attributes maximizes rational decision-making and administrative efficiency. He seems to have designed the ideal-type bureaucracy in a deliberate attempt to describe how a large number of men must be organized in order to promote administrative efficiency in the rational pursuit of given objectives. Optimum rationality and and efficiency appear to be the criteria in terms of which the ideal type intentionally differs from empirical bureaucracies.

The Ideal Type

Before criticizing Weber's method of analysis, a few words must be said about his basic approach and the important methodological contribution he has made. His aim, as previously mentioned, was an objective generalizing science of historical reality, where the meaning of social actions is interpreted in terms of prevailing values. Important as economic forces were in his thinking—note how preoccupied he is with problems of Western capitalism— he considered them as well as all historical processes and social patterns in need of interpretation by a more basic principle, namely, the spirit of a community which gives all social life its meaning. While this basic conception reveals the influence of German idealism, Weber's reformulation of it is under the influence of materialistic philosophy. He conceived of the spirit of a society or of an age not as a supernatural force but as a common value orientation that is reflected in the prevailing, observable beliefs and actions of people. Besides, his interest centered on the interplay between these spiritual values and material conditions of existence, particularly the class structure. If he held that the development of modern capitalism was contingent on the ethical values of Calvinism, for example, he also showed that the nature of religious values depends on the class position of the status group in which they originate: in the case of Protestantism, the urban middle class. Rejecting both the one-sided idealism of Hegel and the one-sided materialism of Marx, he viewed the historical process as governed by the conflicts and combinations between spiritual ideals and material conditions.

In one respect, according to Weber, the method of sociology is unlike that of the natural sciences and like that of social philosophy. Since values give social life its meaning, it is not enough to show that two social conditions occur together or that one produces the other. It is also necessary to interpret these observations in terms of existing values. This is the gist of Weber's concept of *Verstehen*, as I understand it. In another respect, however, the method of sociology parallels that of the natural sciences and contrasts with that of history. Sociology is a generalizing science. Although every historical event is unique, the sociologist must ignore these unique aspects of social events and subsume them under general categories or types in order to generalize about them. Even if history furnishes us only with one instance of a social system, as in the case of modern capitalism, Weber treated it as an ideal type in an attempt to explain its development by deriving generalizations about it rather than by interpreting the configuration of historical conditions that led up to it. This procedure was his solution to the issue posed in the German *Methodenstreit*, notably by Dilthey, Windelband, and Rickert.[23]

The ideal type is an abstraction that combines several analytical elements which appear in reality not in pure form but in various admixtures. In actual bureaucracies, for example, officials are not completely impersonal, not all official business is recorded in writing, and the division of responsibilities is not always unambiguous. To be sure, the ideal type does not correspond to any empirical case or to the average of all cases, but it is inten-

[23] See Wilhelm Dilthey, *Einleitung in die Geisteswissenschaften* (Leipzig: Duncker & Humbolt, 1883); Wilhelm Windelband, "Geschichte und Naturwissenschaft," lecture given in Strassburg, 1894, published in his *Praeludien* (Tuebingen: J. C. B. Mohr, 1907) and Heinrich Rickert, *Die Grenzen der naturwissenschaftlichen Begriffsbildung* (Tuebingen: J. C. B. Mohr), 1902.

tionally designed in this form, as Weber stresses.[24] It is not a substitute for empirical investigation of historical situations but a framework for guiding the research by indicating the factors to be examined and the ways in which the observed patterns differ from the pure type.

A criticism of the ideal type advanced by Schelting is that implicit in Weber's procedure are several different constructs.[25] The two basic ones are the individualizing ideal type, which refers to a specific social system that occurred only once in history, such as Western capitalism, and the generalizing ideal type, which refers to a category that includes many social systems of the same kind, such as bureaucracy. In my opinion, Weber's use of the same procedure in the analysis of these different problems was quite deliberate. He tried to extend Rickert's conception and break through the dilemma posed by Windelband's postulate that one cannot generalize about unique events by treating Western capitalism, a unique historical phenomenon, as if it were a general type, that is, just as he treated bureaucracy. The attempt, however, is doomed to failure. One case cannot yield a general principle. For, as the very term implies, a generalization must refer to more than one case. But how can we possibly know that it does if there is only one case to examine? The relevant requirement of a generalizing science is that it abstracts those elements of unique occurrences that many have in common, thereby transforming them into nonunique cases in terms of the conceptual scheme and making it possible to subsume them under general categories. This is not accomplished by Weber's very different procedure of abstracting those elements of a historical system that reveal its most distinctive features in pure form. The analytical category and the ideal type are two entirely different abstractions from reality. Had Weber selected a few distinctive elements of modern capitalism that it has in common with other economic systems, he could have derived a generalization about the analytical elements of religious systems that promote these characteristic features of capitalism. But he was too interested in the unique aspects of Western capitalism to formulate his problem in this sociological manner, and his ideal type is no adequate substitute for doing so.

The generalizing ideal type is also subject to criticism. Parsons notes that it implies a fixed relationship between various elements, say, specification of responsibility and legal rationality—although these elements may in fact vary independently of one another.[26] Friedrich's objections are that the ideal

[24] *The Theory* . . ., p. 111.

[25] Alexander von Schelting, *Max Weber's Wissenschaftslehre* (Tuebingen: J. C. B. Mohr), 1934.

[26] Talcott Parsons, *The Structure of Social Action* (New York: McGraw-Hill, 1937), pp. 606–609; and his comments in the introduction to Weber, *The Theory* . . ., pp. 13 and 75.

type is neither derived by systematic induction from empirical observations nor by deduction from more abstract concepts and that it implicitly led Weber to introduce value judgments into his analysis.[27] Bendix points out that the procedure of constructing ideal types obscures the very contradictions, conflicts, and compromises in which Weber was especially interested.[28]

A fundamental shortcoming of the ideal type, which underlies many criticisms of it, is that it is an admixture of conceptual scheme and hypotheses. Take the ideal type of bureaucracy. In part, it is a conceptual scheme which calls attention to the aspects of organizations that should be included in the investigation, and which supplies criteria for defining an actual organization as more or less bureaucratized. In addition, however, Weber indicates that these characteristics tend to occur together, that certain historical conditions promote them (such as a money economy), and that the specified characteristics and, in particular, their combination increase administrative efficiency. These are not elucidations of concepts but statements of fact which are assumed to be correct. Whereas concepts are not subject to empirical verification, hypothesized factual relationships are. Only empirical research can ascertain, for instance, whether authoritarian management and impersonal detachment, singly and in combination, always promote administrative efficiency, as predicted, or whether they do so only under certain conditions, or perhaps not at all. But what bearing would such empirical findings have on the ideal type? If we modify the type in accordance with the empirical reality, it is no longer a pure type, and if we do not, it would become a meaningless construct. Since the ideal type confuses statements that have different significance for empirical investigation and theoretical inference, it has serious limitations compared to analytical conceptual schemes.

Ignoring that Weber's analysis of bureaucracy is assumed to represent an ideal type, it can be considered a sophisticated conceptual scheme and a set of interrelated hypotheses, which furnish guidelines for the study of bureaucracies of various kinds, and which can be refined on the basis of research as well as conceptual clarification. In Weber's ideal bureaucracy, for instance, the official's legal authority rests on technical expertness, but in actual bureaucracies, the professional standards of the expert often come into conflict with the administrative requirements of the managerial official, even if the two are the same person. Professional and bureaucratic authority must be distinguished, as Parsons and Gouldner point out,[29] to clarify some of the

---

[27] Friedrich, *op. cit.*, pp. 27–33.

[28] Bendix, *op. cit.*, p. 275.

[29] Parsons, Introduction to Weber, *op. cit.*, pp. 58–60 (footnote 4), and Alvin W. Gouldner, *Patterns of Industrial Bureaucracy* (Glencoe: Free Press, 1954), p. 22.

central issues and conflicts in today's organizations which tend increasingly to be both professionalized and bureaucratized. Another problem is the specification of conditions under which the bureaucratic characteristics Weber delineated further operating efficiency. To cite only one illustration, it is highly questionable that strict lines of authority in an organization have the same significance for effective administration in a hospital as in an army, or in a country where an egalitarian ideology prevails as in Weber's imperial Germany. To refine Weber's theory by the investigation of such problems entails dispensing with the notion of the ideal type.

Elaboration of the Conception of Authority

Turning now to a substantive analysis and clarification of Weber's conception of authority, the focus is on some issues his theory has not resolved. The first question is posed by the description of authority as voluntary imperative control. How can compliance be imperative if it is voluntary? The second problem is that of the origins of authority, especially of the processes through which other forms of power become transformed into legitimate authority. Closely related is a third issue, namely, that of the structural conditions that give rise to authority systems, of the existential determination of the beliefs that legitimate authority.

Authority often originates in other forms of power; for example, the conqueror later becomes the king. In a bureaucracy, the system with which I am most familiar and which I therefore shall use as an illustration, the situation is somewhat more complex. The legal contract into which officials enter by becoming members of a bureaucracy legitimates the authority of superiors over subordinates. Although employees assume the contractual obligation to follow managerial directives, the scope of the formal authority that has its source in the legal contract is very limited. The legal authority of management to assign tasks to subordinates is rarely questioned—there is willing compliance—but this legal authority does not and cannot encourage willingness to work hard or to exercise initiative. Managerial responsibilities require more influence over subordinates than that which rests on their legal obligations.

The bureaucratic manager has the official power of sanction over his subordinates, a typical manifestation of which is the civil service efficiency rating, on which the career chances of officials depend. He may use his sanctioning power directly to impose his will upon subordinates. Such domination does not, strictly speaking, involve the exercise of authority, since his orders are followed to avoid penalties or attain rewards rather than simply because doing so is an accepted duty. An alternative strategy is for the manager to try to expand the scope of his influence over subordinates by obligating them to follow his directives and requests. This strategy involves essentially relinquishing some of his official power in exchange for legitimate authority.

The official position and power of the bureaucratic manager give him opportunities to furnish services to subordinates and, thereby, create social obligations. His superior administrative knowledge, on the basis of which he presumably was promoted, enables him to train newcomers and advise even experienced officials in difficult cases. His managerial status gives him access to top echelons and staff specialists, making it possible for him to channel needed information to subordinates and, what is of special importance, represent their interests with the higher administration or the legislature. In brief, he has many occasions to benefit subordinates and make them indebted. His formal prerogatives and powers make it possible for him to earn their good will merely by not exercising them—for instance, by not enforcing an unpopular no-smoking rule. The manager who discharges his responsibilities by refraining from resort to his coercive powers and by devoting effort to benefiting subordinates obligates them to himself. The advantages they derive from his mode of supervision obligate them to reciprocate by willingly complying with his demands and requests.

This type of personal influence over *individual* subordinates does not constitute the exercise of authority in the specific Weberian sense either. For authority requires social legitimation. Only the shared values of a social collectivity can legitimate the power or influence of a superior and thus transform it into authority. The bureaucratic superior whose managerial practices further the *collective* interest of subordinates creates joint social obligations. Hence, the group of subordinates has a common interest in remaining under this manager and maintaining his good will, which finds expression in shared feelings of loyalty to him and in group norms making compliance with his directives an obligation enforced by the subordinates themselves. The prevalence of such a normative orientation among subordinates legitimates the superior's authority over them.

The distinguishing criterion of authority suggested here is that structural constraints rooted in the collectivity of subordinates rather than instruments of power or influences wielded by the superior himself enforce compliance with his directives. To discharge its joint obligations[30] to the superior, the group of subordinates makes compliance with his directives part of the common norms, which are internalized by its members, and which are socially enforced by them against potential deviants. Such normative constraints

[30] The closely related concept of joint liability is used by Max Weber in his discussion of the Jews' relation to God, which is translated in *Ancient Judaism* (Glencoe: Free Press, 1952), pp. 215–216, and to which my attention was called by Bendix, *op. cit.*, pp. 230–241.

require even the individual who does not feel personally obligated to the superior to submit to his authority. This conception helps to resolve the paradox posed by the definition of authority as a form of social control hat is both voluntary and imperative. Voluntary social action is never devoid of social constraints. From the standpoint of the collectivity of subordinates, compliance with the superior's directives is voluntary, but from the standpoint of the individual subordinate it is the result of compelling social pressures. The compliance of subordinates in authority relationships is as voluntary as our custom of wearing clothes.

Let us recapitulate the main points of the argument and somewhat refine them. Authority usually has its source in other forms of power, specifically, in a situation where a group of people are dependent in vital respects on one person (or another group). Their dependence enables him to coerce them to do his bidding. He can, however, use his power and the resources from which it derives—whether these are superior physical force, wealth, knowledge, or charisma—to furnish services to subordinates and thus obligate them to follow his directives, which makes it unnecessary for him to coerce them. In this manner, coercive power is transformed into personal influence. If the superior's actions advance the common interests of subordinates and make them collectively obligated to him, a further transformation tends to occur as group norms enforce compliance with his directives to repay the joint obligations to him. This is the process by which personal influence turns into legitimate authority. The influence of one individual over another in a pair relationship cannot become legitimate authority, because only the shared norms of a collectivity can legitimate social control and only the collective enforcement of compliance makes the compliance independent of the superior's personal influence over the individual subordinate. But once an authority system has become institutionalized, it can find expression in apparently isolated pairs. A father exercises authority over an only child, since culturally defined role expectations, which are enforced by members of the community, such as teachers and neighbors, constrain the child to obey his father. Such institutionalized authority is typically supplemented by other forms of influence.

The power of sanction formally invested in the bureaucratic official has paradoxical implications for authority. In terms of the conception advanced, the direct use of sanctions by a manager to compel subordinates to carry out his orders does not constitute the exercise of authority. Quite the contrary, it shows that his directives do not command their unconditional compliance. It is this official power of sanction, on the other hand, that makes subordinates dependent on the bureaucratic superior, and this dependence, in turn, is the ultimate source of his authority over them. This paradox is not confined to bureaucracy but is characteristic of all power: its use to coerce others destroys its potential as a source of authority over them. What is distinctive about the bureaucratic case is that the instruments with which an official readily can extend his authority over subordinates beyond the narrow confines of the legal contract are placed in his hands by the formal organization.

In general, a situation of collective dependence is fertile soil for the development of authority, but its development is contingent on judicious restraint by the superior in the use of his power. If he alienates subordinates by imposing his will upon them against their resistance, they will obey only under duress and not freely follow his lead. If, however, he uses some of his power to further their collective interests, the common experience of dependence on and obligation to the superior is apt to give rise to shared beliefs that it is right and in the common interest to submit to his command, and these social values and the corresponding social norms of compliance legitimate and enforce his authority over them, as has been noted.[31] In brief, coercive power and authority are alternative forms of social control, which are incompatible, but which both have their roots in conditions of collective dependence.

The question arises, what are the various kinds of collective dependence in which authority has its ultimate source? Weber calls attention to the importance of "the *monopoly* of the *legitimate* use of physical force" for the power of the state.[32] The transformation of this coercive power by political values and norms produces political authority. Note that this type cuts across Weber's distinction between legal and traditional authority, since traditional political structures as well as rationalized legal ones ultimately rest on the force of arms. The dependence of the followers on a charismatic leader, in contrast, is due to their ideological convictions. Their firm belief in the mission that the charismatic leader represents and symbolizes makes his approval and disapproval more important to them than any other sanctions. This is similar to the dependence created by any personal attachment, such as a boy's infatuation with a girl, except that the ideology makes an entire collectivity dependent on the leader and is, therefore, an essential condition for the development of charismatic authority. A very different source of domination is technical knowledge (real or attributed; quackery will do if superstition gives it credence), which also makes people in need of it dependent on a person. Socially acknowledged superior competence may be considered the basic source of professional authority. Finally, people are

---

[31] See Friedrich's discussion of authority as resting on the "potentiality of reasoned elaboration" of a communication in terms of existing beliefs and values, on the one hand, and as related to the exercise of discretionary power, on the other, in Carl J. Friedrich (ed.), *Authority* (Nomos I), (Cambridge: Harvard University Press, 1958), pp. 28–48.

[32] *The Theory* . . ., p. 154 (italics in original).

dependent on others for their material well-being, notably on their employer and his representatives. This dependence gives rise to managerial authority.[33]

The purpose of presenting these types is not to make a claim for a definitive typology of authority but merely to illustrate that a classification on the basis of the dependency conditions in which authority is rooted does not yield the same types as Weber's classification in terms of legitimating beliefs. Although differences in these legitimating value systems have significant implications for social systems, as Weber's analysis shows, a theory of authority should also come to grips with the structural conditions in which it originates.

Democracy and Bureaucracy

What is the referent of Weber's concepts of authority? In some discussions, he appears to deal with three analytical principles that underlie conformity—convention, ethics, and law.[34] At other times, he seems to refer to political systems—traditional political institutions, revolutionary movements, and modern governments based on rational law. (The limitations of the ideal type may be responsible for Weber's switching between these different conceptualizations.) If his analysis is considered an approach to a theory of political institutions, it is amazing that it does not include a systematic treatment of democracy or the general conception of sovereignty, its locus and its distribution. Democracy is subsumed under the legal order, although Weber makes it clear that a legal order is not necessarily democratic.[35] On the contrary, the prototype of the legal order is the autocratic bureaucracy. "Experience tends universally to show that . . . the monocratic variety of bureaucracy . . . [is] capable of attaining the highest degree of efficiency and is in this sense formally the most rational means of carrying out control over human beings."[36] It is this kind of unsupported and questionable value judgment that Friedrich undoubtedly has in mind when he states that Weber's discussions of bureaucracy "vibrate with something of the Prussian enthusiasm for the military organization."[37]

Weber examines the relationship between democracy and bureaucracy from several perspectives, but he never systematically differentiates the two

---

[33] This conceptualization was suggested by, although it differs from, the classification of organizations in terms of incentives in Peter B. Clark and James Q. Wilson, "Incentive Systems," *Administrative Science Quarterly* 6 (1961), 129–166.

[34] See *The Theory* . . ., pp. 126–132.

[35] *Ibid*, p. 310: "This legality . . . may derive from a voluntary agreement of the interested parties on the relevant terms. On the other hand, it may be imposed on the basis of what is held to be a legitimate authority."

[36] *Ibid*, p. 337.

[37] Friedrich, *op. cit.*, p. 31.

concepts in the manner in which he distinguishes the legal order from the two other types of authority structures. One theme in Weber's analysis is the paradoxical relationship between the two institutions. Some legal requirements further democracy as well as bureaucracy, such as the principle of "equal justice under law," and the emphasis on technical knowledge rather than inherited status prerogatives (achieved instead of ascribed status), both of which help produce a leveling of status differences.[38] Nevertheless, " 'democracy' as such is opposed to the 'rule' of bureaucracy, in spite and perhaps because of its unavoidable yet unintended promotion of bureaucratization."[39] A major reason for this is that bureaucracy concentrates power in the hands of those in charge of the bureaucratic apparatus and thereby undermines democracy.[40]

A related problem with which Weber is concerned is the contrast between political and bureaucratic domination. Under the rule of law, as Bendix notes, "success in the struggle for power becomes manifest in decisive influence upon the enactment of binding rules. To exercise such decisive influence a politician must contend with others like himself in the competition for votes, in political organizations, and in the legislative process of enacting laws and supervising their execution."[41] Political power is apparently viewed as containing elements of the two opposite prototypes, economic power which rests on constellations of interests, and authority which rests on beliefs in its legitimacy. Power in the political struggle results from the manipulation of interests and profitable exchanges—for example, of commitments or "spoils" for votes—and does not entail legitimate authority of protagonists over one another. Success in this struggle, however, leads to a position of legitimate authority. The political struggle occurs not only among politicians but also between them and the executives of bureaucratic organizations to prevent the latter from exploiting their dominant administrative position to usurp political power. A final complication arises in mass democracies, where the political struggle is carried out through large party organizations which tend to become bureaucratized, with the result that the conflict between political and bureaucratic principles manifests itself again in the struggle between the politician who directly appeals to the voters and the regular party official, once more creating the danger that democratic processes become submerged by bureaucratic considerations.[42]

[38] *Essays in Sociology* (New York: Oxford University Press, 1946), pp. 224–228.

[39] *Ibid.*, p. 231.

[40] *Ibid*, pp. 232–235.

[41] Bendix, *op. cit.*, p. 439.

[42] See Max Weber, *Gesammelte Politische Schriften* (Munich: Drei Masken, 1921), pp. 182–183, 201–211, summarized in Bendix, *op. cit.*, pp. 446–447.

These brief excerpts show that Weber discusses the differences and inter-relations between democracy and bureaucracy extensively; nevertheless, he never makes a systematic analytical distinction between them. Let me attempt to draw such an analytical distinction. Two reasons why men organize themselves and others and form an association can be distinguished. First, their purpose may be to settle on common courses of actions, on objectives to be collectively pursued. Second, their purpose may be to implement decisions already agreed upon or accepted, to work together on attaining given objectives. There are other reasons for establishing a social association, for instance, giving common expression to shared values, as in religious congregations, but the discussion here is confined to the first two kinds. The principle of organization must be adapted to its purpose.

If men organize themselves for the purpose of reaching common agreement on collective goals and actions by some form of majority rule, they establish a democratic organization. The specific mechanisms and institutions through which the democratic rule of the majority is effected can differ widely and pose important problems in a large social structure. Whatever the particular institutional solution to these problems, however, the fundamental principle that is expected to govern a democratic organization is freedom of dissent. For tomorrow's majority will not be able to emerge unless today's majority— and, indeed, every majority—relinquishes the right to suppress dissenting minorities, however extremist their views.

If men organize themselves and others for the purpose of realizing specific objectives assigned to or accepted by them, such as winning a war or collecting taxes, they establish a bureaucratic organization. The exact form best suited for such an organization depends on a variety of conditions, including notably the kinds of skills required for the tasks.[43] Strict lines of authority, for example, are probably not conducive to the exercise of responsibility and initiative in a research organization. In any case, the fundamental principle that is expected to govern the specific character and administration of a bureaucratic organization is that of administrative efficiency, that is, the achievement of specified objectives at minimum cost.

In sum, the differentiating criteria between democracy and bureaucracy proposed are whether the organization's purpose is to settle on common objectives or to accomplish given objectives, and whether the governing principle of organizing social action is majority rule rooted in freedom of dissent or administrative efficiency. The distinction is an analytical one, since many organizations have the dual purpose of first deciding on collective goals and

[43] See the typology developed in James D. Thompson and Arthur Tuden, "Strategies, Structures, and Processes of Organizational Decision," in Thompson *et al.* (eds.), *Comparative Studies in Administration* (Pittsburgh: University of Pittsburgh Press, 1959), pp. 195–216.

then carrying out these decisions. As a result, the two principles come into conflict. Unions are a typical example. Democratic freedom of dissent and majority rule are often set aside in the interests of administrative efficiency and effective accomplishment of union objectives. Even if Michels erred in considering this process inevitable, it is undoubtedly prevalent.[44] Another illustration is the tendency of party bosses to circumvent primaries and other democratic processes in the interest of building an efficient machine for winning elections. Although some specific conflicts may be due to corrupt or domineering union or party officials, there is a fundamental organizational dilemma that is independent of individual motives. Democratic decisions are futile without an administrative apparatus strong enough to implement them, but the requirements of administrative efficiency frequently are incompatible with those of democratic decision-making—if only because one organization cannot be governed by two distinct ultimate principles of social action.

In our political system, we have attempted to resolve this dilemma by separating the process of deciding on collective goals and the process of accomplishing these goals into two distinct sets of political institutions—the party and election machinery and the legislative branch of the government, on the one hand, and the executive branch of the government, on the other. The former institutions are expected to be governed by majority rule and freedom of dissent, while the latter are expected to be governed by administrative efficiency. Democratic values demand not only that political objectives be decided by majority rule but also that they be implemented by the most effective administrative methods, that is, by executive agencies whose operations are governed by the principle of efficiency and not by majority opinion. Despite the institutional separation, however, the fundamental dilemma between democracy and bureaucracy recurrently reasserts itself, especially in the form of demands for suppressing freedom of dissent in the interest of national security.

Conclusions

This paper has presented a critical review of Weber's theory of authority and bureaucracy. The ideal-type procedure Weber used in his analysis has been criticized for failing to differentiate between conceptual elaborations and hypotheses concerning the relationship between facts, and also for confusing the distinction between analytical attributes of social systems and

---

[44] Robert Michels, *Political Parties* (Glencoe: Free Press, 1949); for a case study of an exception to the tendencies Michels describes, see Seymour M. Lipset *et al.*, *Union Democracy* (Glencoe: Free Press, 1956).

prototypes of the social systems themselves. The substantive theory has been criticized for focusing primarily on the beliefs that legitimate authority while neglecting to conceptualize systematically the structural conditions that give rise to it. Finally, the lack of a systematic theory of democracy as well as of revolution was noted, despite the prominent part these two problems play in Weber's thinking and writing. Having focused in the paper deliberately on what appear to be limitations of Weber's theory, I would like to close by putting these criticisms into proper perspective.

Perhaps the most difficult task for a scholar is to develop a new approach to the study of reality, a new conception and perspective that fundamentally changes the development of theory and research in a discipline for generations to come. It is no exaggeration to say that Weber was one of the rare men who has done just this. He has shaped the course of sociology, not alone but together with a few others, and it would not be what it is today had he not lived. It is the fate of every scientist, but particularly the great innovator who blazes new trails and points in new direction, that his very success in clearing the path for others makes his own work soon appear crude and obsolete. While this does not hold true for the philosopher, it does for the social scientist, and Weber clearly and self-consciously was a social scientist rather than a philosopher. Much of Marx's work seems crude today; so does much of Freud's; and if much of Weber's does too, as I have suggested, it is because he belongs to this august company.

3. Formal Organization: Dimensions of Analysis

It has been only within the last decade or two that the precise methods of social research developed in interviewing surveys and in observation laboratories have been applied to the study of military services, factories, government agencies, and other formal organizations.[1] Often, however, the research techniques have been adopted without first having been adapted to a new field of inquiry. Quantification, so important for providing evidence in support of generalizations, has often produced an artificial atomization of the organized social structures under investigation. Not that the members of the organization are conceived as Robinson Crusoes on isolated islands. Quite

---

Originally published in 1957.

[1] The term *formal organizations* is used here to refer to social organizations that are formally established for explicit purposes but to include the informal as well as the formalized aspects of such organizations. Herbert A. Simon, Donald W. Smithburg, and Victor A. Thompson define formal organization as "a planned system of cooperative effort in which each participant has a recognized role to play and duties or tasks to perform. These duties are assigned to achieve the organization purpose" [*Public Administration* (New York: Knopf, 1956), p. 5].

the contrary, the emphasis is all on human relations, but as atoms somehow suspended in free space. Specifically, human relations are treated in the analysis as though they were attributes of individuals, and the group structures of which they are component parts as well as the larger organization of which these groups are parts are neglected.

These tendencies are the result of a fundamental methodological problem. Since an empirical study is usually confined to one or two organizations and the investigation of a large sample of organizations is hardly feasible,[2] quantitative evidence for generalizations must be based on the observation of regularities among individual members or subgroups. But, by treating individuals, or even subgroups, as independent units of analysis that can be classified and reclassified according to any one of their characteristics, this procedure necessarily ignores the unique constellation of relationships between groups and individuals in the organization—its *Gestalt*. If, on the other hand, the analysis is focused on the organized whole of interdependent elements, it deals only with a single case and provides no empirical evidence for generalization, no matter how many individuals are observed.

This paper is an attempt to explore this dilemma in the study of formal organizations. For this purpose a secondary analysis of some research findings, which is largely concerned with the effect of impersonal mechanisms of control upon the structure of work groups and the flow of communication in the hierarchy, will be presented first. Four dimensions in the analysis of formal organization are then suggested.

Work Groups on the Assembly Line

The distinct difference between having established personal relations with several co-workers and being a member of a work group is clearly illustrated in Walker and Guest's study of assembly-line workers in an automobile plant. Despite the noise and the fact that hardly any jobs on the assembly line require cooperation between workers, most workers have regular social contacts with a few others stationed nearby. Indeed, over three-quarters of them consider friendly contacts with fellow workers one of the things they like best about their job.[3]

Since the workers are strung out along the line, however, the set of interpersonal relations of each differs somewhat from those of everyone else. Tom and Dick are friends, and both have frequent contacts with Harry, who stands

---

[2] Added in 1974: This is incorrect. Since it was written, numerous studies of large samples of organizations have been conducted; for some illustrations see Part Three.

[3] Charles R. Walker and Robert H. Guest, *The Man on the Assembly Line* (Cambridge: Harvard University Press, 1952), pp. 67–68.

between them; but Tom also often talks to three fellows on his right, who are out of Dick's earshot, and Dick has friendly ties with two men on his left, whom Tom hardly knows. There is no common network of social relationships that unites a number of workers and distinguishes them from others by furnishing a socially agreed-upon definition of the boundaries of the in group. Notwithstanding regular patterns of informal interaction, therefore, work groups do not seem to exist on the assembly line.

This is not merely a matter of arbitrary definition. In the absence of a *shared* set of social relations and a common boundary, there is no single group with which a number of individuals can identify themselves and which, in turn, provides them social support. Perhaps this lack of group support is one of the reasons why assembly-line workers become so quickly and strongly identified with their union.[4] It may also play a major role in the prevalent dislike of work and the high rates of turnover and of absenteeism on the assembly line.[5] Indeed, when the same research team in a second study discovered that work groups sometimes do become established on the assembly line, they also found that absenteeism declined as a result.[6]

The men on the assembly line are divided into sections under different foremen. Merely having the same foreman does not give rise to a group structure in the section: the foreman must help to create it. Most important, the foreman must identify himself with his men as a group and "think of himself as also a member of the group",[7] he sticks up for his men, treats them as equals, and delegates responsibility to them. These things make a foreman a symbol of identification uniting the members of his section. Some foremen, moreover, institute periodic meetings of the entire section. Of particular significance is the establishment of "informal systems of job rotation,"[8] which not only reduce monotony and make men more satisfied with work but also help to create group boundaries. If the men in a section intermittently change their positions on the line, their social situation is no longer very different from that of other work groups: each, sooner or later, finds himself close enough to every one of the others for informal contacts. Opportunities for recurrent interaction among all members of the section promote a common network of social relationships and a cohesive group.

But how could foremen become identified with the workers in their section and still discharge their managerial responsibilities? Walker, Guest, and

[4] *Ibid.*, p. 132.

[5] *Ibid.*, pp. 62–63, 116–117, 119–120. See also Ely Chinoy, *Automobile Workers and the American Dream* (Garden City, N.Y.: Doubleday, 1955), pp. 62–72.

[6] Charles R. Walker, Robert H. Guest, and Arthur N. Turner, *The Foreman on the Assembly Line* (Cambridge: Harvard University Press, 1956), pp. 132–133.

[7] *Ibid.*, p. 135.

[8] *Ibid.*, p. 134.

Turner argue that a successful foreman must play a dual role, representing both his men and the management. It may also be, however, that assembly-line production itself has a bearing on the problem. The unrelenting movement of the conveyor constrains workers to attain a certain output, relieving the foreman of responsibility for their productivity. But, of all his duties, it is only the exercise of control over subordinates that benefits from social distance. Thus, the fact that the conveyor system substitutes in part for the foreman as a mechanism of control makes it possible for him to identify himself with the workers without impeding operations.

To be sure, most of the foremen questioned did not think that assembly-line production facilitates their job. The foreman still has to supervise quality, keep the line manned, and tackle problems of adjustment and morale inevitable in repetitive work.[9]

There is quite a difference, however, between the problems the assembly line creates and those the foreman would have to face in its absence. High rates of turnover and absenteeism make the training of new workers and temporary replacements one of his major responsibilities. To ease the extra burden the absence of a worker places on the rest of the section, the foreman must be skillful in redistributing the work load and in negotiating with management for a quick replacement. The foreman must try to reduce turnover and absenteeism by making the work itself less arduous and the situation as satisfactory as possible. In discharging his responsibility for maintaining quality, he sees to it that the workers' tools are kept in good repair and that the materials they need are delivered to them at the proper time. All these tasks involve helping subordinates rather than making demands on them. The major exception is checking on the quality of performance, but even the significance of such checks is altered by the powerful constraint of the moving line.

Impersonal Constraints and the Flow of Demand

The impersonal constraints exerted by production-line methods change the flow of demand in the organization. The concept of flow of demand is derived from the concepts of origination of action and flow of work developed by Arensberg, Whyte, and Chapple in their studies of patterns of interaction among the members of an organization.[10] Whyte shows, for example, that

---

[9] *Ibid.*, pp. 31–32.

[10] See especially Conrad M. Arensberg, "Behavior and Organization," in John H. Rohrer and Muzafer Sherif (eds.), *Social Psychology at the Crossroads* (New York: Harper, 1951); William F. Whyte, *Human Relations in the Restaurant Industry* (New York: McGraw-Hill, 1948); and E. D. Chapple and Conrad M. Arensberg, "Measuring Human Relations," *Genetic Psychology Monographs* 22 (1940). 3–147.

demands in the restaurant flow not only from management through supervisors down to waitresses and cooks but also from customers via waitresses and pantry personnel to the cooks. The fact that demands are made from two different sources often precipitates problems and conflicts, particularly when the person asked to do something considers himself superior to the one making the request.

Usually, demands flow primarily down the hierarchy from management through supervisors or foremen to workers, although staff experts provide an alternative route. The superior directs operations by giving his subordinates instructions and checking their work. Studies reveal, however, that frequent and detailed instructions and close checking of the subordinates' work is not the best method of supervision; on the contrary, such close supervision actually reduces productivity.[11] In other words, the flow of demand down the hierarchy, even if there are no conflicting streams, seems to impede effective operations.

Assembly-line production reverses the direction of the flow of demand. It is the conveyor that assures coordination and a certain level of productivity, not the directives of foremen. And, where an impersonal mechanism makes most necessary demands on workers, the major task of the foreman is no longer to issue directives but to be a troubleshooter—to come to his subordinates' aid when they have difficulties. Hence, the typical interaction is initiated by a worker's demand for the foreman's help rather than by a demand by the foreman on the worker. This reversal is also manifest on the next level in the hierarchy. It has been pointed out that staff experts not merely advise management but, in effect, give orders to foremen and operators.[12] Foremen often feel that staff officials interfere with their work by making unreasonable demands,[13] but the majority of the foremen in the assembly plant studied considered staff and service personnel helpful and felt free to call on them. When management and experts exercise control by planning assembly-line production, there is no need for issuing many directives to the foreman, and so most of the contacts between the foreman and superiors or staff officials are the result of his requests for help.[14]

---

[11] See Robert L. Kahn and Daniel Katz, "Leadership Practices in Relation to Productivity and Morale," in Dorwin Cartwright and Alvin Zander (eds.), *Group Dynamics* (Evanston: Row, Peterson, 1953), pp. 617–619. Cf. bibliography of the empirical studies on which this summary is based, pp. 627–628.

[12] See Victor A. Thompson, *The Regulatory Process in OPA Rationing* (New York: King's Crown Press, 1950), esp. pp. 430–433.

[13] See e.g., Melville Dalton, "Conflicts between Staff and Line Managerial Officials," *American Sociological Review* 15 (1950), 342–351.

[14] The only foreman for whom Walker, Guest, and Turner (*op. cit.*, p. 91) report quantitative data initiated fewer contacts with his subordinates than they did with him, and many more contacts with superiors and staff personnel than they did with him.

The fact that the foreman is cast in the role of adviser and assistant to his subordinates affects interaction even on the occasions when he makes demands on them. He could not maintain this role if, upon discovering imperfections, he would curtly order a worker to improve the quality of his work. Moreover, since the foreman knows that the standardized quality requirements are generally accepted by workers—he typically thinks they want to do a good job—he is likely to lay the blame for failures upon the changing speed of the line or the worker's inexperience and not on lack of effort. Thus demands for improvement are likely to take the form of guidance and training rather than commands. Workers, finally, are not so prone to blame the foreman if they have difficulty meeting standards as they might otherwise be, because the speeding line absorbs the brunt of their aggression.

The change in flow of demand engendered by the constraints of the assembly line distributes discretion more equitably between superior and subordinates. Although the demands of superiors are often worded as requests, it is difficult to refuse them—much more difficult than it is to refuse requests of subordinates. Demands that flow downward, no matter how polite, control the conduct of subordinates and restrict their freedom of action. To be sure, the foreman exercises control over workers even if demands flow upward; his counsel and guidance, in effect, influence the conduct of workers. Yet when the flow is upward, workers decide when to call upon the superior; not so when the flow is downward. The superior continues to exercise considerable discretion over granting requests for assistance and over what guidance to furnish, but instead of monopolizing discretion he shares it with subordinates.

There is a fair amount of evidence that the exercise of discretion and responsibility increases satisfaction at work. Thus Hoppock finds that the higher the level of skill and responsibility, the greater the job satisfaction.[15] Katz and Kahn confirm this finding, and they also show that on a given occupational level individuals whose superiors permit them to exercise discretion are more satisfied and less often absent from work than others.[16] Feeling free to bring problems to the supervisor, for one thing, is inversely related to absenteeism. Coch and French discovered that factory workers who participate in deciding on a change in production accept the change more readily than those without a voice in making it, perform much better once the change is made, and are less likely to quit.[17] These data support the conclusion that

---

[15] Robert Hoppock, *Job Satisfaction* (New York: Haprer, 1935).

[16] *Op. cit.*, p. 618; and Daniel Katz and Robert L. Kahn, "Some Recent Findings in Human-Relations Research in Industry," in Guy E. Swanson, Theodore M. Newcomb, and Eugene L. Hartley (eds.), *Readings in Social Psychology* (New York: Holt, 1952), pp. 657, 663–664.

[17] Lester Coch and John R. P. French, Jr., "Overcoming Resistance to Change," *Human Relations* 1 (1948), 512–532.

the reversal in the flow of demand, since it increases the workers' discretion, contributes to their satisfaction.

The impersonal constraints of the assembly line decrease the worker's discretion on the job, but the upward flow of demand encouraged by these very constraints increases his discretion in his relationship with his foreman. Hence, assembly-line operations reduce work satisfaction at one point while enhancing it at another. This illustrates that a correlation between two "terminal" variables—a formal condition and its ultimate effect in the organization—can be misleading unless the intervening social processes are considered. Moreover, since it is unlikely that demand flows upward in all sections on the assembly line, it is essential to determine the other conditions in the organization on which the reversal of flow depends. In short, to analyze complex configurations, relationships between two variables must be elaborated externally by inquiring into additional necessary conditions as well as internally by examining intervening variables.

Multiple Consequences and Change in Organization

Assembly-line production is not the only impersonal constraint. Evaluation on the basis of published statistical records of performance is another: precise knowledge of how his work compares with others' constrains every employee to try to improve and so exercises control over operations without any direct intervention by superiors. Indeed, the statistical method of evaluation is a more adaptable mechanism of control than the assembly line. It lends itself to being used not only for manual but also for clerical and even professional work, and it can serve to control qualitative as well as quantitative standards of performance, since a variety of errors and successes can be counted and recorded.

A study of two government agencies reveals that statistical records of performance, too, reverse the flow of demand between supervisor and operating officials.[18] The direct influence the records exert on the performance of officials and the exact knowledge of accomplishments they furnish make it unnecessary for the supervisor to check on subordinates frequently and permit him to let them come to him for advice when needed. In fact, the more a supervisor relied on statistical records in his evaluation, the larger the proportion of interactions between him and them that they rather than he initiated.[19] Even when a supervisor talks to a subordinate about improving

[18] Peter M. Blau, *The Dynamics of Bureaucracy* (Chicago: University of Chicago Press, 1955), pp. 33–40, 101–105. (The former is included here as Chapter 8.)
[19] *Ibid.*, p. 232, n. 7.

his performance, statistical evidence transforms the significance of their conference; what might have been a much-resented critical rebuke becomes an offer of help to make a better record. Evaluation on the basis of a record also makes it possible to give officials considerable discretion in the discharge of their duties. A quantitative record of performance and a conveyor belt are both impersonal mechanisms of control which, be the setting the semiprofessional work in the two government offices or the semiskilled work in the automobile plant, appear to have similar effects upon interaction between superior and subordinates.

Quantitative evaluation has a series of consequences in an organization. Its introduction in one government agency, for example, raised productivity, improved the relations between interviewers and their supervisors, and promoted a detached, impartial attitude toward clients. But it also fostered competitive tendencies which interfered with operations, and these new operating problems gave rise to new practices and patterns of interaction.[20]

The same aspects of the organization that make essential contributions to operations frequently also create conflicts and problems, and the unanticipated consequences of the adjustments instituted to cope with them may, in turn, produce further problems. Hence, there is a continual process of change in the organization.

Dimensions of Analysis

The methodological problems posed here may be dealt with by distinguishing a structural, an organizational, and a developmental dimension in the analysis of formal organizations. There is at least one other dimension, which can be called "environmental": the analysis of the relationships between formal organizations and other social institutions, for example, of the connections between the economic or political system and formal organizations; of the relations between the organization of unions and that of companies in an industry, or of the role of differences in cultural values and norms for organizations. Restricting the discussion here to the three intraorganizational dimensions is not meant to imply that the environmental one is any less important.

Structural Dimension. The fact that it makes a difference whether workers on the assembly line merely have friendly relations with several fellow workers or whether a group structure has developed among them raises the question of how the distinct significance of social structure can be taken into account

[20] *Ibid.,* pp. 44–68. (See Chapter 7 in this volume.)

in systematic research. Ever since the early writings of Durkheim, and even though he modified his own position later, it has been recommended that the study of social structure confine itself to indexes that are independent of the behavior of individuals, such as the laws in a society, or the group's resistance to disruption.[21] This procedure, however, entails the danger of reifying the concept of group structure and ignoring the fact that it refers to a network of social relations between individuals which finds expression in their interaction. In any case, it is possible to investigate the effects of social structure by an alternative method.

This method consists of three steps. First, empirical measures are obtained that pertain to those characteristics of the individual members of the groups that have direct or indirect bearing on their relations to each other, such as group identification, sociometric choices, initiation of interaction, or promotions. Second, the measures that describe individuals in one respect are combined into one index for each group, and this index no longer refers to any characteristic of individuals but to a characteristic of the group.[22] Examples of such group attributes are the proportion of members identified with the group, the average number of in group sociometric choices, the mean and the variance of the rates of interaction, and homogeneity of interests. Third, to isolate a structural effect, the relationship between a group attribute and some effect is determined while the corresponding characteristic of individuals is held constant. An illustration will make this clear.

To test the hypothesis that the free flow of communication within a work group improves the performance of its members, two kinds of data have been collected in fifty work groups of about ten members each: measures of performance for every individual and the frequency with which he discusses his problems with another member of his own work group. We could investigate whether frequency of discussion and quality of performance are correlated in the entire sample of 500. But, if they were, it would show only that individuals who readily discuss their problems with others perform better, not that the network of communication in a group influences performance. A second test would be to divide the fifty groups into those with many and those with few members who readily discuss their problems and to determine whether average performance in the first category of groups is superior. A positive finding in this case, however, might merely be a re-

[21] See Emile Durkheim, *Rules of Sociological Method* (Chicago: University of Chicago Press, 1938), pp. 44–46. For a recent discussion of the issue see Neal Gross and William E. Martin, "On Group Cohesiveness," *American Journal of Sociology* 57 (1952), 546–554.

[22] On the distinction between empirical measures pertaining to individuals and the corresponding ones pertaining to groups see Patricia L. Kendall and Paul F. Lazarsfeld, "Problems of Survey Analysis," in Robert K. Merton and Paul F. Lazarsfeld (eds.), *Continuities in Social Research* (Glencoe: Free Press, 1950), pp. 187–192.

Table 3.1 Performance Scores by Rate and Frequency of Discussion (Hypothetical Example)

Individuals Who Discuss Their Problems	Groups Most of Whose Members Discuss Their Problems	
	Often	Rarely
Often	.85	.65
Rarely	.70	.40

flection of a high correlation between the individual's readiness to discuss and his performance and thus still would not supply unequivocal evidence of the significance of the network of communication for performance. If, on the other hand, individuals are first divided on the basis of their frequency of discussion, and it turns out that within each category of individuals about equally ready to talk about their problems those who belong to groups where frequent discussion is prevalent perform better than those in other groups, then it is demonstrated that the network of communication itself is related to performance (see Table 3.1, where the differences between columns indicate the structural effect of the network of communication on performance). This finding would show that, even when the effect of the individual's discussion rate of his problems on his performance is eliminated, just to be in a group where communication flows freely improves performance—other things being equal. (The assumption is that performance is affected by rather than affects discussions.)

What would account for such a finding, were it obtained? The fact that an individual discusses his problems with others has consequences for them as well as for himself. He may get specific advice, and, even when he does not, the discussion may clarify his thinking. At the same time the others may learn something from his discussion which they can use in their own work, or their self-confidence may be raised by his often coming to them for advice. Moreover, the observation that others have problems, too, and that they feel free to consult one another probably reduces an individual's anxiety over his own problems even before he starts discussing them.[23] It is, therefore, hypothesized that ego's discussions of his problems contribute to the performance of alters as well as to that of ego. (Of course, every member might alternate between playing the role of ego and that of alter, which means that reciprocity prevails in discussions.) If this is correct, and only if it is, one would actually obtain the finding described, that is, a relationship be-

[23] See Blau, *op. cit.*, pp. 105–116. (Chapter 9 in this volume.)

tween the frequency of discussion in the group and performance when the individual's rate of discussion is controlled.

The general principle is that if ego's X affects not only ego's Y but also alters' Y, a structural effect will be observed, which means that the frequency of X in a group is related to Y even though the individual's X is held constant. Such a finding indicates that the network of relations in the group with respect to X influences Y. It isolates the effects of X on Y that are entirely due to or transmitted by the processes of social interaction.

A somewhat different structural effect is reported in a study by Stouffer and his colleagues.[24] Soldiers who have been promoted have more favorable attitudes toward chances of promotion in the army than those who have remained privates. However, soldiers in outfits a large proportion of whose members have been promoted have *less* favorable attitudes toward chances of promotion than others of equal rank in outfits with fewer promoted members. Thus, the frequency of promotions in a group has an unfavorable effect on these attitudes, while the individual's own promotion has the opposite effect. Being promoted raises the individual's status, but the promotion of many other members of his group depresses his status relative to theirs. In short, the promotion of a number of egos decreases the relative status of alters and increases the relative status of egos. Since ego's X has the opposite implications for alters' Y and for ego's Y in this case, the structural effect and that of the corresponding characteristic of individuals are in opposite directions.[25]

Social norms also have structural effects. Workers who firmly believe that it is wrong to be a "rate-buster" are probably less likely than others to exceed informal standards of output. Even workers who see nothing wrong with rate-busting, however, may work slower than they otherwise would if most members of the group believe rate-busting wrong. The reason is, of course, that prevailing social standards are enforced throughout the group and, therefore, influence the conduct of those who do not fully accept them as well as those who do. Again, ego's X influences both alter's Y and ego's Y. If the pressure of the group is successful, however, one-time deviants will not only conform to the expectations of the majority but sooner or later incorporate them in their own thinking. Once this happens and virtually all members of some groups condemn rate-busting while hardly any of others do, it is no longer possible to use the proposed method of determining structural effects. For it requires a sufficient number of individuals who reject the

[24] Samuel A. Stouffer *et al.*, *The American Soldier*, Vol. I (Princeton: Princeton University Press, 1949), pp. 250–254.

[25] Another instance: competitive interviewers in an employment agency produce more than others, but the prevalence of competitiveness in a group reduces its productivity (see Blau, *op. cit.*, pp. 61–65; Chapter 7 in this volume).

norm in groups that, on the whole, accept it and of individuals who accept the norm in groups that, on the whole, reject it. This indicates an important limitation of the method. It reveals only the present, not the past, effects of the normative structure of groups. The prevalence of a normative orientation in a group may have three effects upon deviants: intensify their deviant conduct as a reaction to being alienated from the majority, constrain them to conform against their own convictions, or convert their very thinking. Although all three are effects of the social structure, the last would not find expression in what has here been called a structural effect.

Still another structural effect is illustrated by a finding of Lipset, Trow, and Coleman.[26] If the members of a small printing shop are in substantial agreement on political issues, they are more prone to be active in union politics than if there are considerable political differences among them. It is not whether the members of a shop are liberal or conservative but their consensus that is significant, whatever their political opinion. Wide divergences in political viewpoint among the members of a work group incline them to avoid political topics of conversation to forestall arguments. Sufficient political consensus to provide a basis for cordial discourse, on the other hand, encourages political talk at work, and this stimulates interest in the political activities of the union. In formal terms, if the joint occurrence of X, or of non-X, in ego and alter affects Y, the variance of X in the group will have an effect on Y which is independent of any possible relationship between the individual's X and his Y.

Organizational Dimension   The structure of work groups is, of course, profoundly influenced by the formal organization of which they are parts. Although the analysis of formally established organizations is generally concerned with larger social units than work groups, the distinction between the structural and the organizational dimension is analytical, not one of size. To speak of the interrelations within a social system may refer either to the *social* relations between individuals or groups or to the interdependence of abstract elements in the organization, say, the relationships between personnel policies, supervisory practices, and interaction among workers.[27] The term *organizational dimension* is used to denote the latter type of analysis, whose focus is the configuration of interdependent elements in the organization.

As has been pointed out, the establishment of a relationship between two characteristics of organizations is merely a starting point for elaborating it

[26] Seymour M. Lipset, Martin Trow, and James Coleman, *Union Democracy* (Glencoe: Free Press, 1956), pp. 165–167.

[27] For a more general distinction between "part" concepts and analytical elements see Talcott Parsons, *The Structure of Social Action* (New York: McGraw-Hill, 1937), pp. 30–40.

internally as well as externally. Internal elaboration involves a search for intervening variables, without which the finding that an antecedent condition has a certain ultimate consequence cannot be interpreted and may even be misleading. For example, when it was found that the impersonal control exerted by statistical records of performance gave rise to more impersonal and impartial treatment of clients in an employment agency, one might, on first impression, conclude that impersonality is simply transmitted from the exercise of control down to the contact with clients. Actually, complex intervening processes were responsible for the relationship. Performance records stimulated employment interviewers to concentrate on making many placements and induced them to eliminate all considerations that had no bearing on making placements—in short, all personal considerations—in their treatment of clients. This disinterested approach often created conflicts with clients, which made it difficult for interviewers to remain detached and neither become angry at clients nor modify decisions in order to pacify them. However, the practice developed of relieving the tensions generated by these conflicts by complaining or joking about clients in informal discussions with colleagues. These friendly, *not* impersonal, interactions among interviewers rendered conflicts with clients less disturbing, so that it was easier to maintain an impersonal attitude toward them even at the risk of conflict.[28]

In analyzing an organization, the major independent variables are the formal institutions in terms of which social conduct is organized: the division of labor, the hierarchy of offices, control and sanctioning mechanisms, production methods, official rules and regulations, personnel policies, and so on. The major dependent variables are the results accomplished by operations and the attachment of its members to the organization, as indicated by productive efficiency, changes effected in the community (say, a decline in crime rates), turnover, satisfaction with work, and various other effect criteria. To explain the relationships between these two sets of abstract variables, it is necessary to investigate the processes of social interaction and the interpersonal relations and group structures.[29] In dealing with these patterns of conduct, sociopsychological processes cannot be entirely ignored. To be sure, the student of organization is not concerned with the effects of psychological characteristics but with those of conditions in the organization on social conduct. However, sociopsychological processes are the *intervening* variables drawn on to explain why social conditions give rise to certain patterns

---

[28] Blau, *op. cit.*, pp. 73–95.

[29] For a method of testing the hypothesis that a given intervening variable or set of intervening variables accounts for the relationship between two variables see Kendall and Lazarsfeld, *op. cit.*, pp. 147–151.

of conduct.[30] Statistical records brought about more impartial treatment of clients, for example, because they motivated interviewers to engage in supportive social interaction with colleagues which facilitated excluding all irrelevant personal considerations from their decisions in making placements. In sum, sociopsychological conditions in the organization lead to given processes of social interaction, and these processes must be examined to account for the relationships between conditions in the organization and the results they accomplish.

The external elaboration of a relationship between two factors involves a search for the conditions responsible for their joint occurrence. Is the correlation possibly spurious, resulting from the effects of a common antecedent on both factors? If not, another question can be asked. For example, granted that impersonal mechanisms of control tend to reverse the flow of demand, on what other conditions does the reversal depend? Concern with the significance of a combination of conditions introduces the conception of organization as a configuration of interdependent elements. It is often assumed that the concept of *Gestalt* defies quantitative analysis, but this assumption seems unwarranted.

If the concept of *Gestalt* means that the organized arrangement of elements in a larger whole has a significance of its own, not attributable to the specific character of the elements, multivariate analysis furnishes a method for its systematic investigation. Thus, it is possible to test the hypothesis implied by Weber that administrative efficiency is the result of a combination of various characteristics in a bureaucracy,[31] provided that empirical data on these characteristics and on efficiency can be obtained for a large sample of bureaucratic organizations. Although the empirical measures describe only the elements and not their configuration, the significance of the latter would become apparent in the analysis of variance, for this statistical method would supply information not only on the contribution of each characteristic to efficiency but also on the additional contribution made by their combination. The so-called interaction effects would furnish quantitative measures of the significance of the *Gestalt* by abstracting the effects produced by various factors in combination from the effects of each factor by itself. While the cost in time and money of such a project is great, it is important to realize that there are no inherent obstacles to the systematic investigation of the complex configurations in formal organizations.

[30] This is the main implication of Weber's concept of *Verstehen* [see Max Weber, *The Theory of Social and Economic Organization* (New York: Oxford University Press, 1947), pp. 87–107].

[31] *Ibid.*, pp. 329–241.

Practical problems, however, cannot be brushed aside. Since it is often impossible to establish generalizations on the basis of evidence from a representative sample of formal organizations, substitute methods have to be developed, one of which might be internal comparison. The great variations existing in large organizations have not been sufficiently exploited for systematic research. Guided, apparently, by a mistaken notion of *Gestalt*, many investigators are concerned with the "typical" foreman or the overall pattern of "human relations" in a company instead of deriving limited generalizations from the differences in the organization of the various divisions or departments. However, generalizations about the total configuration cannot be supported by evidence collected in only one organization. A second substitute method, which permits making tentative generalizations about total organizations, might be the secondary analysis of a number of empirical studies of formal organizations.[32]

Developmental Dimension. Change in the organization is the result of the very interdependence between elements that is often assumed to imply a stable equilibrium. Even if there were a perfect organization with no problems, changes in its environment would soon create some. But internal as well as external conditions generate change in the organization, since innovations instituted to solve one problem, as already mentioned, have a variety of repercussions, some of which are likely to produce other problems.

> A mistake we often tend to make is that the world stands still while we are going through the process of a given adjustment. And it doesn't. Facts change, we must keep up with the facts; keeping up with the facts changes the facts. . . . When we think that we have *solved* a problem, well, by the very process of solving, new elements or forces come into the situation and you have a new problem on your hands to be solved.[33]

Interdependence entails dilemmas: efficient operation in a large organization depends on many different conditions, and the practices instituted to establish one of these conditions do not remain solely means for this end but have implications for others; and since the conditions required for optimum operations are diverse, the measures to improve them are often incompatible.

[32] For this to be fruitful, however, research procedures would have to be better standardized or, at least, more accurately reported than they usually are. Research centers that regularly conduct studies of formal organizations, such as those at the University of Michigan and at Yale University, have special opportunities for coordinating various investigations in the interest of deriving generalizations about organizations.

[33] Mary Parker Follett, "The Process of Control," in Luther Gulick and L. Urwick (eds.), *Papers on the Science of Administration* (New York: Institute of public Administration, 1937), p. 166.

For instance, effective administration is contingent on uniform adherence to regulations as well as on adaptability to a variety of specific situations, but bureaucratic pressures compelling strict conformity to rules also give rise to rigidities that interfere with the adaptability needed to handle special cases.[34] Although evaluation on the basis of accomplished results encourages the responsible performance of complex tasks, it simultaneously engenders anxieties that impede decision-making.[35] Assembly-line methods, while increasing productivity, lead to absenteeism and make operations particularly dependent on regular attendance to boot. Incompatibility of means, not simply lack of administrative foresight, is responsible for recurrent problems requiring adjustment in the organization and thus for its continual development.

The pattern of change in formal organizations can be described as a dialectical development. The process of solving some problems while frequently creating others is also a learning process in which experience is gained. On the one hand, efforts at adjustment shift from one problem to another as new difficulties arise when old ones are resolved. After assembly-line production has been instituted, reduction of absenteeism and turnover replaces technical questions of coordination as the major area of concern. On the other hand, as one type of problem recurs, it does not remain the same type of problem, since cumulative experience changes the orientation of the members of the organization toward it. This is so of problems confronting work groups as well as of those confronting management. Work groups experienced in maintaining solidarity against excessive demands of superiors will be less threatened by a new and unreasonably demanding foreman than groups that never had to cope with the problem, just as management will find it easier to combat absenteeism if it has successfully done so on previous occasions.

These processes of development are further complicated by changes in personnel, which result in the loss of accumulated experience despite the profusion of written records typical of bureaucratic organizations. Of particular importance is the fact that knowledge of the networks of informal relations can be acquired only through direct experience. Gouldner shows that a new manager's inevitable ignorance of informal relations constrains him to resort to formal procedures in discharging his responsibilities even if he is convinced that informal procedures are more effective.[36] Similarly, turnover of personnel on lower levels in the hierarchy undermines the

---

[34] See Robert K. Merton, *Social Theory and Social Structure* (Glencoe: Free Press, 1949), pp. 153–157.

[35] Blau, *op. cit.*, pp. 103–104.

[36] Alvin W. Gouldner, *Patterns of Industrial Bureaucracy* (Glencoe: Free Press, 1954), pp. 70–101.

cohesiveness of work groups and threatens informally established cooperative practices.

Conflicts of interests between management and nonmanagerial personnel, and between other groups, are an additional source of dialectical change. What constitutes adjustment for one group may be quite the opposite for the other, since different interests serve as criteria for defining adjustment, and when issues between workers and management have been resolved on one level, new ones on a different level often arise. After satisfactory working arrangements have been agreed upon, management introduces new machines, which then create new problems of adjustment for workers. After the union has achieved the right of collective bargaining, it uses it to raise the issue of pensions. Indeed, independent of conflicts between union and management, the successful attainment of an objective stimulates efforts to make further improvements and seek new fields to conquer, and this succession of goals as they are achieved by more ultimate ones is still another force that produces change in the organization.

In sum, dialectical organizational developments are generated by different patterns of change superimposed upon one another. The process of adjustment in the organization changes the kind of difficulties that demand foremost attention, since new ones arise as old ones are resolved. Simultaneously, experience alters the orientation with which problems are approached. Hence, as efforts at adjustment are turned from one problem to another, their effectiveness tends to increase. There are, however, several different spirals of adjustment of this sort rather than a single one, because conflicts of interests between various groupings in the organization produce diverse conceptions of adjustment. When issues created by these conflicts are settled, the conflicting developments continue and new issues emerge. Thus, the existence of divergent dialectical processes gives rise to yet another dialectical process of adjustment—a spiral linking the other spirals, as it were. The complexity of these developments is further increased by two conditions. Changes in personnel, which are disruptive, notwithstanding attempts to preserve continuity through written records and formalized procedures, reduce the level of adjustment. And the additional demands made on the organization as the result of striving for new objectives once old ones have been successfully attained create new problems of adjustment.

The systematic study of these processes of development requires that the time dimension be taken into account in the investigation of formal organizations. To be sure, there are a number of empirical studies of change in organizations. Richardson and Walker, for example, trace the repercussions of a change in production methods in a factory;[37] Gouldner examines the

---

[37] F. L. W. Richardson, Jr., and Charles R. Walker, *Human Relations in an Expanding Company* (New Haven: Yale Labor and Management Center, 1948).

consequences of a change in management for an industrial organization;[38] Selznick analyzes modifications in an organization resulting from its adaptation to a hostile environment;[39] and Michels deals with the changes generated by the very establishment of a formal organization.[40] But the empirical data for most of these studies were collected at one time,[41] and the patterns of change had to be inferred subsequently either from written records or from other evidence. Although preferable to ignoring change completely, the procedure is far from ideal.

The adaptation of the panel technique to the study of formal organizations would yield reliable evidence on developmental processes. It would involve systematic observation as well as interviewing in an organization at repeated intervals, perhaps a year or more apart. Precise indications of both informal and formal changes would be supplied by this method, and intensive interviewing about the changes discovered and analysis of pertinent records would provide information on the sociopsychological processes leading to them. Although continuous observation for several years, permitting the investigation of changes as they occur, is preferable to collecting data at periodic intervals, it is rarely feasible. Studies based on repeated interviews with the same respondents have greatly contributed to accurate knowledge about change in opinions and attitudes.[42] This panel design, properly adapted to research on formal organizations, may well prove equally fruitful in the systematic study of organizational developments and, specifically, in testing the hypothesis advanced here that such developments are dialectical.

[38] *Op. cit.*

[39] Philip Selznick, *TVA and the Grass Roots* (Berkeley: University of California Press, 1949).

[40] Robert Michels, *Political Parties* (Glencoe: Free Press, 1949).

[41] My own research is no exception. The investigation by Jaques should be mentioned as a notable exception; change in a factory is analyzed on the basis of continuous observation for two and a half years, although no quantitative data were collected [see Elliott Jaques, *The Challging Culture of a Factory* (New York, Dryden Press, 1952)].

[42] See, e.g., Paul F. Lazarsfeld, Bernard Berelson, and Hazel Gaudet, *The People's Choice* (New York: Duell, Sloan & Pearce, 1944).

4.   Structural Effects

Two basic types of social fact can be distinguished: the common values and norms embodied in a culture or subculture, and the networks of social relations in which processes of social interaction become organized and through which social positions of individuals and subgroups become differentiated.[1] Kroeber and Parsons have recently reemphasized the importance of this analytical distinction.[2] Most theoretical concepts refer to one of the two. Weber's Protestant ethic and Sumner's mores exemplify social values and norms, while Marx's investigation of the class structure and Simmel's study of coalitions in triads deal with networks of social relationships.

These concepts refer to attributes of social collectivities, not to those of individuals, but they have counterparts that do refer to characteristics of individuals. Individuals can be described in terms of their orientations and dispositions, just as groups or entire societies can be described in terms of the prevailing social values and norms; and individuals can be distinguished on the basis of their social status, just as communities can be distinguished on

Originally published in 1960.

[1] See, e.g., Robin M. Williams, Jr., *American Society* (New York: Knopf, 1951), pp. 443–448.

[2] A. L. Kroeber and Talcott Parsons, "The Concepts of Culture and of Social System," *American Sociological Review* 23 (October, 1958), 582–583.

the basis of the status distribution in them.[3] These parallels tend to conceal the fundamental difference between the implications of group structure and those of the individual's own characteristics for his conduct. Even socially acquired or socially defined attributes of individuals are clearly distinct in their effects from attributes of social structures.

Systematic social research has often been critized for distorting, if not entirely ignoring, crucial characteristics of social structure.[4] Interviewing surveys have provided much information about the influences of attitudes of individuals and their social status on human behavior, but they have contributed little to our knowledge of the structural constraints exerted by common values and status distributions in groups or communities, because sampling procedures tend to make isolated individuals the focus of the analysis. And while ecological studies have examined social units, they have not, with rare exceptions,[5] separated the consequences of social conditions from those of the individual's own characteristics for his behavior, because ecological data do not furnish information about individuals except in the aggregate. But the systematic analysis of structural constraints requires, as Merton and Kitt have pointed out, the simultaneous use of indices of social structure and of individual behavior.[6] This paper suggests and illustrates a method for isolating the effects of social structure.[7]

Social Values and Norms

Social values and norms are common orientations toward social conduct that prevail in a society or group. Social values govern the choice of objec-

[3] The relationships between measures of individual attributes and of group attributes are discussed by Patricia L. Kendall and Paul F. Lazarsfeld, "Problems of Survey Analysis," in Robert K. Merton and Paul F. Lazarsfeld (eds.), *Continuities in Social Research* (Glencoe: Free Press, 1950), pp. 187–196.

[4] See, e.g., Herbert Blumer, "Public Opinion and Public Opinion Polling," *American Sociological Review* 13 (October, 1948), 542–549.

[5] For example: Robert E. L. Faris and H. Warren Dunham, *Mental Disorders in Urban Areas* (Chicago: University of Chicago Press, 1939).

[6] Robert K. Merton and Alice S. Kitt, "Contributions to the Theory of Reference Group Behavior," in Merton and Lazarsfeld, *op. cit.*, pp. 82–83; see also pp. 70–81. Cf. Samuel A. Stouffer *et al.*, *The American Soldier*, Vol. 2 (Princeton: Princeton University Press, 1949), pp. 242–272, for a notable exception to the tendency of ignoring effects of social structure in survey research.

[7] I have briefly discussed this method in "Formal Organization," *American Journal of Sociology* 63 (July, 1957), 63–65 (see Chapter 3 above). Structural effects are a special type of the "contextual propositions" discussed by Paul F. Lazarsfeld in "Problems in Methodology," in Robert K. Merton *et al.* (eds.), *Sociology Today* (New York: Basic Books, 1959), pp. 69–73.

tives that are experienced as worth striving for, and social norms differentiate between proper and improper conduct.

Since social values and norms are shared, internalized orientations, the most plausible procedure for ascertaining them in empirical research would seem to be to determine, first, what values the members of a number of communities hold and, then, which ones of these are shared by members of any given community. For example, one could administer the F-Scale to a sample of the American population[8] and divide communities on the basis of whether authoritarian values are more or less prevalent. Let us assume that such a study finds that the relative prevalence of authoritarian values in a community is associated with a high degree of discrimination against minorities. (We shall also assume that other relevant conditions have been controlled and that we have evidence that authoritarianism is the antecedent variable and discrimination the dependent one.) Two conclusions could be drawn from this finding: first, if a community has an authoritarian subculture, discriminatory practices will prevail in it; second, if an individual has an authoritarian personality, he will tend to discriminate against minorities.

There is a fundamental difference between these two interpretations: the former implies that social processes external to individual personalities are responsible for the differences in discrimination, the latter that internal psychological processes are responsible. To be sure, the prevalence of authoritarian dispositions in some communities and not in others may well be largely due to differences in their social structures. What the determinants of prevailing values are, however, has no direct bearing on what their consequences are or on how these consequences are effected. These are the issues under consideration here. The individual's orientation undoubtedly influences his behavior. The question is whether the prevalence of social values in a community also exerts social constraints upon patterns of conduct that are independent of the influences exerted by the internalized orientations.

The sociologist assumes that this is the case. But how can one demonstrate that social values and norms exert *external* constraints upon the acting and thinking of individuals if they only exist in the minds of individuals? Durkheim, who is concerned with various aspects of this problem in most of his writings, suggests a specific answer in *Suicide*. After admitting, notwithstanding his social realism, that "social consciousness" exists only in individual minds, he states that the social force it exerts, nevertheless, is *"external to each average individual taken singly."*[9]

[8] T. W. Adorno *et al.*, *The Authoritarian Personality* (New York: Harper, 1950).

[9] Emile Durkheim, *Suicide* (Glencoe: Free Press, 1951), p. 316 (italics in original); see also pp. 309–320 for what may be Durkheim's most perceptive discussion of the problem.

The common values and norms in a group have two distinct kinds of effect upon the conduct of its members. Ego's conduct is influenced by his own normative orientation for fear of his conscience, and ego's conduct is also influenced by alters' normative orientation for fear of social sanctions. In other words, people conform to prevailing norms partly because they would feel guilty if they did not and partly because they gain social approval and avoid disapproval by doing so. This conception is somewhat oversimplified. It ignores, for example, the fact that the strength of ego's normative orientation itself is in part due to the reinforcement it receives from the social sanctions of alters. Despite its oversimplification, however, this analytical distinction makes it possible to demonstrate empirically the external constraints exerted by social values and norms by differentiating them from the influences of the internalized orientations of individuals.

The structural effects of a social value can be isolated by showing that the association between its prevalence in a community or group and certain patterns of conduct is independent of whether an individual holds this value or not. To return to our illustration: if we should find that, regardless of whether or not an individual has an authoritarian disposition, he is more apt to discriminate against minorities if he lives in a community where authoritarian values prevail than if he lives in one where they do not, we would have evidence that this social value exerts external constraints upon the tendency to discriminate—structural effects that are independent of the internalized value orientation of individuals.

Direct Effects

To illustrate the method of analysis suggested above and the distinguishable types of structural effects, data from a pilot study of a public assistance agency will be used.[10] The clients who came to the agency as applicants for general public assistance constituted the poorest stratum in a large American city. The primary job of the caseworker was to determine whether new applicants are eligible for public assistance and to check recurrently whether old recipients continue to be eligible. This involved visiting the clients in their homes and a considerable amount of paper work in the office. Many workers tried to provide some casework service as well, although their ability to do so was limited by their heavy work loads—the average number of cases per worker exceeded 120—and by their lack of training—the ma-

[10] Philip M. Marcus was of great help in the collection and analysis of these data. I am also indebted to the Social Science Research Committee of the University of Chicago, which provided the funds for this study.

jority of workers had only a college degree and no professional training in social work.

Caseworkers were organized into units of five or six under a supervisor. After a period of observation in the agency, the members of twelve supervisory units were interviewed. The analysis presented below is based on these interview responses of sixty caseworkers who were members of twelve work groups. Not quite half of these workers were women; one-third of them were blacks; and one-third had been with the agency less than one year, which indicates the high rate of turnover of personnel characteristic of public assistance agencies.

When caseworkers were asked whether the amount of public assistance should be increased, remain the same, or be decreased, one-half stated unequivocally that it should be increased; the majority of the rest felt that an increase is needed only for certain special cases, for example, clients who must pay high rent; and a few thought that no increase is necessary. Nobody suggested that the amount should be decreased. This item is positively associated with a larger number of other measures of orientation to clients than any other, which suggests that it is indicative of a fairly basic value orientation to clients.

Does the prevalence of proclient values in a group affect the performance of duties of its members independently of the individual's own attitude to clients? The description by workers of what they did when visiting clients provides a measure of their orientation in the performance of duties. It indicates that some largely confined their work to checking on eligibility, whereas others were also concerned with furnishing casework service. To isolate the structural effects of proclient values, groups are divided on the basis of whether or not a majority of group members favors raising the assistance budget for all clients, and within each type of group, individuals are divided into those that favor an increase in assistance for all clients and those that do not. The first section in Table 4.1 shows that individuals with proclient attitudes were more often service oriented in their work than others (compare adjacent columns). It also shows, and this is the pertinent finding, that regardless of their own attitudes, members of groups in which proclient values prevailed were more apt to be oriented toward casework service than members of groups with other values (compare alternate columns). Of the proclient individuals, 60 per cent in proclient groups and 44 per cent in other groups were service oriented; of the other workers, 44 per cent in proclient groups and 27 per cent in other groups were service oriented.

Although the differences in the proportion of service-oriented workers associated with contrasting group values are not large, they are just as large as those associated with contrasting individual attitudes. (The combination of group value and individual attitude made a considerable difference for

Table 4.1   Effects of Value Orientation Toward Clients

	Positive		Not Positive	
	Individual's Orientation		Individual's Orientation	
	Positive	Not Positive	Positive	Not Positive
1. Orientation to work				
Checking eligibility	30%	56%	56%	55%
Intermediate	10	0	0	18
Casework service	60	44	44	27
Total	100	100	100	100
2. Visits to recipients[a]				
Forty or less per month	59	50	44	31
Over forty per month	41	50	56	69
Total	100	100	100	100
3. Delegating responsibility to clients				
Unwilling to delegate	45	22	67	50
Willing to delegate	55	78	33	50
Total	100	100	100	100
4. Involvement with work				
High (worry much)	75	44	89	68
Low (worry little)	25	56	11	32
Total	100	100	100	100
Number of cases	20	9	9	22

Group's Prevailing Value Orientation Toward Clients

[a] This information is taken from performance records; since insufficient information was available for the newer workers the totals for this item in the four columns, reading from left to right, are: 17, 6, 9, 13.

orientation toward work: only about one-quarter of the workers who neither had proclient attitudes nor were in groups where proclient values prevailed were service oriented, compared to three-fifths of those who had themselves proclient attitudes and most of whose coworkers shared these proclient values.) Moreover, other measures of performance reveal the same pattern of relationships with group values. For example, making relatively few field visits generally implied the provision of more intensive services. Individuals with proclient attitudes tended to make slightly fewer visits to recipients than other workers, and whatever the individual's attitudes were, he was more prone to make fewer visits if he was a member of a group in which proclient values prevailed than of a group with different values (see Table 4.1, Visits to Recipients). Although all these relationships are small, their consistency makes it unlikely that they are entirely due to chance.[11]

These findings suggest that the social values that prevail in a work group do exert external constraints upon the thinking and acting of its members. If proclient values prevail in a group, merely checking on the eligibility of clients meets with social disapproval while providing casework services gains a worker approval and respect. But this is not the case if proclient values do not prevail; indeed, the opposite may be the case. In other words, the pro-client values of the members of a group motivate them not only to furnish more intensive service to their own clients but also to express social approval of colleagues who are service oriented and social disapproval of those who are not. In response to those sanctioning patterns, individuals tend to modify their approach to clients.

The conclusion that proclient group values have structural effects on the performance of duties rests on the assumptions that the relationships observed are not spurious and that proclient values are the independent variable in these relationships. Differences in supervision might constitute a correlated bias that accounts for the relationships, but examination of the data reveals that this is not the case. Of course, this does not exclude the possibility of other influential correlated biases, and neither can the possibility be excluded that proclient values are actually consequence rather than antecedent in these relationships. But this is a limitation of cross-sectional studies, not of the method of isolating structural effects. Given more adequate data than those used here for illustrative purposes, this method makes it possible to demonstrate structural effects as firmly as the effects of a characteristic of individuals can be demonstrated.

Inverse Effects

The structural effects of the prevailing values in a group are not necessarily parallel to the effects of the individual's value orientation. In some respects

[11] Structural effects cannot be expected to account for most of the variance in dependent variables, but since there are a mere sixty cases divided into four unequal columns, only large differences would be statistically significant. It was necessary, therefore, to include in the illustrations findings that are not significant at the .05 level. (But it should be noted that each type of structural effect was observed repeatedly.) Since the respondents are not a representative sample, the applicability of tests of significance is questionable in any case. For a recent criticism of the indiscriminate use of statistical tests of significance, see Hanan C. Selvin, "A Critique of Tests of Significance in Survey Research," *American Sociological Review* 22 (October, 1957), 519–527.

proclient group values and the individual's own proclient attitudes have opposite implications for his conduct.

In this agency, clients received money to buy clothing when needed; the caseworker and his supervisor exercised considerable discretion in establishing this need. In some other public assistance agencies, recipients receive a regular clothing allowance, which they spend at their own discretion. Respondents were asked whether they would favor giving such a regular allowance to clients. This change would save the caseworker some tedious and time-consuming work, but it would also deprive him of discretionary power over clients and their welfare.

Individuals with proclient attitudes were *less* willing than others to delegate this responsibility to clients, but the prevalence of proclient values in a group *increased* the willingness to delegate it (see Table 4.1, Delegating Responsibility to Clients)—from one-third to 55 per cent for proclient workers, and from one-half to 78 per cent for others. Proclient values had the same kind of inverse structural effect on the extent to which workers worried about their cases after working hours: individuals with proclient attitudes worried *more* than others, but the members of groups in which proclient values prevailed worried *less* than the members of other groups (see Table 4.1, Involvement with Work).

The fact that an individual is favorably disposed toward clients would be expected to increase his concern for their welfare and the gratification he receives from helping them, and thus to make him eager to exercise responsibilities that permit him to furnish more help to them and that make them grateful to him. If most members of a group share proclient values, their common interest in the welfare of clients will induce them to develop at least implicit normative standards that promote the interest of clients. They are likely to react with social disapproval toward a colleague whose involvement leads him to lose his temper when talking to a client or toward one who uses his discretion not to help clients more but to withhold help from them or to hold a club over their heads. Discussion of such experiences by proclient members of a group may lead to an agreement that the interest of clients is best served by encouraging detachment and the delegation of responsibilities to them. Or these group members may adopt explicit professional standards of social work, according to which a worker should remain detached toward his clients and foster their independence by letting them make their own decisions. The members of groups where proclient standards do not prevail are less apt to adopt professional casework standards.

Such inverse structural effects of social values call attention to the importance of social norms. Since the emotional reaction to proclient dispositions is greater involvement and an unwillingness to delegate responsibility, whereas the welfare of clients is best served by detachment and delegation of responsibility, the workers most interested in the welfare of clients are psychologically least able to provide effective service to them. But the prevalence of positive values in a group promotes the development of casework standards, which curb the psychological consequences of proclient feelings that impede effective service. Professional training in social work probably leads to the internalization of these casework standards, but the untrained workers in this agency had not fully internalized them; if they had, no inverse structural effects would have been observed.

Contingency Effects

The influence of the prevalence of social values in a group may be more indirect than in the examples discussed above. Instead of having an effect on a third variable that is independent of the individual's value orientation, it may determine whether the individual's value orientation and a third variable are related or how they are related. In technical terms, the group values and the individual's orientation may have an interaction effect on a third variable. Conceptually, this implies that the relationship between the individual's orientation and another variable is contingent on the prevalence of this value orientation in his group.

All assistance budgets made out by caseworkers were reviewed by an audit section. Caseworkers tended to accuse auditors of being too rigid about eligibility procedures and too little concerned with the welfare of clients, and conflicts between caseworkers and auditors were frequent. In groups most of whose members were service oriented, the individual's orientation had no bearing upon his conflicts with auditors; seven out of every ten workers, whatever their orientation, reported such conflicts. In groups where an eligibility orientation prevailed, however, the individual's orientation made a pronounced difference; all five of the service-oriented workers reported conflicts with auditors, in contrast to less than half of the twenty-four workers oriented toward eligibility (see Table 4.2). It seems that the chances of conflict with auditors decline only if neither the individual's own orientation nor that of the other members in his group demand that he place serving the interests of clients above strict conformity with eligibility procedures.

The extreme case of contingency effect is the one where the relationship between the individual's orientation and another factor becomes reversed, dependent on the prevalence of the orientation in the group. The extent of involvement with the work had such contingency effects. Respondents were asked how often they worry about their work after working hours, which is the measure of involvement used; then they were asked to exemplify what they worry about. The illustrations of the majority reveal worries about

Table 4.2 Effects of Orientation Toward Work

	Group's Prevailing Orientation			
	Casework Service		Checking Eligibility	
	Individual's Orientation		Individual's Orientation	
	Service	Eligibility	Service	Eligibility
Reported conflicts with auditors				
None	29%	30%	0%	54%
Some	71	70	100	46
Total	100	100	100	100
Number of cases	21	10	5	24

clients: "If they'd have enough to eat over the weekend," "Problems the people have—I hope that a deserted family can manage—I remember the expressions on their faces." But some workers worried about their own performance: "If you mean their personal problems, then the answer is, no; but I worry about the record which is open to the supervisor's checking."

If involvement—that is, extensive worrying—prevailed in a group, there was an inverse relationship between the individual's involvement and whether he worried about clients rather than his own performance, but if involvement did not prevail in a group, these two factors were directly related. The implications of this interaction effect can be clearly seen when percentages are computed horizontally (for each half-row) instead of vertically, as in Table 4.3, Source of Worries. If all the members within any given group were alike in their involvement, 100 per cent of those in groups with much involvement would be highly involved, but none of those in groups with little involvement. In other words, the two central columns (marked by one asterisk) of the table represent the deviants—the lows in groups with much involvement and the highs in groups with little involvement. It is evident that workers mostly concerned with their clients' welfare were deviants in disproportionate numbers in both kinds of groups. They were *more* apt than workers primarily concerned with their own performance to be involved in groups where involvement was rare, but they were *less* apt than the others to be involved in groups where involvement was common.[12] Indeed, they apparently were not at all influenced by the prevailing

[12] Contrary to what this finding seems to imply, differences in supervisory practices were not associated with amount of worrying.

group climate; whether they were in groups where the majority was involved or in groups where the majority was not, about half of these client-identified workers were highly involved. In contrast to only two of the sixteen workers who were concerned about their performance, seventeen of the thirty-two who were concerned with their clients' welfare deviated from the group climate. This suggests that identification with clients is a source of strength which makes a worker somewhat independent of peer group pressures.

This finding has a general methodological implication. Whenever the distribution of value orientations in a group and the individual's value orientation show such an interaction effect on a third variable, the latter differentiates members who tend to deviate from the standards of their own group from those who tend to conform to them, regardless of what these standards are. For this pattern of findings inevitably indicates that the X's have orientation Y *more* often than the non-X's in groups where this orientation is rare but *less* often than the non-X's in groups where it is common, which means that the X's tend to be the deviants whatever the prevailing orientation of the group.

Several studies have investigated the relationship between an individual's social integration among peers or his informal status and his conformity or resistance to group pressure.[13] An important problem is whether social integration increases or decreases resistance to group pressure independent of the kind of pressure involved. The procedure outlined above facilitates the study of the relationship between social position and response to *opposite* kinds of group pressure.

Individuals who were integrated in their work group were more prone than those who were not to deviate from the prevailing group climate in respect to involvement. (Whether a worker was called by his first name by some of the other members of this group, as reported by the others, is the measure of social integration used.) In groups where the majority was involved with their work, integrated workers were slightly less likely to be involved than others, but in groups where the majority was not involved, integrated workers were more likely to be involved than others (see Table 4.3, Status in Work Group). In other words, whether much or little involvement characterized the group climate, the integrated workers were more apt than the rest to deviate from it. Their resistance to group pressure is. indicated by the fact that their involvement was quite independent of the group climate; the proportion of integrated workers who were involved in

---

[13] See, e.g., George C. Homans, *The Human Group* (New York: Harcourt Brace Jovanovich, 1950), pp. 140–144; and Harold H. Kelley and M. M. Shapiro, "An Experiment on Conformity to Group Norms," *American Sociology Review* 19 (December, 1954), 667–677.

Table 4.3 Patterns of Deviancy in Respect to Involvement with Work

	Group's Dominant Climate							
	Much Involvement				Little Involvement			
	Individual's Involvement				Individual's Involvement			
	High	Low*	Total	N**	High*	Low	Total	N**
1. Source of worries								
Client's welfare	47%	53%	100%	19	54%	46%	100%	13
Own performance	89	11	100	9	14	86	100	7
Not asked***				3				9
2. Status in work group								
Integrated	50	50	100	18	50	50	100	16
Not integrated	62	38	100	13	0	100	100	13
3. Self-confidence								
High	50	50	100	8	50	50	100	10
Low	57	43	100	23	16	84	100	19

* These two columns represent the deviants—the lows in much-involved groups and the highs in little-involved groups.
** The number of cases on which the percentages, computed horizontally for each half-row, are based.
*** Respondents who said they never worried, and thus are classified among those with low involvement, could not be asked what they worried about; they are, therefore, not considered in this comparison.

their work was the same in groups with much involvement as in groups with little involvement. One-half of the thirty-four integrated workers deviated from the prevailing group climate, as contrasted with only one-fifth of the twenty-six unintegrated workers.

This finding seems to be typical. If other measures of orientation toward work and clients are substituted for involvement, and if other aspects of informal status are used instead of integration, one also finds superior status among peers associated with the tendency to deviate from the prevailing orientation in a group regardless of the particular content of this orientation.[14] Since it is improbable that deviation creates more liking and respect than conformity, the opposite direction of influence is the plausible inference. The

[14] But informal status was differently related to orientation to the supervisor. For a discussion of the implications of these and similar findings, see my paper, "Patterns of Deviation in Work Groups," *Sociometry* 23 (1960), 245–261.

acceptance and respect of his colleagues provides a worker with social support. His consequent feelings of security apparently permit him to resist group pressures and depart from group norms more readily than can the worker whose insecure position provides strong incentives to improve his standing and to court social approval through strict conformity. This interpretation implies that self-confident workers are more prone to deviate from the prevailing group pattern than those lacking in self-confidence. Indeed, this seems to have been the case (see Table 4.3, Self-Confidence).[15]

Social Cohesion

An important aspect of the network of social relations in a group is the strength of the bonds that unite its members—the group's social cohesion. One possible procedure for measuring group cohesion is to ascertain how strongly each member is identified with the group and compute some average. The objection that such an index does not pertain to the group structure could be met by isolating the structural effects of group identification, using the method suggested in this paper.

Another measure of group cohesion, which Festinger and his colleagues have made popular, is based on ingroup sociometric choices, for example, the proportion of friendship choices made by the members of a group.[16] The conception of cohesion underlying this measure has been criticized by Gross and Martin because it emphasizes "individual perceptions and minimizes the importance of the relational bonds between and among group members."[17] Sociometric measures, however, are indicative of relational bonds, since they are based on reports of choices made by one individual and received by another. Moreover, the alternative the authors propose is not likely to bring us closer to a structural definition of cohesion. They suggest that it should be measured by subjecting groups to disruptive forces of varying degrees and observing when they "begin to disintegrate."[18] But the sign of beginning disintegration would undoubtedly be that some members quit the group, or that some stop attending meetings, and an index based on such signs of disintegration relies as much on the strength of the group ties of individual members as does Festinger's sociometric index.[19]

[15] The measure used is the respondent's confidence in his ability to work without supervision. Several indices of informal status, such as popularity, were directly related to self-confidence, but the index of integration used here was not.

[16] Leon Festinger *et al.*, *Social Pressures in Informal Groups* (New York, Harper, 1950).

[17] Neal Gross and William E. Martin, "On Group Cohesiveness," *American Journal of Sociology* 57 (May, 1952), 554.

[18] *Loc. cit.*

[19] See also Lazarsfeld's discussion of this controversy, *op. cit.*, pp. 55–59.

Nevertheless, Gross and Martin's criticism should not be summarily dismissed. It draws attention to the important distinction between group structure and interpersonal relations. To be sure, interpersonal relations (and relationships between subgroups) are the very core of group structure. But atomizing group structure into its component interpersonal relations is as little justified as reducing groups to the individual personalities who compose them. Group structure refers to the distribution or network of social relations, which may have a significance that is quite distinct from that of the social relations in which specific individuals are involved. Thus, it cannot be assumed that the influence of the network of cohesive bonds in a group is the same as that of the interpersonal bonds of individual group members. The method of isolating structural effects makes it possible to distinguish between these two kinds of influence—those exerted by the prevalence of cohesive ties in a group and those exerted by the integrative ties of the individual members.

Group cohesion is operationally defined in terms of ingroup sociometric choices. Respondents were asked to name the five persons in the agency with whom they were most friendly. The median proportion of ingroup choices is used to divide groups into cohesive and noncohesive ones. Within each type of group, individuals are divided on the basis of whether or not they received ingroup choices. (An alternative procedure would have been to divide individuals by the ingroup choices they *made*. But if we accept the notion that cohesion is related to group attractiveness and wish to hold constant the aspect of the individual's interpersonal relations that is most parallel, received choices, which indicate attractiveness, are preferable to choices made.)

Cohesion in these work groups had structural effects on the approach of caseworkers to clients, that is, effects that were independent of the individual's interpersonal bonds in the group. Respondents were asked, "What are the things clients do that are particularly trying?" The answers of some reveal behavior of clients they considered a personal affront—"Demands get under my skin, or a client's trying to tell me my job," "If they cheat on me it makes me awfully mad"—whereas those of others refer to behavior that is improper or harmful to the client and his family—"They were winos, constantly drunk and beating each other up," "She hadn't even gotten her children the routine inoculations." Thus, some workers reacted in personal terms and objected to behavior of clients when they felt offended, while others reacted in accordance with generally accepted rules of conduct and objected to behavior of clients not primarily because it was discourteous to them but because it was morally wrong.[20]

[20] This distinction is related to Parsons's distinction between particularism and universalism.

The members of cohesive groups were less apt to take personal affront at the behavior of clients than those of less cohesive groups, and this difference persists if the individual's sociometric position is held constant (see Table 4.4, Reaction to Clients). Not much more than one-third of the former, in contrast to over two-thirds of the latter, reacted in personal terms. The prevalence of supportive ties in cohesive groups is a source of emotional strength for their members. The absence of extensive ego support in less cohesive groups throws their members upon other social resources for this support, such as their relations with clients. If an individual defines an interpersonal relationship as a potential source of ego support, he is apt to react in personal terms, feeling insulted or more or less appreciated, but if he does not, it is easier for him to take the view of an outsider and judge the behavior of others in accordance with impersonal criteria. Apparently, it is the general

Table 4.4 Effects of Group Cohesion

	Group Cohesion			
	High		Low	
	Individual's Attractiveness		Individual's Attractiveness	
	High	Low	High	Low
1. Reaction to clients[a]				
Personal	38%	34%	70%	80%
Impersonal	62	66	30	20
Total	100	100	100	100
2. High respect for own supervisor				
Present	76	58	50	41
Absent	24	42	50	59
Total	100	100	100	100
3. Orientation to work				
Checking eligibility	29	59	50	53
Intermediate	18	8	7	6
Casework Service	53	33	43	40
Total	100	100	100	100
Number of cases	17	12	14	17

[a] Since some clients were not asked this question, the column totals for this item, reading from left to right, are: 13, 6, 10, 15.

extensive support of group cohesion rather than the specific intensive support of the individual's own interpersonal ties that promotes an impersonal approach in social interaction with clients. Only group cohesion was associated with this approach; the individual's sociometric position was not.

When asked to choose the best supervisors in the organization, members of cohesive groups were more prone to name their own supervisor than members of less cohesive groups (see Table 4.4, High Respect for Own Supervisor). Independent of this relationship, individuals who received sociometric choices from the ingroup were also somewhat more likely to name their own supervisor than others. Perhaps the fact that a supervisor commands the respect of his workers increases the chances that cohesive ties will develop among them. But it is also possible that the absence of strong ingroup bonds produces strains and tensions which find expression in more critical attitudes toward the supervisor.

A contingency effect is illustrated by the implications of ingroup choices for the caseworker's orientation to his work; that is, group cohesion and its individual counterpart had an interaction effect upon whether a worker was oriented primarily toward checking eligibility or toward casework service. In groups with low cohesion, whether or not an individual received ingroup choices did not influence his orientation, but in groups with high cohesion, individuals who received choices from their peers were less apt than others to confine themselves to checking on the eligibility of clients (see Table 4.4, Orientation to Work). Social support from prevailing cohesive bonds and from specific interpersonal bonds both seem to be necessary to reduce the chances that workers will confine their work to rigid enforce ment of eligibility procedures. The group and the individual measure of ingroup choices also had interaction effects on other indications of strict adherence to established procedures.

Communication Structure

Instrumental as well as socioemotional patterns of social interaction form into networks of social relationships which characterize group structures. The pattern of friendly associations among workers is one aspect of the social structure of the work group, the pattern of communication assumed by their consultations and discussions of problems is another. The two are not unrelated, but neither are they identical.

The procedure used to define the communication structure is a familiar one. Respondents were asked with which colleagues they usually discuss their problems; they were free to name any number of colleagues, either members of their own group or outsiders. On the basis of the ingroup choices, groups are divided into those with relatively dense and those with sparse internal communication networks, and within each type of group, individuals are divided according to whether or not they were named as regular consultants by two or more colleagues. In short, cohesion and communication networks are defined in equivalent terms, both pertaining to social interaction, but the content of the interaction is different.

In several instances, the structural effects of the consultation network were quite similar to those of social cohesion. Both aspects of group structure, for example, had closely parallel consequences for the respect workers accorded to their supervisor. In other cases, however, their impact was different. Thus, the consultation structure did not influence a worker's reaction to the behavior of clients in personal or impersonal terms. In still other respects, the degree of reciprocity in the consultations of a group rather than their frequency had effects that paralleled those of cohesion. For instance, reciprocity in consultation was slightly associated with high productivity (many field visits), and so was group cohesion. Further research with a larger number of groups is needed to derive generalizations about the different implications of various aspects of group structure.

The density of the group's communication network had an interesting double effect on orientations to clients, as indicated by attitudes toward increasing the amount of assistance. Negative attitudes were more common in groups where consultation was frequent than in those where it was rare (see Table 4.5). Whether a worker was regularly consulted or not, he was three times as likely to oppose any increase in the assistance allowance if he

Table 4.5   Effects of Communication Network

	Extent of Communication in Group			
	Much Consultation		Little Consultation	
	Individual's Position		Individual's Position	
	Consultant	Not	Consultant	Not
Orientation to clients				
Negative	25%	36%	8%	9%
Qualified	17	36	42	36
Positive	58	28	50	55
Total	100	100	100	100
Number of cases	12	14	12	22

was a member of a group in which consultation was prevalent than one in which it was rare. This does not mean, however, that the individual's social status—how often he was consulted—was entirely unrelated to his orientation to clients. But whether or not these two factors were related was contingent on the group structure. In groups whose members consulted little, the attitude of consultants toward increasing public assistance did not differ from that of others. But in groups whose members consulted much, consultants were more likely to advocate an increase than nonconsultants. Hence, the group's communication network had two effects on the attitudes toward clients: first, frequent communication fostered more negative attitudes; and second, such communication partly determined whether or not the individual's position in the communication network influenced his attitudes toward clients. Furthermore, while the frequency of consultation in a group was associated with *negative* orientations toward clients, the fact that an individual member of a group where consultation prevailed was often consulted was associated with *positive* orientations.[21]

To interpret this finding, it is necessary to examine briefly the strained relations between caseworkers and clients in this agency. There were many reasons for conflict. Most clients were in dire need and had strong incentive to conceal any slim resources they might have had or otherwise to try to increase the amount of assistance they would get even if this required some dishonesty. Caseworkers, many of whom came to the agency directly from college with idealistic views about helping people, tended to experience what Everett Hughes has called a "reality shock" when they encountered clients who, instead of appreciating their help, lied to them and broke their promises, and whose values were so different from their own. Even when a worker tried to help clients, he sometimes found that they blamed him for limitations the agency's procedure imposed on him. Caseworkers protected themselves against such frustrating experiences by developing and publicly flaunting a hardened attitude toward clients. Their discussions among themselves were dominated by aggressive remarks and jokes about clients. Many workers were undoubtedly much more favorably disposed toward recipients than their statements to colleagues indicated. Even those who clearly had positive attitudes toward clients seemed to feel compelled to present a hardened front by making aggressive remarks about them when talking to colleagues. This pattern of relieving tension appears to be typical of work groups whose members experience conflicts with clients. Most members of this agency did not have a callous attitude toward clients, but expressing anticlient sentiments was the prevailing norm.

---

[21] For similarly contrasting effects of group and individual competitiveness, respectively, see Chapter 7.

The enforcement of social norms requires an effective network of communication in a group. Hence, a group with a strong communication network will be more effective in enforcing the prevailing anticlient norms than one with a weak network. To be sure, the anticlient norms in this organization were not so severe as to include opposition to any increase in the assistance allowance; after all, only a minority of respondents expressed such opposition. However, the more effective the enforcement of general anticlient norms in a group, the greater the chances that some of its members will take an extreme position—one more extreme than that called for by the norms—and this is what the finding shows. Informal status in a group, as data presented earlier suggest, is inversely associated with conformity to the normative orientation toward clients. In groups with communication networks that permit effective enforcement of anticlient norms, nonconsultants, whose low status makes them subject to the full impact of group pressures, therefore have more negative attitudes toward clients than consultants, whose high status removes them somewhat from group control. But in groups where consultation is rare, the status of consultant has less significance, and since, moreover, the prevailing anticlient norms are not effectively enforced in these groups, whether or not an individual is regularly consulted does not influence his orientation to clients. These considerations also explain the seeming paradox: the fact that there is much consultation in a group and the fact that a member of such a group is much consulted have opposite consequences for attitudes toward clients. An effective network of communication increases the group's power to enforce prevailing anticlient norms, but the superior status of consultant in this network enhances a person's power to resist group pressure.

Types of Structural Effects

Robinson has criticized research based on ecological correlations for implicitly assuming that these indicate relationships between the characteristics of individuals, and he has demonstrated that an ecological correlation between, say, the proportion of blacks and the proportion of illiterates in an area does not prove that more blacks than whites are illiterate.[22] Menzel has pointed out, however, that ecological studies may well be concerned with relationships between aspects of social structures without making any assumptions about relationships between attributes of individuals.[23] But

[22] W. S. Robinson, "Ecological Correlations and the Behavior of Individuals," *American Sociological Review* 15 (June, 1950), 351–357.

[23] Herbert Menzel, "Comment on Robinson's 'Ecological Correlations and the Behavior of Individuals,'" *American Sociological Review* 15 (October, 1950), 674.

Robinson's strictures apply also to Menzel's sociological conception. If the psychologically-oriented investigator assumes that ecological correlations *are* due to correlations between traits of individuals, the sociologically-oriented analyst assumes that they *are not*, and neither assumption is warranted. A correlation between divorce rates and suicide rates, for example, might be sociologically interpreted to indicate that anomie in the marital institutions of a society, operationally defined by a high divorce rate, increases suicide rates. This theory clearly implies that the ecological correlation is *not* entirely due to the fact that divorced persons are more apt to commit suicide than married ones; for if it were, much simpler explanations would suffice. To demonstrate that it is anomie, as measured by divorce rates, rather than the psychological state or personality of the divorced individual that is responsible for high suicide rates, it is necessary to show that married as well as divorced persons have higher suicide rates in countries where divorce is frequent than in those where it is rare. This is precisely how Durkheim tested his theory of anomic suicide.[24]

Durkheim, then, some sixty years ago, illustrated the method of isolating structural effects. The essential principle is that the relationship between the distribution of a given characteristic in various collectivities and an effect criterion is ascertained, while this characteristic is held constant for individuals. This procedure differentiates the effects of social structures upon patterns of action from the influences exerted by the characteristics of the acting individuals or their interpersonal relationships. If a structural effect is observed, it invariably constitutes evidence that social processes originating outside the individual personality are responsible for the differences in the dependent variable, since the influences of psychological processes have been controlled in the analysis. The futile arguments of whether or not a certain concept or empirical measure is *really* a social factor can be dismissed if this method of analysis is employed, since its results demonstrate whether social forces or psychological ones produce given effects regardless of the empirical index used to define the independent variable. Take such an individualistic characteristic as intelligence. If it were found that the average IQ scores in fraternities are associated with the scholastic records of their members when the individual's score is held constant, there could be no doubt, provided other relevant conditions are controlled, that the level of intelligence in a fraternity influences performance on examinations through *social* processes (although, of course, the finding would not show whether these processes involve social stimulation of learning or collaboration on examinations).

---

[24] Durkheim, *op. cit.*, pp. 259–276. The hypothesis is confirmed only for men; Durkheim advanced another though related interpretation to account for the suicide rates of women.

A tentative typology of structural effects can be derived by classifying them along two dimensions. The first distinguishes between the consequences of the common values or shared norms of a collectivity and those of its networks of social relationships or distribution of social positions. Second, either of these two basic aspects of the social structure can have direct effects, inverse effects, and contingency effects. (Still another type is that where the variance of a characteristic in a group, rather than its frequency, exerts an influence upon social conduct. But such an association between the variance and an effect criterion usually indicates the impact of a social force even when the characteristic is not held constant for individuals,[25] and therefore this type, which generally requires no special method of analysis, is not discussed in this paper.)

These two dimensions yield six types of structural effects:

1. *Direct structural effects of common values* indicate that the individual's conduct is influenced not only by the motivating force of his own value orientation but also by the social pressure resulting from the shared values of the other members of the group. In a public assistance agency, for example, a worker's positive orientation toward clients seemed to increase his tendency to provide casework services, and the prevalence of a positive orientation in a group also made it more likely that casework services were provided, whatever the individual's orientation.

2. *Inverse structural effects of common values* suggest that group values give rise to normative constraints that counteract the individual's psychological reaction to his own value orientation. Thus, the individual's positive attitude to clients tended to *increase* his involvement with his work and his unwillingness to delegate responsibility to recipients, but the prevalence of positive attitudes in a group tended to *decrease* involvement and unwillingness to delegate responsibility.

3. *Contingency effects of common values* are those in which the distribution of a value in a group influences the correlation between the individual's value orientation and a third variable. In the extreme case, the prevalence of the value in a group determines whether this correlation is positive or negative, and this pattern of findings identifies the deviants. It shows that individuals with a certain characteristic in terms of the third variable are more prone than others to resist group pressures and deviate from group norms, regardless of the specific content of these norms. Whether most members of a group were much involved with their work or little involved, those with an integrated status among peers, for instance, were more apt than others to deviate from the prevailing group climate, and so were workers identified with clients.

---

[25] Only if the distribution of the characteristic is not normal is there a need to control it for individuals when ascertaining the structural effects of its variance.

4. *Direct structural effects of relational networks* abstract the supportive or constraining force exerted by the *configuration* of social relations in a collectivity from the influences of each member's interpersonal relationships or social status. This is illustrated by the finding that group cohesiveness—that is, the prevalence of social ties in a group rather than its members' individual friendship ties—apparently promoted a more impersonal approach to clients.

5. *Inverse structural effects of relational networks* are indicative of the fact that the status distribution or network of social relations in a collectivity has an impact which is the very opposite of that of the individual's social status or his social relations. Since status refers to relative standing, high status of many others and own high status have often opposite implications. A perfect case is the well-known finding reported by Stouffer that a soldier's rank was *directly* associated with favorable attitudes toward the army's promotion system, but the proportion of high-ranking enlisted men in a military unit was *inversely* associated with favorable attitudes.[26] A more complex instance of this type has been observed in the public assistance agency: in work groups where consultation was frequent, *negative* attitudes toward clients were more prevalent than in other groups, but individuals who were often consulted had more *positive* attitudes than those who were not; however, this difference between individuals existed only in groups where consultation was common and not in those where it was rare.

6. *Contingency effects of relational networks* are those in which the association between the individual's social position or relations and another factor depends on the distribution of social positions or relations in the collectivity. This pattern of findings demonstrates that individuals whose social status differs from that of the majority in their group, regardless of the nature of this difference, also tend to have different characteristics in another respect. Contingency effects of status variables identify the implications of minority status as such, just as contingency effects of normative variables identify the correlates of deviancy as such. For example, Zena S. Blau finds that the proportion of widowed in an age-sex category determined the influence widowhood had on the friendships of older people. Among men in their sixties, only a small minority of whom were widowed, the widowed had much less extensive friendships than the married; but among women over seventy, three-quarters of whom were widowed, the widows had slightly more extensive friendships than the married women. Older people whose marital status places them in a minority position among age-sex peers seem to have less chance to maintain friendship ties than others.[27]

---

[26] Stouffer *et al.*, *op. cit.*, Vol. 1, pp. 250–254.
[27] Zena S. Blau, *Old Age in a Changing Society* (New York: New Viewpoint, 1973), pp. 79–83.

This list of effects of social structures is tentative and incomplete. Further refinements are needed, for example, with respect to differences in the nature of the dependent variable, and with respect to the distinction between large societies and small groups. Omitted are influences of those aspects of social structures that are not manifestations of frequency distributions, such as the form of government in a community, because in these cases there are no corresponding individual characteristics to be held constant. However, even if the empirical measure of social structure is not based on a frequency distribution but the theoretical conception implies one, corresponding characteristics of individuals should be controlled. Thus, if we are concerned with the differential impact on social conduct of democratic and authoritarian cultures, rather than with that of political institutions, and use the form of government in a country merely as an inexpensive and indirect index of its culture, we implicitly refer to differences in prevailing value orientations and should control the individual's value orientation in order to distinguish the external constraints of culture patterns from the influences of internalized values.

The method of isolating structural effects presented above underestimates the social constraints of structural differences, since the prevalence of certain shared values or social relationships in some collectivities and not in others, which is taken as given, is also often due to social forces, specifically, processes of socialization. It cannot be simply assumed, however, that any observed group pattern is the result of socialization. Other processes, such as differential selection, might be responsible. Moreover, whatever its plausibility, the claim that the common values of communities are social in origin and the product of processes of socialization is a hypothesis that requires empirical confirmation, and testing this hypothesis involves the use of procedures essentially similar to those discussed in this paper. To demonstrate its validity requires evidence that individuals who do not have a certain orientation but live in communities where this orientation prevails are more apt to develop such an orientation over time than those in other communities. Thus, Lazarsfeld and Thielens use this procedure to show that members of conservative university faculties are more apt to become increasingly conservative as they grow older than members of less conservative faculties.[28] In diachronic as well as synchronic investigations where social structures are defined, explicitly or implicitly, in terms of frequency distributions, structural effects on patterns of conduct must be analytically separated from the influences of the individuals' own characteristics or interpersonal relations.

[28] Paul F. Lazarsfeld and Wagner Thielens, Jr., *The Academic Mind* (Glencoe: Free Press, 1958), pp. 247–250.

5. The Case Study of Work Groups in Bureaucracy

How does one conduct a theoretically-oriented case study that uses quantitative as well as qualitative information? Not enough systematic knowledge on the distinctive problems of the case study has been accumulated to answer this question in general terms. I want to describe here how I carried out a cast study of work groups in two bureaucracies: the decisions I made in designing the study and in collecting the data in the field and analyzing them. Irrational elements often entered into these decisions, and some were obvious blunders, but it is precisely from these that future researchers may learn most.

Of course, I shall not deal with all decisions I made or even all I recorded. Although it might be of interest, I have not endeavored to make a quantitative analysis of my field notes and memos, which occupy nearly three file cabinets. This is merely a case study of a case study; a few cases are selected to illustrate various types of decisions.

Originally published in 1964.

Initial Design

During my last semester in graduate school in the spring of 1948, I wrote many lengthy memos in preparation for my dissertation research, outlining a multitude of problems about bureaucratic work groups that could be studied. As one reads these scores of pages, two basic themes stand out: first, how the formal organization influences the informal organization of work groups and how the latter, in turn, influences the performance of duties; and second, a functional analysis of the informal organization, exploring the distinctive functions of the informal group structure in a bureaucracy. My ideas ranged from broad problems to be explored to quite specific hypotheses. For example, I stated that the various forms taken by the displacement of goals should be ascertained, as should the specific processes through which displacement comes about; I suggested that a basic function of the informal organization in a bureaucracy is to mitigate bureaucratic impersonality; more specifically, I hypothesized that informal relations among colleagues serve the function of relieving the tensions that arise in the contacts of officials with the public.

Some of the hypotheses advanced at this early stage were later abandoned; others were supported by empirical observations, but even these were often modified and refined in the course of research. This process of selection and modification indicates that no claim can be made that hypotheses have been subjected to a rigorous test in such a case study. But the idea that research methods can be classified neatly into hypothesis-testing and insight-supplying ones is misleading, since these are polar types that appear in actual investigations in various admixtures. The double aim is typically to develop and refine theoretical insights that explain reality—for instance, group structures in bureaucracy—and to discriminate between the correct and the false explanatory principles.

It is all too easy to obtain some impressionistic evidence for our broad theoretical speculations. Such evidence, therefore, helps us little in discriminating between diverse or even conflicting theoretical principles. My endeavor to stipulate hypotheses, some in advance of the empirical research and some in the course of it, and to collect at least some quantitative data served the purpose of furnishing a screening device for insights. Those ideas that survived this screening test, while still only hypotheses (since a case study cannot validate general principles of bureaucratic structure), were more apt to be correct than the original speculations. Moreover, the quantitative analysis of specific relations between variables often produced unexpected findings that challenged the imagination and led to refinements of theoretical conceptions.

The significance of a quantitative case study, then, is (1) that it stimulates the kind of theoretical insights that can be derived only from quantitative analysis as well as the kind that result from close observation of an empirical situation, and (2) that it provides more severe checks on these insights than an impressionistic study and thus somewhat increases the probable validity of the conclusions. It is only in retrospect, however, that I have arrived at this general formulation. While I was preparing my study, I was concerned simply in exploiting pertinent theories and translating their insights into specific research problems. This helped me in deciding what kind of formal organization would be most suitable for the study. It was also necessary to prepare a proposal for the Social Science Research Council, which later awarded me a predoctoral fellowship. Last, though not least, the extensive outline of problems and hypotheses became the basis for the development of the research procedures for my case study.

On the suggestion of Robert K. Merton, whose impressive teaching had stimulated my interest in social structure, and from whose criticism and advice I benefited greatly at this stage, I modified my plan and decided to compare groups in two bureaucracies—a public and a private one. I re-formulated my hypotheses in terms of this comparison between government agency and large private firm and spent much time trying to obtain permission for study from one organization of each type. The immediate cause for abandoning this plan was that I was unable to obtain permission for doing this research from any suitable private firm, but by the time I had to make this decision there were other reasons for it, too. My experience with the first agency made me realize that, since I had so much more to learn about social patterns in government agencies, a comparison of groups in two government agencies that differ in some ways but are not too dissimilar might be most fruitful.

In the weeks before I started observation in the first government agency, I designed a detailed schedule of research procedures. This was completed after I had entered the organization and become acquainted with the actual setup. I had earlier decided to use three basic methods—direct observation, interviewing, and analysis of official records—and to employ various quantitative as well as qualitative research techniques under each. Thus, I planned not only to observe whatever I could notice about the relations among colleagues in the office but also to obtain a systematic record of all their social interaction for a specified period; not only to interview selected members of the organization on specific issues but also to administer a semi-structured interview to all members of the work groups intensively studied; not only to read the procedure manual but also to abstract some quantitative information from it.

I put each research problem I had outlined on a 5 × 8 slip, making several carbons, which were cross-classified by the various research procedures to be used to investigate this problem. For example, the slip that dealt with contacts between different sections in the organization was classified under written regulations, interview with management representative, active observation (by which I meant that I would ask questions to clarify what I observed), quantitative observation, self-recording, and interview with officials. The resulting file indicated the different substantive problems that might be studied with any given research procedure.

This schedule served as the basic guide for my study, but it was not intended to be rigid or fixed. As new ideas or new investigation techniques occurred to me in the course of observation, I added them to the file. And when it became that a certain problem could not be studied with a given procedure, or not at all in this situation, I modified the schedule accordingly. I repeatedly went over the file in the early phase of observation, revising it and abstracting lists of problems under the various research procedures, which I carried with me into the field. There I explored how well the various procedures would actually lend themselves to studying the different problems. The revised lists resulting from this exploration were regularly consulted, and they directed my research activities.

I found such a schedule of procedures, somewhat flexible yet exerting some control over the research process, very useful. To be sure, it is possible that I missed some exciting leads because I was too concerned with following a research schedule. It may also be that I failed to collect systematic data I could have obtained because I was too easily intrigued by new possibilities and diverted from following the predesigned procedure. But, whatever the wisdom of my specific decisions, I think that the general principle of using such a research schedule in a case study is sound.

In a bureaucratic field situation, the needs of the organization and not those of the observer determine what occurs and thus what can be studied at any given time. While some events occur regularly, enabling the researcher to determine when to study them, others do not. A change in regulations is introduced, a conference is called, two officials have an argument, and the observer must be ready to turn his attention to these incidents, which may bear on some of his central research problems. The researcher who compulsiveley insists on following his predesigned plan will miss these rare opportunities. Conversely, the one who is seduced by every new lead will find that he has failed to collect information on the theoretical problems that prompted his research. A research schedule that is recurrently revised but quite closely followed guards against these dangers. During the last weeks of observation, I went over my lists carefully, and, while my design was so ambitious that I could not possibly carry out all my plans, I was able to select those items for completion that I considered most important. At the very least, my research schedule prevented me from inadvertently forgetting to obtain some information that was essential in terms of my theoretical framework.

Entry and Orientation

An inteviewing survey of a sample of New Yorkers can be conducted without official permission from anybody, but a field study of a bureaucracy cannot be executed without the explicit permission of management. This poses special problems. While not all respondents selected for a sampling survey agree to be interviewed, and those who do are typically not representative of those who do not, there are known procedures for correcting this self-selection bias. But the problem of self-selection is far more extreme in research on organizations, and it is not easily possible to correct for the bias it introduces. Suppose someone wants to study bureaucratic rigidities and fear of innovation. The very fact that the management gives him permission to conduct his investigation in its organization indicates that it is not resistant to trying something new. It may well be no accident that all old-established bureaucracies I approached refused permission for the study and that both organizations that opened the way were relatively young ones, founded during the New Deal. Perhaps self-selection makes it inevitable that the organizations we study are those in which bureaucratic rigidities are least pronounced.

The members of the organization know, of course, that management has given permission to conduct the study, and this creates another problem. The observer cannot escape an initial identification with management, since the assumption is that management must have a direct interest in the study. In the federal agency, I was suspected of being a representative of the Hoover Commission, which at that time carried out investigations in various branches of the federal government. These suspicions compound the problem posed by the sheer presence of the observer, since people become self-conscious if somebody sits in a corner and watches them, even if he tries to do so unobtrusively. Ultimately, I overcame these difficulties, but not until blunders I committed owing to my inexperience had first intensified them.

On my first day in the federal agency, the district commissioner introduced me to his top assistants, told me that one of them would serve as my guide during my period of orientation, and assigned an office to me where I could read in private the extensive rules and regulations that governed the agency's operations. During the first week, the official who acted as my guide explained the operating procedure to me in lengthy interviews and answered the questions I had after reading the books of rules and regulations. He also introduced me to the supervisors of the various departments, and I had occasion to interview them. During the second week, I further explored the operations of various departments, discovered the quantitative operational records that were kept, abstracted information from them, and revised my research design by adapting it to the concrete circumstances in this agency.

I still spent much time in the private office, and only supervisors and some selected officials had as yet met me; most agents had not, although they had undoubtedly noticed my presence.

This thorough initial orientation was a good preparation for the observation period. The basic knowledge I acquired about the organization and its operations enabled me to translate my general research procedures into specific operational terms appropriate for this field situation, and it helped me to select a suitable department for intensive study. But spending two weeks on becoming oriented to the agency's operating procedures also had serious disadvantages.

At the very start of the intensive observation of Department Y, I was introduced to all its members by a senior official at a meeting and given an opportunity to explain the study briefly. I realized that an observer must explain at the outset who he is and what he wants to do. But I failed to realize that what I defined as the beginning of the actual observation was not the beginning for these agents. I had been seen around for two weeks, and my failure to explicitly clarify my identity earlier gave rumors about me that much time to circulate. The private office and my preoccupation with becoming familiar with a complex bureaucratic structure had blinded me to the fact that I was already being observed by these agents, even though I had not yet started observing them.

I learned from this experience. Six months later, in the study of the state employment agency, I explained the study in a brief talk to the members of Department X the day I set foot in their local office.[1] (It was possible to arrange the preceding one-week orientation in a different location.) It seemed to be easier to establish rapport here than in the federal agency, but whether this was due to the lecture or the experience I had acquired as an observer is a moot point. In any case, the lecture was far less effective than it could have been, as I found out when I gave another lecture at the end of the observation period in the employment agency. The object of this farewell lecture was to illustrate what such a study of social relations seeks to discover; I presented Whyte's analysis of the relation between informal status in a gang and bowling score, plus some of my own preliminary findings on consultations among officials and their discussions about clients. This lecture was much more successful than the first one. Officials were interested, asked numerous questions, and made some revealing comments afterward. One agency interviewer said that there should have been a meeting in which I explained my study at the beginning, not just at the end; apparently she had entirely forgotten that there had been such a meeting. Another inter-

[1] I did the field work in Department X after that in Department Y, but in both the original book and this one, the analysis of Department Y (see Chapters 7 and 8) is presented before that of Department Y (Chapter 9).

viewer, who had not forgotten the earlier talk, mentioned how much more interesting the second one was and how much more relaxed I appeared when giving it.

In the first lecture, I described the objective of the study in general terms, covering such points as the importance of human relations and the need for firsthand knowledge of government agencies. In the second lecture, I illustrated the study's objective with concrete findings. It is evident from the reactions that the second topic would have been a better way to introduce the study than the first. There are a number of reasons: a discussion of actual findings is much more interesting than a mere description of formal objectives, creating some interest at the outset in what the observer has to say and wants to do. Besides, the concrete examples of sociological analysis, judiciously chosen, demonstrate more effectively than hollow-sounding explicit disavowals that the observer is really not an efficiency expert who wants to check up on the work of officials. The evidence the observer furnishes of what he and other social scientists can do, finally, not only affirms his professional identity but also helps to command respect for his research and to motivate respondents to cooperate with it.

The Role of the Observer

After I had been introduced to the members of Department Y in the federal agency, I spent most of my time in the room where they and the members of another department were located. I took every opportunity to become acquainted with these agents, asking them about their work, going to lunch with little groups, slowly beginning to establish some rapport. But I soon became impatient with the slow progress I made and decided that, since I was sitting in this room and watching what was going on anyway, I could use my time more economically by making the quantitative record I had planned of the social interaction among agents. I started this record of all social contacts in the department within a week from the day I had been introduced to its members. This was a serious mistake.

I had just begun to overcome the suspicion and resistance aroused by my entry, and now I employed a technique of observation that the agents found very objectionable and that increased their resistance to the study again. Of course, I explained that I simply wanted to get a systematic record of the social contacts among officials, but this did not overcome the objections of the agents. Even those who apparently believed my explanations considered such a record ridiculous and emphasized that I could not gain an understanding of the agent's job by sitting in the office but must go into the field where the most important work was being done. Others suspected that I was really trying to check on how much time they wasted, as exemplified by the mocking comment one whispered to me when he left the room: "I'm going to the washroom; will be back in two minutes." The continual observation to which keeping such a record subjects respondents makes them self-conscious and is irritating. Evidently I should have waited until my rapport was much better before using this technique (as I did, of course, in the second study). Why did I make the blunder of using it prematurely?

I think the answer is not simply that lack of experience prevented me from knowing how much resistance this method of observing interaction would create in a group not yet fully reconciled to my presence. Common sense should have told me so, had not irrational factors prevented me from realizing it. I was a lone observer in the midst of an integrated group of officials who were initially suspicious of and even somewhat hostile to me and my research. While they were part of the bureaucratic structure, my position was not anchored in it. My anxiety engendered by this insecure position was undoubtedly intensified by the pressure I felt to progress with my observations, since I was not sure whether I could achieve my research aims in the limited time available. It seems (and I use the tentative wording advisedly because I am now reconstructing mental processes of which I was then not fully aware) that I tried to cope with this anxiety by imposing a rigid structure on my research activities. This emotional reaction may have prompted my decision to turn so early from more exploratory observations to the precisely circumscribed and fairly routine task of recording interaction frequencies.

The feelings of insecurity that the bureaucratic field situation tends to evoke in the observer, particularly the inexperienced one, are generally a major source of blunders. This is the fundamental pragmatic reason, quite aside from considerations of professional ethics, why the observer, in my opinion, should not resort to concealment and deception. It is difficult to simulate a role successfully over long periods of time, and if concern over detection adds to the observer's other worries he is not likely to be effective in discharging his research responsibilities. I explained quite openly what I was doing and the aims of my study to any respondent who was interested, the major exception being that I never called it a study of "bureaucracy." (Refraining from deception does not imply, of course, revealing one's hypotheses to respondents, since proper research procedure requires these to remain confidential.)

A few times I did try to conceal something, against my better judgment, and this typically turned out to be a mistake. For example, the negative reaction of agents to the recording of social interaction made me worry about how senior officials would react to my use of this technique. Once, when a managerial official passed my desk, I inadvertently placed my hand over the recording sheet; and another time, when the district commission stopped by my desk and asked me about the research, my concern over his reaction, which proved to be quite unjustified, led me to give a vague and confused answer. Here were two silly blunders that resulted from unnecessary attempts to conceal my research activities.

I was at first suspected of masking my true identity and pretending to be an outside observer while really being a representative of some government commission. My trump card in establishing rapport, therefore, was that I actually was who I pretended to be, and chances were good that this would become apparent in continuing social interaction. I could not have played this trump if I had in fact practiced deception, for doing so entailed permitting my natural behavior in social intercourse to reveal the kind of person I am. There is little doubt that my success in overcoming the strong initial resistance to the study by some union members stemmed from the fact that they perceived my genuine sympathy with their viewpoint, even though I never explicitly expressed my political opinions. As our informal discussions revealed my familiarity with university life and the sociological literature, my claim of being a social researcher was validated.

But the most convincing evidence that I really was not part of the government service was supplied by me inadvertently, often by mistakes I made. When agents, apparently not believing that I was an outsider, came to me for advice on a problem in their cases, my genuine ignorance of the complex official regulations became quite apparent. When I talked too freely to interviewers in the state agency during working hours, having become used to this practice in the federal agency, a supervisor several times told me, politely but firmly, not to interfere with their work. I had made a mistake in not being more careful, but these incidents were to my advantage, since they demonstrated to the interviewers that I was only a tolerated outsider and really not part of the management hierarchy.

As one would expect, I found some officials more easily approachable than others, more interested in the research, and more willing to furnish information. A few seemed quite eager to talk to me and volunteered sensitive information on topics that others were most reluctant to discuss at all; for example, they freely criticized agency procedure and even their colleagues. It is my impression that the best informants in the early weeks tended to be officials who occupied marginal positions in the work group or the organization. Being not fully integrated among colleagues or somewhat alienated from the bureaucratic system may have made these officials more critical of their social environment, less restrained by feelings of loyalty from sharing their criticism with an outsider, and more interested in the approval of the observer than were those who received much social support and approval within the organization.

The marginal position of the observer in the bureaucratic field situation complements the marginal position of these informants, and this entails a danger. The observer may be tempted to rely too much on these officials who make themselves easily accessible to him. If he yields to this temptation, he will obtain a distorted picture of the organization and the group structure. Moreover, if he becomes identified with deviant individuals or cliques, his ability to establish rapport with the majority and his effectiveness as an impartial observer will be impaired.

It is not possible, however, to avoid entirely the self-selection of informants. The observer is no neutral machine that selects respondents purely at random and devotes exactly the same amount of time to each. He can hardly be expected to reject the overtures some officials make to him, not only because his insecure position creates a need for social acceptance but also because his research responsibilities demand that he take advantage of these opportunities for obtaining information. Somewhat marginal officials proved to be an invaluable source of new insights, particularly about dysfunctions of various institutions and practices. Their incomplete integration in the existing social structure made them perceptive observers of it and its shortcomings, and their concern with commanding the observer's respect gave them incentives to share their most interesting observations. The solution to the problem of self-selection of informants is not to ignore this important source of information but to supplement it with quantitative data based on responses from the entire group or a representative sample.

Interest in earning the observer's respect may well be an informant's major motivating force for supplying information and explanations. Respondents make a contribution to the research in exchange for the respect they win by doing so, provided they care about being respected by the observer. The most competent officials can command respect by demonstrating their superior knowledge and skills, but the less competent ones cannot, and this leads some of them to seek to earn the observer's respect by acting as second-hand participant-observers and sharing their inside knowledge and insights with him.

In addition to this difference between respondents variously located in the social structure, there is a difference in the time when they tend to be good informants. During the later phases of the field work, my best informants were no longer largely officials who occupied marginal positions but included some of the most competent and highly respected ones. I think what happened was that once I became accepted as a social scientist my prestige rose, increasing the value of my approval and respect for my respondents. As long as my respect was not worth much, only the marginal officials who commanded little respect in the organization were interested in earning it; but later, when my respect came to be worth more, other officials, too, became interested in earning it.

Finally, a few remarks are in order about the interviews administered subsequent to the observation period. On my last day in the office, many officials whom I asked for interview appointments assumed that the interview would take place during office hours. When informed that the interview would be during off-hours, some were reluctant to devote their own time to it, but group pressures soon came to operate in my favor. (I had this experience in both agencies.) As these potential refusals, who had said they wanted to think it over and that I should call them back, noticed that most of their colleagues made interview appointments with me, a few approached me and said they had decided they could make an appointment now, and most of the others readily made one later. Only two of the thirty-eight respondents in the two departments intensively studied were not interviewed. (Even these two never overtly refused but postponed appointments so often that I finally gave up.)

The question that evoked most resistance was the one on party preference in the last election, notwithstanding my repeated assurance that answers were anonymous and confidential. That this was not due simply to distrust of me is indicated by the fact that one agent said he would be glad to tell me if I would only promise to not use his answer in the research. (I refused to make such a promise.) Since politics is a sensitive area in civil service, agents did not want my report to describe the political preferences of civil servants generally (particularly in 1948, when Henry A. Wallace was a presidential candidate), and this, rather than fear that I would identify individual responses, probably accounted for their reluctance to express their voting preferences. The anonymity of our research reports protects only individuals from exposure and not the groups they are identified with, for our monographs do reveal the characteristics of various groups—civil servants, blacks, Jews, and others. In a situation where the group with which responses will be associated in the final report is apparent, persons identified with this group will not be moved by our assurance of anonymity to reveal characteristics they do not want attributed to their group.

6. The Comparative Study
of Organizations

The comparative method, in the broadest sense of the term, underlies all
scientific and scholarly theorizing. If we mean by theory a set of generalizations that explains courses of events or situations on the basis of the conditions
and processes that produce them, every theory must rest on comparisons of
contrasting cases; for to explain a state of affairs requires that the difference
between it and some other state of affairs be accounted for—why democratic
institutions developed in some countries but not in others, or what political
processes distinguish democracies with multiparty systems from those with
two-party systems. Usually, however, the term *comparative method* is used in a
much narrower sense, though by no means a consistent one. Spencer and
Durkheim, for example, referred by it to virtually opposite methodological
principles. The former's comparative method involves collecting descriptions
of the same institution in many different societies to demonstrate "laws" of
social evolution.[1] Durkheim, who rejected this procedure of the evolutionists,

---

Originally published in 1965.

[1] See the discussion of Spencer's comparative method in Howard Becker and Harry E.
Barnes, *Social Thought from Lore to Science*, 2d ed., Vol. 1 (Washington: Harren Press, 1952).
pp. 748–749.

employed the same term to refer to the establishment of concomitant variations or correlations between two social phenomena.[2]

Although every analysis of organizations entails some explicit or implcit
comparisons, the comparative method in the study of organizations is defined
here more narrowly as the systematic comparison of a fairly large number of
organizations in order to establish relationships between their characteristics.
In short, the term is used here to refer to quantitative comparisons that make
it possible to determine relationships between attributes of organizations—
for example, what other differences are generally associated with variations
in an organization's size, or the degree of its bureaucratization, or its functions. Lest this emphasis on quantitative research be misconstrued, let me
hasten to add that it is not meant to imply a concern with mathematical
models or advanced statistical techniques. These are not at all the focus of
interest. The point made is rather that theoretical generalizations about
organizations are necessarily rooted in comparisons of many that differ in
relevant respects, regardless of how impressionistic the data are on which the
analysis is based. Since some quantitative comparisons are inherent in the
method of constructing theories, such comparisons should be built into the
research procedures from which the theories derive.

The distinctive nature of the comparative approach to the study of organizations, as defined, can be highlighted in juxtaposition with the case-study
approach. Most empirical investigations in the field are case studies of single
organizations. The rationale for this approach is that large modern organizations, which often contain many thousands of members, are too complex to
permit studying more than one or two at a time. While this statement is
obviously correct if the aim is to investigate the attributes and behavior of the
individual members of organizations, it is highly questionable if the aim is to
investigate the characteristics and operations of the organizations themselves.
Many characteristics of organizations can be ascertained quite easily and
without the time and effort required for a survey of a large part of the
membership. In any case, to derive theoretical generalizations from the study
of a single organization, either the conditions in this organization must be
compared to those in others known from the literature, which means that
most of the systematic information collected in the case study are ignored, or
the analysis must center on internal comparisons of the various units within
the organization.[3] The latter procedure tends to constrain the investigator
to focus on principles about the structure of work groups and the behavior
of individual members *within* organizations rather than on principles that

[2] Emile Durkheim, *The Rules of Sociological Method* (Chicago: University of Chicago Press,
1930), pp. 125–140.

[3] On the method of internal comparison, see Seymour M. Lipset *et al., Union Democracy*
(Glencoe: Free Press, 1956), pp. 425–427.

govern the functioning and development of organizations. As a result of these tendencies, empirical studies in the field of organizations have contributed more to our knowledge of human relations and group structures in the context of organizations than to the theory of organizations as distinct social structures. To be sure, the intensive analysis of internal processes possible in case studies can greatly enrich the theory of organization, but only as a complement to inquiries based on comparative studies.

An organization is a system for mobilizing and coordinating the efforts of various, typically specialized, groups in the pursuit of joint objectives. Although an organization could not exist without the individuals who compose its membership, it has characteristics that do not pertain to characteristics of its individual members, such as its size, to name only the most obvious example. The sociological theory of organizations, the economic theory of the firm, and the political theory of the state or government constitute important potential links for interdisciplinary cross-fertilization and comparative research, inasmuch as they deal with diverse kinds of organizations, the organized government in a society being a particular kind of organization, namely, the one with the largest scope.[4] But there is actually little cross-fertilization on this level, in part because the theory of organization is in such a rudimentary state.

The objectives of this article are to conceptualize various dimensions that can be distinguished in the analysis of organizational life, to outline the comparative approach to the study of organizations, and to indicate the theoretical significance of this approach.

Three Foci of Analysis

Three foci of analysis may be distinguished in organizational research, whether concern is with government agencies of industrial concerns, labor unions or political parties, armies or hospitals.[5] The focus of the analysis can

---

[4] This may well be at least as important a distinctive characteristic of the state as the usually emphasized monopoly over the use of force; see Max Weber, *The Theory of Social and Economic Organization* (New York: Oxford University Press, 1947), p. 156.

[5] The conceptualization presented is a revision of one suggested in Blau, "Formal Organization," *American Journal of Sociology* 63 (1957), 63–69; see Chapter 3 above. (Processes of development are not included as one of the three foci in the reconceptualized version because they belong to a different dimension which cuts across the three distinguished here, *not* because I consider them any less important.) A related schema of levels of analysis is presented in Stanley H. Udy, "The Comparative Analysis of Organizations," in James G. March (ed.) *Handbook of Organizations* (Chicago: Rand McNally, 1965), and a somewhat different schema is developed in W. Richard Scott, "Theory of Organizations," in Robert E. L. Faris (ed.) *Handbook of Sociology* (Chicago: Rand McNally, 1964).

be (1) the individual in his specific role as a member of the organization who occupies a certain position in it; (2) the structure of social relations among individuals in the various groups within the organization; or (3) the system of interrelated elements that characterizes the organization as a whole.

First, many studies carried out in organizations center attention on the attitudes and behavior of individual members insofar as they pertain to the functions of the organization. The application of survey techniques to research in organizations invites this focus, expecially if representative samples are used, because sampling surveys make individuals the independent units of analysis. This type of analysis is illustrated by investigations of the attitudes of soldiers in combat, of the career patterns or civil servants and their implications for commitment to the organization, of the influence of the background characteristics of workers on performance of tasks and turnover, or of the conditions that promote work satisfaction. Studies of voting exemplify the same type in respect to the political organization of the government. These studies deal with processes that occur in the context of organizations and often show how the context modifies these processes—for instance, how employment conditions affect work satisfaction or productivity—but they are not studies of organizations and the principles that govern their character and development. *The American Soldier* examines sociopsychological processes, such as those manifesting relative deprivation, but it tells us little about the organization of the army.[6] *Voting* analyzes political processes, such as the crystallization of voting decisions under cross pressure, but it has little to say about the ways in which governments are organized.[7] *Management and the Worker* deals with behavior in work groups, but not the organization of the factory.[8]

A second type of analysis focuses upon the structures of social relations that emerge in the groups and segments in the organization. Since interest centers on networks of social relations and processes of informal communication in groups in this case, data are typically obtained about every member of selected subgroups and the social interaction among them rather than from a sample of individuals dispersed throughout the organization. Examples of this type are studies of the informal organization of work groups (*Management and the Worker* is a pioneering one), of union solidarity among factory workers, of consultation among officials, or of the differentiation of informal status that emerges in social interaction. Here concern is with the social procesess

---

[6] Samuel A. Stouffer *et al.*, *The American Soldier*, 2 vols. (Princeton: Princeton University Press, 1949).

[7] Bernard R. Berelson *et al.*, *Voting* (Chicago: University of Chicago Press, 1954).

[8] F. J. Roethlisberger and William J. Dickson, *Management and the Worker* (Cambridge: Harvard University Press, 1959).

that govern the development of group structures and the effects of these structures on patterns of conduct. The aim is to discover the principles that characterize group life, and the organizational context within which the work groups exist is considered as a set of limiting conditions for the emergence of group structure. The conditions in the larger organization, therefore, are treated as given rather than as problematical; that is, they are not made the subject of the inquiry that needs to be explained.

Third, the analysis may focus on the attributes of organizations themselves, the interrelations between these attributes, and the processes that produce them. In order to determine the relationships between various characteristics of organizations, as an initial step in tracing the processes that give rise to them and explaining them, it is necessary to compare a large number of organizations which are similar in many respects but different in some. Studies on the connections between the size of organizations, their complexity, and the degree of bureaucratization within them illustrate this type, as do investigations of the impact of automation on the division of labor in factories, of the conditions that foster oligarchy in unions, of the implications of dispersed ownership for centralized control in corporations, or of the impact of the shape of the hierarchical pyramid on operations. The focus of interest now is the system of interrelated elements that characterize the organization as a whole, not its component parts. The aim is to discover the principles that explain why organizations develop various characteristics, although the processes underlying the connections observed must often be inferred in the absence of detailed information on the internal structures of and the informal processes in work groups.

Implications. It is evident that the three foci lead to the analysis of quite different, though by no means unrelated, problems. The phenomena that are made the central subject of the inquiry in one kind of analysis are assumed to be given in the others. In the first case, the role attributes and performances of the individual members of organizations are investigated, and the context of the organization and even that of the work group are considered given conditions or stimuli that may affect the roles of individuals. In the second case, social interaction and, particularly, the structures of social relations in groups are analyzed, and the characteristics of the individuals who compose these groups as well as the organizational context are treated as limiting conditions for the emergence of these social processes and structures. In the third case, the combinations of attributes that characterize, organizations as such and the development of these systems of organizing the efforts of various groups in joint endeavors are studied, and both the individual behavior and the group processes that underlie these systems are taken for granted.

The specific criterion for differentiating the three foci—role analysis, structural analysis, and organizational analysis—is whether the variables under consideration describe individuals, groups of interrelated individuals, or organized systems of interrelated groups. Thus, seniority, professional expertness, socioeconomic status, commitment to an organization, and political preference are attributes of individual human beings. But the strength of the cohesive bonds that unite group members and the extent of differentiation of status that emerges among them are variables that refer to groups as such and not to their individual members. Correspondingly, the division of labor among various groups, the degree of centralization of control in an organization, the age of the organization, and its size are characteristics of the organization as a whole that cannot be attributed either to its subgroups or to its individual members.

A complication arises, however, because the variables that *pertain* to a collectivity may be based on data *obtained* either by measuring a property of the collectivity itself or a property of all of its members. Lazarsfeld and Menzel have referred to the former as global properties, such as whether a factory is automated, uses assembly lines, or neither, and to the latter as analytical properties of collectivities, such as the proportion of older workers in a company.[9] The turnover rate in a factory, the average productivity of its labor force, and the proportion of its personnel in administrative positions are analytical properties that clearly refer to the organized collectivity but that are based on data derived from the behavior of individuals. For every analytical attribute that describes an organized collectivity there is a parallel attribute that disinguishes the members within it—the productivity of a worker, or whether an employee occupies an administrative position. But there are no such individual parallels for the global properties of collectivities —only factories can be distinguished by the extent of automation, not the individual workers within a factory. A simple illustration of this contrast is the difference between the age of a firm and the average age of its employees.

Focus on Organizational Attributes. The use of analytical properties—averages, proportions, or rates—as independent variables in organizational or structural analysis raises special problems. Let us assume that a comparative study of welfare agencies found that professionalization, that is, the proportion of caseworkers who have graduate training in social work, is associated with more extensive service to clients. Three interpretations of this finding are possible, depending on whether the focus is on roles, on group structures, or

---

[9] Paul F. Lazarsfeld and Herbert Menzel, "On the Relation between Individual and Collective Properties," in Amitai Etzioni, *Complex Organizations* (New York: Holt, Rinehart and Winston, 1961), pp. 426–435. The other two types of properties they distinguish can be considered special cases of the two noted in the text.

on the organization of the agencies. First, professionally trained individuals may provide more service to clients than untrained caseworkers. Second, the structure of work groups with a high proportion of professionals, perhaps by making informal status dependent on the way clients are treated, may encourage caseworkers, regardless of their own training, to extend more service to clients. Third, agencies with a high proportion of professionals on their staff may be better organized to serve clients, which would be reflected in improved service by individual caseworkers independent of these individuals' own training or the work groups to which they belong. To determine which one of these three different interpretations is correct, or whether more than one or all three are, it is necessary to separate three distinct influences on treatment of clients, that of the individual's own training, that of the professional composition of his work group, and that of the professionalization of the agency in which he works. Statistical procedures for accomplishing this separation have been outlined elsewhere.[10]

It should be noted that the technical criterion by which organizational analysis is distinguished from the two other types is an analytical one that applies to all kinds of organized collectivities, not alone to formal organizations. Cross-cultural comparisons or studies of the relationship between the stage of technological development and the stratification system in different societies involve organizational analysis in the technical sense, although they do not deal with formal organizations. To speak of a formal organization there must exist explicit procedures for organizing the subgroups in a collectivity to further some joint ends. On the basis of this definition, the political system in a society is a formal organization, while the stratification system is not, and neither is the economy, though a firm, of course, is one.

To advance the theory of formal organizations, a focus on organizational analysis is essential. This is not to say that role analysis and structural analysis of the members and work groups in organizations are unimportant, because they can supply evidence on the social processes that account for the systems that emerge in organizations, but this evidence can be used to explain organizational systems only in combination with comparative studies that focus on the relationships between various attributes of organizations themselves.

Social Processes in Organizations

The study of social processes is often contrasted with the study of social structures or that of the interrelations between factors in a system, but it is not

[10] Peter M. Blau, "Structural Effects," *American Sociological Review* 25 (1960), 178–193 (see Chapter 4). The procedure there described for isolating the effects of group structure from those of role attributes can also be used to isolate the effects of organizational attributes from those of the other two.

always entirely clear what the specific distinguishing marks of the analysis of social processes are. One implication of the term is that processes occur over time and that their investigation, therefore, must be diachronic rather than synchronic. Whereas the synchronic study of the interrelations between attributes in a system takes the emergence of these attributes for granted, the diachronic study of social processes traces the sequence of events or occurrences that led to the development of these attributes. An illustration of this difference would be an inquiry into the status structure in a group and the various characteristics associated with superior status, on the one hand, and an inquiry into the processes of differentiation that produced the status structure, on the other. Taking time into account, however, is only a necessary and not a sufficient condition for the analysis of social processes. Thus, panel studies that compare opinions or states of affairs at two points in time do not directly deal with social processes, although they make it easier to infer them than does research at a single point in time.

Analysis of Intervening Links. The analysis of social processes requires the specification of a series of intervening links between an earlier state and a structure that subsequently develops. Thus, the investigation of the process of socialization seeks to trace the many steps that link the behavior and attitudes of parents to the internalized values and personalities that their children ultimately develop. Similarly, the investigation of the process of bureaucratization seeks to trace the sequence of typical events stimulated by the large size and complexity of an organization and eventuating in a formalized system of procedures and hierarchical authority. In brief, the examination of social processes entails the specification of intervening variables that connect initial conditions with their effects in a time sequence.

External as well as internal social processes affect organizations. Research on processes that occur outside the framework of organizations must not make organizations the unit of analysis but must find another more appropriate one. Thus, the study of the processes that give rise to technological advancements and the chain of implications of technological innovations must compare different cultures and not merely different organizations in one society. To investigate the processes that govern career patterns, the occupational roles and career lines must be the focus of the analysis and the occupational experiences of individuals must be followed as they move into and out of various organizations. The student of organizations is not primarily concerned with these external processes but only with the results they produce, which constitute conditions that affect organizations, for instance, the limits set by the state of technological knowledge for organizational developments, or the influence career experiences have for the performance of organizational responsibilities.

The internal processes in organizations include the processes of social inter-action among members that find expression in the emergent group structures and the processes through which the interrelated elements in the total system become organized. The analysis of processes of interaction may deal with the ways in which first impressions affect role expectations and how these in turn affect the conduct of interacting persons, with the exchanges of rewards in the form of advice, help, approval, and respect that shape the relations among group members, and with the modifications in these exchange pat-terns produced by differences in the complexity of the task or in the style of supervision. The aim of the analysis is to explain the differentiated social structures that arise as the result of these processes of interaction among individuals. Whereas this analysis exemplifies the structural focus, the organi-zational focus calls attention to such problems as the processes of increasing differentiation, specialization, mechanization, professionalization, centraliza-tion, or bureaucratization, the conditions that give rise to these processes, and the interplay between them. The aim here is to explain the systems of interrelated characteristics that evolve in various organizations. These are the processes that are of immediate concern to the student of organizations, because they give rise to the configurations of organizational characteristics that develop.

Compass of Social Systems.   Social systems are typically part of broader ones that encompass them and simultaneously constitute the environment of narrower systems they encompass. Work groups are the environment in which individuals act out their roles; the organization of the department is the context within which work groups develop their structure; the total organization sets limits to the ways in which departments can be organized; and the society, including the political order, other institutions, and the state of the technology, provides the social setting that conditions the character of the organizations in its boundaries. Whereas the larger system restricts the developments of those it encompasses, there are also feedback effects from the subsystems to the more encompassing ones, because subsystems are not infinitely pliable but tend to have a minimum of autonomy to which the encompassing system must adjust.[11] Thus, the occupational experiences and professional values of the members of an organization condition the perform-ance of tasks, the informal structures of work groups modify the impact of the incentive system, and the professional requirements of the department of psychiatry set limits to the administrative requirements the hospital administration can impose on it.

[11] See Alvin W. Gouldner, "Reciprocity and Autonomy in Functional Theory," in Llewellyn Gross, *Symposium on Sociological Theory* (Evanston: Row, Peterson), pp. 254–266.

Even in comparative studies only those characteristics of the units under consideration in respect to which they *differ* can be systematically investigated, whereas the characteristics all have in common must be allocated to the next higher level as part of the constant environment. If all work groups under investigation consist of six workers under a supervisor, size cannot be treated as a variable in the analysis of group structure, but the existence of work units of this size must be considered part of the organizational context that conditions the emerging group structures. Similarly, if computers are used in some organizations but not in others, the significance of this aspect of mechanization for other characteristics of the organization can be examined, but if secretaries in all the organizations studied use typewriters, it must be inferred that this aspect of mechanization is part of the technological state of the society that is invariably reflected in its organizations. Whether this inference is correct or not depends on the representativeness of the organizations included in the sample. Regardless of whether the inference about all organizations is warranted, however, the fact that a certain characteristic reveals no variation among all the organizations examined necessitates that it be treated as a given condition of organizational life in this particular research.

Whereas factors that cannot be explained within the framework of a specific investigation must be allocated to a more encompassing system, a full explanation of relationships between factors tends to involve references to a less encompassing system. A theoretical intepretation of an observed relationship between two variables, an antecedent and its effect, entails subsuming it under a general proposition that connects two abstract concepts of which the observed variables are specific manifestations and, in addition, specifying intervening variables that account for the connection.[12] Thus Durkheim explained the relationship between religion and suicide rates by suggesting that an individualistic belief system, by lessening social integration, promotes an egoistic mentality, which affords weak protection against crises.[13]

To explain the correlation between an independent and a dependent variable, the intervening processes that account for the connection are specified, and to explain the principles that govern these intervening processes further entails a shift in compass to a lower level. For example, the relationship between the composition of a group and the status structure that develops in it is explained by taking into account the processes of social interaction that lead to differentiation of status, and patterns of social interaction and exchange can be explained in terms of the psychological processes that

[12] On the latter, see Patricia L. Kendall and Larzarsfeld, "Problem of Survey Analysis," in Robert K. Merton and Lazarsfeld, *Continuities in Social Research* (Glencoe: Free Press, 1950), pp. 147–162.

[13] Emile Durkheim, *Suicide* (Glencoe: Free Press, 1951), pp. 152–170.

underlie them. An explanation of psychological principles, in turn, refers back to the underlying physiological processes, and these physiological processes can be further explicated in terms of chemical ones. But systematic theoretical explanations typically confine themselves to concepts on one level of abstraction. Physiological principles do not help to account for group structures and social processes, and nuclear physics does not aid in clarifying learning theory, though there are undoubtedly indirect connections.

Case Study and Comparative Approach. The aim of organizational analysis is to explain the systems of interrelated elements that characterize various kinds of organizations. For this purpose, the interdependence between different attributes of organizations must be established—their size, complexity, specialization, authority structure, professionalization, bureaucratization, and so forth. To clarify this constellation of attibutes requires an understanding of the social processes through which the different attributes develop and the connections between them evolve. Since the structures of social relations among the members of the organization affect the processes of its development, a knowledge of these informal structures contributes to the understanding of the development of the organizational system. Research has shown, for instance, that the informal organization of work groups exerts important influences on performance, the exercise of authority, and the significance of the incentive system for operations, which indicates that the study of the relationships between these and other factors must take the impact of informal structures into account.

A major contribution of case studies on organizations has been that they have called attention to these informal structures and investigated them intensively. This intensive investigation involved the analysis of the social processes through which the informal structures emerged, such as the process of cooptation that modifies the leadership structure,[14] the sanctioning processes in which output becomes regulated,[15] or the process of exchange of advice that gives rise to status differentiation.[16] Comparative studies of organizations, however, need not repeat such intensive analysis of informal processes, since it suffices for them to take account of the results of these processes that find expression in group structures. Indeed, even the role of informal structures will probably have to be inferred rather than directly investigated in most comparative studies of organizations, for systematic organizational analysis—analogous to all systematic analysis—cannot possibly take all factors

[14] Philip Selznick, *TVA and the Grass Roots* (Berkeley: University of California Press, 1949), pp. 85–213.

[15] Roethlisberger and Dickson, *op. cit.*, pp. 379–524.

[16] Peter M. Blau, *The Dynamics of Bureaucracy*, 2d ed. (Chicago: University of Chicago Press, 1963), pp. 121–164 (see Chapter 9).

that indirectly influence organizational life into account but must treat some as given conditions while inquiring into the interrelations,of the basic features of organizations.

Theoretical interpretations of the relationships between antecedent conditions and their consequences remain inevitably somewhat inferential, it would seem, not only because they subsume relations under propositions on a higher level of abstraction that cannot be directly confirmed in research, but also because they typically conceptualize the connecting process as a series of links too complex for direct empirical testing. The proposition that the antecedent A promotes the occurrence B can be empirically confirmed, provided that operational measures for the two factors exist, by showing that B is more prevalent under condition A than under non-A. If the analysis of social processes means the specification of the intervening variables that link A and B in a time sequence, multivariate analysis should make it possible to test whether the process occurs as specified by ascertaining the relationships between A, all intervening variables, and B. Although this is correct in principle, it is usually impossible to implement such a test in actual practice, because so many intervening links tend to be indicated in process analysis that it is virtually impossible to examine the interrelations between all of them simultaneously.[17] Computers facilitate the simultaneous analysis of many variables, but the capacities of the human mind still limit the number of interrelated concepts that can be simultaneously taken into account in a theory.[18] Although theoretical explanations couched in terms of complex social processes cannot be directly tested, precise specification of these processes makes it possible to predict what combinations of organizational features the processes produce under varying conditions, and these predictions serve as indirect tests for the theory.

Organizational Theory

A theory of organizations, whatever its specific nature, and regardless of how subtle the organizational processes it takes into account, has as its central aim

[17] The principle is the same as that of a game in its normal form, as I understand it. Although game theory does not deal with processes or sequential steps but with single choices between strategies, sequential steps can be taken into account in advance by translating all possible sequences into a game in its normal form and then treating it as one choice between all these possibilities. In actual fact, however, the number of alternatives for games with any degree of complexity is virtually infinite, which makes the formalistic solution of translating successive steps into a game in its normal form useless for practical purposes.

[18] It is, of course, much easier to clarify many successive situations, one at a time, than all of them simultaneously. Even a very good chess player can anticipate only a few moves ahead.

to establish the constellations of characteristics that develop in organizations of various kinds. Comparative studies of many organizations are necessary, not alone to test the hypotheses implied by such a theory, but also to provide a basis for initial exploration and refinement of the theory by indicating the conditions on which relationships, originally assumed to hold universally, are contingent. Strict impersonal detachment, for instance, may well promote efficiency only under some conditions and not at all under others.[19] Systematic research on many organizations that provides the data needed to determine the interrelations between several organizational features is, however, extremely rare. The main reason is that the investigation of the internal structure of a complex organization is so costly in time and effort to make the inclusion of many organizations in a single study design impracticable. One way out of this impasse is to study the major attributes of many organizations and sacrifice any detailed information on their internal structures.

The approach to comparative research on organizations proposed, therefore, would be explicitly restricted to those data that can be obtained from the records of organizations and interviews with key informants, without intensive observation or interviewing of most members, which would make it possible to collect the same data on one hundred or more organizations of a given type in one study. In other words, the research design sacrifices depth of information to achieve sufficient breadth to permit a minimum of quantitative comparison. The very limitation imposed by lack of extensive data on internal structures has a latent function, so to speak, inasmuch as it forces the investigator to focus on the neglected area of organizational analysis rather than on the repeatedly studied role relations and group structures within organizations. It is suggested that this approach, though prompted by methodological necessity, has the potential to contribute greatly to organizational theory. To illustrate the theoretical significance of the comparative approach to organizational research, let us examine how it could help refine Weber's theory of bureaucracy.[20]

Weber's Theoretical Concepts. Weber's analysis of bureaucracy is part of his general theory of types of political order and authority, and it is simultaneously a crucial case of the most pervasive theme in all his writings, namely, the increasing rationalization of modern life. The conceptual scheme in terms of which Weber analizes the typical bureaucracy will first be outlined, and operational measures for these concepts will then be suggested.

[19] See Eugene Litwak, "Models of Bureaucracy which Permit Conflict," *American Journal of Sociology* 67 (1962), 177–184.

[20] Weber, *op. cit.*, pp. 324–341, and *Essays in Sociology* (New York: Oxford University Press, 1946), pp. 196–244.

The large *size* of an organization and the great *complexity* of its responsibilities promote bureaucratization, according to Weber. One aspect of bureaucratization is the elaboration of the *administrative* apparatus in the organization. Bureaucracies also are characterized by a high degree of *specialization*, and their members are trained as specialized *experts* in the tasks assigned to them. Furthermore, official positions are organized in a *hierarchy* with clear lines of authority, the scope of which is precisely circumscribed by impersonal rules. Operations generally are governed by a consistent system of *rules* and regulations. *Impersonal* detachment is expected to prevail in the performance of duties and in official relations. Personnel and promotion policies, too, are governed by impersonal criteria, such as merit or seniority, which assures officials stable *careers* with some advancement in the organization. Weber held that this combination of characteristics tends to evolve because it is necessary for and furthers administrative efficiency.

In analyzing the processes that produce this interdependence among characteristics, Weber implicitly presents a functional analysis of bureaucracy, with rational decision-making and administrative efficiency as the criteria of function. . . .[21] In short, the problems created by one organizational feature stimulate processes that give rise to another, and many such interdependent processes produce the constellation of characteristics of the typical bureaucracy as conceptualized by Weber.

Operational Measures. Operational measures for the characteristics of bureaucratic organizations described by Weber can be obtained by the comparative method here advocated, and it would be sheer waste in most cases to employ more intensive methods to obtain these data. This is evidently the case for the *size* of an organization. Whether size is measured by number of employees of a factory, number of voters for a party, number of beds in a hospital, or total assets of a firm, there is clearly no need to interview all members of the organization to ascertain this information. One index of *complexity* is the number of basic objectives or responsibilities of an organization—a university with graduate and professional schools has more complex responsibilities than a college without them—and another index of it is the number of different locations where the organization operates. Still another aspect of complexity is the degree of *specialization* in an organization, which might be measured by the number of different occupational positions, or by the distribution of the members among various occupational specialities, or by the number of functionally specialized departments. The amount of training required for various positions could serve as an indicator of professional *expertness*, as could the proportion of personnel with a given amount of professional education.

[21] For a summary of this analysis, see Chapter 1.

An index of bureaucratization that has been used in previous research is the relative size of the *administrative* component; that is, the proportion of personnel in administrative or staff positions.[22] Three related measures of the *hierarchy* of authority, which refer to the shape of the pyramid, would be the number of levels in the hierarchy, the average span of control, and the proportion of personnel in managerial positions. The extent to which procedures have been made explicit in formal *rules* is indicated by the existence and size of written procedure manuals and by the specificity of the prescriptions contained in them. Two other measures of an emphasis on uniform standards of performance are whether decisions are routinely reviewed for correctness and the amount of statistical information on operations that is kept in the organization as a basis for executive decisions. The use of such statistical records for the evaluation of the performance of subordinates can be considered an indication of *impersonality*, and so can precisely stipulated personnel policies, as exemplified by civil service regulations. The degree of *career* stability, finally, is manifest in membership turnover and average length of service.

This listing makes evident that the empirical data needed for research on the major characteristics of bureaucratic organizations included in Weber's theory are easily enough accessible to make it possible to obtain them for large numbers of organizations in brief visits to each. To be sure, to examine the various facets of each concept, as Weber does, would require more extensive data than those outlined. To cite only one example, an analysis of organizational authority should not be confined to the shape of the hierarchical pyramid but include other aspects of hierarchical control, such as the degree of centralization in the organization. There is no reason to assume, however, that additional measures suitable for comparative studies, which would complement the original ones and thus allow refinement of the analysis, cannot be devised; for instance, information could be obtained about the level in the hierarchy on which various important budgetary and personnel decisions are made to provide measures of centralization. The crucial point is that intensive investigations of internal structures and processes are neither needed nor appropriate for obtaining the data that pertain most directly to theories of organization.

Empirical data of this kind about a fairly large sample of comparable

---

[22] See, for example, Theodore R. Anderson and Seymour Warkov, "Organizational Size and Complexity." *American Sociological Review* 26 (1961), 23–28; Alton W. Baker and Ralph C. Davis, *Ratios of Staff to Line Employees and Stages of Differentiation of Staff Functions* (Columbus: Bureau of Business Research, Ohio State University, 1954); Reinhard Bendix *Work and Authority in Industry* (New York: Wiley, 1956), pp. 221–222; and Seymour Melman, "The Rise of Administrative Overhead in the Manufacturing Industries of the United States, 1899–1947," *Oxford Economic Papers*, Vol. 3, 1951, pp. 64–66, 89–90.

organizations would make it possible to test numerous hypotheses implied by Weber's theory, such as that the processes of specialization, professionalization, and bureaucratization tend to occur together in organizations. Chances are that research findings would reveal that many hypotheses must be revised, thereby directing attention to needed reformulations and specifications in the theory. Thus, impressionistic observation leads one to suspect that increasing specialization is indeed accompanied by increasing professionalization in some types of organizations, such as hospitals, but that a high degree of "specialization"—in the sense of division of labor—reduces the need for an expertly trained working force in other types, such as assembly-line factories. If this impression should be correct, it would raise the question of the conditions that determine whether an extensive division of labor is associated with a highly trained working force.

Refining Theory. Systematic exploration of the empirical relationships between organizational features would provide a basis for refining the theory of bureaucracy by indicating the conditions on which the concurrence of various bureaucratic characteristics is contingent, by helping to answer some questions Weber did not resolve, and by clarifying problems and issues his theory raises. For example, Weber considers both seniority and merit typical impersonal criteria of bureaucratic advancement. An important question that he never answers is what conditions determine whether promotions are largely based on seniority or primarily on merit, a difference that undoubtedly has significant implications for careers and for the organization. Properly designed comparative studies of organizations could help answer this question.

Whereas Weber implies that the large size of an organization as well as its complexity promotes bureaucratization, recent comparative research indicates that size is unrelated or inversely related to bureaucratization as measured by the proportion of the organization's personnel in administrative positions.[23] It appears that complexity is associated with a disproportionately large administrative apparatus, and large size often goes together with a high degree of complexity, but increasing size as such does not lead to a disproportionate expansion of the administrative apparatus. The question these conclusions raise is whether other aspects of bureaucratization, such as extensive written rules, detailed statistical controls, or impersonal personnel procedures, are associated with both size and complexity independently, in accordance with Weber's assumption, or only with one of the two or possibly with neither.

[23] See references cited in preceding footnote. Cf. also Chapters 17 and 18 in this volume.

An important issue that has been raised concerns the relationship between professional competence and bureaucratic authority. Several authors, including notably Parsons, Gouldner, and Stinchcombe,[24] have criticized Weber's contention that professional expertness is a typical characteristic of bureaucracies which goes together with such other bureaucratic characteristics as strict lines of hierarchical authority and disciplined compliance with the commands of superiors. It has been held that professional principles often conflict with the principles that govern hierarchical administration and that the two are not complementary, as Weber assumes, but rather alternative mechanisms of control and coordination. The empirical question is under which conditions professionalization and bureaucratization, especially as revealed in centralized hierarchical control, are associated in organizations and under which conditions they are not. Comparative research might explore, for instance, whether the association between professionalization and bureaucratization depends on the degree of specialization in the organization, because professional standards facilitate coordination among men in similar fields, reducing the need for bureaucratic mechanisms, whereas they make coordination between widely diverse fields more difficult, increasing the need for administrative mechanisms of coordination.

A related issue of even broader theoretical significance is posed by Weber's implicit assumption that strict hierarchical authority and discipline are universally most effective in achieving efficiency in administrative organizations. One might well wonder whether the Prussian army, which sometimes seems to have served Weber inadvertently as the prototype, is really the ideal model for all organizations, whatever the nature of their responsibilities, the composition of their personnel, and the culture in which they operate.[25] In a democratic culture where subordination under authoritative commands tends to be negatively valued, strict hierarchical control and close supervision may well be less effective methods of operation than delegating responsibilities and permitting subordinates some discretion in their exercise. The greater the professionalization of the staff, moreover, the less effective is control through directives from superiors likely to be. The most effective method for organizing an army, finally, is probably not identical with the

[24] Talcott Parsons, "Introduction," to Weber, *The Theory of Social and Economic Organization*, pp. 58–60 (fn.); Gouldner, *Patterns of Industrial Bureaucracy* (Glencoe: Free Press, 1954), pp. 22–24; and Arthur L. Stinchcombe, "Bureaucratic and Craft Administration of Production," *Administrative Science Quarterly* 4 (1959), 168–187.

[25] According to Carl J. Friedrich, Weber's "very words vibrate with something of the Prussian enthusiasm for the military type of organization"; "Some Observations on Weber's Analysis of Bureaucracy," in Merton *et al.*, *Reader in Bureaucracy* (Glencoe: Free Press, 1952), p. 31.

most effective method for organizing a research laboratory. Comparative studies of organizations could throw some light on these broad issues too.

Conclusions

Three foci of analysis have been distinguished in the study of organizational life: (1) role analysis is concerned with individual members of organizations, their attitudes, and their behavior; (2) structural analysis focuses upon groups of interrelated individuals in organizations and the processes of social association that develop in these groups and give them their form; (3) organizational analysis centers attention on systems of interrelated groups explicitly organized to achieve some joint ends and the constellations of attributes that characterize these organizations. The differentiating criterion is whether the unit of analysis whose characteristics are being compared, and of which, therefore, a fairly large number must be examined, is the individual member, the work group, or the entire organization.

In terms of this criterion, a case study of an organization cannot make the organization the unit of systematic analysis but only the structures of subgroups or the roles of individuals. By the same token, the study of the influence of the environment on organizations would have to employ a research design that includes organizations in a variety of different environments, and since hardly any studies do so, the complaint often heard that we know virtually nothing about the impact of the social setting on organizations is quite justified. Whereas more than three foci of analysis are possible —as just noted, the social setting could be the focus—the three outlined are the major ones in the study of organizational life. The most appropriate method for role analysis is the interviewing survey, for structural analysis, intensive observation of all members of selected groups, and for organizational analysis, the comparative study of many organizations.

A theory of organization seeks to explain the systems of relationships between elements in a structure that characterize organizations. Such explanations involve, like all theoretical explanations, subsuming observed relationships between characteristics under more general propositions and specifying the intervening processes responsible for the connections. A major contribution of case studies that investigate the internal structures of organizations is that they provide specific evidence on these underlying processes, which otherwise must be inferred in organizational analysis. But this is only a potential contribution to organizational theory as long as it stands by itself and is not yet a supplement to the data on constellations of organizational features provided by comparative studies of organizations, which must furnish the main foundation of such a theory. Only systematic comparisons of many organizations can establish relationships among characteristics of organizations and stipulate the conditions under which these relationships hold, thereby providing the material that needs to be explained by theoretical principles, and important guides for deriving these principles. Although comparative research on a fairly large number of organizations is necesasrily restricted to data easily accessible without time-consuming intensive investigations, these are the very data most relevant for organizational theory; for example, Weber's theory of bureaucracy.

PART TWO

Informal Processes in Work Groups

Introductory Remarks

Work groups are primary groups, which Cooley defined when he introduced this important concept as groups "characterized by intimate face-to-face association and cooperation," adding that "the unity of the primary group . . . is always a differentiated and usually a competitive unity." To be sure, work groups are not "fundamental in forming the social nature and ideals of individuals."[1] This is undoubtedly the reason Cooley did not mention them when he gave as the three major illustrations of primary groups families, play groups of children, and neighborhoods of elders. But while work groups evidently have less significance for personality development than the family, they probably have today at least as great significance as neighborhoods in adult life. Most adults—increasing proportions of women as well as most men—spend a good part of their waking hours in their work groups. Thus, work groups provide opportunities for studying the processes of social interaction in which human relations and group structures are formed. The intensive investigation of work groups in formal organizations, moreover, furnishes information on the dynamic processes that occur within organizations and help shape their structure.

In short, case studies that analyze closely the informal processes in work groups of organizations can contribute to a better understanding of both the nature of group life in general and the nature of organizations in particu-

[1] Charles H. Cooley, *Social Organization* (Glencoe: Free Press, 1956), p. 23.

lar. The first four papers in Part Two present such case studies, and the last two discuss some theoretical implications for processes of social integration and social exchange, which are assumed to apply to groups of all kinds. The social processes in work groups examined in this part underlie the formal structures of organizations to be examined in Part Three. Since the comparative study of many organizations will not be able to take into account the informal processes in their thousands of work groups, the information about informal processes derived from detailed case studies in Part Two complements and adds meaning to the statistical analysis of the interrelations between organizational characteristics in Part Three.

The comparison of a cooperative and a competitive work group in Chapter 7 illustrates what I mean by a quantitative case study. Statistical data on a dozen members of a large organization are, of course, not of intrinsic interest. But quantitative data reflecting group processes are useful as checks on the impressionistic insights the observer in the field has, and they often provide clues that guide his further observations and their interpretation. When I gained the impression that one group was more competitive than another, I looked for some objective measure to confirm this observation. The analysis of the quantitative data I obtained not only supported this conclusion but also revealed that an individual's competitiveness improved his or her productivity in one group though not in the other. This suggestive finding, obtained while I was still in the field, directed my attention to other relevant observations, such as the competitive practices used and indications of group cohesion, and it became a crucial element in my attempt to tie the various pieces of pertinent information together and interpret them. [2]

The theme of Chapter 8, which is based on the same case study of a public employment office as Chapter 7, is that statistical records of performance in a bureaucracy make differences in performance socially visible and thereby influence the work of officials and their social relations. Statistical data are often used in sociological analysis; here the tables are turned and a sociological analysis of the bureaucratic use of statistical data is carried out. If I were to write this today, I would rely less on a functional framework than I did twenty years ago, though I still think that a functional scheme is least subject to criticism in the study of formal organizations, because their specified goals supply unambiguous criteria of function and dysfunction. Im-

---

[2] The method of analyzing structural effects discussed in Chapter 4 can be applied to Table 7.1, which yields clearer results, though these do not negate the interpretations advanced. They show that conformity with the prevailing practices in the group raise an individual's productivity. Productivity scores were higher for both competitive individuals in the competitive group (.70) and noncompetitive individuals in the noncompetitive group (.74) than for either the competitive individual in the noncompetitive group (.53) or the two noncompetitive individuals in the competitive group (.42).

plicit in the analysis at the end of the chapter is the principle of social exchange, which becomes the explicit focus of attention in subsequent inquiries. The discussion of specialization here and that of the division of labor in several chapters of Part Three indicate the contrasting perspectives of the same subject matter provided by a case study of one organization and by the quantitative comparison of many, respectively. The case study cannot address itself to the question of what other differences accompany differences in the division of labor, but it furnishes information on the informal practices supplementing the formal division of labor, which is not available in comparative research.

Consultation among officials in a federal agency is conceptualized in Chapter 9 as an exchange process, a formulation that has stimulated the development of the theory of social exchange by Homans and by myself.[3] If social interaction is viewed as involving exchange transactions, some principles of economics, properly adapted, can be applied to its investigation, for instance, principles of marginal analysis. Although I did not use the term *marginal utility*, it is implied by my discussion of why popular consultants, though they enjoyed being treated as experts, lost interest in acting as consultants, and why officials who often needed advice tended to obtain it in mutual consultation partnerships from colleagues whose competence was not superior to their own, because the price in respect of expert advice increased if it was requested frequently. This chapter again uses a functional framework more extensively than I would were I to write it today. It should be stressed that the assumptions made about the various beneficial consequences of the consultation pattern are mere hypotheses, the validity of which would have to be established with more rigorous empirical data than those available in this case study.

A problem usually neglected in research on organizations is their relations to the larger community of which they are part. Chapter 10 deals with one aspect of this problem, namely, the relations of officials in a bureaucracy to the public they serve.[4] (Another aspect of this problem, which will be examined in Chapter 16, is how the broader social context affects the characteristics of organizations.) The main questions raised are how the bureaucratic procedures in a public welfare agency and the informal relations among caseworkers influence their orientations to clients. Integrative relations with colleagues modified the effects of experience in the agency on a

[3] George C. Homans, "Social Behavior as Exchange," *American Journal of Sociology* 63 (1958), 597–606; George C. Homans, *Social Behavior: Its Elementary Forms* (New York: Harcourt, 1961; rev. ed., 1974); and Peter M. Blau, *Exchange and Power in Social Life* (New York: Wiley, 1964).

[4] A collection of studies dealing with these relations is Elihu Katz and Brenda Danet (eds.), *Bureaucracy and the Public* (New York: Basic Books, 1973).

caseworker's treatment of clients and concern with their welfare. Integrated workers learned more quickly than unintegrated ones to adapt bureaucratic procedures in order to provide more services to clients, and the great concern newcomers typically exhibited with the troubles of their poor clients subsided substantially after some time in the agency among unintegrated but not among integrated workers. In conclusion, it is shown how processes of selection rather than experience in the agency may account for some of the observed differences.

The next two papers discuss theoretical inferences that can be derived from these case studies of social processes in work groups. Chapter 11 presents a theory of social integration, to which empirical data from the public welfare agency lend some support, and which was subsequently tested in an experiment by Jones.[5] The central thesis is that for an individual to become integrated in a group requires that others find him both attractive and approachable. This poses a dilemma, however, since endeavors to impress others to prove one's attractiveness simultaneously convey the impression of unapproachable superiority. The interdependence between processes of social integration and processes of status differentiation in groups is analyzed in terms of this dilemma. Principles of social exchange, which were adumbrated in Chapter 9, are used to explain these group processes.

The last chapter of Part Two briefly summarizes the theory of social exchange which I have presented in detail elsewhere.[6] In contrast to Homans's formulation of exchange theory,[7] mine uses as a starting point for the basic assumptions processes of social associations, not psychological processes of individual behavior. After examining the basic assumptions made and noting the ubiquity of social exchange, the concept is delineated by distinguishing social from economic exchange as well as from conduct that does not entail exchange. The conditions under which exchange processes give rise to differentiation of power are specified. The analysis concludes by indicating the new exchange processes that emerge in differentiated social structures, which are at the roots of social legitimation and organization, on the one hand, and social opposition and change, on the other. The explanation of complex social structures requires theoretical principles that go beyond those incorporated in the theory of social exchange, as I state in the final paragraph, but whereas I considered social values the central concepts of such structural theories in this paper, I no longer do so, as Chapters 17 and 18 will show. It is for the study of sociopsychological processes in groups that exchange theory is best suited.

[5] Edward E. Jones, *Ingratiation* (New York: Appleton-Century-Crofts, 1964), pp. 120–142.
[6] Blau, *op cit.*
[7] Homans, *op. cit.*

7. Cooperation and Competition in a Bureaucracy

This paper discusses performance and variations in competitiveness among twelve interviewers in two small sections of a public employment agency.[1] The duties of the interviewers in both sections were essentially alike. They received requests for unskilled workers from employers in the garment industry over the phone. The order forms on which job openings were described were filed in a common pool in each section. Most of the official's time was spent interviewing applicants for jobs. After ascertaining the client's qualifications, the interviewer searched the sectional files for suitable vacancies. If an acceptable job was found, he referred the client to it and later phoned the employer to determine whether the client had been hired.

"The statistics which show how many interviews and how many placements each person in the section did are passed around to all interviewers.

Originally published in 1954.

[1] These data are part of a study on interpersonal relations in two government agencies conducted under a fellowship of the Social Science Research Council, which is hereby gratefully acknowledged. There were seven interviewers in Section A and five in Section B. Seven of the twelve were women.

Of course, you look at them and see how you compare with others. This creates a competitive spirit," said one of the interviewers, voicing the sentiments of most of his fellows. In a period of job shortages, competition took the form of trying to utilize job openings before anybody else did. Interviewers were so anxious to make placements that they even resorted to illicit methods. Said one:

> When you take an order, instead of putting it in the box, you leave it on your desk. There was so much hiding of orders under the blotter that we used to ask, "Do you have anything under your rug?" when we looked for an order. You might leave an order you took on the desk, or you might leave it on the desk after you made no referral. . . . Or, you might take an order only partially; you write the firm's name, and a few things; the others you remember. And you leave it on the pad [of order blanks]. You keep on doing this, and all these orders are not in the box.
>
> You can do some wrong filling out. For instance, for a rather low-salary job, you fill out "experience required." Nobody can make a placement on that except you, because you, alone, know that experience isn't required. Or, if there are several openings [on one order], you put the order into "referrals" [file category for *filled* job openings] after you make one placement. You're supposed to put it into "referrals" but stand it up, so that the others can see it. if you don't, you have a better chance of making the next placement than somebody else. And time and again you see four, five openings on one order filled by the same person. [In one case on file eight out of nine openings on one order had been filled by the same interviewer.]

The major opportunity for competitive monopolization of job openings occurred when they were received from employers. Since illicit practices were concealed from the observer, the extent of competition could not be determined through questioning or direct observation,[2] but it was betrayed by the record of official transactions. The extent to which an interviewer filled the vacancies he had received over the phone with his own clients in excess of chance expectations furnishes an index of competitiveness. (Column 4 in Table 7.1 shows this index; Columns 1–3 present the data on which it is based.)

[2] This is clearly indicated by the comment of one of a group of special interviewers, who were expected to use the job openings of the regular interviewers but usually had great difficulty in doing so: "Oh, they hide everything from us. We got more orders when you [the observer] sat in the middle of that section than ever before. We laughed about it. Interviewers would hand us orders asking whether we could use them—when you were looking. That had never happened before."

Table 7.1 Competitiveness and Productivity in Section A and in Section B

	Openings Received[a] (1)	Referrals Made by Recipient (2)	Ratio of Referrals to Openings (3)	Competitiveness[b] (4)	Productivity[c] (5)	Number of Placements (6)
Section A:						
Adams	34	19	0.56	3.9	0.70	100
Ahman	62	27	.44	3.1	.49	70
Ajax	40	28	.70	4.9	.97	139
Akers	71	32	.45	3.2	.71	101
Ambros	69	18	.26	1.8	.45	65
Atzenberg	106	43	.41	2.9	.61	87
Auble	10	3	.30	2.1	.39	56[d]
Section B:						
Babcock	16	7	.44	2.2	.53	46
Beers	58	19	.33	1.6	.71	62
Bing	51	15	.29	1.5	.75	65
Borden	17	7	.41	2.1	.55	48[d]
Bush	43	19	0.42	2.1	0.97	84
Section A	392	170	0.43	3.0	0.59	590
Section B	185	67	0.36	1.8	0.67	289

[a] The great differences between interviewers in this column show that some were much more successful than other in inducing employers, or telephone operators, to channel requests for workers to them personnally. This form of rivalry does not involve competitive interaction.

[b] Competitiveness index (col. 4): The proportion of job openings received to which the recipient made a referral (col. 3) times the number of members of the section. (This represents the observed divided by the expected frequency of referrals made by the recipient of a job opening.) Base period: First half of April, 1949.

[c] Productivity index (col. 5): The number of placements made (col. 6) divided by the number of job openings available, that is, the number of openings in the section per interviewer. Base period: April, 1949.

[d] The number of placements was adjusted for the two interviewers absent for more than five days during April. Since the sectional numbers of placements were not revised, the values in col. 6 add up to more than the two totals shown.

Structural Conditions and Competitiveness

The members of Section A were more competitive than those of Section B. The fourth and fifth columns in Table 7.1 also show that the interviewer's competitiveness was related to his productivity in Section A (Pearsonian $r = +.92$), but this was not the case in Section B ($r = -.20$). In other words, hoarding of jobs was an effective way to improve an interviewer's placement record only in one of these two groups.

The members of Section B were more cooperative: they discouraged competitive practices by making them ineffective. When they learned about interesting vacancies, they often told one another, but an interviewer who manifested competitive tendencies was excluded from the network of reciprocal information and lost the respect of his co-workers. Any advantage of hoarding jobs was, at least, neutralized by such lack of cooperation, as is indicated by the absence of a relation between competitiveness and productivity in this group. Since competitive practices made an interviewer unpopular and failed to raise his productivity, they were infrequent.

These officials themselves attributed the greater competitiveness in Section A to the ambitiousness of several members: "There is usually one individual who starts it, who becomes a pacesetter. Once it has started, it is too late." The others, so interviewers claimed, have to follow suit. However, the most competitive member of Section A, in recounting her reactions when production records were first introduced, made it clear that this explanation of competition on the basis of personality characteristics is inadequate:

> When they introduced statistics, I realized how fast I worked. I even wanted to drop lower. I didn't mind working fast as long as it didn't show, but when it showed up like that on the record, I wanted to work less. But you know what happened? Some of the others started to compete with each other and produced more than I did. Then I thought to myself, "Since I can do it, it's silly to let them get ahead of me." I'm only human. So I worked as fast as before.

When statistical records made the superior performance of this interviewer public knowledge, she decided to work less, possibly in response to pressures the others had brought to bear upon her. While complaining about her unfair standards, however, the other members of the section also improved their own performance. Consequently, this interviewer, just like the others, felt constrained by colleagues to compete for an outstanding record. One or two members of Section B, on the other hand, were also accused of competitive tendencies, but their colleagues successfully discouraged their expression in monopolistic practices. It is in this sense that the competitive practices of one group and the cooperative practices of the other were social factors, calling for explanation in sociological rather than psychological terms, as Durkheim has long since emphasized.[3]

Differential conditions affected the development of these two groups. First, the supervisor in Section A relied heavily on performance records in evaluating interviewers: "And here, in the production figures, is the answer to the question: How good are you? Here you see exactly how good the work you did was." Interviewers often mentioned the pressure this exerted. "[Especially] around rating time, you get this competition. You don't care whether the best person gets the job, but you try to make the placement yourself." In contrast, the new supervisor in Section B surprised his subordinates by rating them more leniently than they had expected, and not primarily on the basis of production records. Consequently, as one interviewer reported, "we became less anxious about statistics; another experience like that, and we might forget all about placement credit."

Second, a common professional orientation existed only in Section B. While the members of Section A had been assigned, and had received their training, at different times, the majority of those in Section B received their training together after World War II, at a time when intensive counseling had been stressed, since many returning veterans needed occupational advice. One official said of this period:

> When I first came here, in May, 1946, we had a very nice bunch. It was like an all-day consultation; we discussed placements with each other all day long. At that time, the veterans came back, and there was a lot of emphasis on counseling. Nobody asked you how many placements you made, then. The emphasis was on quality, and we consulted with each other all day.

In this situation, the group developed a common professional code, which discouraged speedy placement as constituting defective employment service. In effect, this orientation transformed competitive practices from illegitimate means for desirable ends into illegitimate means for worthless ends. If such practices did occur, they were vigorously opposed on moral grounds as violating the interest of clients. Nevertheless, as will be shown presently, competition could not have been effectively curbed if the supervisor's evaluation practice had engendered acute anxiety over productivity. However, the existence of this code would have made it difficult for the supervisor to judge performance mainly by productivity, since doing so would have stamped him as ignorant of the essentials of good employment service.

[3] Emile Durkheim, *The Rules of Sociological Method* (Chicago: University of Chicago Press, 1938), pp. 110 and *passim*.

No opportunity for the development of a *common* professional code had existed in Section A. Since competitiveness prevailed in this group, the individual whose personal professional standards made him reluctant to compete either became the deviant whose productivity suffered or modified his standards and entered the race with the others.

Third, most members of Section A had been appointed to temporary civil service positions during World War II. They were on probation pending permanent appointments when production records were originally introduced and even afterward remained subject to layoffs due to reductions in staff. Their insecurity led them to strive to impress superiors with outstanding performance. In contrast, all but one of the members of Section B were veterans, whose employment could not be terminated except for cause. As one envious colleague put it, "They felt that nothing could happen to them because they were veterans and had superseniority."

Differences in these three conditions—security of employment, opportunity for the development of a common professional orientation, and the evaluation practice of the supervisor—gave rise to two dissimilar social structures. Productivity was highly valued in Section A and became associated with the individual's standing in the group, while striving for sheer productivity was disparaged in Section B. Thus, whereas the most productive and most competitive member of Section A was considered the best interviewer by her co-workers and was most popular with them,[4] the most productive member of Section B was the least respected and least popular. As a result of these structural differences, cooperative norms prevailed only in Section B.

The interviewers in *both* sections disliked working in a competitive atmosphere. A member of Section A said: "If I see that an interviewer keeps orders on her desk, I take them and put them in the box. . . . Of course, you don't make friends that way." Since the majority in this section, including its most popular members, were highly competitive, to antagonize them was to threaten one's own standing in the group. This deterred interviewers from discouraging competitive practices. Antagonizing a deviant, however, does not endanger one's status. Since a striver was unpopular in Section B, its members could use sanctions freely to combat competitive pactices and enforce cooperative norms.

Social Cohesion and Productivity

Table 7.1 shows that the group most concerned with productivity was less productive than the other group. Fifty-nine per cent of the job openings re-

---

[4] She was most often mentioned by members of her own section in answer to the questions, respectively, "Who are the best interviewers?" and "Who are your friends in the office?"

ceived in Section A were filled, in contrast to 67 per cent in Section B. (The 8 per cent difference is significant on the .01 level.) Another implicit paradox is that competitiveness and productivity were directly related for individuals in Section A but inversely related for the two groups.[5]

Anxious concern with productivity induced interviewers in Section A to concentrate blindly on it at the expense of other considerations. In their eagerness to make many placements they often ignored their relationships with others as well as official rules. Competitiveness in this group weakened social cohesion, while cooperativeness in Section B strengthened it. This difference is indicated by the fact that usually none of the members of Section A spent their rest periods together, whereas all but one (a newcomer) of those of Section B did. Social cohesion enhanced operating efficiency by facilitating cooperation and by reducing status anxiety.

Although the members of both groups had occasion to assist one another, greater effort was required to elicit such cooperation in Section A. The social interaction that occurred in the office during the twenty-four busiest hours of one week was recorded and classified as official and private contacts, that is, those directly concerned with a specific job or client, and all others. The frequency of an interviewer's official contacts with colleagues was related to his productivity in Section A (rank correlation $= +.98$), but not in Section B (rank correlation $= +.08$). This suggests that only interviewers who kept, as one put it, "hopping around all the time" to retrieve job orders that others kept on their desks were able to make many placements in the competitive section. But in the cohesive group, the cooperation needed for making placements occurred as a matter of course, and not only in response to special requests. This effort was not required for high productivity.

To maximize his placements, the interviewer in Section A hoarded jobs and simultaneously tried to prevent others from doing so, thereby antagonizing his co-workers, whose cooperation he needed if he was to do well. The members of this section therefore attempted to conciliate colleagues whom their competitive practices had alienated. Often, shortly after having interfered with her operations, an interviewer paid another a compliment about her work or her apparel. The most competitive interviewer was in the habit of taking time out to joke with her co-workers and was proud of making more placements than anybody else, "nevertheless." Actually, this compensating friendliness, which made her popular despite her competitiveness, helped her to be productive.

[5] For another example of such disparity between individual and corresponding group data, see the discussion of promotion opportunities and attitudes toward promotion in Samuel A. Stouffer *et al.*, *The American Soldier*, Vol. 1, (Princeton: Princeton University Press, 1949), 250–254. Kendall and Lazarsfeld discuss the methodological significance of such findings in Robert K. Merton and Paul F. Lazarsfeld (eds.), *Continuities in Social Research* (Glencoe: Free Press, 1950), pp. 193–195.

In Section A, interviewers had to make special efforts at conciliation in order to make placements, but this was not necessary in Section B. At least, this impression is corroborated by the finding that frequency of private contacts with others was also related to productivity in Section A (rank correlation = +.84), but not in Section B (rank correlation = +.13). The members of the cohesive group, whose operating practices did not put colleagues at a disadvantage, did not have to devote time and energy to solicit and encourage cooperation, since it was not extended reluctantly. Their spontaneous cooperation improved operating efficiency.

Social cohesion also lessened the status anxiety generated by the evaluation system. Such anxiety is most acute in the individual who does not feel integrated in his work group and therefore seeks to derive social recognition from excelling at his task and from approval of superiors. Friendly relations with co-workers made the standing of the individual in the cohesive group independent of his productivity, particularly since fast work was disparaged as a sign of superficial service. The consequent reduction of anxiety in the antiproductivity-oriented group actually raised its productivity.

Fluctuations in productivity illustrate the dysfunction of status anxiety. Section B had not always operated more efficiently than Section A. Its productivity had been lower during the two months preceding the last rating but had abruptly increased then, while that of Section A had declined, as Table 7.2 shows.

Table 7.2   Productivity Before and After Rating

	Section A	Section B
December, 1948	0.64 (619)[a]	0.56 (317)
January, 1949	.70 (941)	.56 (472)
February, 1949 (rating)	.56 (1,342)	.60 (477)
March, 1949	.59 (1,335)	.71 (448)
April 1949	0.59 (1,001)	0.67 (433)

[a] Numbers in parentheses are the numbers of job openings available on which the productivity index—the proportion of these openings that were filled—is based.

The two groups found themselves in different situations before and after they were rated. The members of Section A were familiar with the rating standards of their supervisor, for she had rated them in previous years. Their anxiety led them to work especially hard immediately before the annual rating. The members of Section B, on the other hand, had never before been rated by their new supervisor. They were also concerned about their record but could not calm their anxiety by concentrating on certain tasks, because they did not know what the supervisor would stress; the explanation he gave to his subordinates was too vague and adhered too strictly to official procedures to help them foresee his actual practices. This unfocused anxiety was particularly detrimental to efficient performance. Later, when the interviewers found out that they were not rated primarily on the basis of statistical records, their anxiety largely subsided and their productivity increased. In contrast, the experience of the members of Section A, whose ratings were strongly influenced by their production records, intensified their status anxiety, but when the rating was over this anxiety was no longer channeled into exceptionally hard work, with the result that their productivity declined below that of Section B.

Social cohesion is no guaranty against anxiety in a bureaucracy. Civil service status is too important to officials for them to remain immune to the threat of losing it. But when no such threat is felt, social cohesion reduces anxiety by divesting productivity of its significance as a symbol of status in the work group. Diminished anxiety as well as smoother cooperation then enable those in the cohesive group to perform their tasks more efficiently than the others.

In the absence of social cohesion, competitive striving for an outstanding performance record became a substitute means for relieving status anxiety in Section A. This psychological function of competition is illustrated by the following incident. The interviewers in this section became very irritable, and one of them even became physically ill when a temporary supervisor, who tried to prevent competitive practices, interfered with their method of allaying anxiety.

Status anxiety reduced operating efficiency. Even in the cohesive group, productivity was low when the unknown rating standards of a new supervisor produced acute and diffuse anxiety. Otherwise, however, the cohesive group was more productive, because social cohesion relieved status anxiety by making the individual's standing in the group independent of his productivity. The very competitive striving that undermined the group's cohesiveness also served to lessen the individual's status anxiety in a noncohesive situation. The hypothesis that the cohesiveness of the group and the competitiveness of the individual in the less cohesive group both reduce status anxiety helps to explain the paradox that the *less competitive group* and the *more competitive individuals* in the competitive group were particularly productive.

8.   *Statistical Records of Performance*

At the beginning of this century Max Weber wrote: "The management of the modern office is based upon written documents ('the files'), which are preserved in their original or draught form. There is, therefore, a staff of subaltern officials and scribes of all sorts."[1] For the two agencies observed, this must be supplemented to read that many of these scribes have become statistical clerks, who classify and codify, index and tabulate, these documents before they are relegated to the files.

The preparation of periodic statistical reports constitutes a method for evaluating operations well suited to the administration of large organizations.[2] Dehumanized lists of cold figures correspond to the abstract, impersonal criteria that govern bureaucratic activities. Statistical records provide precise and comparable information on operations quickly and in a concise form that is easily communicated. In these respects, they are superior to descriptive reports. Information on the operations of the entire agency can be simply obtained by adding the statistical data collected by various de-

Originally published in 1955.

[1] Max Weber, *Essays in Sociology* (New York: Oxford University Press, 1946), p. 197.

[2] The significance of statistical records for the administration of large organizations is discussed by Marshall E. Dimock, *The Executive in Action* (New York: Harper, 1945), pp. 128, 143–147. Otherwise, it has received surprisingly little attention in the literature.

partments, whereas the combination of descriptive reports is more cumbersome and less accurate. Quantitative indices uniformly abstract predetermined information and thus facilitate the objective comparison of operations in different departments by eliminating the different biases that necessarily are reflected in descriptive reports written by various officials. Statistical records are also more economical, since they can be prepared by clerks. Finally, these records provide an objective basis for the periodic rating of the performance of officials.

The statistical method is by no means confined to the measurement of production quantity. On the contrary, it was also used in the public employment agency to ascertain facts about performance quality not readily accessible by any other method. To mention only one example at this point: Whether interviewers decided correctly when to send notifications to the unemployment insurance agency could not be checked directly. There were no records of interviews on the basis of which their decisions could have been reviewed, and supervisors could not listen to all interviews. However, the statistical report that showed the relative frequency with which notifications were sent by different interviewers indicated those whose performance probably needed to be corrected.

Statistical techniques are often used in sociological analysis. In this chapter the tables are turned and a sociological analysis of the use of statistical techniques is presented. After examining how the keeping of performance records influenced operations in Department X (which included the two sections examined in the preceding chapter plus a third), a social innovation that developed in response to difficulties produced by these records will be discussed.

Statistical Records: A Mechanism of Control

Quantitative records were used widely in the employment agency. They provided accurate information on various phases of operations, such as the number of requests for workers received from different branches of the industry and the number of placements made. This information enabled higher officials to take the actions they considered necessary to improve operations. Statistical reports were intended to facilitate the exercise of administrative control. However, the collection of data for these reports had consequences that transformed them from an indirect means for controlling operations into a direct mechanism of control.

Social scientists are only too familiar with the fact that the process of collecting information on people's activities influences these activities. The presence of an observer in a work group affects the behavior he wants to study, and the repeated interviews in a panel study of political attitudes increase the political interest of respondents. The distorting influence of the measuring instrument is a serious problem in social research. In this bureaucracy the collection of data on operations, such as the number of interviews each official held, also influenced the interviewer's conduct. The knowledge that his superior would learn how many clients he had interviewed and would evaluate him accordingly induced him to work faster. Far from being a disadvantage, this direct effect constituted the major function of performance records for bureaucratic operations. The supervisor wanted to know the number of interviews completed by each subordinate only in order to take corrective action in case any of them worked too slowly. The fact that the very counting of interviews had induced them to work faster facilitated operations by making such corrective steps superfluous. The use of statistical records not only provided superiors with information that enabled them to rectify poor performance but often obviated the need for doing so.

Until the beginning of 1948 the number of interviews held per month was the only operation that was statistically counted for each interviewer in Department X. (Although detailed statistical reports were kept in the agency, they were presented only for departments as a whole, not for individuals.) As long as jobs were plentiful during the war, this rudimentary record seemed to suffice. However, when jobs became scarce after the war and time and effort were required to find one for a client, this count of interviews had a detrimental effect on operations. One interviewer, perhaps slightly exaggerating, described the behavior of her colleagues at that time in the following terms: "You know what happened then? They used to throw them [clients] out. The same interviewers who engage in all the bad practices now in order to make placements never made a referral then; maybe, when the supervisor was looking. Otherwise, they tried to get rid of them as fast as possible."

Except for the information obtained by direct observation, the number of interviews completed by a subordinate was the only evidence the supervisor had at that time for evaluating him. The interviewer's interest in a good

Table 8.1   Placement Results Prior To and After the Introduction of Detailed Performance Records in Department X

	Job Openings (#)	Place-ments (#)	Jobs Filled (%)
2 months without records (January and February, 1948)	3,944	2,159	55
2 months with records (March and April, 1948)	3,425	2,286	67

rating demanded that he maximize the number of interviews and therefore prohibited spending much time on locating jobs for clients. This rudimentary statistical record interfered with the agency's objective of finding jobs for clients in a period of job scarcity. There existed an organizational need for a different evaluation system.

In March, 1948, two months after Department Head Xavier was put in charge, she instituted new performance records.[3] These were issued monthly and made available to all interviewers. They contained the following eight indices for every interviewer and for each of the three sections in Department X:

1. The number of interviews held
2. The number of clients referred to a job
3. The number of placements (referred client was hired) made
4. The proportion of interviews resulting in referrals
5. The proportion of referrals resulting in placements
6. The proportion of interviews resulting in placements
7. The number of notifications sent to the insurance office
8. The number of application forms made out (for clients with special qualifications)

The introduction of these records improved placement operations considerably. Table 8.1 presents the results of operations during the two months immediately preceding the introduction of performance records and during the first two months they were kept.[4] The number of job openings available depended on labor-market conditions in this seasonal industry and was largely beyond the control of the department. The proportion of job openings filled by placements therefore provides a better index of the effectiveness of operations than does the number of placements. The third column shows that two-thirds of all openings were filled when detailed performance records were kept, whereas only a little more than half of them

---

[3] Alvin W. Gouldner, *Patterns of Industrial Bureacracy* (Glencoe: Free Press, 1954), shows that changes in administrative personnel lead to the introduction of bureaucratic procedures. This explains why extensive performance records were established after a change in departmental administration had occurred, but the existing need for a new evaluation system explains why the new department head introduced this particular innovation.

[4] The comparison of activities before and after they were measured is usually impossible, since no measures for the control period exist. It was very fortunate that the agency-wide records, which had been prepared for many years, provided indices on the operations of this department (but not on those of its individual members). These indices could be used to compare the two periods and thus to estimate the effect of·the introduction of departmental performance records. (Data for both periods are taken from the agency-wide records.)

had been filled before these records were introduced.[5] Apparently, the performance records contributed to the effectiveness of operations.[6]

Statistical reports influenced operations by inducing interviewers to concentrate their efforts on the factors that were measured and would thus affect their rating. The first index, the number of clients interviewed, impelled them to work faster. One interviewer indicated this by saying: "It might influence me, if I saw that I had so many interviews, and somebody else had many more, to try to equalize it." The next two indices, the number of referrals and placements, curbed the tendency to attain speed by neglecting the very objective of employment interviewing, namely, finding jobs for clients. In the words of another interviewer: "There is no tendency to get rid of an applicant, as there was before. Maybe you didn't like an applicant, subconsciously; so you tried to get rid of him without getting him a job. Now, this doesn't happen; since they're measured by placements, everybody tries to find a job for every applicant. It eliminates the subjective element."

The next three indices (the proportion of interviewed clients who were referred, the proportion of referred clients who were placed, and the proportion of interviewed clients who were placed) did not provide any additional information. Interviewers could have derived these percentages easily from the raw figures. Nevertheless, their inclusion in the official record was by no means irrelevant for operations. An interviewer who had been transferred to another department mentioned to the observer that performance records there did not include these proportional indices, "but they have the figures, so you could get the percentages." When the observer remarked that this seemed to be only a technical difference, he said: "Yes, but it really is a different approach. Miss [Xavier] thought very highly of the percentage of placements to people interviewed, or to people referred. Here they think more of the number of placements, rather than the percentage of placements. This is different."

This interviewer was quite correct. In the other department inducements were provided to make as many placements as possible by any legitimate means. The addition of percentage figures in the record of Department X constrained interviewers also to watch *how* they achieved this objective, as the following explanation by one of them shows:

> For instance, I noticed once that my percentage of placements [based on number of referrals] was low. While the *number* of placements was highest on the list, my *percentage* was not so high. So I decided to be more careful and selective in my referrals. The next month, my percentage went way up, to 90 per cent, but the number

[5] This 12 per cent difference is significant on the .01 level.

[6] Other factors might have influenced this difference, such as other actions of the new department head. However, it should be remembered that she was in charge of operations during both time periods.

was smaller than before. This happened only because I had looked
at figures.

These indices prescribed the methods through which results had to be
achieved and therefore provided checks against malpractices. An interviewer
in Department X not only had to place many clients but also had to exercise
care in selecting a qualified client for each job; otherwise the proportion of
his referrals that resulted in placements would have been low. This curbed
the tendency of sending clients quickly and indiscriminately to jobs in the
hope that a large number, though a small proportion, would be hired, which
would have constituted inefficient service to both employees and employers.
Besides, an interviewer had to make an effort to locate jobs for as many
applicants as possible; otherwise the proportion of his interviews that resulted in referrals would have been low. This discouraged attempts to increase
the proportion of placements by such meticulous selection that only the perfectly qualified client is referred, which would have unduly restricted service
to clients.

Interviewers often protested that the "statistics" measured only "quantity" and not "quality." This accusation was not justified. The performance
records measured not only the amount of work done (since the number of
interviews was counted) but also whether certain objectives were accomplished (since the number of placements was counted) and whether this
was done by prescribed methods (since the proportional indices were included). They induced officials to maintain certain qualitative as well as
quantitative standards in their performance.

To be sure, these records did not indicate all aspects of performance.
Indeed, the decision to exclude a factor also influenced operating practices.
Since the number of counseling interviews held per month was not included
in the departmental report, interviewers rarely asked permission to give one.
These time-consuming interviews would only have interfered with making a
good showing on the record. This corresponded to the departmental policy
of restricting counseling service and facilitated operations by reducing the
number of occasions on which supervisors had to refuse permission for
these interviews.[7]

---

[7] This discussion is not intended to imply that the departmental records took into account
all relevant aspects of operations. They may be criticized, for instance, for disregarding
the quality of placements made; workers can be sent to and hired for jobs that are more
or less suitable for them. It should be noted that the neglect of this factor was due not to
the technical limitations of quantification (without denying that such limitations exist)
but to a policy decision. It would be simple, and not very expensive, to measure some aspect of placement quality, for example, by ascertaining over the telephone whether clients
still hold their jobs after three months and whether they have received any wage raise.
The reason that this was not done was an explicit or implicit administrative decision that
the cost of obtaining this information outweighed the contribution it would make to
operations.

Since the omission of indices influenced operations, performance records tended to contain all elements that superiors considered important. When the number of interviews alone had been counted, interviewers had been little concerned with placement. If only the six factors pertaining to the placement process had been considered, interviewers would probably have neglected other operations. By making a part of their record the number of applications taken and the number of notifications sent, the department head tried to guard against neglect of these two time-consuming operations. As a result of the need for taking many subtle phases of operations into account, performance records tend to grow in complexity. A single-index record had been replaced by an eight-index record in this department. In the federal agency that will be discussed in the next chapter, where operations were more complex, the statistical report contained sixty categories!

As effective control mechanism, performance records served several functions for operations. First, it has already been noted that they increased productivity. Second, they facilitated hierarchical control over operating officials. Procedures governing operations were often modified when interpreted by lower hierarchical levels. If the department head had relied on rules that showed how qualified clients must be selected for referral, for example, these might have been modified by supervisors, and again by interviewers. The use of the proportion of referred clients who were hired as one element in the evaluation of subordinates enforced careful selection more effectively than rules could, because it identified the interest of interviewers with being selective in their referrals. This strengthening of uniform administrative control is especially important in a large organization, in which policy-makers are many hierarchical levels, and often hundreds of miles, removed from the operating officials whose work they are expected to control.

Third, these records enabled superiors to institute changes in operations quickly and effectively. New procedures are not always opposed, but sometimes they are, and usually a period of adaptation is required before they become fully effective. By altering the performance record or the relative emphasis on various factors, higher officials can induce lower echelons to change their practices immediately. The introduction of extensive statistical records in Department X illustrates this, and so does an incident that occurred in the federal agency. Its director once found himself far short the number of cases the agency was expected to investigate annually. Thereupon, he announced that any official who would complete a certain number of cases during the next three months would receive an outstanding rating. This one element of the performance record, number of cases completed, was given absolute weight for a limited time. As a result, many officials worked much faster than they usually did, and the quota was met.

Fourth, use of performance records improved the relations between supervisors and interviewers. The supervisor's responsibility for operations required him to criticize subordinates whose performance was inadequate, as a means of improving it. This task was greatly disliked, since such criticism was often resented, and resentful subordinates were less cooperative. Performance records either relieved the supervisors of this duty or reduced the resentment it created. Sometimes they were substituted for verbal criticism, as a supervisor indicated when he was asked whether he discusses performance figures with his subordinates: "Yes I do. I always send them around. I used to discuss them more before we had these records. Now, I just let them speak for themselves. That's all I want." Even if a supervisor actually talked to an interviewer about the ways of improving his performance, the existence of statistical data transformed the nature of these discussions. Instead of telling the interviewer that *he* considered his performance inadequate, the supervisor tried to help him improve his record. Finally, the onus for giving a low rating was partly removed from the supervisor because he could transfer responsibility to the record of the official. Since these records reduced the chances for the development of conflict and antagonism, they made possible a more cordial and cooperative relationship between subordinates and their supervisor.

Dysfunctional Consequences

Statistical records facilitated the job of the supervisor by providing him with information that he would have otherwise had to ascertain laboriously, and by improving his relationships with subordinates. It might be expected, therefore, that superiors favored the exclusive use of quantitative indices for evaluating subordinates, a method of evaluation that would eliminate personal considerations in accordance with bureaucratic principles. This, however, was not the case. Superordinates on all levels explained that it would be impossible to judge all aspects of performance on the basis of these indices alone. "You can't reduce a man to a statistic." The validity of this opinion can hardly be questioned. Nevertheless, it is possible to examine how the structural position of superordinate officials constrained them to hold this opinion so firmly.

The evaluation of subordinates is a major responsibility of supervisors. If the evaluation were based entirely on statistical indices, this responsibility would be reduced to a clerical task, the application of a mathematical formula to a set of data. This would not only make the job of the supervisor less interesting for him but also undermine his authority over subordinates. The fact that the civil service rating of officials depends on the judgment of their supervisor, which means that it is not directly determined by quantitative indices, is an important source of supervisory authority. In opposing the more extensive use of these indices for evaluation, supervisors were opposing threats to their authority. Actually, the rating procedure of the employment agency stipulated that three of the five elements in the rating must *not* be based on statistical records. This preserved the authority of supervisors and thus their ability to discharge their duty of directing the work of interviewers.

Reliance on quantitative indices alone in evaluating subordinates would have been dysfunctional for operations by undermining the supervisor's authority. Completely ignoring these records, once they existed, was also dysfunctional, since it alienated subordinates, as the following report illustrates:

> My supervisor gave me a low rating [before performance records
> had been introduced] because my production wasn't high enough.
> I told him that he had no way of estimating my production, since
> he didn't keep any records. Then they introduced statistics. I was
> high on those statistics. I thought, "Maybe this is a good thing."
> But my rating was low again. So I saw that this type of supervisor
> will use the statistics his own way, to prove that he's right in the
> first place.

The performance indices of this interviewer, which had been outstandingly high, as he said, dropped abruptly after the second rating, and remained low. Although a different supervisor, whom he liked, had been in charge of this section for a year, this interviewer continued to make a poor showing on the records. This experience had apparently made him permanently uninterested in improving his performance as measured by these records, which he frequently criticized. The preparation of performance records set up expectations; by disregarding them, the previous supervisor had not only antagonized an interviewer but also destroyed their effectiveness as incentives.

Experiences of this kind inspired the recurring comment, "Figures can't lie, but liars can figure." Statistical indices constitute a neutral instrument; their effectiveness depends on the way they are used, or misused. Since statistical records influence operations directly, methodological errors do not merely lead to mistaken conclusions but disrupt operations in bureaucracies. The use of an inadequate sample in the federal agency illustrates this. The departmental supervisor there was responsible for having his subordinates complete one hundred cases a month. Although some cases required only a few hours work, while others took many weeks, these differences were probably canceled in a sample of a hundred cases. The supervisor discharged this responsibility by requiring that each agent complete eight cases a month, much too small a number to expect such cancellation of differences. As a result, officials postponed finishing a lengthy case in order to meet the quota by working on short ones or failed to complete cases, saving them for the next month, if they had already met the quota. The decisions concerning the work schedule, in principle based on the relative urgency of the various cases, were distorted by the "methodological" error of using too small a sample.

Another dysfunction results from the fact that indices are not perfectly related to the phenomena they purport to measure. Since interviewers were interested in maximizing their "figures," they tried to do so by various means. Occasionally, a client who had been temporarily laid off expected to return to his former job within the next few days. After confirming this with the employer, the interviewer made out a job order and referred the client to this job. In this way he improved his number of referrals and of placements (and the corresponding proportional indices) without having accomplished the objective that these indices were designed to measure, that is, finding a job for a client. Sometimes an interviewer even went a step further; if a client said he expected to return to his former job in four weeks, the interviewer asked him to return to the office then and "referred" him to his own job, wasting the client's time and his own.

These tendencies constitute a form of *"displacement of goals* whereby 'an instrumental value becomes a terminal value.' "[8] An instrument intended to further the achievement of organizational objectives, statistical records constrained interviewers to think of maximizing the indices as their major goal, sometimes at the expense of these very objectives. Interviewers avoided operations that would take up time without helping them to improve their record, such as interviewing clients for whom application forms had to be made out,[9] and wasted their own and the public's time on activities intended only to raise the figures on their record. Their concentration on this goal, since it was important for their ratings, made them unresponsive to requests from clients that would interfere with its attainment.[10] Preoccupation with

[8] Robert K. Merton, *Social Theory and Social Structure*, 3rd ed. (New York: Free Press, 1968), p. 253 (italics in original).

[9] Supplementary indices are designed to curb such tendencies; since the number of application forms made out was also counted, interviewers would be expected not to avoid this task. But if there are too many indices, most will be disregarded, and a few considered as important. Thus interviewers disliked taking applications, since they did not think performance on this index would outweigh the loss of time involved. Of the sixty indices in the federal agency, less than half a dozen were considered "really" significant by officials.

[10] Merton shows how red tape, an official's refusal to make clearly warranted exceptions to rules, results from displacement of goals upon regulations (*op. cit.*, pp. 253–256). Such apparent overconformity with rules might often be the result of performance records, which constrain officials to maximize certain factors in the interest of their careers.

productivity also affected the interpersonal relations among interviewers, and this constituted the most serious dysfunction of statistical reports.

Interviewers had reacted to the introduction of performance records with hostility and continued to dislike them vehemently. Their negative attitudes were similar to those of manual workers toward production quotas, intensified by the fact that "working on production like in a factory" had negative status implications for these white-collar workers. Since those with outstanding records shared this aversion, it cannot be explained as merely an expression of resentment for being put in an unfavorable light. The main reason for their antagonism against quantitative criteria of performance was often voiced by interviewers in forceful language:

> The worst thing about these records is that they create competition between interviewers to an extent that is—disgusting. . . . They lead to competition and to outright falsification. I don't say that all do that, but it happens. . . . You can't expect anything else. If you make production so important, some people will feel that they have to increase their figures by any means. The only way you can stop it is by discontinuing the production records.
>
> And I didn't have to compete with my fellow-workers [in my former job], hustling for jobs all the time. I enjoyed my work much more before they introduced statistics. I don't like to have my work counted, like in a factory. It makes for poor morale, and for poor selection, I'm afraid. They aren't as careful on account of statistics. I'll bet all of them told you they don't like statistics.

The significance of competitive interaction within Sections A and B has been analyzed in Chapter 7. Now a dysfunction of performance records for the interaction between sections and for the operation of Section C will be examined.

Specialization

All handicapped clients who came to this public employment office were referred to Section C of Department X, where special efforts were made to find suitable jobs for them. The special interviewers there had received training for dealing with handicapped workers and locating employment for them. Different procedures governed their operations, allowing more time for interviewing and providing more opportunity to discuss problems with the supervisor, who was responsible for only three subordinates.

The specialized section enabled the agency to provide this extra service at less cost and with least interference with other operations. Only a small proportion of interviewers had to be given additional training and expert supervision. Exceptional cases did not interfere with uniform operations or with the use of evaluation standards but became typical cases in this small section. Interviewers in other sections, oriented toward speedy referral of their clients, disliked special cases and might therefore have treated handicapped clients inconsiderately; they would have had to, since performance records identified their career interest with working rapidly. The performance records identified their career interest with working rapidly. The performance of special interviewers was evaluated by different criteria, and frequency of placements carried less weight. This allowed special interviewers to become interested in the problems presented by their handicapped cases. Interviewers in other sections were glad to be able to rid themselves of handicapped clients by transferring them to Section C. The three special interviewers, on the other hand, all of whom had volunteered for this assignment,[11] preferred working with these clients. The statement of one of them is typical: "I like it much better. This is a challenge. If you see one interesting case during the day, you feel your job is worthwhile; you feel satisfied. Over there, you can go for weeks without coming across one [pause] outstandingly interesting case. Of course, all people are interesting as individuals."

All sections of this division provided specialized service, but their specialization was based on occupational categories. Each section dealt with clients in certain occupations and handled the corresponding job openings. The specialization of the handicapped section cut across these categories. Special interviewers dealt with handicapped clients in all occupations in the clothing industry. They therefore had the right to obtain job openings from the files of any section. Interviewers and supervisors in charge of those files were obligated to allow special interviewers to select any job for their clients and to cooperate with them for this purpose.

Evaluation on the basis of performance records inhibited such cooperation. Interviewers anxious to make many placements needed all the job openings they had and therefore hindered rather than helped special interviewers who tried to find jobs for their handicapped clients. One of the special interviewers expressed this difficulty vividly: "Oh, they hide everything from us. . . . It's a matter of self-protection for them. They started the production records a year ago, and it made it very difficult for us."

However, patterns of reciprocity developed between interviewers, and these reduced the tendency to hide job orders from specialists. The members of Section C accepted for service also the most disturbing clients, those who got very excited or made scenes in the office. The possibility of transferring

---

[11] All three special interviewers had, or had had, minor physical handicaps.

these clients to the special section greatly relieved other interviewers, who often made such remarks as: "If they are too difficult, they go to [Section C]; they have the really difficult applicants." In exchange for this service, interviewers in other sections became less reluctant to cooperate with special interviewers who looked for jobs, as one of these specialists indicated when asked how he locates jobs for his clients: "This is an area of difficulty. However, most of the time the interviewers are very glad to let us place somebody on their orders. . . . Like they say, one hand washes the other; when they have a difficult client and want to send him over, we never make an issue of it but are glad to take him."

Superior officials justified the practice of transferring uncooperative as well as handicapped clients to Section C by explaining that this section is responsible for both physically and mentally handicapped applicants. Excitable clients were defined as emotionally disturbed and therefore transferred. This rationale for the modification of a procedure does not explain its functional significance. Indeed, this practice cannot be accounted for in terms of Section C's external function of providing more extensive help for clients whose occupational handicaps entitled them to it. Clearly, the most uncooperative clients were not entitled to such special consideration. However, this practice contributed to Section C's internal function of relieving other interviewers of tasks that interfered with regular operations. Excited clients who had to be calmed disrupted operations even more than handicapped clients whose interviews were more complicated. Only by handling both groups did Section C relieve the other sections of most exceptional cases, thus contributing to the uniformity of operations and enabling other interviewers to concentrate on speedy placement of clients.

Perhaps an even more important function of this unofficial practice was the restoration of effective service to handicapped applicants, which had been impeded by competitive tendencies. The transfer of uncooperative clients to Section C was tolerated by superiors, but it was not made official. The members of this section therefore exercised some discretion over the acceptance of such clients. Since serving uncooperative clients was not their official duty, they put other interviewers under obligation by doing so. To be able to transfer their difficult clients to Section C, interviewers in other sections had to cooperate with special interviewers who looked for job orders. By assuming this additional responsibility, Section C could discharge all its responsibilities more effectively, despite the obstacles that the existence of performance records had created.

9. *Consultation among Colleagues*

The next case to be examined is a department in a federal agency, one of nine district agencies of a bureau with headquarters in Washington. The district commission was responsible "for enforcement practices designed to bring about uniform application of the provisions [of two federal laws]"[1] in two eastern states. This required the inspection of business establishments to institute faithful adherence to these relatively new laws. If violations were found, which was the case in about half the inspected firms, future compliance was ordered. Serious violations, especially if repeated, resulted in legal action.

Department Y, the unit under intensive study, had eighteen members. The department supervisor was in charge of sixteen agents and one clerk. The principal duties of agents were carried out in the field. Cases of firms to be investigated were assigned to them individually by the supervisor. Processing a case involved an audit of the books and records of the firm, interviews with the employer (or his representative) and a sample of employees, the determination of the existence of legal violations and of the appropriate action to

---

Originally published in 1955.

[1] From the 1948 *Annual Report* of this bureau, which is not cited in full to preserve anonymity; for the same reason, the terms of offices, officials, and office forms have been changed.

be taken, and negotiations with the employer. The time spent on a case varied between half a day and several months. On the average, an agent worked seventeen hours on an investigation.[2]

The agent had to evaluate the reliability of the information he obtained— since the concealment of violations occurred, of course—and had to decide whether violations had taken place on the basis of a large and complex body of legal regulations. This was a difficult task, which often required extensive research and consultation with the supervisor or with an attorney on the agency's staff. Upon completion of a case, a full report was written. All these activities were carried out in the office. Besides, agents sometimes interviewed employees or negotiated with employers in the office and had to attend biweekly departmental meetings as well as occasional special conferences. An average of 42 per cent of their working time was spent in the office.

A few of the background characteristics of the members of Department Y were the following: Only one of these eighteen officials had been with the agency for less than five years, and eleven had more than ten years seniority. Three agents were women, the rest men. The clerk and one agent were the only blacks in this group. The majority, thirteen officials, were veterans, since postwar reductions of personnel had primarily affected nonveterans. Seven officials had college degrees, and one had a higher degree. Two of the agents, trainees transferred from different assignments within the last year, had the civil service grade CAF-7; two had the grade CAF-9; the others were CAF-8's, earning between $4,100 and $4,800 in 1949. The supervisor had a higher and the clerk a lower grade. All agents did the same type of work, but especially difficult cases were most frequently assigned to CAF-9's and never to trainees; CAF-9's also occasionally assisted the supervisor in his work.

Department Y and another department with similar responsibilities shared one room. A visitor coming from the employment agency would have found this room small, quiet, and relatively empty. There would be no long lines of waiting clients, and half the forty desks would not be occupied, since many agents were in the field. At most of the other desks, agents would be sitting by themselves, reading or writing. At a few desks, two individuals might be taking. These pairs might be an agent in conference with the supervisor, a secretary taking dictation from an agent, a client being interviewed by an agent, or two agents engaged in a discussion.

If the visitor had been shown around the premises of the district agency's headquarters, he would have found a third department of agents in an

---

[2] However, the completion of the average case took thirty-one days from the date of assignment because appointments had to be arranged at the convenience of the public and because each agent worked on about a dozen cases simultaneously.

adjoining room and would have been told that two slightly larger departments were located in other towns. Near the elevator, he would have seen the "front office," the rooms of the district commissioner, his assistant, and the superintendent. The latter, the immediate superior of department supervisors, was in charge of the operations of all agents and was considered by them to be their "real boss." Next door was the office of the senior attorney responsible for legal action and advice, whose staff was located on another floor.

Down the corridor were the rooms of the section that selected the firms to be investigated, the file section, the stenographic pool, and the public information section. Finally, the review section received all completed cases and checked them for errors. Its major function was to assure that all decisions made by the agency's personnel were legally correct, but it also provided superiors with information on the quality of the performance of subordinates. Any mistake found had to be corrected by the agent who had made it, and this fact became part of his official record. Agency looked upon reviewers as taskmasters who made their jobs difficult.

In this chapter on Department Y, the process of decision-making will be examined. The accuracy of official decisions, which had to be justifiable in a court of law, was of crucial importance to the government; yet it was often extremely difficult to determine unequivocally how the general regulations applied to a particular case. In response to this problem, patterns of cooperation developed among agents, which transformed the mental process of making decisions into a social process. . . .

The Pattern of Consultation

Official provisions were made to assist agents with their difficult cases. Decisions of specified complexity or significance—for example, if the amount of money involved exceeded a certain sum—had to be authorized by the supervisor, who, in turn, had to obtain authorization from his superiors in special cases. Similarly, if an agent encountered a problem he could not solve, he was expected to consult his supervisor, who, if he could not furnish the requested advice himself, gave the agent permission to consult a staff attorney. Agents were not allowed to consult anyone else directly, not even their colleagues.

This rule requiring agents to come to their supervisor with their problems was an integral part of the authority structure of the agency. The supervisor was responsible to his superior for the legal accuracy of all actions taken in his department. In order to be able to discharge this responsibility, he had the authority to control all official decisions of his subordinates. As a last resort, he could correct mistakes when he reviewed their cases and order agents to revise the erroneous actions they had taken. Since this involved much wasted effort and sometimes bad public relations, two other ways of exercising authority were more efficient. First, the supervisor could prevent mistakes by advising agents in difficult cases or by guiding them to expert legal consultants. The requirement that they see him when they had problems, that is, in cases in which mistakes were most likely, facilitated his control over decisions for which he was held responsible.[3] Second, he could discourage the repetition of types of decisions he considered erroneous, because his evaluation of subordinates influenced their career chances.[4] To use this evaluation judiciously and as an effective control device, he had to be able to place responsibility for all decisions made. This would have been impossible if a half-dozen agents had collaborated on a case. The rule prohibiting consultation with colleagues was designed to prevent such collaboration.

Agents, however, were reluctant to reveal to their supervisor their inability to solve a problem for fear that their ratings would be adversely affected. The need for assistance and the requirement that it be obtained only from the supervisor put officials under cross pressure. "They are not permitted to consult other agents. If they have a problem, they have to take it up with me," said the department supervisor. Yet an agent averaged five contacts per hour with his colleagues. Hardly any of these were officially required, since each agent worked independently on the cases assigned to him. Some of them were purely private conversations, but many were discussions of their work, ranging from simple requests for information that could be answered in a sentence to consultations about complex problems.

This unofficial practice had developed in response to a need for advice from a source other than the supervisor. Anxiety over the correctness of his findings and actions, on which his rating was based, inhibited the agent in the process of making decisions and raised doubts in his mind regarding the validity of the decisions he had made. Consulting the supervisor, the only legitimate source of assistance, could not relieve the anxiety generated by concern over his opinion of an agent's competence. On the contrary, this anxiety induced agents to conceal their difficulties from the supervisor, as one of them explained: "I try to stay away from the supervisor as much as possible. The reason is that the more often you go to the supervisor, the more you show your stupidity." At best, even if an official had made correct tentative decisions, repeatedly asking the supervisor for confirmation would

[3] Another reason for this requirement was that attorneys, since they did not officially evaluate agents, might have been overrun by agents seeking advice if the supervisor had not provided a screen.

[4] Indeed, observation after a change in supervisors indicated that agents adapted their investigation procedures to the supervisor's interpretation of regulations.

reveal his inability to act independently, which would also affect his rating adversely. Their need for getting advice without exposing their difficulties to the supervisor constrained agents to consult one another, in violation of the official rule.[5]

Requests for information were a time-saving device, which must be distinguished from other consultations. An agent who did not recall a regulation or a reference often turned to ask a colleague instead of conducting a lengthy search. Since any agent might have this knowledge, depending primarily on the kinds of cases on which he had recently worked, proximity largely determined who was asked. An official requested information from his neighbors or from a colleague who passed his desk. This lack of discrimination had the result that every agent was often consulted.

When an agent had trouble solving a problem, on the other hand, he was more selective in his choice of consultant. The sixteen members of Department Y were asked with whom they usually conferred when they encountered difficulties. Seven agents were named by two or more colleagues in answer to this question, namely, all but two of the nine agents whom the supervisor considered highly competent, but none of the seven whose competence was below average.

Competence was clearly related to popularity as a consultant, but consultations were not confined to a few experts. A record was kept of all contacts between agents that lasted for three minutes or more. Most of these discussions were consultations. Two particular officials who spent at least fifteen minutes during thirty hours of observation together in such conferences are defined as a consultation pair. These relationships are presented in Figure 9.1. The sociogram does not show any "stars," but, except for the position of one individual (Y-2), two "chains" (Y-8—Y-14—Y-13—Y-10—Y-6—Y-11—Y-9—Y-15, and Y-16—Y-12—Y-7), and four agents without a link.

Most of these officials had one or two regular partners with whom they discussed problems. One partnership involved two agents whose competence, as indicated by the supervisor's rating and the estimation of colleagues, differed greatly, which suggests that one generally advised the other. Typically, however, each member of a pair was in the habit of consulting the other. All four agents without partners were experts, and three of them were

[5] The close relationship between the agent's concern with his rating and the need for unofficial consultation is indicated by the following incident: At a departmental meeting, the supervisor announced, "Any time an agent asks me a question, this has to be recorded in his diary." This made consulting the supervisor an official "black mark" on the agent's record. A week later, one of the most popular consultants in Department Y told his friends at lunch: "You know, these questions are terrible! At the last meeting, [the supervisor] told them they're not supposed to ask him questions. When they do, he'll write it in their diary. Now, instead of going to him, they all come and ask me questions."

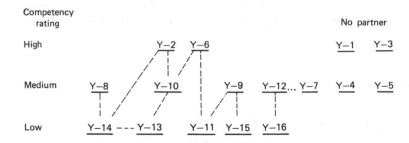

Figure 9.1. Sociogram of consultation conferences between agents. *Position on vertical axis:* last civil service rating by supervisor. *Number by which agents are designated:* rank order of esteem among colleagues (derived by averaging the rankings made by all other members of the department when asked to group agents in terms of their competence).

also very popular consultants.[6] These three were by no means isolated from the exchange of advice. On the contrary, they participated so widely in it that they did not spend much time with any single co-worker.

A consultation can be considered an exchange of values; both participants gain something, and both have to pay a price.[7] The questioning agent is enabled to perform better than he could otherwise have done, without exposing his difficulties to the supervisor. By asking for advice, he implicitly pays his respect to the superior proficiency of his colleague. This acknowledgment of inferiority is the cost of receiving assistance. The consultant gains prestige, in return for which he is willing to devote some time to the consultation and permit it to disrupt his own work. The following remark of an agent illustrates this: "I like giving advice. It's flattering, I suppose, if you feel that the others come to you for advice."

The expert whose advice was often sought by colleagues obtained social evidence of his superior abilities. This increased his confidence in his own decisions and thus improved his performance as an investigator. Such a popular consultant not only needed advice on fewer occasions than did others, but he could also distribute discussions of his own problems among several colleagues, since most of them were obligated to him for his assistance. Besides, to refrain from asking any particular individual too many questions helped to maintain his reputation as an expert. Consequently, three of the most popular consultants had no regular partner.

[6] The fourth agent had only recently been assigned to Department Y and was not yet integrated into the consultation pattern. (The term *experts* simply refers to agents whose competence was highly esteemed.)

[7] William F. Whyte's concept of "mutual obligation" suggested this formulation of consultation as an exchange of values. See the discussion of the significance of exchanges of obligations for social cohesion in his *Street Corner Society*, rev. ed. (Chicago: University of Chicago Press, 1955), pp. 256–258 and *passim*.

All agents liked being consulted, but the value of any one of very many consultations became deflated for experts, and the price they paid in frequent interruptions became inflated. One of them referred to the numerous requests for his advice by saying, "I never object, although sometimes it's annoying" (see also statement quoted in note 5). Being approached for help was too valuable an experience to be refused, but popular consultants were not inclined to encourage further questions. [8]

The role of the agent who frequently solicited advice was less enviable, even though he benefited most directly from this unofficial practice. Asking a colleague for guidance was less threatening than asking the supervisor, but the repeated admission by an agent of his inability to solve his own problems also undermined his self-confidence and his standing in the group. The cost of advice became prohibitive if the consultant, after the questioner had subordinated himself by asking for help, was in the least discouraging— by postponing a discussion or by revealing his impatience during one. To avoid such rejections, agents usually consulted a colleague with whom they were friendly, even if he was not an expert. One agent explained, when asked whether he ever consults a colleague whom he considers outstandingly competent: "I sometimes would like to, but I'm hesitant. I always have the feeling that I don't have the right to pick his brain. I ask the ones I know well because I don't feel any reluctance about asking them."

The establishment of partnership of mutual consultation virtually eliminated the danger of rejections as well as the status threat implicit in asking for help, since the roles of questioner and consultant were intermittently reversed. These partnerships also enabled agents to reserve their consultations with an expert whom they did not know very well for their most complicated problems. They could therefore approach him in these cases with less fear of courting a rejection. If the complexity of a problem prevented the agent from solving it, he needed expert guidance. Often, however, anxiety over the correctness of his findings rather than lack of knowledge interfered with his ability to arrive at decisions. In this situation, the counsel of a colleague who was not outstandingly competent could furnish the reassurance that facilitated decision-making.

The prevailing practice of consulting colleagues removed the agent from the isolation in which he otherwise would have been, since his work on his own cases officially required hardly any contact with co-workers. The evidence it supplied that he was not alone in having difficulties and the knowledge it provided that advice could be obtained without revealing his troubles

---

[8] The expert who was most encouraging toward queries from others was most frequently consulted and best liked by the other members of the group. As a result, he became, in some respects, its informal leader. His great willingness to assist others was his price for maintaining this position.

to the supervisor lessened his anxiety about making decisions. The repeated experience of being consulted did so even more effectively. By reducing such anxiety, this unofficial practice made the job less strenuous for agents and improved their ability to make accurate decisions in general and not only in those cases where a consultation took place.

However, consulting others also had disadvantages. It was a source of possible conflict with the supervisor, since it violated an official rule. Although the supervisor tolerated consultations, he did express his disapproval of agents "who are shopping around for the answers to their questions." Moreover, admitting ignorance by asking many questions lowered the groups's estimation of an agent and his own self-confidence. The more competant an official was, the greater was his reluctance to admit inability to solve a problem. But even experts needed assistance in making difficult decisions.

Consultation in Disguise

An agent who worked on an interesting case and encountered strange problems often told his fellow agents about it. All members of the department liked these discussions and considered them educational. One expressed her disappointment that superiors sometimes discouraged them by saying: "I wish they would not frown upon it. I used to like our gabfests. You used to learn so much discussing cases somebody came across, which you would never get. I guess they feel that you waste too much time thay way." The fact that agents devoted their free time to such discussions—lunch periods were filled with them, despite occasional protests, "No shoptalk!"—indicates that they were enjoyed. Officials found it interesting to hear how unusual problems were solved, perhaps after suggesting a possible solution themselves.

Generally, the discussant did not solicit the opinions of his listeners. For instance, an agent explained that one of the experts occasionally discussed a case with him: "He mentions a problem once in a while, because he finds it interesting. I'm sure that he's not going to ask *my* opinion.[9] Usually, you don't want the opinion of somebody else in these discussions. What you're doing is thinking out loud." Even when no advice was expected and none was given, these presentations of complex cases assisted the speaker in solving his problems. They were consultations in disguise.

Making decisions in an investigation involved the coordination of many pieces of information, the selection of the appropriate regulations from a large

---

[9] The speaker, in his own opinion as well as in that of others, was far less competent than the agent to whom he referred.

body of such regulations, and the appraisal of the specific data in terms of these legal principles. Anxiety resulted in "blocking" of ideas and associations, which increased the difficulties inherent in this intellectual process. The agent who attempted to arrive at decisions while sitting alone at his desk defined the situation as preparing the case for submission to the supervisor. His anxiety, engendered by the supervisor's evaluation of his decisions, interfered most with clear thinking in this situation. Instead of trying to make important official decisions, an agent could discuss the interesting aspects of his case with one of his colleagues. This situation, defined as a discussion among friends, did not evoke anxiety. On the contrary, it destroyed the anxiety that pervaded the decision-making process.

The listener was not merely a friend but a fellow specialist in solving the problems that occurred in investigations. This created the possibility of interruption if the suggested interpretation required correction. A listener might remind the speaker that he forgot to take some factor into account or that the data lend themselves to alternative conclusions. The assent implicit in the absence of interruptions and in attentive listening destroyed the doubts that continuously arose in the process of making many minor decisions in order to arrive at a conclusion. The admiration for the clever solution of the problem advanced, expressed by interested questions and appreciative comments, increased the speaker's confidence in his partial solutions while groping for the final one. By reducing his anxiety, "thinking out loud" enabled an official to associate relevant pieces of information and pertinent regulations and thus arrive at decisions which he might not have thought of while alone.

These discussions of problems were functional substitutes for consultations. They served the same functions for the discussant without having the same disadvantages for him. An explanation of a complex case did not violate the rule against asking other agents for advice, and it did not threaten the speaker's prestige or his self-confidence. In contrast to asking a question, presenting an interesting discussion *enhanced* the respect of his colleagues for an agent. Of course, this was the case only if his conclusions were correct; presenting false conclusions that were corrected by his listeners hurt an agent's standing in the group.[10] Agents who were not confident of their abilities, therefore, did not feel so free as experts to present their own solutions of problems. Besides, experts more often worked on intricate cases with unusual problems that others found interesting. Consequently, they, the very agents most reluctant to admit ignorance by asking for advice, were in the best position to use this substitute for consultations.

---

[10] However, whereas the questioner had to pay the price of admitting inferiority a priori, the discussant was able to elicit confirmation of his accurate decisions and help in arriving at them without paying this price.

The recognition of both participants in a consultation that one provided an intellectual service to the other raised the status of the consultant and subordinated or obligated the questioner to him. These were the inducements for the consultant to give advice and, simultaneously, the cost incurred by the questioner for receiving it. Discussions of interesting problems, on the other hand, were not recognized as providing a service to the speaker, and he did not start them because he experienced a need for *advice*[11] Manifestly, both he and the listeners, who sometimes commented, participated in these discussions because they were stimulating. The fact that they facilitated his solving of problems was disguised from the speaker as well as from his listeners; this was a latent function of such discussions.

In the absence of awareness that a service was furnished, no need existed for the speaker to reciprocate for the help he did, in fact, obtain. He did not subordinate or obligate himself to listeners. Such inducements were unnecessary for finding an audience, since interest in the problem and its solution supplied sufficient motivation for listening. This constituted the major advantage of consultations in disguise over direct consultations. Only a service intentionally rendered creates obligations, which make it costly.

The advantages of these discussions occasionally induced an agent who needed advice *deliberately* to disguise his consulation. The following comment refers to this practice: "[Casey] asks me sometimes, too, but he does it with a lot of finesse. He will just seem to ask what my opinion is, not as if he were worried about the question." Such manipulative attempts to obtain advice without reciprocating by acknowledging the need for the other's help were resented. A discussion had to be interesting to make listening and commenting intrinsically rewarding. This was the case only if the problem discussed was actually unusual and if the speaker manifested his own interest by appearing absorbed in presenting his solution rather than worried about its correctness. If his advice was needed, the agent demanded that the respect due him be paid by *asking* for his assistance. An official whose deliberate disguise of a consultation was discovered created resentment without averting loss of esteem. Only discussions that were genuinely stimulating facilitated decision-making without cost.

The practice of consulting co-workers, directly or in disguised form, served social, as well as psychological, functions. First, it transformed an aggregate of individuals who happened to have the same supervisor into a cohesive group. The recurrent experience of being dependent on the group, whose members furnished needed help, and of being appreciated by the

[11] For example, a highly competent agent mentioned that he sometimes asks others questions but distinguished these from his discussions: "And often I want to share an experience with somebody, discuss an interesting problem. . . . I already know what the answer is, but I want to see if he catches the gimmick."

others in the group, as indicated by their solicitations for assistance, created strong mutal bonds. Requests for information, which were indiscriminately made of any agent nearby, permitted all agents, even the least competent ones, to experience being needed by several other members of the department. Social cohesion, in turn, contributed to operations in a variety of ways.

Second, consultation among colleagues made more effective law enforcement possible because it improved the quality of the decisions of agents. Every agent knew that he could obtain help with solving problems whenever he needed it. This knowledge, reinforced by the feeling of being an integrated member of a cohesive group, decreased anxiety about making decisions. Simultaneously, being often approached for advice raised the self-confidence of an investigator. The very existence of this practice enhanced the ability of all agents, experts as well as others, to make decisions independently, even when they were alone in the field.

Third, discussions of problems increased the agent's interest in his work and his knowledge about it. They provided not only opportunities for learning, from the examples of experts, how intricate problems can be solved, but also incentives for becoming more skillful in this task since the presentation of an ingenious solution raised an agent's standing in the group. These stimulating discussions, moreover, contributed to the great interest that agents took in their work and their professional pride in being responsible for such complex duties. Most federal officials, in contrast to those in the state agency, considered the interesting and important nature of their tasks the most attractive feature of their job. Such work satisfaction furnishes inducements for exerting greater efforts. Its existence, and that of social cohesion, are perhaps particularly important for the American civil servant, who does not enjoy the emoluments of high status and authority that fortify the esprit de corps of his European counterpart, the *Herr Geheimrat*.

Fourth, the pattern of consultations stabilized the relationships among the members of the department and forstalled conflict. It gave agents accurate knowledge of the differences in proficiency among them, as indicated by the close correspondence between his colleagues' ranking of an agent's competence and that of the supervisor, who had evaluated every case (rank correlation $+.93$; see also Figure 9.1). Besides, officials *socially* acknowledged the superior ability of others in the process of asking for advice and in the course of listening admiringly, sometimes in a small group, to presentations of clever solutions of problems. This reduced the chances of friction when agents were differently rewarded for their performance. A high rating, or even a promotion, was less likely to create resentment against the supervisor or the agent involved, since his superior competence had been socially recognized in advance. Indeed, promotion expectations in this department were most realistic. Only two agents expected to become supervisors within ten years, the same ones who were considered to be the two most competent members of Department Y by all co-workers and the by supervisor.[12]

The mechanisms through which these functions were fulfilled also entailed dysfunctions. Thus the pattern of interaction tended to reinforce competence differentials in the process of making them known. The high esteem of agents frequently consulted reinforced their self-confidence as investigators at the expense of lessened self-confidence on the part of others. Furthermore, by creating social cohesion, this pattern also generated resistance to the frequent transfers of personnel from one department to another. Agents disliked being transferred because they felt loyal to their departmental group and because it required adaptation to new consultation relationships. Finally, this practice weakened the authority of the supervisor. It decreased not only the frequency with which agents consulted him but also their respect for his judgment, which they compared unfavorably with that of their most competent colleagues. The comment of one agent is typical: "If you can't get an answer from [either one of two agents], the likelihood of getting an answer from any supervisor is remote." It is quite possible that the anxiety evoked by consulting the supervisor, and its absence in consultations with colleagues, produced a bias in favor of the advice received from peers. In any case, the fact that his judgment did not command their full respect diminished the supervisor's control over subordinates and made it more difficult for him to discharge his responsibilities.[13]

Conclusions

Consultation among agents greatly contributed to effective operations in this enforcement agency, albeit at some social cost. At least, the data strongly suggest this inference, although they do not permit it to be directly tested. This would require that changes in competence over an extended period be related to participation in the consultation pattern, which could not be done in this study.

The question arises why the rule proscribing these consultations persisted despite their important functions for the organization. The supervisor preferred that agents consult him because his control over operations was weakened by their failure to do so. Another possible reason for this prohibition is related to the official character of bureaucratic rules. Since agents were permitted to consult their supervisor, they were not held responsible

[12] These evaluations were independent of the present grade of agents; of the two most esteemed, one was a CAF-9 and the other a CAF-8. (The second CAF-9 in the department ranked fifth in the estimation of his colleagues.)

[13] For a study of consultations in another organization, see Herbert A. Shepard, "The Value System of a University Research Group," *American Sociological Review* 19 (1954), 456–462.

for decisions made on the advice of the supervisor. Permission to consult colleagures would have given official recognition to the fact than an agent may not have been responsible for all the mistakes in his cases; one of his consultants may have been. This would have interfered with the rigid allocation of bureaucratic responsibility, whereas tolerating consultations without officially permitting them did not.[14]

This explanation, however, is not entirely satisfatory. After all, an advisory staff makes recommendations without relieving the line official of the responsibility for acting on them. To be sure, to place agents who were responsible line officials simultaneously in the position of an advisory staff to one another would have involved a major reorganization of the official responsibility structure, but it would not have been impossible.

The fact that consultations were tolerated suggests that their unofficial character was incidental to their relative newness. To treat them as deviations from formal requirements may well be less fruitful than to consider them modifications of the structure, a stage in its development. A basic reorganization had actually taken place in this agency, and it was tolerated by superiors, although it had not yet received official sanction.

The formal requirements of a bureaucratic organization give rise to operational problems. In the state agency, competitive hoarding of jobs and conflict with clients constituted such problem areas. In the federal agency, different problems were crucial for operations, such as that of decision-making. The solving of these problems necessitated changes in the patterns of interaction among officials as well as in their operating practices. The network of interpersonal relations among agents differed from that among interviewers because the two had developed in the course of finding solutions to different common problems. Thus competence influenced the relations between agents more than those between interviewers, since it was more relevant for consultations than for discouragement of competitive tendencies.

The pattern of consultation produced a new dynamic situation, not a stable equilibrium. It simultaneously generated cohesive bonds among peers and differentiation of status between them. It made an agent's standing in the group dependent on his competence, and it forced some agents socially to acknowledge their inferior competence while making an integrated position in the group of vital significance for them. These dynamic processes of adjustment had not yet been officially acknowledged and institutionalized. Formal adjustments occur slowly, in part because existing powers have vested interests in the status quo, as illustrated here by the interest of the supervisor in being the one whose tolerance of unofficial consultations makes subordinates obligated and increases their dependence on him.

[14] Official rules that are usually not enforced also increase the discretionary power of superiors over subordinates.

10. Orientation Toward Clients in a Public Welfare Agency

Public assistance differs in important respects from other branches of social work. Since furnishing financial aid to those in need is legally recognized as a public responsibility, such assistance is administered by public welfare agencies, whereas casework and group work are generally carried out by private agencies. The welfare agencies in metropolitan communities are larger and more complex than private social work agencies, often having a thousand employees or more and consisting of numerous divisions which provide many services besides financial assistance. Another distinctive characteristic of public welfare is that most of the "caseworkers" who administer assistance are not professionally trained social workers but have only a college degree and possibly a few courses in social work. Welfare agencies have not been successful in attracting professionally trained personnel not only because of their low pay but also because the ideology of professional social workers depreciates work in public assistance.

This paper is concerned with the orientation of caseworkers toward clients in a public welfare agency in a large American city, and particularly with

Originally published in 1960.

the ways in which the organizational and social context of the agency influenced their orientation.[1] Merton's concept of role set calls attention to the "complement of role relationships which persons have by virtue of occupying a particular social status."[2] Thus the status of caseworkers in the welfare agency involves individuals in role relationships with superiors in the organization, with clients, and with co-workers, and each of these relationships has some bearing on the way they perform their role as caseworker.

The first question to be raised is that of bureaucratic constraints. The administrative procedures that have necessarily become established in such a complex organization impose limits upon role relationships and operations. Training, supervision, and accumulated experience help the caseworker to adapt his role to the bureaucratic requirements. What are the consequences of these bureaucratic conditions for his orientation toward recipients of public assistance? A second problem is posed by the role relationship between caseworker and clients. How does the experience of meeting recipients and encountering difficulties in dealing with them affect the worker's approach? His relationships with peers and integration in his work group constitute a third important source of influence upon the caseworker's orientation toward recipients. Finally, the significance of the absence of a role relationship should be noted. Since they are not professionally trained, caseworkers are not actual members of a professional group of colleagues (although professional social work is a meaningful reference group for some of them).

The data for the study were collected in 1957 in a large public welfare agency.[3] The agency was responsible for administering general public assistance, but it also provided medical and legal aid, help with employment, industrial training, child placement, and several other services. The main duty of the caseworker was to determine whether new applicants were eligible for public assistance and to continue to check whether recipients remained eligible. He was also expected to furnish sufficient casework service to encourage clients to become self-supporting again and to see that they obtained the services from other departments as needed. These tasks re-

[1] For a study that deals extensively with the orientation to clients in a public employment agency, see Roy G. Francis and Robert C. Stone, *Service and Procedure in Bureaucracy* (Minneapolis: University of Minnesota Press, 1956). A study that deals with the influence of the community on the orientations to recipients in a public welfare agency is reported in Edwin J. Thomas," Role Conceptions and Organizational Size," *American Sociological Review* 24 (1959), 30–37.

[2] Robert K. Merton, *Social Theory and Social Structure*, 3rd ed. (Glencoe: Free Press, 1968), p. 423.

[3] I am indebted to Philip M. Marcus for assistance in the collection and analysis of the data, and to the Ford Foundation as well as to the Social Science Research Committee of the University of Chicago for financial support. I also want to acknowledge William Delany's helpful suggestions for revising the paper.

quired familiarity with agency procedures and involved a considerable amount of paper work in the office as well as visiting clients in their homes. Caseworkers spent about one-third of their time in the field. Large case loads and high turnover of personnel created special difficulties for discharging these responsibilities. More than one-half of the caseworkers were men, and one-third were blacks.

The research concentrated on twelve work groups, each consisting of five or six case workers under a supervisor. After a three-month period of observation devoted to collecting some systematic data as well as general impressions, pertinent information was abstracted from agency records, and the members of the twelve work groups were interviewed. A central focus of the interview, which lasted from one to two hours, was the respondent's orientation toward clients. Only those items that analysis revealed to be salient as well as reliable are used in this paper. Although such interview responses cannot hope to capture all subtle aspects of the caseworker's approach to clients, they do indicate some basic differences in approach.

Bureaucratic Constraints

Caseworkers often complained about the bureaucratic restraints under which they had to operate. Many of them felt that the agency's emphasis on following procedures, and particularly the requirement to investigate closely each recipient's eligibility, made it impossible for them to provide the kind of casework service that would benefit clients most:

> They always talk about social work, but actually you can't do anything of the kind here. For instance, I had one case which I wanted to send to [another agency], but my supervisor said, "You can't. You would have to make a case plan first, and we can't do that."

These were the words of a worker who had been with the agency only a few months. Newcomers not only voiced such complaints most often (although they were by no means alone in doing so), but they also frequently criticized old-timers for having grown callous and inflexible in the course of having become adapted to the bureaucratic organization.

Implicit in the opinions of caseworkers were two contradictory explanations of compliance with official procedures. On the one hand, compliance was ascribed to externally imposed restraints that prevented workers from following their own inclinations and furnishing good casework service. On the other, the old-timers' conformity to procedures was attributed to their rigidity, resulting from their overadaptation to the bureaucratic organization. As a matter of fact, neither of these explanations is entirely accurate.

Bureaucratic constraints actually became internalized, but adaptation to them did not increase rigidity.

The impact of the bureaucratic organization on service to clients cannot be directly determined without comparing different agencies that are more or less bureaucratized. While this is not possible in a study confined to caseworkers in one organization, an indirect estimate of this impact can be made. Since bureaucratic pressures are, in large part, transmitted to workers through their supervisors, their influence can be inferred from a comparison on the orientations of workers under supervisors who stress strict adherence to official procedures and under supervisors who interpret procedures more liberally. On the basis of their description of a day in the field, workers were classified as being primarily oriented either toward checking eligibility in accordance with procedures, or toward providing some casework service. Only one quarter (seven of twenty-nine) of the workers under supervisors who emphasized procedures were oriented toward casework service, in contrast to three fifths (nineteen of thirty-one) of those under less procedure-oriented supervisors.[4]

Some caseworkers were subject to less bureaucratic pressure than others, and this was reflected in their work, but few if any escaped the penetrating impact of bureaucratization. The summer camp program illustrates this. A number of free placements in children's camps were made available to the agency each year. Caseworkers who often deplored the lack of funds that made it impossible to help clients beyond supplying them with the bare necessities of life, and who sympathized particularly with the plight of children, would be expected eagerly to take advantage of this opportunity to provide special services and to compete for the few placements available. Actually, most workers were not at all interested in making camp referrals, looking upon it as an extra burden rather than an opportunity, although the actual amount of work involved was quite small. Moreover, service-oriented workers were no more likely to make referrals to summer camps than others.

This general apathy toward the camp program indicates that, although many caseworkers complained about being restricted in their endeavors to serve clients by bureaucratic restraints *externally* imposed upon them, they had actually internalized bureaucratic constraints to a considerable degree. To be sure, some workers defined their responsibilities less narrowly than others, partly in response to differences in their superiors' interpretations of agency policies. But even a broader definition of the caseworker's bureau-

---

[4] Supervisors were classified on the basis of descriptions by their subordinates. But regardless of how a given worker described his supervisor, the worker was less apt to be service-oriented if the other subordinates described the supervisor as emphasizing procedures than if they did not.

cratic responsibilities limited their scope to certain recurrent services, and referring children to camps was an extraordinary service, not part of the regular routine.

The very complexity of official procedures in this large organization served to promote adaptation to bureaucratic practice. In order to help his clients, a caseworker had to know agency procedures and to work within their bounds. But it was impossible in a few days or weeks to learn and understand, let alone to administer, the many rules and regulations that governed operations. New employees were overwhelmed by the complexity of their administrative duties and had to devote several months, often much of their first year, to becoming familiar with agency procedures. Newcomers who were unable or unwilling to master the pertinent regulations and perform their duties in accordance with them either found their job so unsatisfactory that they soon left or, more rarely, performed their tasks so poorly that they did not survive the probation period. Most of the caseworkers who remained with the agency for any length of time had come to accept the limitations of official procedures and, indeed, to incorporate them into their own thinking, because doing so was a prerequisite for deriving satisfaction from the job and performing it adequately.

Internalized bureaucratic constraints tended to govern the decisions and actions of caseworkers, their protestations against bureaucracy notwithstanding. However, the data reveal that adaptation to the organization and its requirements did not increase rigid adherence to procedures at the expense of casework service. Caseworkers who had been with the agency for a long time can be assumed to be better adapted to it than newcomers, for reasons already noted. (The fact that less than one-half of the workers with more than one year of employment, compared to three-quarters of the newcomers, mentioned bureaucratic conditions as one of the things they liked least about the job supports this assumption.) Old-timers, however, were less likely than newcomers to confine their work to checking eligibility. One-half of the forty-two workers with less than three years of service but only one-third of the eighteen workers with at least three years of service were primarily oriented toward eligibility procedures. Another finding indicates a similar decrease in rigid compliance with official procedures with increasing experience. Agency rules required workers to be on time, and repeated tardiness was penalized. The time sheets showed that none of the newcomers were late for work more than once every other month, whereas half (nineteen of thirty-nine) of the workers with more than one year seniority were.

Apparently, adjustment to the organization did not lead to greater bureaucratic rigidity; on the contrary, it was the insecurity of the newcomer, not thoroughly familiar with procedures and not yet adapted to the bureaucratic organization, that produced rigid adherence to official rules. The more experienced worker's greater understanding of procedures and better adaptation to them made him less confined by them,[5] with the result that he was more likely than a newcomer to go beyond checking eligibility in his contacts with clients and provide some casework service.

Reality Shock

> There are two things you learn on this job, particularly if it is your first job. First, you become less idealistic. You realize that people are not always honest—that you cannot always accept what they say. Then, you learn to work within a framework of rules. You realize that every job has rules and that you have to work within that framework.

This statement of a perceptive caseworker who had been with the agency for not quite one year indicates the two major problems that confront the newcomer. Often fresh out of college, not only is he faced by a complicated set of procedures, but he also encounters clients who are very different from what he had expected and with whom he must establish a working relationship.

Most persons who took a job in the welfare agency were partly motivated by an interest in working with and helping poor people. They tended to look forward to establishing a warm, although not intimate, relationship with deserving and grateful clients, and considered the caseworker as the agent of society who extended a helping and trusting hand to its unfortunate members. Newcomers generally deplored the "means test" and cared little about protecting public funds by investigating whether clients meet eligibility requirements, feeling that a trusting attitude should accompany financial aid in the best interest of rehabilitation. While a few caseworkers were motivated to seek their job by very different considerations, such as a desire to dominate people, they were the exceptions. The attitudes of most new caseworkers toward clients were strongly positive, if somewhat sentimental and idealistic. Contacts with clients put these views to a severe test, which often resulted in disillusion.

Recipients of public assistance constitute the most deprived segment of the population, especially in a period of relative prosperity. In this northern metropolis, disproportionate numbers of them were blacks, in-migrants from

[5] The same relationship between knowledge of procedures and lack of rigidity was observed in another bureaucracy; see Peter M. Blau, *The Dynamics of Bureaucracy*, rev. ed. (Chicago: University of Chicago Press, 1963), pp. 245–246.

the South, unmarried mothers, alcoholics, and generally people with handicaps in the labor market. The mores and folkways of most of these people
were quite different from those prevailing in the American middle or working class. Strong moral condemnation of desertion, illegitimacy, or physical
violence, for example, was not part of the values of their subculture. Such
differences in values and customs made it difficult for middle-class workers
to maintain their positive feelings for clients, but another factor was even
more important in changing their orientation. Clients were in dire need,
since the assistance allowance, originally set low, never caught up with the
inflationary trend. They were, therefore, under strong pressure to conceal
what slim resources they might have had and try to get a little more money
from the agency, even if this required false statements. People under such
deprived conditions tend to look upon government organizations as alien
forces that must be tricked into yielding enough money for survival, and
consequently some clients, although by no means all, tried to cheat. The
situation in which recipients found themselves made honesty a luxury.

The new caseworker was typically full of sympathy for clients' problems.
But as he encountered clients who blamed him personally for not helping
them enough, even though agency procedure limited him, and clients met
his trusting attitude by cheating and lying, the newcomer tended to experience a "reality shock,"[6] just as new teachers do whose first assignment is an
overcrowded class in a slum.[7] This disillusioning experience might make a
worker bitter and callous, or induce him to leave the job. Those who did
not have either of these extreme reactions tended to change their orientation
to clients.

Finding out that people one has trusted have lied is a threatening experience. It implies that one has been made a fool of and that others are laugh-
ing behind one's back at one's naïveté. To protect his ego against these
threats, a caseworker is under pressure to change his orientation toward
clients. If he anticipates deception by distrusting the statements of recipients,
their lies no longer pose a threat to his ego. And if he loses his personal interest in them, their attitudes cease to be significant for his self-conception,
making his ego still more immune against possible deception and other
conflicts. In short, the *situational context* of public assistance, by producing a
reality shock, tends to create a distrustful and uninterested orientation
toward recipients.

As a result of reality shock, one would expect that caseworkers lose some
of their interest in clients and concern with their welfare during their first

[6] This concept has been introduced by Everett C. Hughes in his studies of professional
careers.

[7] See Miriam Wagenschien, "Reality Shock," (unpublished Master's thesis, University of
Chicago, 1950).

year in the agency. The data confirm this hypothesis. Of the newcomers, 57 per cent reported that they worried sometimes or often about their cases after working hours; of the workers with more than one year of service, only one-third did (this proportion was the same for those with one to three years and those with more than three years seniority). Personal involvement with clients, that is, the proportion of workers who considered it important to be liked by clients, decreased similarly after one year of service.

A less simple pattern, however, was revealed by the relationship between seniority and deriving satisfaction from clients, as Table 10.1 shows. Contacts with clients were a major source of work satisfaction for three-quarters of the newcomers. This proportion decreases, as expected, to considerably less than one-half for workers with one to three year seniority; but it increases again to more than three-quarters for old-timers with more than three years of employment. The proportion of workers who particularly enjoyed helping clients manifests the same pattern—a drop after one year and a rise after three years. Again, workers with one to three years of seniority were somewhat more likely to think that clients often cheat than either newcomers or old-timers. These findings suggest that the reality shock has some effects that are temporary as well as some permanent ones.

Having come to the agency with idealistic views about poor people, newcomers tended to be much concerned with helping recipients. Contacts with clients constituted the most gratifying aspect of their work, not only because of their positive feelings toward clients, but also because they had few alternative sources of satisfaction on the job. Still unsure about procedures and not yet having become friendly with many colleagues, newcomers were not likely to find much gratification in their work at the office, where the necessity to make decisions and submit them to the supervisor aroused their anxieties, and where the friendly interaction among other caseworkers underlined their own relative isolation. The disillusioning experience of the reality shock often alienated the caseworker from clients. After he had been with the agency for some months, he tended to lose much of his concern with helping clients and to derive less satisfaction from working with them.

Table 10.1 Seniority and Source of Work Satisfaction

Major Source of Work Satisfaction	Newcomer (%)	1–3 Years (%)	Old-Timer (%)
Client contacts	76	43	83
Other sources	24	57	17
Number of cases	21	21	18

But as the worker learned to adapt to the reality shock by becoming less involved with clients, contacts with them ceased to be a threatening and unpleasant experience. Moreover, as he became increasingly conversant with agency procedures and acquired skills in applying them less rigidly, the worker could furnish more effective casework service, and this made contacts with clients once more a source of work satisfaction for him.

The continuing lack of involvement of the old-timer might be considered a residue of the reality shock. After three years of experience, however, the old-timer was again as apt as was the newcomer to find satisfaction in his work with clients. But whereas the gratification of the newcomer was rooted in his interest in recipients and their welfare, that of the old-timer, who generally lacked such a personal interest in clients, stemmed from his superior skill in providing effective service. The workers who did not find the exercise of this skill an interesting challenge probably left the agency in disproportionate numbers, and this selective process may well partly account for the finding that those who had remained with the organization for more than three years obtained more satisfaction from contacts with clients than those with one to three years seniority.

Peer Group Support

The finding that newcomers, despite their positive feelings, were less likely than other workers to go beyond checking eligibility and to offer casework services to clients has been interpreted by suggesting that lack of experience and familiarity with procedures engendered insecurities and anxieties that lead to rigid adherence to procedures. If this interpretation is correct, then conditions other than experience that lessen feelings of insecurity should also promote casework service.

Friendly relations with colleagues are a source of social support which helps reduce the anxieties and insecurities that arise in the work situation. Individuals who were somewhat isolated from colleagues, therefore, were expected to be less oriented toward casework service than those with extensive informal relations with peers. Indeed, this seemed to be the case. Two measures of social support from peers were the caseworker's popularity in the organization (how often others named him as a colleague with whom they were friendly), and his integration in his work group (whether he was called by his first name by other members of his own work group). Whichever index was used, over one-half of the workers with social support from peers were service oriented, in comparison with not quite one-third of those without such social support.

Table 10.2 Seniority, Integration, and Orientation

Orientation Toward Clients	Newcomer Integration		1–3 Years Integration		Old-Timer Integration	
	Low (%)	High (%)	Low (%)	High (%)	Low (%)	High (%)
Eligibility procedure	67	50	67	33	13	50
Intermediate	11	8	11	0	38	0
Casework service	22	42	22	67	50	50
Number of cases	9	12	9	12	8	10

Apparently, friendly relations with peers decreased the tendency of workers to confine themselves rigidly to checking eligibility,[8] just as accumulated experience did. The influence of both social integration in the peer group and experience (seniority) on the service orientation of workers[9] is presented in Table 10.2. The data in adjacent pairs of columns show that social support from integrative relations with co-workers encouraged casework service only among workers with less than three years of experience, but not among old-timers. If the two categories of caseworkers who had been with the agency less than three years are combined, 22 per cent of the unintegrated, in contrast to 54 per cent of the integrated, were service-oriented. But after three years, whether workers were integrated among peers or not, the proportion of service-oriented ones was 50 per cent. This suggests that social support from colleagues is significant for service to clients only as long as lack of experience engenders anxieties that impede service. Since the worker who has become fully adapted to the organization and its procedures in several years of employment experiences little anxiety in his or her work, the anxiety-reducing function of friendly relations with peers has no bearing on his or her performance.

Experience decreased rigid concern with procedures considerably among unintegrated caseworkers but had much less impact on the orientation of

[8] An alternative interpretation of the finding would be that service orientation made workers more popular among colleagues, but other data suggest that the interpretation presented is probably the valid one. Thus the interpretation implies a direct relationship between popularity and self-confidence, and also one between self-confidence and a service orientation, and the data confirm both of these inferences.

[9] The pattern of findings is quite similar if the index of popularity rather than that of integration is used, and also if several other measures of orientation to clients are substituted for the one shown in the table. (Integration in the ingroup rather than popularity in the organization is the measure presented in the tables, because there are too few popular newcomers to make meaningful comparisons.)

integrated workers, as a comparison of alternate columns in Table 10.2 shows. Among the integrated, the proportion of procedure-oriented workers declined somewhat after the first year only to increase again after the third. Among the unintegrated, in contrast, two-thirds of the workers were procedure oriented for the first three years, but this proportion dropped sharply to one out of eight after three years of experience. This finding probably indicates that experience frees the worker from being rigidly restricted by procedures, and thus fosters casework service, not simply because it increases a worker's technical competence but specifically because his increased competence lessens his feelings of insecurity and anxiety. The unintegrated worker, whose anxieties are not already relieved by social support from peers, is therefore the one most apt to become less rigid with increasing experience.

Social support from colleagues and accumulated experience can be considered functional substitutes for each other with respect to service to clients. Both seemed to reduce anxieties and rigidities, and thus to foster casework service, but their effects were not cumulative. If workers were experienced, integration did not increase their tendency to be service oriented, and if they were integrated, experience hardly increased service. (As a matter of fact, there is some indication that the combined influence of much experience and social support from peers was the very reverse of that of either condition alone. After three years of employment, integrated workers were somewhat *more* likely to be procedure oriented than unintegrated ones. This could be interpreted as showing that a certain amount of anxiety serves as an incentive to go beyond merely checking eligibility. Workers who were too secure had no incentive to do more than that, and those who felt too insecure were too rigid to do more. The integrated workers without several years of experience and the highly experienced but unintegrated ones, on the other hand, whose anxieties presumably had been mitigated without having been entirely eliminated, were most apt to go beyond checking eligibility and provide some casework service.[10])

While the implication of social integration among peers for casework service was largely similar to that of years of experience, the significance of integration for the concern workers expressed about helping clients was

[10] Although it is hazardous to venture an explanation of a single reversal, this one deserves to be mentioned, because it calls attention to forces that are often neglected in sociological studies of administrative organizations, including my own. In our reaction against scientific management and purely rational models of administrative behavior, we have tended to overemphasize the significance of informal relationships and paid insufficient attention to the formal administrative structure, the significance of incentives, and related problems. See on this point Alvin W. Gouldner, "Organizational Analysis," in Robert K. Merton *et al.* (ed.), *Sociology Today* (New York: 1959) pp. 400–412.

opposite of that of experience. Fully twenty-eight of the thirty-four integrated workers were sufficiently concerned to worry, at least occasionally, about their cases after working hours, in contrast to only twelve of the twenty-six unintegrated workers. Integration in the work group was, then, directly related to this manifestation of interest in the welfare of clients, but experience, as previously noted, was inversely related to it. This remains true if the associations of both factors with worrying are examined simultaneously, as Table 10.3 shows. Caseworkers who were integrated among peers were more apt to be greatly concerned about their cases than unintegrated workers, whatever their seniority (compare adjacent pairs of columns). Experience, on the other hand, reduced the tendency to worry much about recipients, both among integrated workers (from 67 per cent for newcomers to 40 per cent for old-timers) and among unintegrated ones (from 44 to 25 per cent).

Table 10.3   Seniority, Integration, and Concern

Concern (Worry about Cases)	Newcomer Integration		1–3 Years Integration		Old-Timer Integration	
	Low (%)	High (%)	Low (%)	High (%)	Low (%)	High (%)
Often or sometimes	44	67	22	42	25	40
Rarely	44	25	22	25	0	50
Never	11	8	56	33	75	10
Number of cases	9	12	9	12	8	10

These findings suggest that peer group support served to absorb some of the impact of the reality shock. The unintegrated worker, without such social support, experienced the full force of the reality shock, which constrained him to shield his ego by developing a hardened attitude toward clients. Ego support from integrative relations with peers made a worker less vulnerable, enabling him to cope with disagreeable experiences with recipients without feeling threatened and thus reducing his need for protecting his ego by becoming indifferent toward clients. Among unintegrated workers, therefore, the proportion who never worried increased from 11 per cent during the first year of employment to 75 per cent after three years, but there was no corresponding increase among integrated workers (compare alternate columns in the third row of Table 10.3). Social support from colleagues helped integrated workers withstand the reality shock and thus permitted them to maintain a greater concern for clients and their fate. Moreover, workers whose interest in helping clients led to worrying and made them vulnerable had particularly strong incentives to seek social support by fostering integrative relations with colleagues. The data do not enable us to tell whether integration increased concern or concern enhanced the chances of integration, or whether both influences occurred. In any case, however, they point to the conclusion that integration in the work group served to lessen the impact of the reality shock . . . .[11]

The way the colleague group promoted adjustment to the reality shock was apparently by encouraging its members to displace aggression against clients in conversations among themselves. Caseworkers often expressed very callous attitudes toward recipients in joking and talking with one another. For instance, when a worker went to interview a neurotic client, a colleague bid farewell to her with the words "Don't push him over the brink," to which she responded "Anything to get your case load down." Or, a worker proudly displayed his strictness by telling another about having discontinued assistance for a recipient when finding a Christmas tree and presents at his home, and ended by saying "A dirty thing to do, right at Christmas." Workers often seemed to be actually bragging about how unsympathetic they felt toward clients and how harshly they treated them. Indeed, even those workers who had impressed the observer with their sympathetic and understanding attitude toward recipients joined in this aggressive banter. To be sure, these workers might have deceived the observer by simulating a positive orientation in their statements to him and their behavior with clients when under observation by him; a systematic check, however, confirmed the initial impression. In five of the twelve work groups, a quantitative record was kept of all anticlient statements made during section meetings and conferences with the supervisor. A worker's tendency to make anticlient statements in these interactions was not at all related to his attitude to clients, as indicated in the interview.

Aggressive jokes or remarks about clients were typically made at these meetings and conferences after some disagreement or conflict, and the common laughter or indignation helped to reunite the conflicting parties. In other words, anticlient statements were a mechanism for reaffirming social solidarity among colleagues. Since they readily served this function, caseworkers had incentives to make aggressive statements against recipients, regardless of their attitudes toward them, as a means for healing breaches in interpersonal relations that might otherwise fester and become disruptive

---

[11] The findings permit, however, still another interpretation from which this conclusion would not follow. Perhaps certain personality types, such as dependent individuals, were more likely than others to worry about clients and also more likely to foster integrative relations with colleagues. The assumption made in the text is that the relationship between integration and worrying is not spurious, that is, not simply due to personality differences that affect both these factors.

conflicts. Moreover, since older workers, who had generally less considerate attitudes toward clients than newcomers, tended to occupy dominant positions in the work groups, newcomers were under pressure to prove by joining in the anticlient raillery that they were "regular fellows" and disprove the suspicion that they were naïve and sentimental about clients.

Displacing aggressive feelings aroused by conflicts with clients in the fairly harmless form of ridiculing them and displaying a hardened attitude toward them in discussions with colleagues may have helped to prevent such aggressive reactions from crystallizing into an antagonistic attitude to clients; but a caseworker's opportunity for doing so depended on the extent of his informal relations. The unintegrated worker's inability readily to relieve the tensions produced by conflicts with recipients in this fashion may be one reason why he was more prone than the integrated worker to develop a callous, unconcerned attitude toward clients as a means of avoiding such tensions. Processes of selection, however, may also have contributed to the observed differences in worrying about the welfare of clients. Perhaps workers who worried left the agency in disproportionate numbers, and unintegrated worriers were even more apt to do so than integrated ones, whose friendly relations with peers made the job relatively more attractive. This pattern of turnover could also account for the findings presented in Table 10.3.

Conclusions

Two important components of a professional orientation, in social work as well as in other occupations, are an interest in serving clients and the ability to furnish professional services. These are, of course, not the only elements in professionalism, but they are of special interest in the study of public assistance, because they become particularly problematical in the context of the administration of public welfare. The necessity to adapt to the bureaucratic procedures of complex welfare organizations creates obstacles for service, partly by diverting energies to learning the official regulations and administering them, partly by engendering anxieties and rigidities, and partly by the limitations imposed by internalized bureaucratic constraints. Furthermore, conflicts with clients, resulting primarily from the requirement to check their eligibility for assistance, jeopardize the interest in extending services to them. Finally, since the large majority of the personnel of public assistance agencies are not professionally trained, it is especially pertinent to ask what substitutes for such training, if any, promote a concern with the welfare of clients and an ability to serve them.

To be sure, untrained workers cannot be expected to have the skills to provide intensive casework, and there is no measure of such professional competence available in any case. We are concerned here merely with the worker's ability to cope with official procedures without restricting himself simply to checking eligibility—his or her ability to maintain an orientation to casework service. Although newcomers were most vociferous in their criticism of agency procedures, their approach to clients tended to be most limited by them. Experience was a functional substitute for professional training, which enabled workers to render more extensive services to clients. It apparently reduced the caseworker's anxieties about his work and thus freed him or her from being rigidly confined by procedures. Social support from integrative relations with peers also lessened anxieties and inflexibilities and, consequently, encouraged service to recipients.

Concern with the welfare of clients, too, was reinforced by integrative relations with colleagues, probably because their peer group relations mitigated the impact of the reality shock that workers experienced in their early contacts and conflicts with clients and thus obviated the need to adapt to such conflicts by developing a callous attitude toward clients. Experience, however, did not contribute to an interest in the welfare of clients; on the contrary, it reduced concern with their welfare.

In sum, experience increased the caseworker's ability to serve recipients but decreased his or her interest in doing so. Peer group support promoted the worker's concern with helping clients as well as his or her ability to help them. Friendly relations with peers, moreover, constituted a source of work satisfaction which may well have reduced turnover.[12] This possibility raises the question of how differences in the tendency to leave the agency affected the findings.

The relationships between seniority and the orientations of caseworkers to recipients were in all likelihood not entirely due to the influence of experience but partly to processes of selection. Since friendly relations with colleagues make the job more attractive, integrated workers have more reason to remain than unintegrated workers. Hence, factors that make the job unsatisfactory would be expected to increase the quitting rate of unintegrated workers, whose interpersonal relations do not hold them back, more than that of integrated workers.[13] One such dissatisfaction might be a worker's

[12] Over one-third of the integrated workers, but less than one-tenth of the unintegrated ones, spontaneously mentioned friendly relations with colleagues as one of the things they liked best about the job.

[13] Lack of integration in combination with another source of job dissatisfaction might have motivated workers to leave. By itself, lack of integration in the ingroup evidently did not have this effect, as shown by the finding that the proportion of unintegrated did not decrease with seniority (see last row of Table 10.3). Lack of popularity in the organization, on the other hand, might have induced workers to leave; for the proportion of the unpopular did decrease with seniority (from four-fifths among newcomers to one-third among workers with more than one year of service).

inability to extend the scope of his activities beyond the fairly routine and uninteresting task of checking eligibility; another one might be the anxiety caused by contact with severely deprived recipients. If workers who feel restricted by procedures leave the agency in disproportionate numbers, there will be fewer procedure-oriented workers among those with several years seniority than among those with little seniority. And if the restrictions of procedures increase the quitting rate of unintegrated workers more than that of integrated ones, the differences in procedure orientation between old-timers and newcomers will be pronounced among unintegrated but not among integrated workers. This is precisely what Table 10.2 shows. Similarly, if worry about clients encourages quitting, and if worry exerts a stronger influence on the turnover of unintegrated than that of integrated workers, it follows that there are fewer worriers left after several years, and that the difference in worrying associated with length of service is greater among unintegrated than among integrated workers. This is precisely what Table 10.3 shows. In short, the pattern of findings may be due either to these processes of selection or to the influence of experience discussed earlier. The most plausible assumption is that both factors contributed to the observed differences.[14]

Professional training in social work not only imparts knowledge and skills but also has an important socializing function; namely, to inculcate an orientation toward clients that combines impersonal detachment with serious concern for their welfare. The untrained workers in the agency studied probably suffered even more from not having undergone this process of socialization than from lack of professional knowledge and skills. To be sure, beginners were typically much concerned with helping clients, but they were not prepared for the shock of actually meeting recipients and, particularly, for coping with their own reactions to either the sympathy-evoking plight or the threatening aggression of recipients. The worker's untutored response to the tensions produced by these experiences was to become emotionally involved, or to escape by leaving the agency, or, perhaps most often, to lose concern with the welfare of clients as a means of avoiding these tensions. Such ego-defensive reactions would probably have been much rarer if the initial concern of workers with the welfare of recipients had been fortified

---

[14] There is still another factor that may have contributed to these differences, namely, promotions to supervisor. Perhaps the promotion chances of procedure-oriented workers were better than those of workers who showed little interest in official procedures; perhaps individuals who worried about their cases were more likely to be promoted to supervisor than those who expressed less concern with their work; and perhaps popularity among colleagues decreased a worker's interest in becoming a supervisor. These processes of selective advancement might have contributed somewhat, though hardly very much, to the observed differences between newcomers and old-timers.

by a detached attitude which made them less dependent on clients, just as ego support from integrative relations with colleagues reduced the likelihood of such reactions. To produce a detached service approach—the peculiar combination of a strong interest in furthering the welfare of clients and a detached attitude toward them—is an important function of professional training in social work.

11. *A Theory of Social Integration*

A fundamental dilemma of social life is that between being looked up to and being liked by associates. Both the respect and the affection of our associates are important to us, but our efforts to win the one often hurt our chances to win the other. Suppose a colleague has asked us to comment on the first draft of a paper he has written. If we make penetrating criticisms, this may increase his respect for our competence, but it will hardly endear us to him; and if we make only complimentary remarks, he may feel more favorable toward us but see no reason to respect our judgment. Although he benefits from supportive comments as well as from valid criticisms, he benefits from them and reacts to them in different ways, involving for us either a gain in respect at the expense of warm acceptance or a gain in intimacy at the cost of respect.

This dilemma between commanding respect (which implies a superordinate relationship) and winning friendly acceptance (which implies an egalitarian one) is deeply rooted in group life.[1] It calls attention to the com-

---

Originally published in 1960.

[1] The significance of this dilemma has been stressed by Bales. For an early study see Robert F. Bales and Fred L. Strodtbeck, "Phases in Group Problem Solving," *Journal of Abnormal and Social Psychology* 46 (1951), 485–495.

plex social processes through which individuals become integrated in groups and groups develop social structures. Concern here is not with differences in personality that predispose individuals to seek satisfaction in one kind of personal relationship rather than another, but with processes of exchange in groups and the conflicting demands they make on the members.[2] This paper attempts to analyze the processes through which individuals become integrated in groups, and it presents a tentative theory of social integration.

Social Attraction

A group is distinguished from an aggregate of individuals by the social bonds that unite the members into a more or less cohesive social structure. These are bonds of social attraction. A cohesive group is one whose members are strongly attracted to one another. The concept of attraction refers to favorable sentiments toward others which find expression in an inclination to engage readily in social intercourse with them. Of course, only individuals can experience such feelings and manifest such conduct. Networks of sentiments between persons and patterns of interaction in groups, however, indicate attributes of social structures and not of individuals.

Bonds of social attraction can be looked at from two perspectives: how *attracted* each person is to the group, and how *attractive* each person is to the rest of the group. The first perspective, which is that of Festinger and others in the tradition of Group Dynamics,[3] is adequate for such problems as the influence of group standards on behavior but not for the analysis of group structure and the integration of individuals in groups. A person's strong attraction to a group clearly does not make him an integrated member of it. Indeed, the conception of reference group directs attention to the fact that people are attracted to and influenced by groups of which they are not members at all.[4] To be sure, unless one is attracted to a group for some reason, he is not likely to become a member, but this attraction merely supplies him with a goal yet to be achieved. Only if he can make himself attractive to the other members will he attain an integrated position among them. A

[2] For a theory that deals extensively with the psychological processes underlying these patterns of interaction in groups see John W. Thibaut and Harold H. Kelley, *The Social Psychology of Groups* (New York: Wiley, 1959). A different approach to the study of exchange processes is presented in William H. Schutz, *FIRO* (New York: Rinehart, 1958).

[3] See Leon Festinger *et al.*, *Social Pressures in Informal Groups* (New York: Harper, 1950), pp. 164–166; and Dorwin Cartwright and Alvin Zander, *Group Dynamics* (Evanston: Row, Peterson, 1953), pp. 73–78.

[4] Robert K. Merton and Alice S. Kitt, "Contributions to the Theory of Reference Group Behavior," in Robert K. Merton and Paul F. Lazarsfeld (eds.), *Continuities in Social Research* (Glencoe: Free Press, 1950), pp. 47–51.

person is considered to be integrated in a group if the other members find him sufficiently attractive to associate with him freely and accept him in their midst as one of them.

The central sociological problem is what social processes are set in motion as every member of the group seeks to become or remain attractive to the others. Of special interest is the case of the face-to-face group in the process of formation, where all members have yet to achieve integration and where the group's cohesiveness depends on their concern with doing so. But the patterns in already established groups probably differ only in degree, particularly if there is a considerable amount of turnover of membership.

There are a number of factors that make a person attractive to others. If he has high social status in the society at large, they are likely to find him more attractive than if his social status is low. If his values and theirs are similar, they are more likely to enjoy association with him and to be interested in having him as a companion. If the personality needs he expresses in social interaction are complementary to their needs, they may derive some special gratification from him that draws them to him.[5] In general, if a person's qualities are valued by the other members of the group, he will tend to be attractive to them. However, every individual has a large repertory of qualities, and which of these find expression in his conduct in a given group is, of course, not a matter of chance.

A person who is motivated to attain an integrated position in a group has strong incentives not simply to wait until the others discover his good qualities but to exert effort to prove himself an attractive associate. He will try to impress them. This involves, essentially, revealing characteristics that he assumes to be positively valued by the others and concealing those he expects to be negatively valued. Goffman's perceptive discussion of this strategy of "impression management," as he calls it, shows in detail how people seek to control the image they present in social situations and thus the impressions they make.[6] Creating an impressive image of one's self is a complicated process. When one enters a group, he must infer from the few immediately available clues what the values of the others are, predict on the basis of this inference which of his qualities would make a favorable impression, and adapt his conduct accordingly. Moreover, his very concern with making a good impression is likely to interfere with his ability to do so, unless it remains below the threshold of his full awareness as well as theirs. If

[5] Theodore Newcomb points out that both similar and complementary interests, although they seem to be opposites, make social interaction more rewarding ["The Prediction of Interpersonal Attraction," *American Psychologist* 11 (1956), 575–577].

[6] Erving Goffman, *The Presentation of Self in Everyday Life* [University of Endinburgh Social Science Research Centre Monograph No. 2 [Edinburgh Social Science Research Centre, 1956)], pp. 22–23, 152–162, and *passim*.

they suspect him of deliberately putting up a front, they will not consider his behavior a reliable indication of his actual qualities but will instead discount it, and he will have made an unfavorable impression. And if he becomes too self-conscious about putting his best foot forward, he is likely to trip over his own feet and thus make a poor impression. Creating a good first impression is a subtle form of bragging, but its success depends on its being so subtle that it does not appear to be bragging at all.

Despite these pitfalls and difficulties, people often manage to create a good impression. But making a favorable impression is not a sufficient condition for becoming integrated with the other members of a group. It is important in this connection to distinguish between feeling attracted to a person and acting upon the feeling by seeking to associate with him. If a person has impressed others with his outstanding qualities, they will feel attracted to him. But in a group situation other feelings and expectations will arise that prevent them from giving expression to their feeling of attraction in social interaction.

Reactions to Being Impressed

Paradoxically, the more attractive a person's impressive qualities make him appear to the others in a group, the more reluctant will they be, at least initially, to approach him freely and to draw him into friendly social intercourse. There are several reasons for this. Attraction to an individual makes us vulnerable and creates a need for defenses. If we are not interested in associating with somebody and do so only as the occasion demands it, he cannot hurt us by rejecting us; but, if we find him attractive, his possible rejection poses a threat against which we shall try to protect ourselves by resisting the temptation to make overtures to him. Indeed, this fear of being rejected by one who has demonstrated his impressive qualities is quite realistic. We are most impressed by qualities that are superior to our own and to those we usually encounter. Given this comparative frame of reference, a person whose qualities impress us is unlikely to find ours impressive. In a social situation, moreover, where many of us have been impressed by him and feel attracted to him, he is in a position to choose among a large pool of available companions, and this increases the chances that any one of us will be rejected. Hence the first reaction to being impressed is a defensive reluctance to initiate social contacts for fear of rejection.

It now becomes necessary to dispense with the fiction that there is *one* person who tries to impress the other members of the group. Actually of course, every member wants to make a favorable impression on the others, particularly (but not only) in new groups. Indeed, every member has three formal roles in this interaction: first, each member is ego, the person who seeks to impress others; second, each member is alter, one of the others to whom ego wants to become attractive; third, each member is also alter ego, one of the individuals with whom ego competes for the attraction of alters.

Since it can be assumed that everybody likes to be popular among his peers, the members of a group compete *with* one another for being highly attractive *to* one another. The more successful ego is in impressing others in their role as alter with his outstanding qualities, the more will he antagonize them in their role as alter ego, because his impressive qualities threaten their popularity in the group. In contrast to economic markets, where a firm's competitors are distinct from its customers (other firms which sell the same product are generally not its customers), a group member's competitors are identical with the "customers" whose output of attraction is the object of the competition for popularity. Every member has an interest in withholding evidence of his attraction to others, since manifestations of it would give them a competitive advantage over him by contributing to their popularity. The reluctance freely to express attraction to others in the group is not merely a psychological defense mechanism but a strategic weapon in the competition for popularity.

The structural constraints of the competitive context reinforce the defensive tendencies toward which fear of rejection predisposes the members of groups. Each individual is interested not only in suppressing his attraction to another but also in defending his standing in the group by preventing the others from becoming too attracted to that person. Once we have convinced ourselves that a person is not so attractive as he appears, we will convey this opinion to others, for example, by ostentatiously turning away while he tells a story, thereby raising doubts in their minds about his attractiveness. Since the best defense is an offense, defensive tactics merge with the strategy of creating a good impression. An individual may shift the conversation from a topic on which another person has an opportunity to be impressive to one on which he has. He may even take advantage of the fact that the others, too, are threatened by a person who appears to be very impressive and try to make him look ridiculous. This, if successful, is a most effective strategy; it means impressing others by doing what they wanted to have done but did not quite dare to do themselves. It is often possible to deflate the image a person has presented of himself because the competitive situation encourages group members to present inflated images.

Why do people feel attracted to a person who has impressed them with his superior qualities? The answer is probably that his qualities raise in them the expectation that they will benefit from associating with him. In a work group they may look forward to being advised by such a competent colleague; at a party, to being entertained by such an amusing companion; and in any situation, to being seen in such distinguished company. By creating a favorable impression, therefore, a person implicitly promises others that they will benefit from associating with him. To be sure, he can live on credit for a while, because it would be a breach of etiquette to make demands on him too quickly. But as long as the impressions he has created is all the others have to go by, he does live on credit. An impostor is an individual who is skilled in extending his credit far beyond his resources. Deliberate deception, however, is merely the extreme case of a much more common phenomenon, namely, the misrepresentations typically made by those who are anxious to make a good impression.[7]

When we make inferences from the impression a person creates, we are not so much interested in simple facts as in evaluations, for example, not in how many years he has played the piano but whether he plays it well. Thus we expect a person to present an evaluation rather than a mere factual description of himself in social interaction. Of course, an individual can hardly be completely objective in evaluating his own qualities. If he must compete with others to prove his attractiveness, he is under particularly strong pressures to present too high an evaluation of himself, creating an impression that raises expectations he will not be able to live up to. In sum, competition for popularity constrains members of a group to present an inflated image of themselves which exposes them to ridicule and embarrassment, on the one hand, and to take advantage of one another's weaknesses rather than express feelings of attraction and support, on the other.

If such competitive processes were to prevail, the group would undoubtedly disintegrate. The crucial theoretical point is that, although a person's integration in a group depends on his being attractive to the others, the social processes generated by pervasive concern with making a good impression create an impasse that makes social integration impossible. What prevents disintegration and promotes cohesiveness is the tendency of group members *not* to remain preoccupied with appearing impressive but to redirect their efforts to cope with the problems posed by the impending impasse.

Demonstrating Approachability

The very characteristics of a group member that impress others also make him appear unapproachable to them. His superior qualities, which make associating with him inviting, also raise doubts in the minds of others as to whether he will find them attractive associates and threaten their own standing in the group; and these doubts and threats give rise to defensive

[7] Goffman emphasizes how tenuous is the distinction between true and false impressions (*ibid.*, pp. 37–44).

tactics. Unless he can break through these defenses, he will not be able to achieve an integrated position in the group.

An important method for penetrating the defense of other group members (but not the only method, as will be seen presently) is for a person to demonstrate that, even though he has attractive qualities, as he has already shown, he is quite easily approachable. Completely reversing his earlier strategy of presenting only the most impressive parts of his self, he now flaunts his weaknesses. Having first impressed us with his Harvard accent and Beacon Hill friends, he may tell a story that reveals his immigrant background. After having talked only of the successes he has enjoyed in his career, he may let us in on the defeats he has suffered. Having earlier carefully protected himself against ridicule or even made jokes at the expense of others, he may relate an incident that makes us laugh at, as well as with, him. Whatever the content of his remarks, they show him as a person willing to admit his shortcomings. (Situations where a modicum of social integration must be achieved quickly, such as parties, furnish good illustrations of such changes in strategy from creating an impression to demonstrating approachability.)

Such self-depreciating modesty is disarming—literally so, since it obviates the need for defenses. As the listeners sympathize with a person's troubles or smile at his blunders, they will feel drawn to him, because he ceases to be a threat against which they have to protect themselves. By calling attention to his weaknesses and demonstrating his approachability, a person gives public notice that he withdraws from the competition for superior standing in the group and that all he wants to accomplish with his attractive qualities is to win full acceptance as a peer. Self-depreciation thus removes the threat his attractiveness has posed for the other members and induces them to act upon their feeling of attraction to him by engaging him in social intercourse. It consequently contributes to social integration.

When a member surrenders his claim to superior standing in the group, he invites others to follow his example; and the more members who do so, the easier it becomes for the rest to do likewise. The first person at a gathering who relates how he once committed a terrible faux pas makes a self-depreciating statement. His admission may well encourage others to talk about social blunders they have made. Once most members of the group have reported such incidents, for still another to tell about his faux pas is not so much self-depreciation as an attempt to establish a link with the rest. If members of a group are characterized by similar experiences or attributes, particularly if these set them apart from the majority in the community, this is a common bond. After one has discovered the characteristics of most of the others, he can link himself to them by indicating that he shares some of these characteristics, for example, that his ethnic background is the same as theirs. Establishing such links is a substitute for self-depreciation, for it also serves to show that an individual does not seek superior standing but only acceptance as a peer. Each member's demonstration that he considers himself no better than the rest and merely seeks acceptance as an equal makes it easier for the others to let their hair down, too, and these social processes promote mutual attraction and group cohesiveness.

The question arises whether self-depreciation may not have social consequences that are the very opposite of those here ascribed to it. Do we not often react to ostentatious modesty with embarrassment rather than with warmth and acceptance? Indeed we do, but only under certain conditions. If a person whose qualities we admire modestly admits to some shortcomings, this will increase our liking for him and not cause us discomfort. But if a person whom we do not find attractive insists on revealing his shortcomings, the chances are that we shall be embarrassed; for his exhibition of modesty is a claim for acceptance that our failure to be attracted to him prevents us from honoring, and when the expectations of one person are not fulfilled by others, embarrassment arises, as Goffman points out.[8] Self-depreciating modesty does not make one attractive, it merely activates already existing feelings of attraction by reducing the reluctance to express them. Therefore, unless the weaknesses a person admits are less salient qualities than those with which he has impressed others, he will not have demonstrated that he is approachable as well as attractive but, instead, will have provided evidence that he is, all things considered, really unattractive.

The main thesis advanced here is that for a person to become fully accepted and integrated in a group he must prove himself not only attractive but also approachable. Impressive qualities that make a person attractive simultaneously discourage others from freely approaching and accepting him. Concern with winning acceptance in a peer group, therefore, puts an individual under pressure to shift his strategy from impressing others to demonstrating his approachability. These strategies are beautifully illustrated in *Brideshead Revisited*, where the speaker describes his wife as adept in "first impressing the impressionable with her chic and my celebrity and, superiority once firmly established, changing quickly to a pose of almost flirtatious affability."[9]

Some Empirical Data

It is, of course, not possible to present empirical tests of all the hypotheses implied by the above theory. Even quite limited empirical checks, however,

[8] Erving Goffman, "Embarrassment," *American Journal of Sociology* 42 (1956), 264–271.

[9] Evelyn Waugh, *Brideshead Revisited* (New York: Dell, 1956), p. 220.

serve to curb fruitless speculation and clarify conflicting assumptions. A theory according to which a given variable may have contradictory consequences may be suspected of making unscientific assumptions that are inherently untestable. Thus the conception that a mother's unconscious rejection of her child may find expression either in overt rejection or, through reaction formation, in strong attachment is, without further qualification, intrinsically untestable. The same is true of the notion that the socioeconomic position of a class manifests itself either in class consciousness or in the very opposite—false consciousness. The statement that outstanding qualities make a person more attractive to others (thus increasing his chances of integration) and less approachable (thus decreasing these chances) is equally meaningless without further specification, since it predicts both a direct and an inverse correlation between superior qualities and social integration.[10]

It is possible, however, to derive a more precise inference from the theory. If group members are classified on the basis of two attributes, common sense would lead us to expect that those with two positive qualities have the greatest chance of being accepted by their peers, and those with two negative qualities, the least chance. In contrast, the theory implies that the members who are positive on the more salient attribute (and hence attractive) and negative on the less salient one (and hence also approachable) are most likely to win the acceptance of their peers. And the members who are negative on the more salient but positive on the less salient attribute are expected to be least likely to be integrated. In short, the theory predicts that the greatest contrast in integration is not between the plus-plus and the minus-minus-category but between the plus-minus and the minus-plus category.

A study of twelve work groups in a public assistance agency furnishes data that can be used to test this prediction. Each work group consisted of five or six caseworkers under a supervisor. (Responses from supervisors are not included in the analysis here.) The use of first names among peers, since it was not standard practice in this agency, was indicative of friendly acceptance. Whether a caseworker was or was not called by his first name by some of the other members of his own work group, as reported by the others, is the measure of integration employed.[11]

---

[10] Robert F. Bales calls this type of conception "flip-flop hypotheses" [*Interaction Process Analysis* (Cambridge: Addison-Wesley, 1950), pp. 117–120]; they may also be called "heads-I-win tails-you-lose theories."

[11] A worker's integration, as here defined, was directly related to the frequency with which he received social contacts from colleagues in the office, and it was also directly related to the extent of his contacts with other members of his own work group during lunch and coffee breaks. Since social integration is expected to find expression in being readily drawn into social interaction by peers, these two findings help to validate the index of integration used.

Respondents are classified on the basis of both sociometric status and background characteristics. Thus popularity—the number of "friendship" choices received from outsiders as well as from the ingroup—is presumably indicative of attractive qualities, whatever the specific attributes that attract others to any given individual. Background characteristics also make a person more or less attractive, but their residual effect that is not already reflected in the sociometric choices is undoubtedly a less salient force than that manifested in these choices. Experienced old-timers, for example, are generally more attractive associates but, partly for this very reason, less approachable ones than newcomers—workers who had been with the agency less than one year. (Although old-timers are not necessarily more attractive than newcomers, they were so in this agency; that is, there was a direct relationship between seniority and popularity.) If popularity is held constant, the implications of seniority for attractiveness have been largely removed, so to speak, and the remaining influences of seniority are probably due primarily to its unapproachability component.

The naïve assumption would be that newcomers are less integrated in their work group than equally attractive old-timers. The expectation derived from the theory, on the other hand, is that popular newcomers, as individuals who are easily approachable as well as attractive, are most likely to be integrated among peers—more so than popular old-timers—and that unpopular old-timers are least likely to be integrated—less so than unpopular newcomers. The upper rows in Table 11.1 show that this was the case. The

Table 11.1   Social Consequences of Popularity and Seniority

| | Popularity | | | |
| | Popular Seniority | | Unpopular Seniority | |
	Old-Timer (++) (%)	Newcomer (+−) (%)	Old-Timer (−+) (%)	Newcomer (−−) (%)
Integrated	69	100	31	47
Not integrated	31	0	69	53
Total	100	100	100	100
Often consulted	65	25	38	6
Rarely consulted	35	75	62	94
Total	100	100	100	100
Number of cases	26	4	13	17

sharpest contrast is between popular newcomers, all of whom were integrated, and unpopular old-timers, only one-third of whom were. The distinctive significance of being not only attractive but also approachable becomes still more evident than in the table if one singles out the most integrated workers (those called by *most* members of the ingroup by their first name). Only 35 per cent of the twenty-six popular old-timers were highly integrated despite their attractiveness, in contrast to all four of the popular newcomers, whose attractiveness was complemented by greater approachability (and, among the unpopular workers, 8 per cent of the thirteen old-timers and 18 per cent of the seventeen newcomers were highly integrated). This pattern of findings differs sharply from the cumulative effects the same two factors had on other aspects of the caseworker's position in his work group, such as his status as a regular consultant to colleagues (lower rows of Table 11.1). Both popularity and seniority, independently, increased the chances of being named often by colleagues as a consultant, so that their effects were cumulative. Popular old-timers were the most prone to be consulted, and unpopular newcomers the least.

The prestige and manners of people with a middle-class background are likely to make them less easily approachable than those who originated in the working class, particularly for others who themselves have a working-class background, as did most caseworkers in the agency. When father's occupation is substituted for seniority, the impact of popularity and socio-economic origin on integration again confirms the theoretical expectation (Table 11.2). A worker's attractiveness, as indicated by his popularity, significantly enhanced his chances of integration in his peer group only if it was combined with a working-class origin, which made him readily ap-

Table 11.2 Social Consequences of Popularity and Social Origin

	Popularity			
	Popular Father's Occupation		Unpopular Father's Occupation	
	Nonmanual $(++)$ (%)	Manual $(+-)$ (%)	Nonmanual $(-+)$ (%)	Manual $(--)$ (%)
Integrated	43	83	38	41
Not integrated	57	17	62	59
Total	100	100	101	100
Number of cases	7	23	8	22

proachable. Attractiveness enhanced the likelihood of integration for persons from working-class homes from 41 to 83 per cent, but hardly that for persons from white-collar homes (38 and 43 per cent). (Whether the same results would be obtained in an organization the majority of whose members have a middle-class background is, of course, a question that cannot be answered on the basis of the available data.) Four other background factors may have the same implications for approachability as seniority and socio-economic origin—whether a caseworker is white or black, Protestant or not, male or female, and old or young. (Except for a relationship between age and seniority, there were no significant relationships between any two of the six background variables.) Five of the six tables that indicate the influence of both popularity and one of these characteristics reveal the predicted pattern; that is, the plus-minus category contained the highest proportion of integrated workers, and the minus-plus category, the lowest.

While any one of these findings could also be interpreted differently, the theory advanced provides a single explanation for all of them. Moreover, the same results are obtained if sociometric measures other than popularity are used as indications of attractive qualities. When the effects of respect (being named by peers as one of the best caseworkers in the group) and the same background characteristics are determined, all six findings are in agreement with the specific prediction. The respected workers with a "low" background were most often integrated among peers, and the workers who were not respected with a "high" background were integrated least often, regardless of which of the six background factors is under consideration. Finally, when the frequency of being consulted by colleagues is substituted as the sociometric measure in these tables, four of six show the expected contrast in integration between the plus-minus and the minus-plus category. Although not all these tests are independent, the fact that fifteen of eighteen confirm the prediction is suggestive. These findings do not prove the theory, of course, but they seem to support one inference derived from it, namely, that individuals who have characteristics that make them approachable as well as some that make them attractive have the best chance of winning acceptance in their peer group.[12]

[12] The theory implies that group members display *first* impressive qualities, to prove their attractiveness, and *then* some unimpressive ones, to demonstrate their approachability; but the data presented furnish no information on such time sequence, which makes it the more remarkable that they support the central hypothesis. Although no direct evidence on the sequence of these patterns is available, a bit of indirect evidence is contained in a systematic study of social interaction at evening parties. (I am indebted to David Riesman, Jeanne Watson Eisenstadt, and Robert Potter for giving me access to the tables and memos of their sociability project.) The relationships between guests were classified as strangers, expanding acquaintances (people who were just starting to become friendly), and various categories of closer associates. Strangers were particularly likely to present a "polished,

Social Differentiation

An attempt to analyze processes of social integration in abstraction from other group processes is likely to be misleading, since it leaves out of consideration the influence the latter forces have upon the former. Thus people are not exclusively concerned with the position they occupy in the group in which they presently find themselves, as the previous discussion may wrongly have implied. They have various other interests as well—such as obtaining satisfaction in their work, to name only one—and these also influence their interaction. Moreover, a group member's attractiveness to others depends not so much on his clever strategies in impressing them as on his actual qualities and performance, because social reality is not a mirage. Indeed, a basic difference between group life and more transient, isolated social relations— say, that between salesman and customer—is that members of a group have an opportunity to check the reliability of their first impression, in subsequent interaction with a person and in comparing one another's impression of him. Finally, social acceptance as an equal is not the only form social attraction to a person may take, and other forms appear not to be contingent on approachability, as the data presented in Table 11.1 indicate. Old-timers are presumed to be less approachable than newcomers, and this had the expected effect on their chances of being accepted on a first-name basis. Despite their greater unapproachability, however, old-timers were more attractive consultants than newcomers, even when popularity (or respect, as a matter of fact) is held constant. These considerations raise some questions concerning the earlier conceptualization.

Unapproachability has indirect as well as direct social consequences, just as does impressive behavior, and for the same reasons. If a person appears to have outstanding qualities, others will be attracted to him but will also infer that he may well not be attracted to them, because past experience tells them that people with superior qualities are generally not easily approachable. On the basis of the same past experience, however, people will also infer that an aloof and unapproachable person probably has outstanding qualities, otherwise he would not be so self-assured. And since people do make these inferences, self-assured and even arrogant conduct can serve as a strategy to impress others (hence people cultivate poise). But whether one

---

completed, or admirable [image] . . ., creating as positive and acceptable a view of themselves as possible." In contrast, expanding acquaintances were more likely than any other category to share with one another private experiences and feelings; there was "much less of the defensive style that involves putting up a pleasing front." This suggests that strangers at sociable gatherings first try to impress one another and that demonstrating approachability is the next step in establishing closer social bonds. (Established friends, however, again spend much time in presenting a favorable image to one another.)

employs this strategy or another to impress the members of a group, he still must cope with the defenses his implicit claim of superiority arouses in them. Sooner or later, he must prove his approachability or face the consequences.

This, however, is an alternative that has not yet been considered. A person may be willing to face the consequences of having impressed others and, instead of appeasing their defensive reactions, live up to the expectations his outstanding qualities have raised. Others expect some benefit from associating with a person who apparently has superior qualities, and, if he provides those benefits, he furnishes them incentives for associating with him. For example, a worker's superior competence motivates his colleagues to associate with him to obtain his advice. Or a person's sparkling wit at social gatherings induces his acquaintances to invite him to make their parties a success. An individual's ability to live up to the expectations of others depends not only on his capacity to supply desired services but also on his having the sagacity to refrain from presenting too impressive a front at first. The diffident person is one who anticipates this and carefully manages to raise only expectations that he can easily meet or even surpass.

There are, then, two different methods of dealing with the problem posed by the defensive reactions that occur in groups as each member tries to prove his attractiveness to the others. The situation at this stage may be described figuratively as an attractive force behind a defensive barrier that prevents its activation. The person who demonstrates his approachability lessens the attractive force somewhat but lowers the barrier enough to make it easy for others to associate with him. The person who provides services does not lower the barrier but increases the attractive force so much that the others are constrained by self-interest to relinquish their defenses and associate with him.

A member of a group who utilizes his superior qualities for the benefit of others not only makes himself an attractive associate but also earns respect and deference. By rendering significant services, he establishes social obligations. If he helps the rest of the group to attain important objectives, collectively or individually, they will be under obligation to him. The respect his demonstrated ability commands and the obligations his services create will induce others to follow his suggestions and defer to his wishes. Their deference is his reward for past contributions and his incentive for continuing to contribute in the future. These social processes, then, in which some members come to command the respect and deference of others, give rise to social differentiation in the group.[13]

[13] See Peter M. Blau, "Social Integration, Social Rank, and Processes of Interaction," *Human Organization* 28 (1959–60), 152–157.

Exchange Processes and Group Structure

The theory can now be reformulated briefly: A group is cohesive if bonds of social attraction unite its members. For social integration to prevail in a group and a cohesive unit to develop,[14] its members must be concerned with attracting one another. To prove himself an attractive associate, each member will seek to impress the others with his good qualities. But the resulting competition for popularity and defensive reactions against letting one's self be impressed by others threaten to lead to an impasse in which social integration would be impossible. If groups do not disintegrate, and many obviously do not, it is because other social processes forestall it.

In the course of the competition that motivates group members to reveal their best qualities to one another, it becomes evident that some have abilities that permit them to make important contributions to the achievement of common or individual goals. These contributions are a source of social attraction. Their significance forces other members to override their own defenses and seek to draw the person who makes them into the group and associate with him. At the same time the obligations incurred by the rest of the group to a member who contributes to the achievement of their goals constrains them to repay him with respect and deference. In short, the very processes required for social integration in a group give rise to other processes that lead to social differentiation. Hence social differentiation seems inevitable. (To state that some form of social differentiation is inevitable in face-to-face groups does *not*, of course, imply that all existing forms of social inequality are necessary prerequisites of collective life.)

The attraction and deference of other members to one who furnishes valued services intensify their need for integrative bonds simultaneously with relieving his. Since the benefits he has to offer make the others eager to associate with him, and since his abilities command their respect, he attains and sustains a secure position in the group without having to demonstrate his approachability. The others, however, are anxious to prove themselves attractive associates without having as yet been successful in overcoming one another's resistance to expressing feelings of attraction. Besides, paying respect and deference to him undermines their self-confidence, and it threatens the impressive image they have tried to present to one another,

---

[14] Group cohesiveness is here defined as the prevalence of integrative bonds among group members, but the cohesiveness of a group cannot be measured simply by adding the degrees of integration of all its members. A method for distinguishing the significance of cohesiveness (an emergent group attribute) and that of integration (a characteristic of individual members) is presented in Blau, "Structural Effects," *American Sociological Review* 25 (April, 1960), 178–193 (see Chapter 4).

thus increasing their need for social support. Under these conditions a group member will be under pressure to dispel the defenses of others and induce them to accept him as a peer by demonstrating his approachability. In doing so, he turns to his advantage the fact that by his deference he has already given the rest some evidence of his willingness to surrender any claim to a superordinate position. These tendencies give rise to bonds of mutual attraction. Thus it appears that processes of social integration also promote differentiation and that processes of social differentiation, in turn, help to strengthen the group's integrative forces.

Following Homans's suggestive conceptualization,[15] these patterns of social interaction may be looked upon as exchange processes. A person with superior qualities that enable him to provide services that are in demand receives the respect and deference of others in a group, which bestows superordinate status upon him, in exchange for rendering these services. A person who is not able to offer services that are in demand must settle for a lower position in the group. He can exchange his ready acceptance of others like him and his conformity to group norms for their acceptance of him. To put it into a somewhat different perspective, he wins social acceptance in exchange for ceasing to compete for superior standing in the group and for the contribution to social integration he thereby makes.

In conclusion, two important tasks required to improve the theory here suggested should be mentioned. The first is to derive operational hypotheses from the theory and test them in empirical research. One such hypothesis and preliminary tests of it have been presented. Many others have been implicit. To illustrate by making another hypothesis explicit: a person's tendency to demonstrate his approachability in a group to which he is attracted is expected to vary inversely with his ability to render valued services to its other members. The second task is to extend the theory and systematically analyze the dynamics of the exchange processes discussed. A few brief examples of these further dynamic processes must suffice at this point. Since deference is a high price, group members will search for ways to obtain needed services at less cost. They will be motivated to improve their own qualifications for furnishing those services. A person who succeeds in doing so not only can dispense with services for which he had to pay with deference but also earns the respect of others who up to then had merely accepted or liked him. Those unable to make any contributions that win them at least limited respect may leave the group, and new members with greater potentials may be recruited in their place. Group members may also exchange services with one another, instead of receiving them from one with

---

[15] George C. Homans, "Social Behavior as Exchange," *American Journal of Sociology* 63 (1958), 597–606.

superior abilities in exchange for deference.[16] Such practices threaten the position of the informal leader or leaders of the group. To avert this threat, informal leaders often seek to fortify their position by winning the loyalty or even affection of the others.[17] Positive sentiments toward the leader make deferring to his wishes and complying with his requests less onerous for others—not so much of a burden from which they will try to escape. These tendencies also reflect the dilemma posed at the beginning of this paper. Group members who are liked by associates experience pressures to become concerned with earning their respect, and those who command the respect of others are constrained to devote efforts to courting their affection.

[16] See Peter M. Blau, *The Dynamics of Bureaucracy*, rev. ed. (Chicago: University of Chicago Press, 1963), pp. 130–131 (see Chapter 9.)

[17] An alternative strategy may be for the leader to form a coalition with the most popular member of the group [see Philip E. Slater, "Role Differentiation in Small Groups," *American Sociological Review* 20 (1955), 300–310]. But leaders who remain unpopular are unlikely to maintain their position for long, particularly in cohesive groups [see George A. Theodorson, "The Relationship between Leadership and Popularity Roles in Small Groups," *American Sociological Review* 22 (1957), 58–67].

12. *Social Exchange*

Most gratifications of human beings have their source in the actions of other human beings. To experience excitement in sexual pleasure or contentment in love, to enjoy intellectual stimulation or relaxing diversion, to achieve professional recognition or a happy family life, to satisfy the lust for power or the need for acceptance—to attain any of these ends requires that one induce others to behave in certain ways. The fact that many rewards men seek can be obtained only in social interaction is what underlies the conceptualization of interaction as social exchange.

Basic Assumptions

The basic assumptions of the theory of social exchange are that men enter into new social associations because they expect doing so to be rewarding and that they continue relations with old associates and expand their interaction with them because they actually find doing so to be rewarding. Associating with another person may be intrinsically rewarding, as in love and in sociability, or it may bring rewards that are extrinsic to the association itself, such as advice from a colleague and help from a neighbor. In either

Originally published in 1968.

case, the desire to satisfy some want is assumed to underlie the association. As Simmel put it: "Social association refers to the widely varying forms that are generated as the diverse interests of individuals prompt them to develop social units in which they realize these interests, be they sensual or ideal, lasting or fleeting, conscious or unconscious, causally impelling or teleologically inducing."[1] To be sure, not all needs or interests are satisfied directly in social interaction, as hunger illustrates, and not all social interaction is primarily governed by an interest in rewards, since irrational forces and moral values also influence it. But many aspects of social life do reflect an interest in profiting from social interaction, and these are the focus of the theory of social exchange. Far from being confined to strictly rational conduct oriented toward material gain, however, the theory is intended to encompass all striving for rewarding social experiences, including the desire to further humanitarian ideals or spiritual values as well as the pursuit of personal advantage and emotional satisfaction.

The conception of social interaction as an exchange process follows logically from the assumption that men seek to obtain rewards in their social associations. If a man is attracted to others because he expects associating with them to be rewarding to himself, he will wish to associate with them in order to realize the anticipated rewards. Likewise, for them to engage in social interaction with him, they must also have an interest in doing so. But their interest in associating with him depends, according to the assumption, on their expectation that interacting with him will be rewarding to them. To implement his desire to associate with them, therefore, he must demonstrate to them that associating with him would benefit them. In brief, to reap the rewards expected from attractive potential associates, a man must impress them as a desirable associate by implicitly conveying the promise that social interaction with him will be rewarding for them too.

A person who derives benefits from associates is under obligation to reciprocate by supplying benefits to them in turn. People often go out of their way to do favors not only for friends but also for mere acquaintances and even for strangers, and they thereby create social obligations. The individual who fails to discharge his obligations and reciprocate in some form for benefits received robs others of incentives to continue to befriend him. Besides, such an individual is likely to be accused of ingratitude. This very accusation indicates that reciprocation for favors freely given is expected, and it serves as a social sanction to discourage men from forgetting their obligations. Gratitude, as Simmel noted, "establishes the bond of interaction, of the reciprocity of service and return service, even when they are not guaranteed by external coercion."[2]

[1] Georg Simmel, *Soziologie* (Berlin: Duncker & Humblot, 1908), p. 6 (my translation).

[2] Georg Simmel, *The Sociology of Georg Simmel* (Glencoe: Free Press, 1950), p. 387.

When obligations for benefits received are discharged by providing benefits in return, both parties profit from the association, and their exchange of rewarding experiences fortifies the social bond between them. A man who helps others earns their gratitude and appreciation, and he puts them into his debt, which promises to bring him further rewards in the future. These advantageous consequences of doing favors are undoubtedly a major reason why men frequently go to great trouble to help others and enjoy doing so. Giving is, indeed, more blessed than receiving, for having social credit is preferable to being socially indebted. To be sure, there are men and women who selflessly work for others without thought of reward and even without expecting gratitude, but these persons are virtually saints, and saints are rare. Other people also act unselfishly sometimes, but they require a more direct incentive for doing so, if it is only the social acknowledgment that they are unselfish. Such social approval is, of course, a very significant reward individuals seek in social interaction.

Defining Social Exchange

Exchange is not restricted to economic markets: social exchange is ubiquitous. Neighbors exchange help with chores; discussants, ideas; children, toys; friends, social support; politicians, concessions. The novice must meet the demands of the group to find acceptance in it. Colleagues exchange advice, and if the superior competence of one prevents the rest from reciprocating in kind for his advice, they discharge their obligation by paying their respect to his abilities and thus raising his status. Even the lover whose only apparent concern is to please his girl seeks to win her affection in return for his devotion. Groups and organized collectivities, too, are engaged in social exchange. For example, the medical profession receives exclusive license to practice medicine in return for assuming the obligation to meet the health needs of the community, or a political party makes concessions in its program to an interest group in return for support at the election booth.

Homans developed the first systematic theory that focuses on social behavior "as an exchange of activity, tangible or intangible, and more or less rewarding or costly, between at least two persons."[3] Of special concern to Homans are the psychological processes that motivate men to engage in exchange, and the psychological reductionism of the theory has been criticized by other sociologists. Homans was, however, by no means the first to call attention to social exchange. Anthropologists had earlier discussed the

[3] George C. Homans, *Social Behavior: Its Elementary Forms* (New York: Harcourt, 1961), p. 13.

significance and pervasiveness of the exchange of gifts and services in simpler societies. For instance, Mauss presented in 1925 a general analysis of gift exchange in such societies.[4] But anthropologists were not the first to observe this phenomenon either.

Given the ubiquity of social exchange, it is perhaps not surprising that social philosophers have discussed it ever since antiquity. Aristotle's *Nicomachean Ethics* (1162a34–1163a24) deals extensively with social exchange, which he distinguishes from economic exchange by saying that it "is not based on stated terms, but the gift or other service is given as to a friend, although the giver expects to receive an equivalent or greater return, as though it had not been a free gift but a loan." Many writers of the intervening centuries, such as La Rochefoucauld (1664), Mandeville (1714), and Adam Smith (1759), have been intrigued by the exchange nexus observable in much of social life.[5] More recently, a conception of exchange is implicit in Whyte's discussion of the obligations of a gang leader; it is explicit in Blau's analysis of consultation in a group of government officials; and it is an underlying element in Thibaut and Kelley's theory of dyads and triads.[6]

The pervasiveness of social exchange makes it tempting to explore the fruitfulness of the concept by trying to apply it to all social conduct. But the concept of exchange loses its distinctive meaning and becomes tautological if all behavior in interpersonal relations is subsumed under it. Although much of social conduct is oriented toward expected returns from others— indeed, more than we usually think—not all of it is.

The concept of exchange can be delimited with the aid of some illustrations of why a man gives money to others. First, he may do so because they stand in front of him with guns in a holdup. While this could be viewed as an exchange of his money for his life, it seems preferable to exclude the results of physical coercion from the definition of the term "exchange." Second, a man may donate money to charity because his conscience demands that he help the poor, without expecting gratitude in any form from them. While this could be viewed as an exchange of his money for the internal approval of his superego, here again it seems preferable to exclude conformity with internalized norms from what is meant by the term "exchange." Third, an uncontrollable impulse may compel a man to squander his money;

---

[4] Marcel Mauss, *The Gift* (Glencoe: Free Press, 1954).

[5] François La Rochefoucauld, *The Maxims* (London: Oxford University Press, 1940); Bernard Mandeville, *The Fable of the Bees* (Oxford: Clarendon, 1957); and Adam Smith, *The Theory of Moral Sentiments* (London: Bell, 1892).

[6] William F. Whyte, *Street Corner Society* (Chicago: University of Chicago Press, 1943); Peter M. Blau, *The Dynamic of Bureaucracy* (Chicago: University of Chicago Press, 1955), which is partly reprinted in Chapter 9; and John W. Thibaut and Harold H. Kelley, *The Social Psychology of Groups* (New York: Wiley, 1959).

such behavior motivated by irrational drives does not entail any exchange either. Finally, a man may give alms to beggars because he enjoys receiving their expressions of deferential gratitude and discontinue giving them money if they fail to react with such expressions. This last case illustrates social exchange, whereas the others delineate the boundaries of the concept. In brief, the concept of exchange refers to voluntary social actions that are contingent on rewarding reactions from others and that cease when these expected reactions are not forthcoming.

Social and Economic Exchange

The very term *social exchange* is designed to indicate that social interaction outside the economic sphere has important similarities with economic trans-actions. Above all, the expectation that benefits rendered will yield returns characterizes not only economic transactions but also social ones in which gifts and services appear to be freely bestowed. Moreover, the economic principle of eventually declining marginal utility applies to social exchange as well. Advice from an expert colleague is worth much to a man who needs help with a problem, but once the problem has been clarified, additional counsel is no longer as valuable. No matter how much two friends enjoy talking to each other, after a certain amount of time together they will become less eager to continue their discussions. The more a man concen-trates on obtaining a given social reward rather than others, the more the significance of the alternatives forgone will impinge upon his consciousness, making this reward relatively less significant. All of these examples manifest the marginal principle in social life.

There are, however, also important differences between social and strictly economic exchange. The most basic difference is that the obligations in-curred in social transactions are not clearly specified in advance. In eco-nomic transactions the exact obligations of both parties are simultaneously agreed upon: a given product is sold for a certain price. Both commodities may change hands at the time the agreement is reached, or a contract is made that stipulates precisely the obligations either party has to discharge in the future. In social exchange, by contrast, one party supplies benefits to another, and although there is a general expectation of reciprocation, the exact nature of the return is left unspecified. Indeed, it must remain un-specified, since any attempt to specify it in advance destroys the social meaning of the transaction by transforming it into a merely economic one. Doing a favor has an entirely different social significance from making a bargain. If a man does a service for another and then indicates what the return for this service should be, he reveals that he does not want to consider the service a favor but prefers to make it part of a bargain; he thereby insists on keeping the relationship businesslike and refuses to enter a more sociable association. If the recipient immediately states what return he will make, he reveals the same disinclination to enter a sociable relation.

Social exchange, therefore, entails supplying benefits that create diffuse future obligations. The nature of the return is invariably not stipulated in advance, cannot be bargained about, and must be left to the discretion of the one who makes it. Thus, if a person gives a dinner party, he expects his guests to reciprocate in the future. But he can hardly bargain with them about the kind of party to which they should invite him, though he expects them not simply to ask him for a quick lunch if he has given a formal dinner for them. Generally, a man expects some expressions of gratitude and appreciation for favors he has done for others, but he can neither bargain with them over how to reciprocate nor force them to reciprocate at all. Any attempt to assure repayment for one's generosity discloses that it was really not generosity in the first place. The distinctive significance of social obligations requires that they remain unspecific, and the fact that social, as distinguished from economic, commodities have no exact price facilitates meeting this requirement.

Since the recipient is the one who decides when and how to reciprocate for a favor, or whether to reciprocate at all, social exchange requires trusting others, whereas the immediate transfer of goods or the formal contract that can be enforced obviates such trust in economic exchange. Typically, however, social exchange relations evolve in a slow process, starting with minor transactions in which little trust is required because little risk is involved and in which both partners can prove their trustworthiness, enabling them to expand their relation and engage in major transactions. Thus, the process of social exchange leads to the trust required for it in a self-generating fashion. Indeed, creating trust seems to be a major function of social exchange, and special mechanisms exist that prolong the period of being under obligation and thereby strengthen bonds of indebtedness and trust. In the ceremonial gift exchange of the *kula* among the Trobriand Islanders, for example, returns for gifts received at one expedition can be made only at the next, many months later, and hasty reciprocation is generally condemned.[7] In our society, similarly, it is considered improper to reciprocate for a gift or return an invitation too quickly. The condemnation of posthaste reciprocation stimulates the growth of trust by constraining exchange partners to remain under obligation to each other for extended periods.

Social benefits are also less detachable from the source that supplies them than are economic commodities. At one extreme is the diffuse social support

[7] Bronislaw Malinowski, *Argonauts of the Western Pacific* (New York: Dutton, 1961), pp. 210–211.

derived in a love relationship, the significance of which depends entirely on the person who supplies it. At the other extreme are such economic goods as shares in a corporation or money, the value of which is completely independent of the supplier. Most social benefits are intermediate between these extremes, having a value that is extrinsic to the exchange relations in which they are supplied but having this value modified by the significance of these relations. A man who consults a colleague is interested in good advice, whatever its source, but his personal relation with the consultant makes it more or less easy for him to ask for assistance and to understand the advice he receives. (Although in the economic sphere the services of the friendly corner grocer may be preferable to those of the impersonal supermarket, such personal relations generally encroach less on economic than on social exchange.)

Economic exchange may be considered a special case of the general phenomenon of exchange, with social exchange being the excluded residual category. When goods and services are given a price in terms of a single medium of exchange, economic transactions are institutionalized. Their price defines the value of commodities independent of any particular exchange relations, making this value separable from that of other benefits accruing in these relations, and it permits exact specification of the obligations incurred in economic transactions. Economic institutions, such as the impersonal market, are designed to exclude other considerations than price from exchange decisions. Many social benefits have no price, either because they are never traded on an economic market, as is the case with social support, or because they are not so traded in this instance, as exemplified by the advice from a friend in contrast with that from a professional consultant. These are the benefits that enter into social exchange, which means that their supply is not contingent on stipulated returns, though there is a general expectation of reciprocation. The fact that the return is at the discretion of the one who makes it gives social exchange its fundamental significance for developing bonds of trust and friendship, and mechanisms such as the social norms prohibiting bargaining and hasty reciprocation tend to protect this discretion. The most important benefits involved in social exchange, furthermore, do not have any material value on which an exact price can be put at all, as exemplified by social approval and respect.

Exchange and Power

A paradox of social exchange is that it serves not only to establish bonds of friendship between peers but also to create status differences between persons. The *kula* exchange described by Malinowski, for instance, "provides every man . . . with a few friends near at hand, and with some friendly allies in the far-away, dangerous, foreign districts."[8] The potlatch of the Kwakiutl, on the other hand, is a system of giving away valuables in which "status in associations and clans, and rank of every kind, are determined by the war of property," as Mauss noted.[9] An important function of gift exchange in simple societies is, in the words of Lévi-Strauss, "to surpass a rival in generosity, to crush him if possible under future obligations which it is hoped he cannot meet, thus taking from him privileges, titles, rank, authority, and prestige."[10] In modern society, too, supplying benefits to others serves sometimes as an expression of friendship for them and at other times as a means for establishing superiority over them.

A person who gives others valuable gifts or renders them important services makes an implicit claim to superior status by obligating them. A benefactor is not a peer but a superior on whom others depend. If they return benefits that adequately discharge their obligations, they deny his claim to superiority, and if their returns are excessive, they make a counterclaim to superiority over him. Continuing mutual exchange strengthens bonds between equals. But if they fail to reciprocate with benefits that are as important to him as his are to them, they validate his claim to superior status. In simple societies the resulting differentiation of status seems to be rooted in the institutionalized significance of one-sided benefactions, while in modern societies it is typically due to unilateral dependence on a supplier of needs.

The recurrent unilateral supply of important benefits is a basic source of power. A man with resources at his disposal that enable him to meet other men's needs can attain power over them provided that four conditions are met, as suggested in a somewhat different formulation by Emerson.[11] First, they must not have resources that the benefactor needs, otherwise they can obtain what they want from him in direct exchange. Second, they must not be able to obtain the benefits he has to offer from an alternative source, which would make them independent of him. Third, they must be unable or unwilling to take what they want from him by force. Fourth, they must not undergo a change in values that enables them to do without the benefits they originally needed. If these four conditions are met, they have no choice but to comply with his wishes and submit to his power in order to obtain the needed benefits. The four alternatives to compliance are assumed to be

[8] *Ibid.*, p. 92.

[9] Mauss, *op. cit.*, p. 35.

[10] Claude Lévi-Strauss, "The Principle of Reciprocity," in Lewis A. Coser and Bernard Rosenberg, *Sociological Theory* (New York: Macmillan, 1964), p. 85.

[11] Richard M. Emerson, "Power-Dependence Relations," *American Sociological Review* 27 (1962), 31–41.

exhaustive; in their absence, the supply of important services inevitably generates power.

Under specifiable conditions, then, exchange processes give rise to a differentiation of power. A man who commands services others cannot do without, who is independent of any services at their command, and whose services they can neither obtain elsewhere nor take from him by force can attain power over them by making the satisfaction of their needs contingent on their compliance with his directives. By acceding to his wishes, they reciprocate for the benefits he supplies. The exchange balance is restored as unilateral services are compensated by an imbalance of power. The man who recurrently supplies needed services to others makes them dependent on and obligated to him, and their accumulated obligations constrain them to comply with his wishes lest he cease to supply further services. Their indebtedness to him takes the form of a pool of willing compliance on which he can draw at his discretion whenever it is to his interest to impose his will upon them.

The compliance of men with another's wishes and his consequent power, with which they repay him for services received, may appear to be no different from other social rewards that enter into exchange transactions. Yet there is a basic distinction between the differentiation of power and mutual social exchange, just as there is a basic distinction between social and economic exchange. The distinguishing criterion lies in the answer to the question, Who has discretion over the repayment? In economic exchange, neither party can exercise discretion over making the return, since the exact conditions of repayment are specified when the initial transaction takes place. In mutual social exchange, the nature and timing of the return are decided on by the one who makes it, that is, the recipient of the original benefit. In power relations, on the other hand, the return is made on the demand of the one to whom it is owed, that is, the supplier of the original benefit. Accumulated obligations and unilateral dependence transfer the power of discretion over the return from the debtor to the creditor and transform an exchange relation between peers into a power relation between superior and subordinate.

Secondary Exchange

The study of complex social structures must take into account the social forces that emerge in them and that are not observable in face-to-face interaction. To be sure, the concept of exchange itself refers to emergent properties of social relations that cannot be reduced to the psychological processes that motivate individual behavior. Exchange theory is concerned with the interaction processes that emerge as individuals seek rewards in social relations, whatever the psychological forces that lead each to want certain rewards. The differentiation of power in a collectivity gives rise to still other social processes in the complex structure, and these may be conceived of as constituting a secondary exchange that becomes superimposed upon the primary one characteristic of interpersonal relations.

Power makes it possible to enforce demands, and these demands are judged by those subject to the power in terms of social norms of fairness. The fair exchange of power by a ruler or ruling group elicits social approval, whereas unfair demands that are experienced as exploitative or oppressive evoke social disapproval. Thus, a secondary exchange—of fairness in the exercise of power in return for social approval by subordinates—emerges as power becomes differentiated in a collectivity. The social forces set into motion by this secondary exchange lead to legitimation and organization, on the one hand, and to opposition and change, on the other.

Collective approval of power legitimates that power. If people profit from the way they are governed by those in power and consider the demands made on them to be fully justified by the advantages the leadership provides, common feelings of loyalty are likely to develop as they communicate to one another their approval of the leadership. Their joint obligations to the leadership tend to find expression in social norms that make compliance with its directives mandatory. The collectivity of subordinates repays those in power for the benefits derived from their leadership by enforcing the leaders' directives as part of the enforcement of the collectivity's own social norms, that is, by legitimating the leadership's authority. For the distinctive characteristic of legitimate authority is that a superior's commands are obeyed, not because of his sanctioning power, but because of the normative pressure exercised among the subordinates themselves, particularly once these normative constraints have become institutionalized. Authority, in turn, promotes organization.

Collective disapproval of power engenders opposition. People who share the feeling of being exploited and oppressed by the excessive demands of those in power are inclined to communicate their grievances to each other. A wish to retaliate by striking down the oppressors is often kindled in these discussions, in which men receive social support for their aggressive feelings. An opposition ideology may be adopted that further justifies and reinforces the hostility against existing powers. It is out of such shared discontent that opposition movements develop: for example, that people band together to organize a union against their employer or a radical party against their government. Such opposition is an important catalyst of basic social change.

A prime determinant of social conduct is the institutionalized system of values in a society: the distinctive values that define the ingroup's identity, the common standards of morality and of achievement, the values that legitimate governing authority and organization, and the ideologies that sometimes foster opposition to those in power. Guided by these values, people often set aside immediate self-interest and considerations of exchange; for instance, the professional's standards may require him to help clients, disregarding the return he receives from them.

However, social values and norms largely set broad limits on conduct without prescribing it in detail. Within these limits, people are free to pursue their interest in social rewards, and considerations of exchange do apply. While social norms prohibit lying and cheating in order to get advice from another, they permit inducing him to give advice by expressing genuine respect or by any other means not specifically proscribed. Both common values and exchange principles influence social conduct, and neither may be neglected in studying it. Of particular importance in the analysis of social life is the modifying influence social values have on the rewards in which men are interested. Patriotic or opposition ideals often inspire men and women to make great material sacrifices, for these values make furthering the common cause more rewarding for them than material gain.

Exchange theory is most directly concerned with face-to-face relations, and thus it must be complemented by other theoretical principles that focus on complex structures with institutionalized values. However, even in the study of complex structures, exchange theory has something to contribute.

PART THREE

The Formal Structure of Organizations

Introductory Remarks

We turn now from inquiries into the social processes in work groups of organizations to inquiries into the interrelated characteristics of organizations themselves that compose their structures. All the papers in Part Three are based on research of the Comparative Organization Research Program, which has been supported for more than a decade, first at the University of Chicago and then at Columbia University, by successive grants from the National Science Foundation (GS-553, GS-1528, GS-27073, and GS-28646X), for which I am most grateful. To analyze the relationships between characteristics of organizations—for example, their size and their administrative hierarchy—requires data from many of them, which were usually collected by interviewing informants (senior managers) in all those of a certain type or a sample. Since the comparative approach obtains information of wider scope but less depth than a case study, substantive insights are gained from the analysis of the quantitative data rather than from intimate knowledge of informal relations and practices.

Having changed the procedure of data collection in my studies of the nature of organizations, I later also changed the procedure of data analysis. Both of these changes were prompted by my theoretical interests. To discern how some conditions in organizations influence others requires not only data on many cases, which a case study cannot supply, but also controlling various correlates of a given condition to abstract its particular influence on another, which is not feasible in contingency tables. This is the reason I switched from using contingency tables in earlier studies to regression analysis in later ones, having become familiar with regression procedures while collaborating with Otis Dudley Duncan on a research monograph. This methodological change entailed a cost as well as a gain, however. Whereas contingency tables make the interaction effects that reflect the distinctive significance of the constellations of several organizational attributes apparent, interaction effects are easily overlooked and must be specially searched for in regression analysis. But I think that the refined empirical and theoretical analysis regression procedures make possible is worth this cost of possibly failing to detect some interaction effects.

The first study conducted as part of the Comparative Organization Research Program, presented in Chapter 13, still uses contingency tables and centers attention on such interaction effects that reveal the combined impact of configurations of organizational attributes. It deals with the personnel agencies of state and local governments, based on data that had been collected by the Public Personnel Association and that its officers kindly made available for analysis, on which Heydebrand and Stauffer worked with me. Some of the conceptual problems examined already in this early paper, such as structural differentiation and the distinction between two forms of division of labor, became major foci of my later theoretical work. Most conclusions are highly inferential, partly owing to the questionable reliability of the precollected questionnaire data and the crudeness of the operational measures based on them, and at least one must be considered erroneous in the light of subsequent research, namely, that organizational size is unrelated to the proportionate size of the administrative component. Moreover, the higher-order interaction effects discussed, though interesting, are open to doubt. But several of the inferential conclusions have been confirmed by subsequent findings based on reliable data from several studies, for example, those pertaining to the relationships between professional qualifications and decentralization, size and administrative economies, and structural complexity and these economies. At the end, the paper points out the danger of making implicit assumptions of functional integration in organizational analysis, which is a more critical view of functional conceptions than that in earlier papers.

The study of 254 government finance departments in Chapter 14, for which original data were collected, illustrates continuities in organizational research, but it also reveals some discontinuity. On the one hand, it is explicitly designed to test generalizations inferred in the foregoing study with more reliable data from a different type of government agency, with emphasis on the relationship between professional qualifications and hierarchical authority, and it tests its own findings by confronting them with preliminary data from still another type of government agency. On the other hand, the procedure of analysis changes in the middle of the paper from comparing percentages, which is the method I used heretofore, to regression analysis, which is the one I have used since. Subsequent research has corroborated the generalizations derived here about the significance of qualifications for decentralization, the conditions that promote vertical differentiation into a multilevel hierarchy of authority, and the two contrasting shapes the organizational pyramid assumes. One interpretation advanced with tortuous reasoning must be rejected, however. There is no evidence that professional qualifications are part of a configuration of factors that fosters the development of multilevel hierarchies, and the finding in the paper that qualifications and levels are unrelated when other conditions are controlled should be taken at face value.

Chapter 15 turns to organizations of quite a different kind, namely, academic institutions, in order to inquire how conditions in universities and colleges and, particularly, the colleague climate influence the orientations of faculty members to research and to their institution. This somewhat revised section from a book is included to illustrate the significance of structural effects and a procedure for ascertaining them that does not have the limitations of the one employed in Chapter 4. (The operational measures are described in detail and all simple correlations between them are presented in the original source.) The question usually asked about the associations of faculty research with university salaries and appointment policies is whether they result simply from processes of selection or reflect actual influences of incentives that prompt faculty members to engage more in research than they would under different conditions. We shall see that there is a third possibility, to wit, that university salaries and policies affect the research climate in the academic community and thereby increase, or possibly decrease, the research involvement of its individual members. The significance of research in the academic stratification system creates the paradox that an academic institution enhances the loyalty it commands among its faculty by appointing faculty members whose research qualifications make them less loyal than are others.

To indicate how influences of their environmental context on organizations can be systematically investigated, another slightly revised section of a book, on which I collaborated with Schoenherr, is presented in Chapter 16. (In this case too, detailed descriptions of the variables and all their simple correlations are found in the original source.) The research deals with 1,201 public employment security offices, one of which was the subject of the case study twenty years earlier that is partly reported in Chapters 7 and 8. Effects of the organizational context as well as of the community environment on these offices are examined. The use of a product term to test an interpretation advanced exemplifies how the investigation of interaction effects can be incorporated into regression analysis. Three substantive problems studied are the influence of population heterogeneity in the community on the specialization among the various employment offices in it; the significance of the labor supply in the community for the personnel composition of an office; and the effects of agency size on the span of control of supervisors in local offices and thereby on the agency's administrative economies.

A deductive theory of the differentiated formal structure of organizations is formulated in Chapter 17, based on empirical regularities observed in employment security agencies and their subunits. The objective is to organize generalizations supported by extensive empirical data into a deductive system, in which two higher-order propositions logically imply nine lower-order ones. Concern is with the structure of differentiated positions in and components of organizations, not with goals or values, as it is in Parsons's theories, nor with psychological motives and individual behavior, as it is in Homans's. My understanding of deductive theorizing is much influenced by Braithwaite's exposition.[1] But he stresses the importance of unmeasured theoretical terms, and while I use such concepts—for instance, coordination, homogeneity, feedback—I do not explicitly include them in the propositions, which is a shortcoming of this formulation. Since this paper was published in 1970, a number of mathematical models based on the theory advanced have been developed by other authors.[2]

The final chapter applies the theory to quantitative data from several other types of organizations and elaborates it. Tests with six sets of data from five different types of organizations support the generalizations advanced. Whereas my endeavor in the original formulation was to construct a deductive system of propositions, all of which are directly supported by empirical

[1] R. B. Braithwaite, *Scientific Explanation* (Cambridge: University Press, 1968).

[2] See, for example: Norman P. Hummon, "A Mathematical Theory of Differentiation in Organizations," *American Sociological Review* 36 (1971), 297–303: Marshall W. Meyer, "Some Constraints in Analyzing Data on Organizational Structures: A Comment on Blau's Paper," *American Sociological Review* 36 (9171), 294–297; Bruce H. Mayhew *et al.*, "System Size and Structural Differentiation in Military Organizations: Testing a Harmonic Series Model of the Division of Labor," *American Journal of Sociology* 77, No. 4 (1972), 750–765; Bruce H. Mayhew *et al.*, "System Size and Structural Differentiation in Formal Organizations: A Baseline Generator for Two Major Theoretical Propositions," *American Sociological Review* 37 (1972), 629–633; Richard I. Savage, "Sociology Wants Mathematics," Florida State University Statistics Report M 274 (January 1973); Kenneth Land, "The Structure of Work Organizations" (chapter in forthcoming book); David D. McFarland, "A Dynamic Theory of the Growth and Structure of Organizations" (in press; manuscript, September 1972); and David D. McFarland, "Organizational Structure as Generated by Branching Process" (in press; manuscript, February 1973).

evidence, the reformulation here introduces theoretical assumptions that go beyond the empirical data and from which even the most basic earlier generalizations are deducible. Inasmuch as I introduce more than one assumption to explain why increasing organizational size generates differentiation, the question remains which of these, if any, further research will corroborate as the probably valid theoretical explanation.[3] It should also be pointed out that the concluding concise formulation of the theory is provisional and in need of further explication and refinement. A Durkheimian social realism, which contrasts with Homans's methodological individualism,[4] continues to characterize my theoretical orientation.

[3] For a preliminary attempt to use the data on universities and colleges to discriminate among these assumptions, see Peter M. Blau, *The Organization of Academic Work* (New York: Wiley, 1973), pp. 258–270.

[4] George C. Homans, *The Nature of Social Science* (New York: Harbinger, 1967).

13. The Structure of Small Bureaucracies

IN COLLABORATION WITH WOLF V. HEYDEBRAND AND ROBERT E. STAUFFER

Why does Weber's analysis of bureaucratic structure continue to be regarded as the classic on the subject half a century after it was written, despite the many, often justified, criticisms that have been directed against it? Does this merely reflect a romantic regard for one of the great old men of social theory? We think not. Weber's great contribution is that he provided a framework for a systematic theory of formal organization; the fact that his analysis has certain limitations does not detract from this important achievement.

A theory of bureaucratic structure should meet two basic requirements. Above all, it must be concerned with the interdependence among structural attributes of complex organizations and not take these characteristics of the structure as given and merely examine the decisions or behavior of individuals in the context of complex organizations. The focus of Weber's theory is precisely on this interdependence among various characteristics of the

Originally published in 1966.

organizations themselves. In addition, a theory of bureaucracy should account for the connections between organizational attributes by analyzing the social processes that have produced these connections. It is not enough, for example, to indicate, as Weber did, that impersonal authority in which personnel can readily be replaced and the use of formalized procedures tend to occur together in bureaucracies, we would also like to know what processes are responsible for this joint occurrence. Gouldner's analysis of managerial succession, though based on a single case, vividly shows how the exigencies of the role of a new manager constrain him to resort to formalized procedures, thereby helping to explain why recurrent replacement of personnel tends to be associated with formalized methods of operation.[1]

Generally the numerous case studies of organizations that have been carried out in recent decades have complemented Weber's analysis by investigating the social processes within bureaucracies, particularly the informal processes and their significance for the formal organization. At the same time, however, the focus of these studies on informal relations and practices in *one* organization has had the result that investigators lost sight of the central problem of bureaucratic theory, namely, what the interrelations between various structural attributes of formal organizations are. This problem can only be studied by comparing different organizations and not through the intensive analysis of a single case.

At the core of Weber's theory, in contrast, are the structural attributes of bureaucracy and their relationships, in the narrow sense of "structural" as referring to the differentiation of social positions along various lines. At the outset, Weber stresses that responsibilities in a bureaucracy "are distributed in a fixed way as official duties,"[2] elaborating later that this involves a systematic division of labor and often a high degree of specialization. Complementing this specialization is the requirement of "thorough and expert training,"[3] which means that many positions in the organization are occupied by professionally or technically qualified specialists. The formal status hierarchy is a third fundamental characteristic of bureaucracy: "The principle of hierarchical office authority is found in all bureaucratic structures."[4] Finally, the emphasis upon written communication and official documents in bureaucracies makes the employment of many clerks necessary, "a staff of subaltern officials and scribes of all sorts."[5]

---

[1] Alvin W. Gouldner, *Patterns of Industrial Bureaucracy* (Glencoe: Free Press, 1954), pp. 45–101.

[2] From *Max Weber*: *Essays in Sociology* (New York: Oxford University Press, 1956), p. 196.

[3] *Ibid.*, p. 198.

[4] *Ibid.*, p. 197.

[5] *Loc. cit.*

We propose to return to Weber's approach in this paper and to analyze the interrelations among these four structural attributes of bureaucracy and their implications for operations—the division of labor, professionalization, the hierarchy of authority, and the administrative staff of clerks. To be sure, Weber's analysis is not confined to these four but encompasses other formal characteristics of organizations that are not structural in the narrow sense of referring to aspects of status differentiations,[6] such as the rules governing operations, the stable careers of officials, and the impersonal orientation that prevails in bureaucratic relations. In this study, however, attention is restricted to the four organizational attributes indicated, and two others— size and an effect criterion. The investigation is based on data from about 150 public personnel agencies, which represent most of the larger organizations of this type in North America.

Method

The systematic study of bureaucratic structure necessitates a method of inquiry adapted to the purpose as well as an appropriate theoretical approach. The variables under investigation must be structural characteristics *of* the bureaucracies themselves, such as a status distribution in the organization, rather than merely attitudes or behaviors of the individuals *in* these bureaucracies. Moreover, the research design must involve the systematic comparison of a fairly large number of organizations, and not just a few cases assumed to be typical, in order to determine how variations in some characteristics affect variations in others. The important point is that such large-scale comparisons are required not only to test theoretical propositions once they have been formulated, but also initially to formulate and refine the theory.

When Weber portrayed a typical bureaucracy in bold strokes, on the basis of comparative analysis on a wide historical scale, he surely did not intend to suggest, as a simplistic interpretation sometimes assumes, that all the characteristics he outlined are highly correlated under all conditions. On the contrary, the complex interdependencies he traces clearly imply that the relationships between any two characteristics of bureaucracies often depend on and are modified by a third factor or even by a combination of several others. Our empirical data strongly confirm this crucial insight that the various aspects of bureaucratic structure interact in their effects on each other. In other words, it is usually not possible to state simply what the relationship between two organizational attributes is, because it depends on one or more other attributes. We suspect that such higher-order interaction

[6] The term *status* is used here in its broader sense as complementary to role and synonymous with social position, not in the narrower sense that restricts it to hierarchical distinctions in social position.

effects are a fundamental characteristic of social structures. In any case, given these complex interrelations in bureaucracies, the next step in refining the theory of formal organization is to specify the conditions under which different relationships hold. Such specification requires the quantitative analysis of concomitant variations in a fairly large number of cases.

The organizations selected for the study are public personnel agencies, which are the executive agencies of the civil service commissions that administer the personnel policies of state and local governments. The sample consists of all members of the Public Personnel Association who returned a questionnaire about their agency in a survey administered by the Association in 1958.[7] Returns were received from nearly half the member agencies (252 of 528). Althought he sample is not representative, it includes most of the larger public personnel agencies in the United States and some in Canada,[8] with the bias of self-selection working against smaller agencies and those least identified with the merit principles of civil service. All but seven of the fifty state agencies are in the sample, as are most of the agencies of the largest American cities, some of counties, and a few miscellaneous agencies, such as that of the TVA.

Public personnel agencies are small bureaucracies. Nearly two-fifths of the 252 organizations represented had a total staff of fewer than five persons. These were excluded from the investigation, since the status distribution measures used have little validity if constructed on such a small base. This leaves 156 cases for analysis, with a slightly lower total in most tables because of no answers. Even after these tiny bureaucracies have been eliminated, the median staff of the rest is only between sixteen and seventeen persons, and a mere seventeen agencies have a staff of more than 100. Agencies are divided into small ones with a staff of less than twenty (but at least five) and larger ones with a staff of twenty or more. This division close to the median separates agencies all of whose members can easily have frequent face-to-face contact from those whose somewhat larger size makes it unlikely that every member knows all others well.[9]

[7] These data were kindly made available to us for statistical analysis by Kenneth O. Warner and Keith Ocheltree, to whom we are indebted not only for doing so but also for helpful advice. We also gratefully acknowledge grant GS-553 from the National Science Foundation, which supports the Comparative Organization Research Program, whose first report this paper is.

[8] There are only fourteen Canadian cases, four provincial and ten city agencies. Since tabulations showed that these do not essentially differ from the corresponding agencies in the United States, they have not been eliminated from the analysis in order to maximize the number of cases. The U.S. Civil Service Commission and its Canadian counterpart were excluded.

[9] Theodore Caplow specifies twenty members as the upper limit of a primary group, "in which each member interacts with every other member"; "Organizational Size," *Administrative Science Quarterly* 1 (1957), p. 486.

The six variables under consideration are size, four attributes of internal structure, and a weighted measure of operating cost. The internal structure can be considered to have two major dimensions: specialization, which is a mechanism to deal with task complexity; and bureaucratic coordination, which is a mechanism to deal with the organizational complexity introduced by specialization. Specialization can be subdivided into the division of labor in the organization and the degree of professionalization of its staff. Two mechanisms of bureaucratic coordination are the hierarchy of managerial authority and the administrative apparatus.

The following are the operational measures for these four structural attributes—two aspects of specialization and two kinds of coordinating mechanism:

1. *Division of Labor:* the number of distinct occupational titles pertaining to the nonclerical staff, not counting those indicative of status differences within a specialty rather than different specialties.[10] Dichotomized between three and four specialties.[11]

2. *Professionalization:* the proportion of the operating staff (excluding managers as well as clerks) who are required to have, at least, a college degree with a specified major. Dichotomized at 50 per cent.[12]

[10] Thus, "Personnel Technician I" and "Personnel Technical II" were counted as one specialty. Since the absolute number of occupational titles is closely related to size, the question arises whether a relative index of the division of labor would not be preferable to an absolute one. But such a relative index—the ratio of occupational positions to size of staff—is just as much negatively associated with size as the absolute index is positively associated with it.

[11] In this case, the basic procedure for determining the cutting points of the dichotomies was modified for substantive reasons. The basic criterion for dichotomizing was to come as close to the median as the initial categories on the IBM cards permitted. Since the middle category was sometimes fairly large, and since elimination of the agencies with a staff of under five changed the proportions, the numbers of cases in the two classes of the dichotomy are often not the same. Two exceptions to the use of this criterion were made for conceptual reasons. Division of labor was dichotomized between three and four to avoid calling agencies with only three different positions highly differentiated, as would be required if the median were used, and professionalization was dichotomized above the median lest agencies with a single professional on the operating staff be defined as highly professionalized. These decisions about cutting points were made before the substantive analysis of cross-tabulations was carried out.

[12] Although agencies were divided on the basis of whether less than 50, or 50 per cent or more, of the operating staff are required to have the specified professional qualifications, the differences are actually more extreme, since the distribution is bimodal. In more than four-fifths of the less professionalized agencies there are no professional requirements for any position, and in more than three-quarters of the professionalized ones professional qualifications are required of the entire staff. The reason for excluding managerial personnel from this index is to assure that no relationship between professionalization and management hierarchy can be due to lack of independence of the two measures. Managers in professionalized agencies generally are also required to meet professional qualifications.

3. *Managerial Hierarchy:* the ratio of men in managerial to those in non-supervisory positions among the nonclerical staff, excluding those for whom neither alternative was indicated.[13] Dichotomized at one to three.[14]

4. *Administrative Apparatus:* the proportion of clerks among the total staff.[15] Dichotomized at 60 per cent.

A weighted measure of cost is employed to investigate one of the implications of the various aspects of administrative structure for operations. The index of operating costs is the ratio of the salary budget of the personnel agency itself to the total payroll for the entire civil service personnel under its jurisdiction—specifically, whether this ratio exceeds one-half of one per cent or not. This measure adjusts cost not only to the magnitude of the agency's operations but also to regional variations in standard of living. It even takes into account, to some extent, that it is more difficult to administer highly qualified than unskilled personnel, since such differences are reflected in the denominator. While this is an adjusted measure of operating costs, it is not a reliable measure of efficiency, inasmuch as it does not take into account either the scope of personnel services provided or the quality of performance.

Although the organizations under investigation are not a representative sample of a larger universe, statistical tests have been performed to furnish an external criterion for deciding whether or not to place some confidence in the complex relationships observed.[16] The use of these tests rests on the assumption that a given pattern of differences observed would be unlikely to occur by chance in a sample drawn from a hypothetical universe of similar organizations.

[13] Actually, the nonclerical personnel had been classified by respondents into four categories—deputy directors, heads of major divisions, journeymen, and apprentices. The index is the ratio of the first two to the last two. Positions that were not classified by respondents might be staff consultants or ambiguous cases.

[14] Since this excludes clerks, it corresponds to considerably more than three subordinates per manager—probably about seven.

[15] This is the only index that uses total staff in the denominator. The index provides a narrow operational definition of administrative staff; a wider one would include other positions responsible for maintaining the organization, such as bookkeepers.

[16] The statistic developed by Leo A. Goodman has been used; "Modifications of the Dorn-Stouffer-Tibbits Method for 'Testing the Significance of Comparisons in Sociological Data'," *American Journal of Sociology* 66 (1961), 355–363. In a few cases, the criterion for the assumption of a normal distribution that each cell contain at least five observations was not met; interpretation there should proceed with caution. We gratefully acknowledge John Wiorkowski's assistance in performing the statistical tests, and Leo Goodman's advice.

Professionalization and Managerial Authority

Professional qualifications undoubtedly lessen the need for close supervision, other things being equal. We had expected therefore that the ratio of managers to operating officials would not be as high in organizations with a professional staff as in those where most of the staff is not required to meet professional qualifications. The reasoning was that a high managerial ratio implies a narrow span of control, with few subordinates per manager, and such a narrow span of control is often assumed to be associated with close supervision. Contrary to expectations, however, professionalized public personnel agencies are more likely to have a high ratio of managers than other agencies under most conditions, though not under all. Unless one is willing to believe that professionals are being more closely supervised than employees with less training, which seems improbable, this finding calls for a reappraisal of the significance of the managerial ratio. Instead of making a priori assumptions about closeness of supervision, let us start with the attributes of bureaucratic structure this ratio directly reflects, and proceed with the analysis before drawing inferences that are consistent with the data.

The managerial ratio indicates whether the administrative authority rooted in formal status in the hierarchy is centralized in the hands of relatively few officials or distributed among a larger number. To be sure, how centralized actual decision making is in the organization depends not only on the degree of centralization in the formal hierarchy but also on other conditions, such as the delegation of responsibilities by superiors to subordinates. No information is available on these conditions, nor on closeness of supervision. The ratio singles out for attention an attribute of the formal status structure, not an aspect of operations, specifically, the extent to which authority positions are centralized rather than being more widely dispersed in an organization.[17]

A centralized hierarchy of managerial authority is least likely to develop in small professionalized organizations, as Table 13.1 shows. In small agencies with a professional staff, in other words, the probability of a high ratio of managers to subordinates is greatest. Only 16 per cent of these agencies have a centralized management (low ratio), whereas about two-fifths of the less-professionalized small and of either kind of larger agencies do. Professionalization and centralization of authority are inversely related in smaller agencies but not in larger ones. Further analysis reveals, however,

---

[17] The span of control is also indicative of the formal status hierarchy, and not of supervisory practice. The average span of control depends on the number of levels in the hierarchy as well as on the ratio of managers. No data on the number of levels are available. Though the ratio is not equivalent to the average span of control, the two are undoubtedly highly correlated, because variations in number of levels cannot be very large among organizations few of which have a staff of more than 100.

Table 13.1 Per Cent with Centralized Hierarchy* by Size and Professionalization

Professionalization***	Small Agencies	Large Agencies**
Low	38(61)	41(32)
High	16(31)	43(20)

Note: The difference in the left column is significant (at the 0.05 level).

* The managerial hierarchy is *centralized* when the ratio of non-clerical personnel in managerial positions to non-clerical personnel is non-supervisory positions, excluding those listed as neither, is less than one to three; it is *dispersed* when the ratio is one to three or more.

** *Small agencies* have a total staff of less than 20 (but five or more); *large agencies* have a total staff of 20 or more.

*** Professionalization is *low* when the proportion of the operating staff (excluding managers as well as clerks) who are required to have, at least, a college degree with a specified major, is less than 50 per cent; *high* when it is 50 per cent or more.

that these two factors are also inversely related in larger agencies provided that certain conditions are met.

Table 13.2 indicates that a centralized hierarchy of official authority is less prevalent in professional than in other organizations in three of the four comparisons, the only exception being those larger agencies that have a low ratio of administrative personnel. Professionalization reduces the likelihood

Table 13.2 Per Cent with Centralized Hierarchy by Size, Professionalization, and Administrative Apparatus

	Small Agencies		Large Agencies	
	Administrative Apparatus[a]		Administrative Apparatus[a]	
Professionalization	Low	High	Low	High
Low	35(31)	40(30)	29(17)	53(15)
High	11(19)	25(12)	47(15)	38(13)
Difference	−24	−15	+18	−15

Note: The difference between differences in cols. 1 and 3 is significant (at the 0.05 level); that between cols. 2 and 4 is not.

[a] The administrative apparatus ratio is *low* when the proportion of clerks among the total staff is less than 60 per cent; *high* when it is 60 per cent or more.

of centralization of authority not only in smaller agencies, whatever the administrative ratio (-24, -15), but also in larger ones if the administrative ratio is high (-15), though not if it is low ($+18$). The sharpest contrast is between the nineteen smaller professionalized agencies with a low administrative ratio, a mere 11 per cent of which have a centralized hierarchy, and the fifteen larger professionalized agencies with a high administrative ratio, 53 per cent of which do. The two questions to be answered are, first, why the negative relationship prevails in most situations and, second, what accounts for the deviant case. The answers suggested are admittedly post hoc interpretations.

Professional training may be assumed to make a person more self-directing in his work. It was on the basis of this assumption that we had expected— incorrectly, as it turned out—that agencies with a professional staff would have a low ratio of managers. Identification with professional standards, however, tends to make a man working in an organization not only less dependent on direct supervision but also more aware of the broader implications of his job and more interested in seeing to it that agency policies and operations do not violate professional principles. Such a person is likely to detect problems that escape the notice of one without professional qualifications and to want to have administrative procedures modified to remedy these problems. The professional's informed concern with helping shape agency procedures and policies is at the root of the recurrent conflict between professionals and administrators, but it is simultaneously a resource available to the organization for improving operations.

Management cannot give professionals free rein, since there is often a genuine conflict between professional and administrative considerations. Yet if management seriously frustrates professionals in the exercise of their responsibilities, it not only courts the danger of dissatisfactions and defections from the organization but also fails to take advantage of an important resource at its disposal, which includes the professional's interest in perfecting operations as well as his expert knowledge. For management to channel the initiative of professionals into administrative improvements instead of stifling it requires frequent contact and close collaboration between managers and professionals. Though conflicts between professional and administrative concerns are inevitable, the best chance for advantageous compromise is probably provided by extensive communication between the officials responsible for professional and those responsible for administrative decisions. The higher the ratio of managers, with few subordinates for each, the greater are the opportunities for frequent discussions in which problems can be explored, dissatisfactions expressed, and conflicts reconciled.

A high managerial ratio, which implies a dispersed management, promotes extensive vertical communication in the hierarchy of authority. It facilitates downward communication, which makes it easier for superiors to direct the work of subordinates and check up on them. But it also facilitates upward communication, which makes it easier for subordinates to convey information to superiors and to influence administrative decisions. Our original expectation had exclusively focused on the significance of a high managerial ratio for downward communication, whereas the data suggest that its significance for upward communication is the more crucial here. To encourage upward communication by appointing a high proportion of managers is particularly important for organizations with a professional staff, because only by doing so can they take full advantage of the contributions professionals are capable of making.

Professionalization and centralization of authority appear to be alternative methods for organizing responsibilities. Since professional qualifications enhance a man's ability to see the implication of his work and place it into a wider context, professionals can contribute to coordination in an organization; the task of management is to draw upon these contributions and fit them into the administrative framework. This requires a sufficient number of managers to work in close collaboration with the professional staff. If the staff lacks professional training, on the other hand, it can make only limited contributions to coordination, and the task of management is, consequently, to effect coordination largely on its own rather than to collaborate with operating officials for this purpose. A hierarchy in which authority is concentrated in the hands of relatively few managers serves distinctive functions in such a situation, because it makes it possible to achieve coordination through centralized planning by a small headquarters group and then issuing pertinent directives to the staff. The limitations on discretion centralized planning and direction impose upon the staff are undoubtedly more objectionable to professionals than to men whose lack of expertness would make it hard for them to exercise much discretion. To be sure, a centralized structure makes it more difficult for the relatively few managers to keep in close touch with operating officials and supervise them closely. But modern administration has devised substitute methods for obtaining information on operations and checking on the work of subordinates that do not require frequent direct contact, such as detailed statistical records of performance.[18]

[18] One might even speculate whether the very fact that a low ratio of managers facilitates close supervision does not make it particularly *inappropriate* for a nonprofessional staff. The experienced manager in charge of a nonprofessional staff is more likely to be tempted to supervise too closely if conditions permit than is the manager in charge of expert professionals. Since a low ratio facilitates close supervision (which research shows to be detrimental to performance), and since the inclination to resort to close supervision is greatest if the staff is not highly skilled, a low ratio of managers may be most dysfunctional for operations with an unskilled staff.

In the absence of a professionally trained staff, according to these considerations, a centralized hierarchy of authority has important advantages for an organization and comparatively few disadvantages. Its major advantage is that it can meet the need for coordination through centralized planning. In a relatively large organization, however, this requires an adequate administrative apparatus of clerks to maintain the channels of communication that are essential for coordination from a central headquarters. This interpretation brings us back to the findings in Table 13.2, because it suggests why a centralized hierarchy is more likely to develop in agencies that are not professionalized than in professionalized ones if they are small or if they are larger and have a high administrative ratio, and why this is not the case for larger agencies with a low administrative ratio. Professionalization as well as centralization, in turn, depend on the division of labor.

Structural Differentiation

Expansion in size has a pronounced impact on the structural differentiation of functional specialties within the organization. An advanced division of labor with four or more occupational specialties is found in only 14 per cent of the ninety-two small public personnel agencies but in 66 per cent of the sixty-two larger ones. A minimum size is virtually required for the development of several distinct functional positions in an organization.[19] In contrast to this strong influence on the division of labor, size exerts little influence on the three other bureaucratic attributes under investigation. Thus, a high administrative ratio is as likely to be found in larger agencies as in small ones.[20] There is no significant difference between larger and small agencies, moreover, either in the likelihood that their staff is professionalized or in the likelihood that their authority structure is centralized. Although size has no

[19] In the extreme case, such a relationship is a mathematical necessity—agencies of less than four persons could not possibly have four or more positions—but none of the agencies had a staff of less than five.

[20] Whereas other studies of organizations found that the administrative ratio declines with size, this is the case only after a certain size has been reached. This is probably the reason for the difference in findings—since our data are primarily based on fairly small organizations. See Seymour Melman, "The Rise of Administrative Overhead in the Manufacturing Industries of the United States, 1899–1947," *Oxford Economic Papers* 3 (1951), 89–90; Reinhard Bendix, *Work and Authority in Industry* (New York: Wiley, 1956), 221–222; Theodore R. Anderson and Seymour Warkov, "Organizational Size and Functional Complexity," *American Sociological Review* 26 (1961), 23–28; and Wolf H. Heydebrand, "Bureaucracy in Hospitals; An Analysis of Complexity and Coordination in Formal Organizations," (unpublished Ph.D. dissertation, Department of Sociology, University of Chicago, 1965).

Table 13.3 Per Cent with Centralized Hierarchy by Professionalization and Division of Labor

Division of Labor[a]	Professionalization	
	Low	High
Rudimentary	33(64)	31(36)
Advanced	50(28)	26(23)

Note: The difference in the left column is not significant at the 0.05 level.

[a] The division of labor is *advanced* when the non-clerical staff represents four or more occupational specialties; *rudimentary* when it represents less than four.

direct effect on these factors, it has distinct indirect effects that modify their interrelations and condition their significance for operations.

Structural differentiation, which is typically a consequence of expanding size, in turn affects other characteristics of the organization. It has implications for professionalization and for centralization: the pattern revealed by the resulting relationships supports the previous conclusion that professionalization and centralization are alternative modes of organization, the existence of one being somewhat incompatible with that of the other. The division of labor promotes either professionalization or centralization but not both, and whether it promotes the one depends on the absence of the other. Thus, the chances that the hierarchy of authority becomes centralized increase with advances in the division of labor only if the staff is not professional, and not at all if it is professional, as Table 13.3 shows. About one-third of the agencies with a rudimentary division of labor have a centralized structure, whatever the degree of professionalization, and even slightly fewer of the more differentiated agencies that are professionalized, compared to one-half of the more differentiated agencies that are not professionalized.[21] In brief, task differentiation seems to further the development of a centralized hierarchy of authority unless the organization is professionalized.

The conclusion that the influence of the division of labor on the management hierarchy depends on professionalization is, however, suspect. The relationship in Table 13.3 is not significant, and size has not been controlled, although it is known to have a strong impact on the division of labor and some bearing on the two other variables. But controlling for size does not destroy the pattern observed; on the contrary, it accentuates it. In both

[21] The pattern is complementary when percentages for the data in Table 13.3 are computed with professionalization as the dependent variable. Differentiation tends to promote professionalization in the absence of centralization but not when it is present.

Table 13.4　Per Cent with Centralized Hierarchy by Size, Division of Labor, and Professionalization

	Small Agencies		Large Agencies	
	Professionalization		Professionalization	
Division of Labor	Low	High	Low	High
Rudimentary	36(53)	19(26)	18(11)	60(10)
Advanced	50(8)	0(5)	50(20)	33(18)
Difference	+14	−19	+32	−27

Note: The difference between the pooled differences in cols. 1 and 3 and those in cols. 2 and 4 is significant at the 0.05 level (One-half observation, or 10 per cent, was substituted for the zero cell, because variance cannot be estimated by the method used for cells with zero observations.)

smaller and larger agencies, as Table 13.4 indicates, an intensification of the division of labor raises the likelihood of the emergence of a centralized hierarchy if the staff is not professionalized, but it actually lessens this likelihood if it is professionalized; these differences are statistically significant. When the staff lacks professional qualifications, the proportion of centralized hierarchies *increases* with growing task differentiation in smaller agencies (+14) as well as in larger ones (+32). When the staff meets professional requirements, in contrast, the proportion of centralized hierarchies *decreases* with growing task differentiation in both smaller (−19) and larger (−27) agencies. Holding size constant magnifies the interaction effect of differentiation and professionalization on centralization. This confirms the conclusion that structural differentiation promotes the emergence of a centralized hierarchy only in the absence of professionalization; in its presence, it does not and may even have the opposite effect.

The division of labor in an organization can take two entirely different forms. On the one hand, it may involve the subdivision of the overall task of the organization into specialized responsibilities that permit, and indeed require, greater utilization of expert specialists. This development is illustrated by the difference between a hospital medical staff consisting of general practitioners and one composed primarily of specialists. On the other hand, the division of labor may entail the fragmentation of responsibilities into simple assignments with routine duties that require minimal skills. The assembly line factory is an extreme example of this tendency. Since many professionals are essential in the one case while few are needed in the other, the extent of professionalization in a public personnel agency indicates which one of these two forms the division of labor has taken. Specialized differentiation of tasks (an advanced division of labor in combination with professionalization) and routinized differentiation of tasks (an advanced division of labor in the absence of professionalization) pose different administrative problems.

Routinized differentiation, which minimizes the need for professional experts, maximizes the need for managerial coordination. Centralized planning and direction are effective means for coordinating fragmented duties performed by a relatively untrained staff. Routinized differentiation accordingly enhances the likelihood of the development of a centralized authority structure.[22] Specialized differentiation does not pose the same problem of coordination for management as routinized differentiation does, because tasks are not as fragmented, because professionals are qualified to assume wider responsibilities, and because management gains advantages from eliciting their contributions to coordination instead of imposing directives from a central headquarters on them. A centralized management has great disadvantages in a professionalized organization, as has been noted. Hence, specialized differentiation does not enhance the likelihood of the development of a centralized hierarchy.

In sum, structural differentiation in public personnel agencies sometimes is accompanied by greater professionalization of the staff and sometimes by greater centralization of authority, and whether it leads to the elaboration of one depends in part on the absence of the other of these two alternative modes of organizing responsibilities. An advancing division of labor that is associated with professionalization raises entirely different administrative problems from one that is not. The former makes adequate *upward* communication especially important, without which management is deprived of some of the contributions the professional staff can make. To encourage upward communication requires a high ratio of managers dispersed throughout the organization. The subdivision of labor among a staff lacking professional qualifications, in contrast, makes adequate *downward* communication particularly important, without which the coordination of diverse simple routines cannot be accomplished. A centralized hierarchy of authority facilitates such coordination, provided that it is complemented in organiza-

---

[22] The conclusion that routinized differentiation creates a need for centralization, and the earlier conclusion that centralization in larger agencies depends on an adequate administrative staff, together imply that routinized differentiation should lead to the expansion of the administrative apparatus. The data give some support to this inference. The proportion of agencies with a high administrative ratio increases with growing differentiation neither in small agencies nor in larger professionalized ones but only in larger agencies lacking professionalization, from 18 per cent of eleven cases to 60 per cent of twenty. This difference barely fails to reach the conventional level of statistical significance, being significant at the 0.07 level.

tions beyond a minimum size by a sufficient administrative staff of clerks to maintain the essential lines of communication. These considerations suggest that, in an organization, a high ratio of managers is of special importance for upward communication and a high ratio of clerks for downward communication.

Implications for Operating Costs

How do various conditions in the bureaucratic structure affect operating costs? To be sure, it would be of great interest to examine the significance of differences in the administrative structure for other aspects of operations as well as cost, but the data necessary for this purpose are not available. There is no denying the importance of budgetary considerations in government agencies and most other formal organizations; the study of operating costs is consequently a good starting point for clarifying the implications of bureaucratic attributes for operations. The weighted measure of operating costs, to repeat, is whether or not the salary budget of the public personnel agency exceeds one-half of one per cent of the total salary budget for the civil servants under its jurisdiction.

Structural differentiation, on the whole, lowers operating costs. Whereas exactly one-half of the ninety-eight agencies with a rudimentary division of labor operate at relatively high costs, 35 per cent of the fifty-four with an advanced division of labor do. Since larger agencies also operate on the average at lower costs than smaller ones, and since size and the division of labor are strongly related, the question arises whether task differentiation or operating on a large scale actually produces these cost reductions. The answer is that both lead to economies, as Table 13.5 reveals, but their effects are not cumulative. Small undifferentiated agencies are most likely to operate at high costs. Either an increase in differentiation or an increase in size tends to reduce operating costs, but the occurrence of both does not reduce them

Table 13.5   Per Cent with High Costs* by Size and Division of Labor

Division of Labor	Small Agencies	Large Agencies
Rudimentary	55(77)	33(21)
Advanced	23(13)	39(41)

Note: The difference in the left columns is significant at the 0.05 level.

* Agencies in which the salary budget of the agency itself is 0.5 per cent or more of the total payroll for entire civil service personnel the agency administers.

further. Although task differentiation, which usually accompanies growth, effects economies, it simultaneously destroys the economic advantage that operating on a large scale otherwise has (the right-hand value is the lower one in the first but not in the second row of the table).

The significance of professionalization for operating costs closely parallels that of the division of labor. Table 13.6 shows that operations are most likely to be costly in small agencies with few professionals. Professionalization greatly lessens the likelihood of high costs in small organizations (from 60 to 31 per cent), though only there, just as is case for differentiation. The finding that professionals, despite the higher salaries they command, lower the cost of operations in small agencies implies that they make contributions to administrative efficiency—apart from those their expert skills make to performance quality, which are not reflected in the cost measure. Operating on a larger scale without professionals, however, also lessens the likelihood of high costs (from 60 to 28 per cent), and professionalization in larger organizations has, if anything, a detrimental effect on operating economy, in sharp contrast to its beneficial effect in small organizations. These data suggest that professionalization, as well as differentiation, has two contradictory implications for operations.

Table 13.6 Per Cent with High Costs by Size and Professionalization

Professionalization	Small Agencies	Large Agencies
Low	60(61)	28(32)
High	31(29)	43(28)

Note: The difference in the left column is significant at the 0.05 level.

Differentiation and professionalization influence operations directly, and they also produce changes in the organizational structure that have indirect repercussions for operations. The direct effects are most evident in smaller organizations, and the indirect ones, which have opposite implications for operations, in larger organizations. Task differentiation has the manifest purpose of raising efficiency, and it achieves this purpose in small agencies. At the same time, however, differentiation increases the internal complexity of the organizational structure. While the immediate purpose of professionalization is to improve performance quality, the findings indicate that it also raises efficiency in small agencies. The reason may be that the ability of professionals to fit their own tasks into a wider framework contributes to the overall coordination in organizations sufficiently small to permit regular face-to-face contacts among the entire staff, but much less so in larger organizations with several departments. Separate departmental groups of professional specialists increase the structural complexity of an organization, just as does the division of labor. Internal complexity gives rise to problems, which are reflected in operating costs, as can be seen most clearly when complexity is viewed as a condition that modifies the basic influence of size on operating costs.

Simple agencies exhibit an economy of scale, whereas complex ones do not. Whether the division of labor or professionalization is taken as the indication of structural complexity, larger organizations tend to operate at lower costs than smaller ones if their structure is simple, but not if it is complex (see Tables 13.5 and 13.6). Internal complexity nullifies the economic advantage operations on a large scale have in its absence, because it gives rise to problems of communication and coordination in larger organizations. While this is self-evident in the case of the division of labor, it requires explanation in the case of professionals, whose coordinating ability has been noted. Professionals who are "locals" and identify themselves with the organization in which they work have been distinguished from "cosmopolitans," who are primarily oriented to the wider group of professional colleagues anywhere.[23] It seems reasonable to assume that locals predominate in smaller organizations and cosmopolitans in larger ones. The broader context into which professionals tend to fit their own tasks is the work of the organization for locals, but the work of fellow specialists outside for cosmopolitans. The very identification of professionals with their responsibilities that leads the locals in an organization to converge in their orientations leads the cosmopolitans to diverge. Professionals in larger organizations, often working in diverse departments and oriented to different professions outside, consequently intensify problems of communication. The interpretation suggested is that the problems of communication produced by professionalization as well as by differentiation in larger agencies account for the adverse effects of these structural complexities on operations. This interpretation implies that complexity no longer has adverse effects once mechanisms to deal with problems of communication have been developed. The data support this inference.

Organizational complexities destroy the economy of scale that is otherwise observable, but appropriate bureaucratic mechanisms for coping with the problems posed by these complexities restore the economy of scale. Table 13.7 reveals that, among simple organizations with a rudimentary division of labor, a larger scale of operations tends to reduce costs, whether the administrative ratio is low (-15) or high (-29). Among complex or-

---

[23] Alvin W. Gouldner, "Cosmopolitans and Locals," *Administrative Science Quarterly* 2 (1957–58), 281–306, 444–480.

Table 13.7   Per Cent with High Costs by Size, Division of Labor, and Administrative Apparatus

Division of Labor and Administrative Apparatus	Small Agencies	Large Agencies	Difference
Rudimentary:			
Low administrative ratio	51(41)	36(14)	−15
High administrative ratio	58(36)	29(7)	−29
Advanced:			
Low administrative ratio	12(8)	50(20)	+38
High administrative ratio	40(5)	25(20)	−15

Note: The difference between the differences in rows 1 and 3 is significant at the 0.05 level; that between rows 2 and 4 is not.

ganizations with an advanced division of labor, however, a larger size tends to raise costs if the administrative ratio is low (+38) and reduce them only if it is high (−15). The same pattern appears when professionalization is substituted for the division of labor, as shown in Table 13.8. In the absence of professionalization, an increase in size lessens the likelihood of high costs, whatever the administrative ratio (−31, −30), but in professionalized agencies, an increase in size raises the likelihood of high costs (+32) unless the administrative ratio is high (−13).

An adequate administrative apparatus to maintain channels of communication can meet the problems created by structural complexity in organizations beyond a minimum size; thereby it reinstates under complex conditions

Table 13.8   Per Cent with High Costs by Size, Professionalization, and Administrative Apparatus

Professionalization and Administrative Apparatus	Small Agencies	Large Agencies	Difference
Low:			
Low administrative ratio	55(31)	24(17)	−31
High administrative ratio	63(30)	33(15)	−30
High:			
Low administrative ratio	28(18)	60(15)	+32
High administrative ratio	36(11)	23(13)	−13

Note: The difference between the differences in rows 1 and 3 is significant at the 0.05 level; that between rows 2 and 4 is not.

Table 13.9   Per Cent with High Costs by Size, Division of Labor, and Managerial Hierarchy

Division of Labor and Managerial Hierarchy	Small Agencies	Large Agencies	Difference
Rudimentary:			
Dispersed hierarchy	50(54)	23(13)	−27
Centralized hierarchy	65(50)	50(8)	−15
Advanced:			
Dispersed hierarchy	11(9)	39(23)	+28
Centralized hierarchy	50(4)	39(18)	−11

Note: The difference between the differences in rows 1 and 3 is significant at the 0.05 level; that between rows 2 and 4 is not.

the economy that accrues to large-scale operations under simple conditions without it. A centralized authority structure serves equivalent functions, although only for task differentiation and not for professionalization. If the division of labor is rudimentary, as Table 13.9 indicates, operating costs tend to decline with expanding size regardless of the management hierarchy (−27, −15) but if the division of labor is advanced, costs tend to rise with expanding size (+28) unless the hierarchy is centralized (−11). Centralization of formal authority facilitates the coordination of diverse tasks—a major problem in differentiated larger organizations. The pattern of findings in Table 13.9 corresponds closely to those in Tables 13.7 and 13.8. Since centralization and administrative apparatus are not significantly related, and neither are division of labor and professionalization, the three sets of findings are not redundant but actual replications. The combined influence of professionalization and centralization does not, however, reveal the same pattern. This is hardly surprising in the light of the earlier indications that a centralized hierarchy is not a suitable coordinating mechanism for a professional staff.

In short, procedures instituted to meet some problems often have repercussions in the organizational structure that create new problems. These conflicting influences had to be inferred from the analysis. Thus, both the division of labor and professionalization lower operating costs, as manifest in the data from small agencies, but they simultaneously increase the structural complexity of the organization. Operating on a larger scale also lowers operating costs, as revealed by the data from simple agencies, though not by those from complex ones (because of the disturbing influence of complexity). Structural complexity raises problems of communication in larger organizations which, if unresolved, impede effective operations, as implied by the findings that complexity eliminates the economic advantage of larger agencies but administrative mechanisms that meet problems of communication reestablish this advantage.

Conclusions

The interrelations among four bureaucratic attributes in American public personnel agencies have been analyzed—task differentiation, professionalization, the management hierarchy, and the administrative apparatus. It is noteworthy that all six zero-order relationships between any two of these four organizational attributes are insignificantly small, not one making a difference of as much as 12 per cent. Even when size is controlled only one of the six reveals a significant difference (that between professionalization and centralization). It is primarily in the higher-order interactions that distinct relationships become apparent. This creates methodological difficulties, since many more than the 150 cases of organizations here available would be needed to explore adequately the intricate interrelations. But it is also of substantive significance, for these higher-order interactions reflect and provide empirical validation for the theoretical conception of social structure, which implies a complex interdependence between elements rather than correlations between pairs of attributes unaffected by other conditions.[24]

Professionalization plays a dual role in the bureaucratic structure, being in some respects the counterpart of the division of labor, and in others that of the authority hierarchy. Just as does an advanced division of labor, professionalization lowers costs, engenders structural complexities that produce communication problems, and requires the assistance of an administrative staff. On the other hand, it seems to be an alternative to a centralized authority structure. Whereas the analysis of operating costs implies that professionalization increases problems of coordination and communication, its inverse relationship to centralization suggests that it helps meet problems of coordination, but only if complemented by a dispersed management. Although these findings appear contradictory, they can readily be reconciled. The inverse relationship between professionalization and centralization means, after all, nothing else than that a professional staff is usually accompanied by a large and dispersed managerial component. This does not in the least conflict with the interpretation that professionalization intensifies problems of communication. To be sure, professionals also make some con-

[24] Hubert M. Blalock, Jr., stresses the importance of taking explicitly into account such higher-order interactions in sociological theory; "Theory Building and the Statistical Concept of Interaction," *American Sociological Review* 30 (1965), 374–380.

tributions to coordination, particularly by detecting problems and proposing knowledgeable solutions for them. For these contributions to be realized in effective coordination, however, an adequate staff of managers is essential to work in close contact with professionals, and to implement their proposals as well as solicit them. The effectiveness of a professional staff, in sum, depends on its being complemented by an adequate managerial component and in larger organizations also by an adequate administrative component. These are required to meet the problems of coordination and communication professionalization raises, notwithstanding the ability of professionals to help solve these problems.

A systematic analysis of bureaucratic structure, like the one attempted here, seeks to discover the consistent interrelations among organizational attributes. Consistent patterns cannot be found in all the data; those that can are singled out for attention. While such selectivity is inevitable in exploratory research, it creates the danger of conveying an impression of greater functional integration in the structure than actually exists. It should be mentioned as a caveat, therefore, that functional relationships, though often implicit in the analysis, by no means prevail throughout the bureaucratic structure. There are numerous elements that reveal no positive feedback from their consequences to make them functional for operations. To cite only one example: an increase in size promotes task differentiation but not the expansion of the administrative staff. This is a dysfunctional consequence, since task differentiation lowers operating costs only in small agencies but raises them in larger ones unless supplemented by an adequate administrative staff.

The general conclusion suggested by the analysis is that the complex interrelations and higher-order interactions observed in the organizational structure are more likely to be functionally adapted by feedback than the separate attributes themselves. Feedback processes seem to produce not so much the elimination of dysfunctional elements as a greater functional interdependence among them in the bureaucratic structure. A refined conception of functional interdependence is implicit here, which would neither simply mean that the elements in a social structure are interrelated nor assume that each one of them serves important functions, but which would refer specifically to the fact that the complex, higher-order relationships among elements in the structure have been adapted by feedback to minimize dysfunctions. The interdependence is functional, although the specific factors may not be. External circumstances and vested powers often impose conditions on organizations that are dysfunctional for operations; feedback processes can at best minimize dysfunctions within this framework beyond their control.

14. *The Hierarchy of Authority in Organizations*

Advances in the social sciences do not occur in straight lines of uniform progress, as the recurrent rediscoveries of half-forgotten classics indicate, be it Simmel's analysis of conflict or Durkheim's of the division of labor, the insights of Karl Marx, Adam Smith, or even Plato. But neither does the development of sociology move in circles or simply fluctuate between alternative theoretical approaches. There is some continuity, and there is some progress. The analysis of pattern variables by Parsons and Shils surely is a refinement of Toennies's concepts of *Gemeinschaft* and *Gesellschaft*, for example, and the research of Lipset, Trow, and Coleman clearly advances our knowledge of union democracy far beyond Michels's theory of oligarchy which inspired it. The pattern of scientific development may be described as dialectical. Mounting criticisms of one approach lead to concentration on another designed to overcome the first's shortcomings; yet the second approach is likely, in due time, to reveal limitations of its own that encourage still other lines of scientific attack. But slowly some progress is made.

Originally published in 1968.

The study of formal organizations is a case in point. Weber's theoretical analysis, which has long dominated the field, was increasingly criticized for presenting an idealized conception of bureaucracy and for examining only its formal characteristics and ignoring the informal modifications that occur in actual practice. In response to this criticism, research on organizations concentrated on informal relations and unofficial practices, the attitudes of individual members and their observable behavior. The resulting studies of the informal organization of work groups and the actual performance of duties in bureaucracies have undoubtedly contributed much to our understanding of these complex structures. While complementing Weber's approach, however, the new focus neglected the basic theoretical problem to which he addressed himself. One question a student of organizations may ask is how the existing conditions in a bureaucracy affect attitudes and conduct, for instance, why bureaucratic conditions stifle initiative and what the processes involved are.[1] But there is another question that can be asked, namely, why certain conditions emerge in organizations in the first place, for example, what determines the development and the characteristics of the authority structure. Weber was concerned with the second problem—explaining the configurations of bureaucratic conditions—whereas recent research focused on the first—investigating their consequences for individuals and groups—to the virtual exclusion of the second, in part because the case study method usually employed is not suitable for answering the second question.

A theory of formal organization, as distinguished from a theory of group life in a bureaucratic context, seeks to explain why organizations develop various characteristics, such as a multilevel hierarchy or decentralized authority. To furnish these explanations requires that the characteristics of organizations are not taken as given but the conditions that produce them are the very object of the inquiry. Thus one may ask how the qualifications of an organization's staff influence the structure of authority in it, or generally what conditions affect the shape of the hierarchy, which are the two problems posed in this paper. In order to answer this kind of question, it is necessary to compare different organizations and not merely to study the influence exerted on behavior by the conditions found in a single case. The method of comparison might involve analyzing bureaucracies in different historical periods, which was Weber's approach; or intensive examination of two contrasting forms of organization, as in Stinchcombe's study cited below; or quantitative comparisons of many organizations and multivariate analysis of their characteristics. The last procedure is adopted here.

[1] See Robert K. Merton, *Social Theory and Social Structure*, 3d ed. (New York: Free Press, 1957), pp. 195, 249–260.

The assumption made in choosing this procedure is that the analysis of the interdependence between organizational attributes based on systematic comparisons of large numbers of organizations promises to contribute most to organizational theory. If the ultimate aim of this theory is to derive general principles that explain the emergence of structures with various characteristics, the first step must be to advance more limited generalizations that specify the conditions that affect the development of different characteristics. Quantitative comparisons permit such specification. The analysis of the authority structure to be presented is based on data collected from several hundred government agencies. Only agencies of a specific type are directly compared, to eliminate the disturbing influence of differences between types; but the results of one such study are confronted with those of another, to discern whether conclusions are confined to a single type. The inquiry is restricted to the formal attributes of organizations, since it was not possible to collect data on informal patterns and individual attitudes in hundreds of government agencies. This limitation of the approach to organizational research here adopted may well give rise in the future to different approaches not similarly limited to easily accessible data. But the prospect of a possible countertrend in the future should not deter us now from exploiting the scientific contribution that systematic comparisons of even relatively simple organizational traits can make at the present stage of knowledge.

The exposition is deliberately designed to call attention to continuities in bureaucratic theory and research, and the paper also seeks to reveal the role that theoretical speculations which go beyond the empirical evidence play in establishing continuities between different investigations. The research reported is conceived within the framework of Weber's theoretical tradition; it follows his approach of studying the interrelations between formal conditions in bureaucratic structures, rather than the individuals and human relations within them, and it deals with two substantive issues his theory poses—the relationship between expertness and authority, and the significance of the formal hierarchy of offices. Moreover, the continuities from one empirical investigation to another are indicated as the tentative interpretations of earlier findings are tested and refined in a subsequent study. I shall try to illustrate that advancing highly speculative generalizations in interpreting empirical findings serves important scientific functions, for such inferential conjectures are the basis for the cumulation of scientific knowledge, provided that they are followed up by further research. The only connection between different empirical investigations, and hence the only source of cumulation, is the generalizations derived from each that go beyond its limited evidence.

Professional and Bureaucratic Authority

The relationship between the expert qualifications of a professional staff and the bureaucratic authority vested in a hierarchy of offices poses an interesting theoretical issue. Professionalism and bureaucracy have much in common, such as impersonal detachment, specialized technical expertness, and rational decision-making based on universalistic standards. There are also divergent elements, however, and professional principles often come into conflict with the requirements of bureaucratic authority. Weber implied that the professional authority rooted in expert technical knowledge and the bureaucratic authority rooted in a hierarchy of offices with legitimate claims to disciplined compliance tend to occur together, both being distinctive characteristics of complex rational organizations. "The role of technical qualifications in bureaucratic organizations is continually increasing."[2] But, in addition, "each lower office is under the control and supervision of a higher one."[3] The assumption that professional expertness and bureaucratic discipline are simply two aspects of the rational organization of large-scale tasks not only conflicts with the prevailing impression that professional work suffers if subjected to bureaucratic discipline, but it also has been questioned on both systematic theoretical and empirical grounds.

In a well-known footnote, Parsons criticizes Weber for confounding two analytically distinct types of authority.[4] Professional authority rests on the certified superior competence of the expert, which prompts others voluntarily to follow his directives because they consider doing so to be in their own interest. Bureaucratic authority, in contrast, rests on the legitimate power of command vested in an official position, which obligates subordinates to follow directives under the threat of sanctions. Superior knowledge is not required for bureaucratic authority (expert knowledge is not what authorizes the policeman to direct traffic, for example, or what induces us to obey his signals), whereas it is essential for professional control, and mandatory compliance is enforced by coercive sanctions in the bureaucratic but not in the professional case. Gouldner similarly stresses the difference between the influence exerted on the basis of technical competence and the compelling authority in a bureaucratic hierarchy, and he derives from this distinction two contrasting forms of bureaucracy—"representative" and "punishment-centered."[5]

[2] Max Weber, *The Theory of Social and Economic Organization* (New York: Oxford University press, 1947), p. 335.

[3] *Ibid.*, p. 331.

[4] Talcott Parsons, "Introduction," *ibid.*, pp. 58–60.

[5] Alvin W. Gouldner, *Patterns of Industrial Bureaucracy* (Glencoe: Free Press, 1954), esp. pp. 21–24.

Research results also challenge Weber's assumption that technical expertness and hierarchically enforced discipline typically occur together. Stinchcombe's comparison of two industries suggests, for example, that the technical skills of construction workers, which contrast with the low level of skill in mass production, promote rational performance and therefore serve as a substitute for the bureaucratic hierarchy through which the work in mass production is rationally organized.[6] Thus technical expertness and hierarchical authority seem to be alternative, not complementary, principles of organization. Udy's research on the organization of production in 150 nonindustrial societies arrives at parallel results.[7] He finds that several bureaucratic characteristics, including a hierarchical authority structure, are directly correlated with one another but not, or even inversely, with several rational characteristics, including specialization, which may be considered a primitive forerunner of technical expertness, and so may rational work procedures in general. Udy concludes: "Bureaucracy and rationality tend to be mutually inconsistent in the same formal organization."[8] It is noteworthy that both of these studies do not deal with advanced levels of professionalization but with rather rudimentary forms of expert qualifications.

The various components of professionalism must be distinguished in analyzing its implications for hierarchical authority in organizations. Fullfledged professionalization entails not only expert skills but also a body of abstract knowledge underlying them, a self-governing association of professional peers, professional standards of workmanship and ethical conduct, and an orientation toward service. Some of these factors may easily come into conflict with the discipline required by bureaucratic authority. Research indicates that a professional orientation toward service and a bureaucratic orientation toward disciplined compliance with procedures are opposite approaches toward work and often create conflict in organizations.[9] Besides, the identification of professionals with an external reference group may well lessen their loyalty to the organization.[10] It is also reasonable to expect that conflicts arise as decisions made strictly on the basis of professional standards

[6] Arthur L. Stinchcombe, "Bureaucratic and Craft Administration of Production," *Administrative Science Quarterly* 4 (1959), 168–187.

[7] Stanley H. Udy, Jr., " 'Bureaucracy' and 'Rationality' in Weber's Organization Theory," *American Sociology Review* 24 (1959), 791–795.

[8] *Ibid.*, p. 794.

[9] See e.g., Roy G. Francies and Robert C. Stone, *Service and Procedure in Bureaucracy* (Minneapolis: University of Minnesota Press, 1956).

[10] See Alvin W. Gouldner, "Cosmopolitans and Locals," *Administrative Science Quarterly* 2 (1957–58), 281–306, 444–480; Theodore Caplow and Reece J. McGee, *The Academic Marketplace* (New York: Basic Books, 1958), esp. p. 85; Everett C. Hughes, *Men and Their Work* (Glencoe: Free Press, 1958), esp. p. 137; and Peter M. Blau and W. Richard Scott, *Formal Organizations* (San Francisco: Chandler, 1962), pp. 64–74.

are recurrently set aside for the sake of administrative considerations by bureaucratic authorities. All these conflicts refer to fairly advanced aspects of professionalization. But Weber's concern was not so much with these components of professionalism as with technical expertness, which he held to be an integral part of hierarchically organized bureaucracies. The findings of Stinchcombe and Udy imply, however, that even a moderate degree of technical expertness conflicts with bureaucratic authority.

Yet there can be no question that hierarchically organized bureaucracies do employ personnel with expert training and qualifications. As a matter of fact, formal organizations typically *require* their staff to meet certain educational or technical qualifications, and these requirements indicate that a minimum of expertness is indeed an integral part of the bureaucratic structure. If expertness itself is, nevertheless, incompatible with some elements of strict bureaucratic authority, as the findings cited suggest, the question is how it modifies the structure of authority in organizations. The present paper addresses itself first to this problem of how variations in the qualifications of the personnel affect the authority structure in formal organizations, and it then turns to the question of how other conditions affect the hierarchy of authority.

A simple working hypothesis for investigating the first problem can be derived from a few plausible considerations. Entrance requirements that assure that the agency staff (meaning all personnel, in line as well as "staff" positions) has relatively high minimum qualifications might be expected to lessen the need for guidance and close supervision. The implication is that such expert requirements widen the span of control of managers, increasing the number of subordinates under each,[11] and therefore reduce the proportion of managerial personnel in the organization, because each superior can supervise more subordinates if they are experts than if their lower skills necessitate much guidance and checking. These inferences, which appear straightforward and perhaps even self-evident, suggest as an initial hypothesis that expert requirements decrease the ratio of managerial to nonsupervisory personnel in organizations, which widens the average span of control.

Study of Public Personnel Agencies

This hypothesis was tested as part of a previously published study of 156 public personnel agencies,[12] and a brief summary of the pertinent results

[11] The assumption that less close supervision widens the span of control is made explicit by A. Janger, among others. "If the manager practices close supervision, . . . then he is decreasing the number of people he can supervise. He broaders his span by granting them more authority" ["Analyzing the Span of Control," *Management Record* 22 (July-August, 1960), 9].

[12] Peter M. Blau, Wolf V. Heydebrand, and Robert E. Stauffer, "The Structure of Small Bureaucracies," *American Sociological Review* 31 (1966), 179–191 (see Chapter 13).

suffices to introduce the problems investigated in subsequent research. The data were collected by the Public Personnel Association through questionnaires to its members. They pertain to the executive agencies of the civil service commissions of most state and major local American governments, with the bias of selection favoring larger agencies and those identified with merit principles. These agencies are small bureaucracies, with a median staff of not quite seventeen (even after the ninety-six with a staff of less than five were eliminated from the analysis). The measure of expertness is whether the operating staff, excluding both managerial and clerical personnel, is required to have a college degree with a specified job-related major.[13] The only available information on the hierarchy of authority is the ratio of managers to nonsupervisory officials.[14]

The employment of experts with stipulated educational qualifications does not reduce the proportionate size of the managerial staff in public personnel agencies. On the contrary, under most conditions, though not under all, agencies that require their employees to meet relatively high qualifications are more likely than others to have a high ratio of managers. Expertness, moreover, seems to prevent other conditions from reducing the proportion of managers. An increase in the division of labor tends to decrease the managerial ratio in the absence of expert requirements but increase it in their presence. The hypothesis that the expertness of the operating staff widens the span of supervisory control and consequently is reflected in a low ratio of managers is clearly negated by these results.

In the light of these negative findings we reconceptualized the meaning attributed to the managerial ratio. Since it does not appear reasonable that better-trained personnel officers are more closely supervised than those lacking similar qualifications, the initial assumption that a higher ratio of managers is indicative of closer supervision must be questioned. An alternative interpretation of the significance of this measure, which is compatible with the findings, is that a low ratio of managers implies a centralized authority structure, with managerial authority concentrated in the hands of comparatively few officials. When administrative authority is centralized in few positions, management presumably is carried out largely by a central headquarters that issues directives to the operating staff, whereas management in a structure with a large proportion of authority positions probably entails

[13] The measure was dichotomized in contingencies tables on the basis of whether at least half of the operating staff has to meet this requirement, but the actual distribution is bimodal, and in most organizations either all of the staff or none of it has to meet this educational requirement.

[14] The criterion of manager was being head of a division rather than a journeyman or apprentice, which probably includes most supervisory personnel in these small agencies, though some chiefs of small sections may have been excluded, particularly in the few large agencies (only seventeen have a staff of more than one hundred).

more reciprocal adjustments as the result of the greater opportunities for communication between managerial and operating personnel.

The difference in assumptions between the original and the revised interpretations of the managerial ratio should be made explicit. The initial formulation assumed that few managers with a wide span of control imply less close supervision, which permits subordinates to exercise more autonomy in their work. The reconceptualization assumes that few managers imply a centralized authority structure, which encourages management through one-sided directives with little feedback from operating levels, thus reducing the autonomy of subordinates. The empirical data, though they were the basis for the revision, are not adequate to validate either set of assumptions. However, the reconceptualization permits some suggestive conjectures.

Appointing employees with expert qualifications and instituting a centralized authority structure appear to be alternative modes of organization, which are somewhat incompatible. This conclusion is in broad agreement with the one reached by both Stinchcombe and Udy in their empirical studies, as well as with the theoretical distinction Parsons makes between professional and bureaucratic authority. But our research specifies the source of the incompatibility. What is inappropriate for an organization staffed by experts is a hierarchy in which official authority is centralized in the hands of few managers. It seems paradoxical that more managers are required to direct employees with superior qualifications than those less well trained. The explanation lies in the implications of a low ratio of managers already adumbrated and in the implications of expert qualifications.

Expert training may be expected to make a man not only more independent in the performance of his duties but also more aware of the broader implications of his work and more capable of detecting operating problems and finding solutions for them than is an untrained person. Experts are more likely to resent having their discretion limited by managerial directives than are employees whose lesser skills make some guidance welcome. In addition, experts can make greater contributions to the improvement of operating procedures than men without specialized training. Hence, feedback communication from the operating staff is especially valuable for management if this staff consists of experts. To take full advantage of the contributions experts can make to operations, management must facilitate the flow of upward communication. A low ratio of managers tends to discourage upward communication, however, inasmuch as a small contingent of managers can most easily direct operations by issuing orders from a central headquarters to the staff. A high ratio of managers increases opportunities for communication between officials responsible for administrative and those responsible for operating decisions. Such extensive two-way communication is of special importance if the personnel has expert qualifications, not alone

because experts tend to be more alienated by one-sided directives but particularly because they make greater contributions through feedback than
persons with poorer qualifications.

In short, the interpretation suggested is that the added significance the
expertness of the staff lends to the free flow of upward communication in
organizations accounts for the association between expert requirements and
a high ratio of managers. We were able to muster a bit of indirect evidence
in support of this interpretation in the study of public personnel agencies.
An expert staff improves operating economy in very small agencies, with a
personnel of less than twenty, but it impedes economy in larger agencies
unless the clerical staff is relatively large. In agencies of sufficient size to
make communication a serious problem, the absence of an adequate clerical
apparatus to maintain channels of communication has an adverse effect on
operating economy if and only if the staff consists of experts.[15] This finding
implies that expert qualifications of operating officials enhance the importance of communication, indirectly supporting our interpretation.

Nevertheless, the generalizations we advanced rest on shaky grounds.
They are based on data from only one kind of organization, a specific type
of government agency. Besides, public personnel agencies are very small,
while bureaucratic theory presumably deals with large organizations. (It
should be noted, however, that the stereotype of the huge government bureaucracy with a staff of thousands is misleading as far as particular agencies
of state and local governments are concerned, most of which probably have
less than one hundred employees.) Moreover, the only measure of the hierarchy of authority available, the proportion of managers, is clearly insufficient to analyze this complex institution. Finally, the inference that expertness promotes a decentralized authority structure is highly speculative, since
the implication is that decision making is decentralized, but a large proportion of managers is not necessarily indicative of decentralization of *decision-
making*. One might even argue that, on the contrary, the *smaller* the proportion of managers, the more likely will they be to delegate responsibilities
to subordinates in order to lighten the burden of their duties.

Study of Government Finance Departments

A study of 254 finance departments of state and local governments made it
possible to test the hypothesis that staff expertness leads to decentralization

---

[15] Blau *et al.*, *op. cit.*, p. 189, Table 8 (see Table 13.8 above). Among larger agencies *with*
an expert staff, 60 per cent of those with a low but only 23 per cent of those with a high
clerical ratio operate at high cost; whereas in larger agencies *without* an expert staff, high
cost is as unlikely with a low (24 per cent) as with a high clerical ratio (33 per cent).

of responsibilities, and further to explore the conditions that influence the structure of authority in organizations. Original data were collected for the purpose of this study by National Opinion Research Center interviewers from informants (senior managers) in the major finance department of each government. The universe consists of the departments in all states, all counties with a population of more than 100,000, and all cities with a population of more than 50,000, in the United States, except those with a staff of fewer than twenty or with no subdivision of responsibilities into two or more units.[16] The sample comprises the entire universe, and information was obtained from 96.6 per cent of these organizations. Although responsibilities vary, nearly all departments maintain financial records and preaudit disbursements, and the majority are also responsible for postauditing other departments, investment management, and fixed-asset accounting. The median department has a staff of sixty, six major subdivisions, and four hierarchical levels.

A number of the questions raised by the conclusions of the earlier study can be answered by this research. Another type of government agency has now been investigated, making it possible to check whether the previous findings merely reflect some special conditions in personnel work. The organizations under examination are larger, with a minimum size of twenty instead of five and a median of sixty instead of seventeen, and a larger number of cases is available for analysis, increasing the reliability of findings. Of greatest importance is the fact that a variety of measures of the structure of authority were deliberately designed to permit refinement of the earlier inferences. Information was obtained on the proportion of managerial personnel, specifically defined as all officials with supervisory duties; the number of levels in the hierarchy (the mean for the various divisions); the average span of control—number of subordinates—of first-line supervisors and that of middle managers; the proportion of their time managers spend on supervision; and the hierarchical level on which various specified decisions are made, furnishing direct indications of delegation of responsibilities and decentralization of authority. The index of expert requirements is the proportion of the staff expected to have a college degree, roughly parallel to the index used in the other study,[17] and departments are dichotomized on the basis of whether at least one-fifth of the total personnel (which is about

[16] Data on these smaller departments were also obtained, in this case by mail questionnaire, but they are not included in the present analysis.

[17] Although the number required to have a college degree in accounting was ascertained as well, which would furnish an index exactly parallel to that used in the previous study, this number was so low (an average of one-tenth of the staff) that the less stringent requirement— college degree whatever the major—is considered to be the preferable index of staff expertness.

two-fifths of the nonclerical personnel) is expected to meet the requirement of college graduation.

The basic finding reported from the study of public personnel agencies is confirmed by this research on another type of government agency; a high ratio of managerial personnel is more often found in finance departments with a large proportion of college-trained experts than in those with comparatively few employees so qualified (Table 14.1, row 1).[18] The more extensive data of the second study make it possible to stipulate the structural implications of the higher ratio of managers in organizations with many experts. The employment of an expert staff seems to give rise to vertical differentiation, increasing the number of managerial levels in the organization. The number of hierarchical levels tends to be larger in departments requiring of its personnel relatively high educational qualifications than in those with lower requirements (row 2). The span of control of first-line supervisors is, on the average, somewhat narrower if the staff has superior qualifications than if it does not (row 3).[19] The span of control of middle managers (those between the top executive and first-line supervisors) is, by contrast, wider in agencies with well-trained personnel than in others (row 4). But these middle managers have many fewer subordinates in any case, averaging less than two, than first-line supervisors, whose median is six subordinates. Supervisors have typically broader responsibilities than operating officials, and very few of them report to the same superior; expert qualifications presumably broaden the responsibilities of operating employees, which is reflected in a parallel reduction in the number reporting to the same supervisor. This consistent inverse association between scope of responsibilities and width of span of control clearly indicates that a narrow span of control must not be assumed to be indicative of closeness of supervision.[20]

The employment of personnel with superior qualifications raises the proportion of managers in an organization apparently because it tends to increase the number of managerial levels and decrease the span of control of first-line supervisors. The question arises how the extra managerial manpower is utilized in departments with a highly qualified staff. The time esti-

---

[18] The implicit assumption that proportion of managers is inversely associated with span of control over the operating level is strongly supported by the data. The proportion of departments in which first-line supervisors average six or more subordinates is 72 per cent in the 151 with a managerial ratio of less than one-quarter and 20 per cent in the 102 with a higher managerial ratio.

[19] A parallel result, showing complexity of task to be inversely related to width of span of control, is presented in Gerald D. Bell, "Determinants of Span of Control," *American Journal of Sociology* 73 (1967), 100–109.

[20] Bell has some direct evidence on closeness of supervision, which shows it to be unrelated to span of control (*ibid.*, p. 106).

Table 14.1   Training Requirements and Authority Structure

| | Proportion of Staff Required To Have B.A.[a] | | |
Percentage of Finance Departments (in Cols. [1] and [2]) in Which:	Low (1)	High (2)	Yule's Q (Gamma) (3)
1. The proportion of managers exceeds one-quarter of the total personnel	35(147)	48(106)	.27
2. The number of levels is four or more	36(148)	51(106)	.29
3. The mean span of control of first-line supervisors is six or more	56(147)	44(106)	−.23[b]
4. The mean span of control of middle managers is 1.6 or more	38(135)	54(100)	.32
5. The average manager spends more than two-fifths of his time supervising	52(145)	38(106)	−.29
6. Division heads make budgeting or accounting decisions	40(122)	54(86)	.26[b]
7. An official below the director recommends promotions and dismissals	30(147)	45(104)	.32

[a] Since this variable is not associated with size, it is not necssary to control size.

[b] All relationships are significant below the .05 level except these two, which are significant on the .08 and .06 levels, respectively.

mates of informants permit tentative answers to this question. If much of the staff is college trained, managers are less likely to spend most of their time in actual supervision than if it is not (Table 14.1, row 5, based on the mean for all managers), and this is the case for first-line supervisors as well as higher managers. The finding that superiors of experts devote comparatively little time to actually supervising them helps to explain why their narrow span of control does not imply close supervision. Managers in departments with highly qualified personnel seem to spend more time than other managers on professional work of their own which keeps them in touch with the problems encountered by the operating level.[21] Such greater involvement in actual operations on the part of managers of an expert staff,

[21] One might think that the finding could also be interpreted to show that departments with many experts have more complex responsibilities and their managers devote more time to planning and administration, but the instructions were that such activities be included under supervision, and virtually the only activity excluded, except for top executives, would be work of one's own.

compared to other managers, may well improve their qualifications to discuss technical problems of the work with their subordinates and thus to take full advantage of the greater opportunities for communication that the smaller numbers of subordinates per superior create.

The question of prime interest is whether the hypothesis that expertness promotes decentralization, which rested merely on inferential conjecture, is confirmed by the directly pertinent data from finance departments. This is in fact the case. Responsibilities of various kinds tend to be delegated by management to lower levels in agencies where the staff has relatively high qualifications. Thus budgeting and accounting decisions are more likely to be made by division heads rather than the department director himself if the staff includes many college-trained men than if it includes few (Table 14.1, row 6). The likelihood that an official below the top executive recommends promotions and dismissals is also greater in agencies with many experts than in others (row 7). Parallel relationships with expertness, though they are somewhat less pronounced, are revealed by other indications of decentralization of responsibilities, such as the top executive's policy to let his division heads make most decisions, and the fact that first-line supervisors, not higher officials, formally evaluate the performance of nonsupervisory employees. In sum, managerial authority over decision-making appears indeed to be more decentralized in organizations with large proportions of trained experts than in others.

Multilevel Hierarchies

The finding that superior qualifications of the personnel in government agencies encourage delegation of responsibilities is not surprising. But what is unexpected is that such superior qualifications are also associated with vertical differentiation into multilevel hierarchies. It is generally assumed that the proliferation of hierarchical levels in organizations is a sign of over-bureaucratization that is incompatible with the rational work of trained experts, and the results of Udy's study of primitive production organizations point to this conclusion.[22] However, the finding here implies the opposite, namely, that multilevel hierarchies in organizations occur together with superior training which contributes to rational operations. This raises the question of what conditions in contemporary American agencies promote hierarchical differentiation.

A multilevel hierarchy is associated with eight basic characteristics of finance departments: (1) The number of levels increases with increasing

[22] Udy, *loc. cit.*

size, that is, the number of employees (Pearsonian zero-order correlation, .51).[23] (2) Although the zero-order correlation between number of levels and number of major subdivisions[24] is virtually nil ($-.05$), there is an inverse association between the two when size is controlled ($-.34$). (3) The wider the average span of control of middle managers, the larger is the number of levels in the hierarchy (.27). (4) Automation in the form of computers is associated with multiple levels (.34). (5) Explicit written promotion regulations encourage hierarchical differentiation (.22). (6) The number of levels increases the more weight written examinations have for promotions (.24), and it decreases the more weight seniority ($-.22$) and supervisory evaluations ($-.16$) have for promotions.[25] (7) Decentralization of responsibility for promotions and dismissals is correlated with multiple levels (.18). (8) The larger the proportion of employees required to have college degrees, finally, the larger the number of levels (.16).

Since so many factors are associated with hierarchical levels, partial correlations were computed between each of the eight and number of levels holding constant the other seven. The results of this regression analysis, which provide the basis for the further discussion, are presented in Table 14.2. The multiple correlation between all eight factors and levels is .65. These characteristics of finance departments explain 43 per cent of the variance in hierarchical levels, with most of the difference being due to three factors—size, divisions, and automation.

Some reflections on the considerations that probably influence the decision to add new levels in the hierarchy can serve as a starting point for interpreting these associations. As an organization expands in size and complexity, it is likely that additional major divisions are established, which increases the number of officials directly responsible to the department director and overburdens him with supervisory responsibilities. To lighten this administrative load of the top executive and free him to devote more time to his primary executive functions, a few assistant directors may be installed on a new level to whom the division directors report and who in turn report to the director, just as the creation of the U.S. Secretary of Health, Education, and Welfare constituted an intermediate level between the President and officials who formerly reported directly to him. The introduction of such a

[23] Regression analysis is used here, partly because the number of levels is a genuine continuous variable and so are most independent variables, and particularly because this procedure makes it possible to examine partial associations while holding all seven other correlates constant.

[24] The criterion of "major subdivision" is a division whose head reports directly to the department director (or his deputy, if he has a single deputy).

[25] Only the weight of written promotion examinations is considered in the subsequent analysis, since the two other factors are complementary to it.

Table 14.2   Correlations with Number of Levels in the Hierarchy

Independent Variable	Zero-Order Correlation	Partial Correlation	Standardized $B*$	Regression Error	Data on Employment Agencies: Zero-Order Correlation
1. Number of employees	.51	.50	.53	.06	.60
2. Number of major divisions	− .05	− .32	− .30	.06	.19
3. Span of control of middle managers	.27	.11	.09	.05	.31
4. Automation (computers)[a]	.34	.23	.19	.05	.53
5. Explicit promotion regulations[a]	.22	.04	− .03	.06	.33
6. Weight of examinations in promotions	.24	.13	.12	.06	[b]
7. Decentralization of promotion decisions[a]	.18	.12	.09	.05	.19
8. Proportion of staff required to have B.A.	.16	.03	.02	.05	− .00

[a] These three factors are dichotomous and were used as dummy variables in the regression analysis. All others are continuous variables except weight of examinations, which was coded in four categories

[b] No corresponding variable is available for the employment security study.

new level of assistant directors would account for the inverse association observed between levels and major subdivisions because the few "super-divisions" headed by the assistant directors, not the former divisions, would now be defined as the "major subdivisions" by the criterion used. This change would also help to explain why number of levels and span of control of middle managers, which includes assistant directors, are correlated without controls (.27) but are no longer significantly related once size, subdivisions, and other conditions are controlled (.11). The assumptions here are that the assistant directors, whose establishment increases levels, have a particularly wide span of control—hence the zero-order correlation—but that the introduction of this new level occurs usually in large agencies and reduces the number of major subdivisions—hence the considerably lower correlation under these controls.

Differentiation into a multilevel hierarchy has evident advantages for expanding organizations, according to these conjectures. In fact the number of levels in finance departments increases with increasing size, as previously noted; so does the number of major subdivisions, however (the zero-order correlation between size and subdivisions being .43, nearly as large as that between size and levels, .51). Not all large agencies have many levels and few major divisions. The inverse association between levels and subdivisions when size is controlled implies the existence of two contrasting departmental structures, one that is primarily differentiated horizontally into many major divisions and one that is primarily differentiated vertically into many levels. The question is what conditions discourage horizontal differentiation—which places an excessive administrative burden on top management—and encourage vertical differentiation instead.

The clue for answering this question is provided by the other major correlate of number of levels, namely, automation, which reveals a substantial association with it (.34) that persists when other conditions are controlled (.23). Although extending the hierarchy has administrative advantages for the top executive of a large organization, it also removes him increasingly from the operating level and makes it difficult for him directly to control operations and keep tight reins on them. This loss of close contact with the operating level is a serious disadvantage for a director who relies largely on direct supervision for control, but it is not such a disadvantage if top management has instituted indirect mechanisms of control and can exercise with their aid sufficient influence on operations by setting policies and formulating programs. The automation of accounting procedures through computers is just such an impersonal mechanism of control in finance departments. It places much controlling influence over operations into the hands of the top executives whose decisions determine the overall setup of the automated facilities and the nature of the computer programs, thereby obviating the need for much direct supervision. The assembly line serves similar functions in factories.[26] Since automation serves as a control mechanism that greatly reduces the main disadvantage of multilevel hierarchies, it furthers their development.[27]

The general principle suggested is that conditions in organizations that make the reliable performance of duties relatively independent of direct intervention by top management further the development of multilevel hierarchies. Advanced technological equipment, inasmuch as it mechanizes operations and makes them to some degree self-regulating, often serves this function. The mechanization of facilities is not the only condition that affects the reliability of performance, however. Regardless of how automated operations are, top management must rely on its managerial staff

[26] Blau and Scott, *op. cit.*, pp. 176–178.

[27] It is also possible that the causal direction is the opposite from that assumed above, which would mean that agencies with multiple levels are more likely than others to introduce automation, quite possibly because they benefit particularly from its function as a control mechanism.

to implement its objectives and administer its policies. Herein lies the significance of promotion procedures for the hierarchy. Explicit promotion regulations furnish uniform standards that all higher officials must have met. But these standards assure top management that higher officials will have adequate qualifications for their responsibilities only if they stipulate that promotions be based primarily on examinations designed to test these qualifications rather than on seniority or the possibly idiosyncratic evaluations of supervisors. A significant correlation between the weight of written examinations in promotions and number of levels remains when other conditions are controlled (.13), but the correlation between the existence of promotion regulations and levels disappears when the weight of examinations and other conditions are controlled (.04). The reason probably is that only promotion regulations that give merit examinations much weight guarantee that all managerial officials have certain minimum qualifications and thus reduce top management's reluctance to lose direct contact with the operating level by establishing intervening layers in the hierarchy.

The more top management trusts the middle managers who constitute its administrative arm to discharge their responsibilities in accordance with its guidelines and directives, the more inclined it will be in all likelihood to delegate responsibilities to them. The implication is that the degree of confidence top executives place in their managerial assistance will promote decentralization of authority as well as multilevel hierarchies. If this surmise is correct, it could explain why the zero-order correlation between number of levels and decentralization (.18) is reduced to a point that falls just short of significance at .05 when other conditions that affect management's trust are controlled (.12).

Entrance requirements that demand comparatively high qualification of employees undoubtedly improve their abilities to perform their duties without close supervision. The interpretation advanced implies, therefore, that the proportion of the agency personnel expected to have college degrees and the number of levels in the hierarchy are positively related. As a matter of fact, such a positive zero-order correlation has been observed (.16), but controlling other conditions reduces this correlation to the vanishing point (.03). The proportion of employees with college training is not strongly associated with any of the other control variables under consideration, but it is somewhat correlated with four of them (between .12 and .14), its most pronounced zero-order correlation being that with decentralization (.14). A plausible explanation of this pattern of findings can be derived if expert qualifications are viewed as simply one element in a configuration of conditions indicative of operations that are relatively self-regulating and independent of direct intervention by management. As part of this configuration, the qualifications of employees are associated with the development of multilevel hierarchies. But once the other factors that manifest independence of managerial intervention are controlled, including those to which expert qualifications directly contribute, such as decentralization, the entire significance of qualifications for the hierarchy has been taken into account, and they are no longer associated with the number of levels.

Two Contrasting Types

In conclusion, some inferences about two contrasting types of formal organization will be drawn from the associations with multilevel hierarchy observed. One of these types may be considered the modern organization governed by universalistic standards; the other represents the old-fashioned bureaucracy.

A fundamental issue confronting the executives of organizations is whether to manage primarily by means of direct or indirect controls. Management through direct controls entails keeping in close touch with operations and issuing corrective orders whenever necessary. Management through indirect controls involves devising impersonal control mechanisms that constrain operations to follow automatically the policies and programs specified by top executives. The substitution of indirect mechanisms of control for direct control requires that an orientation to abstract universalistic standards replace reliance on personal judgments. The development of these impersonal control mechanisms is most likely if technical considerations and effective performance are supreme values, whereas ideological commitments and particularistic solidarities have little significance.[28]

Today the prototype of an impersonal control mechanism is the computer, which dramatically illustrates how technological facilities automate operations and simultaneously give top management—whose decisions govern the basic computer setup—much control over them without requiring frequent direct intervention. Not only the operations themselves but also the recruitment of employees and that of the managerial staff tend to become standardized in the modern organization in terms of universalistic principles of effective performance. Explicit personnel regulations stipulate merit criteria for employment and for advancement to managerial positions, relieving top management of administrative tasks, lessening the influence of personal bias and variations in judgment over personnel decisions, and assuring minimum qualifications. Both the automation of the work process and the merit standards that the managerial and operating staff must meet contribute to the reliable performance of duties and help to make operations comparatively self-regulating within the framework of the organization's objectives and

---

[28] It is evident that this orientation is inappropriate for certain kinds of organizations, such as religious congregations or ideological political parties.

management's policies. These conditions reduce management's need to keep close direct control over operations and, consequently, often give rise to major changes in the hierarchy. To wit, vertical differentiation creates a multilevel hierarchy, which usually decreases the number of major divisions whose heads report to the agency director and increases the span of control of these division heads, and responsibilities become decentralized. The strongest pressure to institute impersonal mechanisms of control, and thus the conditions that facilitate these structural changes, comes from the expanding size of organizations.

In short, the modern organization is characterized by a tall, slim hierarchy with decentralized authority. The opposite type, which may be called an old-fashioned bureaucracy, has a squat hierarchy with authority centralized at the top. In this case, which is most prevalent in smaller organizations, the top executive maintains tight control over operations by directly supervising many division heads, assigning each of them only few subordinates, refraining from introducing intermediate levels that would increase his distance from the operating personnel, and delegating few responsibilities. The lesser interest in impersonal mechanisms of control under these circumstances is reflected in the rare instances of automation and in the nature of the personnel policies. Explicit regulations that specify personnel qualifications are infrequent; promotions are largely left under the discretion of management; and insofar as promotion standards do exist, they tend to give weight to seniority and personal judgments of superiors rather than objective merit criteria, thus implicitly enhancing the importance of loyalty at the expense of that of technical competence.

A final question to be raised is whether these conclusions concerning two contrasting types of formal structure apply to all work organizations (those employing people to perform tasks), or only to government agencies, or perhaps only to government finance departments. The methodological point made in the introduction bears repeating in this connection: generalizing beyond the data is necessary for scientific cumulation because such generalizing supplies the sole connection between different empirical studies. The finding that multilevel finance departments in the United States have fewer major divisions than others of the same size, for example, can neither be negated nor confirmed by research on other organizations, for the association between levels and divisions in another type of agency simply has no direct bearing on it. Only if the investigator is willing to advance generalizations that refer to broader concepts than his empirical data—all work organizations or vertical differentiation of any kind—is it possible to replicate or refute conclusions and ultimately to develop a scientific theory.

Hence the empirical findings from the study of finance departments are deliberately used to suggest tentative principles about work organizations in general, to be tested and appropriately modified in future research, just as the inferences drawn in our earlier study were tested and refined this one. Some indication that the conclusions about hierarchical structure are at least not restricted to finance departments is provided by a preliminary analysis of data on quite another type of government agency. The state employment security agencies in this country are large roof organizations, each consisting of a state headquarters and an average of forty local offices dispersed throughout the state, and their median size is more than ten times that of finance departments. Despite these differences, most of the factors associated with multiple levels in finance departments reveal similar zero-order correlations in state employment agencies, even though several of the measures are far from identical (compare the last with the first column in Table 14.2). Controlling size tends to increase the similarity; for instance, number of divisions and number of levels are inversely correlated when size (after logarithmic transformation) is controlled in employment security agencies $(-.37)$, as they are in finance departments $(-.34)$.

These parallels lend some credibility to the claim that the propositions about hierarchical differentiation suggested in this paper are fairly general principles about work organizations, or in any case about the government agencies among them, though further research will undoubtedly call for revisions and refinements. The tentative conclusion is that impersonal mechanisms of control, such as automation and merit personnel standards, help transform flat structures in which the chief executive exercises much personal control into multilevel hierarchies with decentralized authority.

15. The Colleague Climate and Faculty Orientations in Academic Institutions

Universities and colleges are complex organizations, and conditions in them vary widely. The problem to which this paper addresses itself is how the varying conditions of academic life influence the orientations of faculty members to work in their discipline and to their own institution. Which characteristics of academic institutions affect the interest and involvement of faculty members in research, and does the colleague group exert a distinctive effect on research? Which characteristics of universities and colleges influence the allegiance of their faculty members to them, and how does the colleague group influence this allegiance? The data imply that academic salaries and university promotion policies influence faculty research not so much by providing incentives as through processes of selection, but that they nevertheless affect the work of faculty members already selected by creating a colleague climate conducive to research. The analysis also reveals that the

Originally published in 1973.

significance of faculty qualifications and work orientations for allegiance to the local institution poses a paradox, which has its roots in the academic stratification system.

It is a basic sociological assumption that the social environment influences the attitudes and activities of individuals. An implication of this assumption is that the composition of the colleague group in a university or college has structural effects on the academic orientation and work of individuals, for example, on their concern with research. If faculty members with superior qualifications are more interested in research than others, the colleague climate in a faculty with superior qualifications is expected to enhance the research interests of individuals beyond the degree of interest their own qualifications would engender in another environment. To test this hypothesis requires that the effects on a person's research orientation and involvement of his colleagues' qualifications be analytically separated from those of his own.

The procedure previously suggested for this purpose[1]—using contingency tables to separate the influences of an individual's own and his colleagues' traits on a dependent variable—has been justly criticized on two grounds. If characteristics of individuals that are continuous variables are held constant in contingency tables using two or three categories, they are in fact not effectively held constant, and what appears in the tables like an effect of the characteristics of others in his environment may actually be an effect of his own characteristics that have not been fully controlled.[2] Second, even assuming that characteristics that are unquestionably the independent variable, such as sex, are adequately controlled for individuals, the finding that their prevalence in a group is related to certain attitudes does not demonstrate a structural effect of these characteristics in the social environment on these attitudes, because other factors correlated with their prevalence may have produced the effect.[3]

Both criticisms can be met in the analysis to be presented, which therefore provides an opportunity to show that structural effects can be discerned and to indicate the proper method for doing so. First, the regression procedures to be employed, in contrast to contingency tables, effectively control all other independent variables in the equation as partial coefficients reveal the relationship between any one and the dependent variable. Second, most of the conditions in universities and colleges affecting a given de-

[1] Peter M. Blau, "Structural Effects," *American Sociological Review* 25 (1960), 178–193 (see Chapter 4).

[2] Arnold S. Tannenbaum and Jerald G. Bachman, "Structural Versus Individual Effects," *American Journal of Sociology* 69 (1964), 585–595.

[3] Robert M. Hauser, "Context and Consex," *American Journal of Sociology* 75 (1970), 645–664.

pendent variable will be held constant when examining the structural effects of the colleague climate. By controlling the conditions known to account for one half or more of the variation in a dependent variable *among* academic institutions when analyzing the effects of the colleague climate, the likelihood that its observed effects are really due to unknown correlates of it is greatly diminished.[4] Structural effects of the colleague climate in universities and colleges on orientation to and involvement in research as well as on orientation to the local institution will be investigated.

Method

The sample consists of 2,577 faculty members in 114 academic institutions.[5] The sampling procedure involved three steps. First, a sample of universities and colleges was drawn from all those that granted four-year degrees in the liberal arts in 1964. The likelihood that an academic institution is included in the sample was made proportionate to its size, except that institutions of superior quality were selected in disproportionate numbers. Second, the sampling of departments within an institution was designed to make the probability of inclusion proportionate to the size of departments. Six departments (or combinations in the case of very small ones) were selected from every institution, and which ones of four broad fields these represented was systematically rotated. Third, the rate at which individuals within a department were selected are inversely proportionate to its size, so that a higher percentage of the members of small than those of large departments are included. Lists of faculty members in the selected departments were updated, and those who are still graduate students were eliminated. The number of faculty responses per institution ranges from four to fifty-nine, with a mean of twenty-three and a median of twenty-one. The return rate was 65 per cent. Faculty members from better institutions are overrepresented in the sample.

The results of three regression analyses are shown in Table 15.1, and those of one in Table 15.2, together with the zero-order correlations. The beta weights indicate the direct effects of a given independent on the dependent

[4] The importance of controlling other factors in multivariate analysis when investigating structural effects is noted in the critical comments on Hauser's article by Allen H. Barton, *American Journal of Sociology* 76 (1970), 514–517. Hauser's main criticism of structural or contextual effects (repeated in his reply to Barton, *ibid.*, p. 519) that they may be spurious due to unknown correlates is quite meaningless without specifying what the correlates might be, because any empirical finding not based on a controlled experiment can be similarly dismissed by saying that it may have been produced by some unknown correlates.

[5] I am grateful to Talcott Parsons and Gerald M. Platt for making the results of this faculty survey of theirs available to me to be analyzed together with the data on institutional characteristics I collected from administrators and published sources.

variable when all other variables included in the analysis are controlled, and the simple correlations indicate the corresponding associations without controls. The independent variables are presented in the tables in the order of their assumed causal sequence. The substantive meaning of the difference between a simple correlation and the corresponding beta weight depends on these assumptions about the causal order among variables. A difference accounted for by other independent variables assumed to be antecedents of the one under consideration (shown in the rows above it) indicates a spurious association and thus no effect, whereas a difference accounted for by variables assumed to be consequences of the one considered (shown in the rows below it) indicates indirect effects mediated by these intervening variables. The discussion of the findings in the text supplies decomposition coefficients that specify how much of the indirect effect of an independent on the dependent variable is mediated by a certain intervening variable.

To isolate the structural effect on research orientations of the colleague climate, a regression analysis of the research orientations of the faculty members sampled is performed, introducing as independent variables *both* the proportion of faculty respondents in each individual's institution who have Ph.D.'s or advanced professional degrees and whether the individual himself or herself has one. Three regression analyses are presented, one for a person's actual *involvement* in research, one for the *obligation* to publish research, and one for the *weight* research has for promotions to tenure positions at the institution, in all three cases as reported by faculty respondents.[6] Other institutional conditions affecting research orientations are included as independent variables in the regression analyses, and so is a person's broad discipline (whether or not it is a natural science). The analysis is intended to meet the criticisms raised against cruder procedures used earlier for identifying structural effects. As noted above, the objection that contingency tables do not effectively control independent variables does not apply to regression analysis, in which variables are effectively controlled. The second criticism was that effects attributed to a given structural difference— in the case at hand, differences in the proportion of the faculty with advanced

---

[6] The three measures are as follows. (1) Involvement: five-point score, with one point each for the answers to the questions whether the respondent is engaged in research, whether he is engaged in research or creative activity, whether he has received research support in the last three years, and whether he expects to publish (used only for individuals). (2) Obligation: in a list of what "*are* faculty obligations at your institution," the item "to publish my research" (five-point score for individuals; percentage agreeing for institution). (3) Weight: "At this institution it is very difficult for a man to achieve tenure if he is not engaged in research." (Five-point score for individuals; percentage agreeing for institution.) Although the number of faculty respondents per institution is small, this is not a serious problem, since all individuals from various institutions with similar characteristics are considered together in the regression analysis.

degrees—may actually be the result of entirely different factors correlated with these differences. But since two-thirds of the variation among institutions in faculty qualifications and three-fifths of those in research orientations can be accounted for by known antecedents, it seems not very likely that some undiscovered institutional correlate of faculty qualifications really is responsible for the observed effects of colleague qualifications on research orientations.

The results of all three regression analyses are presented in Table 15.1 side by side to facilitate comparison. Very small beta weights are more than twice their standard error, because the number of cases is so large, and those that are less than .10, though they will be mentioned, should be considered trivial. The last row of the table illustrates such trivial effects. Natural scientists put slightly more emphasis on research, in all three respects, than faculty members in other disciplines. It is surprising that natural scientists are only a little more involved in research than scholars in other disciplines once the greater proportion of natural scientists with advanced degrees ($r = .22$) is controlled. The slim difference in research activities (column 1) is reflected in a similar difference in research obligations (column 3), and promotions also seem to depend slightly more on research in the natural sciences than in other fields (column 5).

Structural Effects on Research

Faculty members who have advanced degrees are actively involved in research substantially more often than those who do not, but they are no more likely to report that research is given much weight in promotions to tenure in their institution (columns 1 and 5, row 6, Table 15.1). This is precisely the difference one would anticipate on the assumption that respondents accurately report the weight research has in their institution, which should not be affected by their own training, and that their reports of their own research activities are also fairly accurate, since better trained persons are expected to be more involved in research than others. Hence the findings help validate the measures used. Research obligations are influenced by the individual's own training, but only to a small degree (column 3), which suggests that research obligations reflect primarily institutional personnel practices rather than the individual's training for and interest in research. Indeed, the individual's obligations have a considerably higher correlation with the weight research has in the institution (.63)—and his own statement of what this weight is (.62)—than with his research involvement (.34). Yet a person's own training does color his response concerning obligations, though the question was worded as a factual statement (whether publishing their re-

Table 15.1   Three Measures of Research Emphasis

	Research Involvement		Research Obligations		Research Weight for Tenure	
	1. Beta Weight	2. Simple Correlation	3. Beta Weight	4. Simple Correlation	5. Beta Weight	6. Simple Correlation
Institution						
1. Size	−.03		−.01		−.01	
		.28		.40		.44
2. Percentage of graduate students	−.06*		.12**		.14**	
		.28		.45		.51
3. University	.08**		.26**		.26**	
		.34		.51		.53
4. Salaries	.19**		.16**		.26**	
		.42		.50		.57
Colleague climate						
5. Percentage with advanced degrees	.22**		.15**		.14**	
		.48		.52		.55
Individual						
6. Advanced degree	.26**		.07**		−.03	
		.42		.29		.22
7. Natural scientist	.04*		.05**		.04*	
		.16		.16		.14
	$R^2 = 30; n = 2577$		$R^2 = .37; n = 2399$		$R^2 = .43; n = 2518$	

* More than twice its standard error

** More than three times its standard error.

search *is* an obligation of faculty members at the institution), which indicates that the answers are not purely factual reports but to some degree express internalized feelings of obligations.

The colleague climate exerts a pronounced influence on the research involvement of individuals, independent of the individual's own training and of institutional conditions—an influence nearly as strong as that of his or her own training (column 1, row 5, Table 5.2). Since we just saw that faculty members who have advanced degrees are more involved in research than those who do not, the proportion with advanced degrees on the faculty, the measure of colleague climate, is indicative of prevalent research activities as well as qualifications. The colleague climate also influences research obligations and the weight research has for promotions, but not so much (columns 3 and 5). Unless many faculty members have the advanced training that fosters research interests and activities, administrators and personnel committees are unlikely to give much weight to research in promotions, and faculty members are unlikely to experience strong obligations to publish research. (The emphasis on research in an academic institution probably has a reciprocal effect on qualifications, attracting more faculty members whose advanced training makes them interested in research.) Although these promotion policies and obligations undoubtedly influence the degree of actual involvement in research, they do not account for the influence of the colleague climate on this involvement. For adding measures of research weight and obligations to the independent variables in column 1 virtually does not reduce the direct effect of colleague climate on research involvement ($b^* = .21$, compared to the original .22).

Whether a faculty member's research interests are stimulated or stifled in an academic institution depends on his colleagues, on how many of them have completed graduate education, which has socialized as well as trained them for research, and which makes it probable that they are actually engaged in research. The discussions of such colleagues about their research experiences—the problems encountered and the exciting discoveries made— with those who share research interests, and primarily with them, are incentives likely to activate any latent interest in research a person may have. To become a genuine member of a colleague group of this kind, one must be involved in research and thus be able to participate fully in the discussions about research. Colleagues with research skills facilitate one's own research by tending to give advice when needed, since being asked for advice is a welcome sign of respect for their superior skills, and they make working on research more gratifying by furnishing attentive listeners interested in hearing about promising leads and suggestive results. These processes of social exchange are a continual source of rewards for scholarly endeavors and create group pressures to engage in scholarly research by depriving those failing to do so of social rewards. In colleague groups whose members are not identified by their training and experience with research, opposite normative pressures tend to stifle the individual's research interests; here the often arduous process of scholarship is not rewarded with social approval but frequently ridiculed with such phrases as "publish or perish."

Higher average faculty salaries in academic institutions promote greater emphasis on research, in all three respects considered. They have a direct effect on each of the three expressions of the importance of research, which is stronger on the weight of research in promotions than on research obligations and involvements, as row 4 in Table 15.1 shows. This direct effect is complemented by an indirect one mediated in all three cases mostly by the proportion of faculty members with advanced degrees (decomposition coefficient: for weight, .10; for obligation, .11; for involvement, .16). The indirect effects are readily explained: the faculties with better research qualifications recruited with higher salaries make it possible to give research more weight in promotions, increase research obligations, and produce a colleague climate that fosters active involvement in research. [Twice as much of the influence of salaries on research involvement is mediated by the climate of qualified colleagues (decomposition coefficient, .16) as by the individual's own qualifications (.08), and the differences are still more pronounced for weight of research and for research obligations.]

But what accounts for the direct effect of salaries on the three manifestations of research emphasis? It may well be the greater research abilities that are reflected in higher salaries even when formal qualifications are controlled. On this assumption, the direct effects of salaries on research orientations can be explained in the same terms as their indirect effects mediated by formal qualifications. The productive scientists and scholars who command better salaries encourage making tenure appointments dependent on research, strengthen research obligations, and promote active involvement in research. The influence of a climate of superior colleagues on the individual's tendency to be engaged in research is greater than the direct effect of colleague climate in row 5 (of column 1) implies, inasmuch as the direct effect of salaries in row 4 as well as their indirect effect mediated by colleague climate (together, .35) also partly reflect this influence.[7] High salaries have a "snowball effect" on scholarly research in an academic institution, because they not only attract more productive scholars and scientists but consequently create a colleague climate that further stimulates scholarly activity.

Effects of Institutional Policies

The extent of graduate training in an academic institution influences the various aspects of research emphasis in ways that are complementary to the influences of an individual's own advanced training. The fact that an institution is a university granting Ph.D.'s (a dummy variable) has a pronounced direct effect, regardless of other conditions, on the weight research has for

---

[7] Whereas the beta weights and the decomposition coefficients pertaining to the same independent and dependent variable in a regression analysis can be added (and must sum to their simple correlation), the beta weights of different independent variables (those in different rows) must not be added, although they do indicate independent influences that together are greater than either.

promotions and on the faculty's research obligations, and the proportion of graduate students has independent direct effects further increasing the weight of research and research obligations. (See the beta weights in rows 3 and 2, columns 5 and 3, of Table 15.1.) These direct effects are supplemented by indirect effects of both university status and percentage of graduate students on both weight of research for tenure and research obligations, which are mediated by higher salaries and the better qualified faculties they attract. (The decomposition coefficients of salaries and qualifications together are similar in the four cases, varying only between .19 and .25.) In contrast, the research involvement of individuals is mostly indirectly and hardly directly affected by their being in universities with many graduate students. When other conditions are controlled, the remaining positive relationship of research involvement with university status is small and that with percentage of graduate students has even turned into a slight negative relationship (column 1). The pattern of influence of universities with much graduate work is the reverse of that of the individual's own advanced training, which has direct effects increasing research involvement substantially but research obligations little and weight of research in appointments not at all, as we have seen (compare the three beta weights in row 6 with those in rows 2 and 3).

These findings help answer the question of whether the stronger orientation to research in universities with many graduate students is attributable to a more stimulating academic environment or to different administrative practices. The direct effects clearly indicate that universities granting Ph.D.'s, and to a lesser extent all institutions with many graduate students, have personnel practices that differ from those in undergraduate colleges, giving more weight to research in faculty appointments and obligating their faculties to publish research. When other conditions are controlled, university status and proportion of graduate students hardly affect the extent to which faculty members are actually engaged in research, which seems to imply that the differences in personnel policies do not create an academic environment more conducive to research in institutions concentrating on graduate work than in undergraduate colleges. This is not correct, however, since it ignores indirect effects. Both university status and percentage of graduate students indirectly promote research involvement, as the considerable simple correlations in column 2, which are not spurious, show. Individual faculty members in universities with many graduate students are more likely to be engaged in research than are those in undergraduate colleges because they themselves are better trained (decomposition coefficients, .07 and .06 for university and graduate students, respectively) and particularly because their academic environment consists of more stimulating colleagues, who are better trained (.13 and .12) and command higher salaries (.10 and .13).

The substantial differences in research orientations accompanying variations in institutional size (number of faculty) also raise the question of whether differences in colleague environments or in administrative practices between large and small institutions are responsible. In this case the answer the data give is different, as row 1 in Table 15.1 indicates. Although the simple correlations show that large academic institutions exhibit more research emphasis in all three respects, the beta weights reveal that size itself makes no difference in any of them once other conditions are controlled. Large institutions are more likely than small ones to be universities and have more graduate students, which partly accounts for the greater weight of research for tenure appointments and for the greater research obligations in them (together, the decomposition coefficients are .22 in both cases), and *individuals* in them are more likely to have advanced degrees, which accounts for a slight part of the influence of size on research involvement (.06). The major reason for the more pronounced research orientations in large academic institutions, however, is the superior colleague environment, as indicated by the formal qualifications of colleagues and the salaries they command (together, .23 for weight; .27 for obligations; .23 for involvement).[8]

Faculty members generally have both more and better qualified colleagues in their own field in large than in small academic institutions. The small number of members in most departments in a small institution means that most social contacts on the job are with colleagues in other departments, who cannot provide the same stimulation and social support for research as can colleagues in one's specialty. The number of colleagues in the same discipline who are trained and interested in research tends to be sufficiently large in large academic institutions to stimulate specialized scholarly interests and thereby increase active involvement of faculty members in research as well as their obligations to publish and the weight they give to research in promotions. Whereas the comparatively strong research emphasis in universities concentrating on graduate work results in good part from distinctive administrative policies in universities, that produced by large size does not result from different administrative policies in large and small institutions. This is implied by the finding that size, in contrast to both university status and percentage of graduate students, has no direct effect on the weight of research in tenure appointments. The *indirect* effect large size, independent of extent of graduate training, does have on the weight of research in tenure decisions seems to be due primarily to the greater commitment to research of faculty members in large institutions, which presumably affects their personnel recommendations. These greater research commitments in turn are apparently attributable to the stronger peer group pressures exerted by the

---

[8] Since individual's own salary is not controlled, these figures somewhat overestimate the three mediating effects of colleague climate.

larger and better qualified colleague groups that share specialized interests in large academic institutions.

Before concluding this section, let us examine briefly how the weight of research in an institution influences faculty obligations to publish and how both affect actual involvements in research, assuming that the causal sequence is weight—obligations—involvement.[9] The weight of research in senior appointments (if added to the independent variables in Table 15.1 in a regression analysis of obligations) exerts the dominant influence on the obligations of faculty members to publish research ($b^* = .48$; $r = .63$).[10] The importance of research for tenure appointments in an institution is the main immediate determinant of faculty research obligations—though this finding does not indicate whether incentives or selection are responsible— and it mediates some of the other influences on obligations.

Faculties of universities concentrating on graduate work express stronger obligations to publish than those of undergraduate colleges largely because research has greater weight in university appointments (decomposition coefficient for university status, .34; for percentage of graduate students, .32), which supports the interpretation that these effects represent differences in personnel policies between universities and undergraduate colleges. The influence of salaries on research obligations is also primarily accounted for by the greater weight of research in the appointment decisions of institutions paying better salaries (.39), and the beta coefficient of salaries becomes actually negative ($-.08$) when weight as well as other conditions are controlled. The main reason that salaries and research obligations are associated is that institutions paying higher salaries have more stringent research requirements for appointments. The negative beta weight might reflect a lesser concern with salaries of the individuals most committed to research, though this is sheer speculation.

[9] Weight is measured by aggregate faculty responses in an institution, whereas obligations are measured by individual responses, for a substantive and a methodological reason. Substantively, the weight of research for promotions is an institutional characteristic but obligations are experienced by individuals. Methodologically, the high zero-order correlation between the aggregate responses concerning weight and obligations (.94) creates problems of multicollinearity making it inadvisable to use both as independent variables in a regression analysis. The correlation between weight defined by aggregate responses and obligations defined by individual responses is considerably lower (.63). The difference is of some substantive interest, indicating that the basic influence on publishing obligations is the weight of research in the institution and that individual variations in feelings of obligations tend to cancel one another when the answers of the various individuals in an institution are aggregated.

[10] The beta weights of all independent variables are: size, .01; percentage of graduate students, .05*; university, .10**; salaries, —.08*; colleague climate, .10**; individual's degree, .07**; natural scientist, .05**; weight of research, .48**. The R^2 is .42.

A faculty member's active involvement in research is affected only indirectly by the weight of research in promotions, not directly as would be expected if incentives were operative. This conclusion is based on a regression analysis of involvement with weight and obligations included as independent variables together with those in Table 15.1. The direct effect of the weight of research in promotions on research involvement is close to zero ($b^* = .04$), though it has indirect effects ($r = .42$). The importance of research for an institution's tenure appointments increases the research activities of faculty members primarily because it raises their own research qualifications (decomposition coefficient, .08) and because it furnishes them with more research-oriented colleagues, as indicated by their better qualifications (.15) and the better salaries they command (.13). The individual's research obligations have some direct effect on his or her research involvement ($b^* = .06$), but most of the association between the two ($r = .34$) is indirect, resulting in smaller part from the individual's own training (.07) and in larger part from the colleague climate (.11 for colleague training and .08 for salaries). None of the direct effects of the other independent variables, shown in column 1 of Table 15.1, is altered by more than .03,[11] which means that the interpretations suggested need not be modified.

The findings imply that an academic institution's personnel policies affect the research activities of faculty members in two ways but not in a third. The dependence of promotions on research does not appear to motivate individuals who are not already inclined to engage in research. Appointments based on research raise research involvements by governing the selection of persons committed to research and by consequently providing a colleague climate that stimulates research interests. Indications are that the academic qualifications of a faculty member's colleagues influence his research involvement no less than his own.

Allegiance to Local Institution

Although the comment is often made that faculty members today have little loyalty to their university or college,[12] three-fifths of those interviewed agree with the statement, "My allegiance to my present *institution* is very strong." This reveals considerable institutional loyalty, granting that it is easier to

[11] All the beta weights in this regression equation are: size, $-.02$; percentage of graduate students, $-.07**$; university, $.05*$; salaries, $.17**$; colleague climate, $.21**$; individual's degree, $.25**$; natural scientist, $.05*$; weight of research, $.04$; research obligations, $.06*$. The R^2 is .31.

[12] See, for example, Christopher Jencks and David Reisman, *The Academic Revolution* (Garden City, N.Y.: Doubleday-Anchor, 1969), p. 14.

express loyalty verbally than in action. Not all universities and colleges command the same allegiance, of course. The findings suggest that faculty attitudes to their own institution depend not alone on its attraction but also on the extent to which these attitudes are diverted by a cosmopolitan orientation to outside reference groups.

Three characteristics of an academic institution affect the allegiance of their faculty members to it, as indicated by a five-point score expressing the individual's strength of allegiance. A fourth factor, the institution's location, affects faculty loyalty only in small colleges. Small colleges in the Northeast command less allegiance from their faculties than those in the three other regions of the country, perhaps owing to the proverbial cosmopolitanism of Easterners, but there are no corresponding differences by location in institutions with a faculty of more than 165, probably because other conditions have overriding importance in larger academic institutions. Since there are nearly three times as many faculty members in larger than in these small academic institutions, the influence of location on allegiance, which is confined to the small ones, is hardly apparent in the regression analysis of all faculty members, as the first row in Table 15.2 shows. (Since regression analysis ignores such interaction effects, these must be looked for by using special procedures.)

Row 2 in Table 15.2 indicates that faculty members express less allegiance to public academic institutions than to private ones, be they religious or secular. The religious ties of many faculty members to denominational colleges and universities may account for their stronger allegiance, but religion cannot account for the similar difference in allegiance between private secular and public institutions.[13] The impersonal conditions in public academic institutions do not invite strong personal commitments to them. This conjecture is supported by the finding in row 3 that large academic institutions command less loyalty of their faculties than small ones, independent of other conditions, inasmuch as large size also implies greater impersonality. The stronger personal bonds among faculty members in a small college strengthen local attachments. The impersonality of large places, universities no less than cities, weakens local bonds and fosters cosmopolitan perspectives.

Inbreeding promotes faculty loyalty, as the fourth row in Table 15.2 indicates. The larger the proportion of recently appointed faculty members who have degrees from the same institution, the greater is the allegiance of faculty members to it. The finding presumably reflects the greater identification

---

[13] Although the dummy variable of private secular institution has a negative simple correlation with allegiance, it has a positive direct effect supplementing that of religious institution if both are used in a regression analysis instead of the dichotomy public-private; since the two have parallel effects, the dichotomy public-private, which combines them, is used instead.

Table 15.2   Allegiance to Local Institution

	Beta Weight	Simple Correlation
Institution		
1. Northeast	−.02	−.02
2. Public	−.07**	−.13
3. Size (log)	−.16**	−.17
4. Inbreeding	.16**	.16
Colleague climate		
5. Percentage with advanced degrees	.08*	−.13
6. Percentage who emphasize teaching	−.14**	.13
Individual		
7. Advanced degree	−.06*	−.08
8. Emphasis on teaching	.21**	.28
9. Research involvement	−.10**	−.18
10. Undergraduate contacts	.08**	.15
11. Tenure position	.28**	.30
$R^2 = .21$; $n = 2552$		

* More than twice its standard error.
** More than three times its standard error.

with a university or college of faculty members who received their education there. Unfortunately, this inference cannot be tested, since no information is available about where particular individuals obtained their degrees.

The factor that exerts the strongest influence on a faculty member's loyalty to his academic institution is that he has a tenure appointment (row 11 in Table 15.2).[14] Until the university or college makes a commitment to an individual by giving him a tenure position, he is naturally hesitant to make a strong commitment to it. Dressel and his colleagues similarly find "that there is a progression from orientation to discipline to department to university as one rises in rank." They go on to explain:

> The younger assistant professor has few friends in his new job. . . . As he gets older he makes more friends; at first they

[14] Placing the dummy variable of whether the individual has a tenure position in the last row is not meant to imply that it necessarily follows orientations to academic work in a causal sequence. No causal assumptions about the individual characteristics in the last four rows in Table 15.2 are made.

come from his department and then from the larger university in which he works. As he publishes fewer papers than anticipated, and receives less acclaim from his discipline, he turns to others with whom he daily interacts for job-related rewards. Thus his attachment to the discipline weakens as he is pulled into the social web of the university. [15]

A faculty member's own academic qualifications and those of his colleagues have opposite effects on his local allegiance. Individuals who have completed advanced training express slightly less allegiance to their academic institution than those who have not (row 7 in Table 15.2). Moreover, a faculty member's involvement in research further reduces his commitment to his place of employment (row 9). One reason why the individual's formal qualifications have so small a *direct* negative effect on his local commitment in the table ($-.06$) is that part of their negative effect is *indirect*, mediated by the greater research involvement usually accompanying superior qualifications (decomposition coefficient, $-.04$). Well qualified academics actively engaged in research tend to be enmeshed in the wider community of scientists or scholars in their discipline, and their cosmopolitan reference groups limit their local commitments.

The superior qualifications of a person's colleagues in the institution, on the other hand, strengthen his or her allegiance to the academic community (row 5). While his own superior qualifications make a person less dependent on the academic institution where he works, his colleagues' superior qualifications make it a more attractive place for him. The structural effect of superior faculty qualifications is the reverse of that of superior individual qualifications on allegiance. Although these opposite influences are small, other influences reveal the same kind of reversal in stronger form.

Individual faculty members who emphasize the importance of teaching are considerably more loyal to their local institution than those who do not (row 8 in Table 15.2). The frequency of a faculty member's contacts with undergraduates, which is another indication of interest in teaching, further strengthens loyalty to his or her university or college (row 10). Here we have the prototype of Gouldner's academic locals, who are much dedicated to undergraduate education and exhibit firm loyalties to their college.[16]

The more prevalent an emphasis on teaching is in an academic institution, by contrast, the less loyalty does it command from its faculty (row 6). For better or for worse, teaching does not have as high standing in academic circles as scholarly research, which puts teachers at a disadvantage in their

---

[15] Paul L. Dressel *et al.*, *The Confidence Crisis* (San Francisco: Jossey-Bass, 1970), p. 79.
[16] Alvin W. Gouldner, "Cosmopolitans and Locals," *Administrative Science Quarterly* 2 (1958), 446–447.

relations with colleagues, and which helps to account for the reverse structural effect of teaching concerns on allegiance. A predominant interest in teaching draws a faculty member closer to his academic institution, not only because he derives gratification from educating students there, but also because he probably fails to obtain gratifications in meetings with colleagues in the discipline outside, where his teaching quality is not known and his lack of published research makes him unknown. Since a teaching reputation is largely confined to the local scene, teachers tend to have stronger commitments to their local institution. Given the superior standing of research and researchers, however, a prevailing emphasis on teaching in the institution and among its faculty diminishes the attraction of the institution and of its members for most academics, who typically have internalized the academic norm of scholarly research and respect those who practice it even if they themselves do not. Widespread preoccupation with teaching accordingly tends to lower the value of an academic community in the eyes of most faculty members and reduce commitments to it.

Paradoxically, then, the very qualities of faculty members that make them attractive colleagues and enhance commitments to the institution where they work make them less committed to the institution, and the qualities that raise a faculty member's own loyalty to his college or university reduce that of his colleagues. The source of the paradox is the academic prestige system. Scholars and scientists whose accomplishments are well known in the wider academic discipline are respected colleagues, and their presence increases the allegiance of others to an institution, but they themselves are less dependent on and attached to their local institution. By the same token, faculty members whose limited academic reputation restricts their opportunities and strengthens their allegiance to the local institution are less desirable colleagues, and large numbers of them weaken commitments to an academic community.

Conclusions

Research has superior academic standing and earns a man or woman higher social status than teaching. Orientations to academic work and institutions reflect this in a number of ways. Fully trained faculty members are more interested and involved in research and emphasize teaching less than those who have not completed advanced training. Researchers command higher salaries than teachers. Affluent academic institutions tend to utilize their financial resources to recruit faculties predisposed to research, whereas poorer institutions stress the importance of teaching. Universities require evidence of research abilities, but little evidence of teaching abilities, at least of their graduate faculties, who train the most advanced students and have the highest prestige.

An academic institution's investment of economic resources in faculty members qualified for and interested in research has "snowball effects." Its direct effect on the amount of scholarly research in the institution is supplemented by indirect effects, for it not only increases the proportion of faculty members interested and actively engaged in research but by doing so creates an academic environment of research-oriented colleagues that further promotes research involvement. Whether an individual's research potentials become activated or suppressed depends in part on the colleague climate in his institution, specifically, on the prevalence of research skills and orientations among colleagues, which stimulates his own research interests and exerts group pressures on him to engage in research. The advanced training of the faculty in an institution has a structural effect on research, as well as an effect due to each individual's own training, because the better trained individuals who are more concerned with research create a structure of colleague relations that has an independent effect intensifying research concerns and activities. University policies that make appointments and promotions dependent on research have a catalytic effect similar to that of investments in faculty salaries. Although such personnel procedures do not seem to serve as incentives for individuals to engage in research but largely act as screening devices for selecting faculty members whose training predisposes them to research, they thereby produce a colleague climate in the university that provides additional inducements for becoming more involved in research.

The paradox the academic stratification system produces is that attributes associated with differences in reputation have opposite effects on the loyalty to the local institution of the faculty members possessing them and that of their colleagues. The superior reputation of researchers reduces their commitment to their academic institution, for they are in demand elsewhere, and simultaneously increases the commitments of their colleagues, for their reputation raises the institution's and makes it a more desirable place. Similarly, the inferior reputation of teachers strengthens their allegiance to their university or college, since they have few alternative opportunities, and simultaneously weakens the allegiance of their colleagues, since their emphasis on teaching lessens the institution's attraction for academics. The underlying principle, which unquestionably also applies to the stratification systems outside academia, is that high-status attributes, virtually by definition, create a demand for a person in many places, thus diminishing that person's exclusive attachment to any one place but intensifying the attachments of others to the one where he or she is found.

16. Effects of Community Environment and Organizational Context

IN COLLABORATION WITH RICHARD A. SCHOENHERR

Organizations are, of course, influenced by the social context in which they exist and operate. But most research on organizations confines itself to inquiries into their internal structure and ignores the influences of the environment on it. To be sure, authors of case studies of organizations sometimes speculate about such contextual influences, for example, the effects on an agency of the government that established it, on a work group of the economic Depression that occurred when the observations were made, on a firm of conditions in its market, or on an organization of the city in which it is located. However, a case study of one organization cannot derive, let alone test, generalizations about organizations, and this applies to environmental influences on the organization, just as it does to the relationships between internal characteristics of organizations. Systematic comparison of many organizations is necessary to ascertain general effects of their social contexts on them. This paper illustrates a method for the quantitative analysis of the effects of the community environment and the organizational context on the characteristics of organizations.

Originally published in 1971.

Many organizations are part of larger organizations. Factories belong to companies, which in turn are owned by parent corporations. Local government agencies are segments of departments, and these departments are part of the executive branch of the government. The larger organization to which subsidiary organizations belong are considered their organizational context. The large organization typically contains not only its subsidiary organizations but also a headquarters, which often includes a substantial share of the total personnel.

The (subsidiary) organizations under study are 1,201 local employment security offices, which includes all such offices in the United States that had at least five employees and one supervisor in addition to the office manager in 1966, when the data were collected. These offices are responsible for providing public employment service and for administering unemployment insurance benefits. Some offices have both responsibilities, others only one of the two, and still others are yet more specialized, which in most cases involves employment services for only certain occupations or for only one industry. These offices are branches of fifty-one state employment security agencies. (One of the fifty states had no local office with at least five employees and one supervisor, but there are offices and "state" agencies in two jurisdictions that are not states—the District of Columbia and Puerto Rico.) The characteristics of a state agency constitute the organizational context of its local offices, and the population characteristics of the place where offices are located constitute their community environment.

Method

The procedure used for the contextual analysis of the influence of agency attributes on office attributes is to classify every local office by the characteristics of the agency to which it belongs, as well as by its own, and then to use the contextual variables together with the office variables in multiple regression analysis. Variations among local offices within a state cannot be influenced by contextual variables, because the values of these variables are identical for every local office in a given state. The 1,201 local offices can therefore assume only a maximum of fifty-one different values with respect to contextual variables. But the procedure does not ignore the variations among offices within a state in their own characteristics, and it consequently provides a more conservative estimate of contextual influences than would be obtained by alternative procedures. This can be illustrated by applying two alternatives to the analysis of the influence of agency size on office size. The zero-order correlation between the contextual variable of agency size and the size of the 1,201 offices is .32, whereas the zero-order correlation for fifty-three agencies between their own size and the mean size of the local offices in them is .65. The reason for the great difference is that the former correlation is depressed by the within-state variance in size of offices, whereas the latter ignores this variance. The substantive meaning is that the method of contextual analysis directs attention to the extent to which the entire variability among local offices is influenced by their organizational context, which is different from asking what the relationships are between agency characteristics and average office characteristics.[1]

Information on the community environment is based on census sources, notably the *County and City Data Book*. There are, of course, differences in the local environment among the various offices in a state, but all those in the same community are described by the same environmental variables. For offices located in places with more than 25,000 inhabitants, the city is considered to be the community context, and for offices located in smaller places, the entire county is.[2] This decision was necessitated by the fact that the sources do not supply data on places with fewer than 25,000 inhabitants, but there is reason to assume that offices in small towns often also serve the surrounding countryside, which makes the decision not completely arbitrary. A dummy variable is used to indicate that county rather than city was coded as the environmental context. The use of this dummy variable in the regression analysis (whenever it makes an appreciable difference) results in the influence of city size being split between the dummy variable (reversing sign) and the variable of population size, and the two must be interpreted together. Most community variables are based on data from the 1960 U.S. Census.

The multiple regression analysis treats a given office characteristic as the dependent variable and introduces as independent variables those referring to the agency context, the community context, and the relevant antecedent conditions within the local office itself. Thus, there is a considerable number of independent variables in most regression problems. To keep this number within bounds, contextual variables that do not have a zero-order correlation of more than .20 with the dependent variable are not considered, except in a few cases in which theoretical considerations make it advisable to include them. But smaller partial regression coefficients are accepted as meaningful.

---

[1] The term *context* is used here in the conventional sense of referring to conditions external to the unit under consideration (local office), not in the specialized sense in which it is used in D. S. Pugh *et al.*, "The Context of Organization Structures," *Administrative Science Quarterly* 14 (1969), 91–114.

[2] Alaska and Puerto Rico have no counties; election districts and *municipios*, respectively, are used to code environmental characteristics for offices in small communities in these two jurisdictions.

Inasmuch as no reliable measures for the services provided in every local office are available, the only way to infer how office characteristics influence services is from the relationships between these characteristics and the services performed in the entire agency, for which reliable measures exist. Hence, though agency services as well as other agency variables are always treated as independent variables in the regression analysis (which is necessitated by the technique of contextual analysis), the relationships will sometimes be interpreted as indicative of the influence of office attributes on services in the larger agency. Otherwise, both agency and community context are assumed to precede the characteristics of local offices in the causal sequence. No assumptions are made concerning the relative precedence of agency context and community environment.

Specialization

The fact that an entire office has specialized functions is one of three expressions of specialization, the other two being its internal division of labor and the number of functional sections within it. The most specialized offices furnish employment services to a limited group of occupations—for example, those in the garment industry—while general offices responsible for both unemployment insurance and employment service are at the opposite extreme, with offices responsible for either one but without occupational restrictions being classified as intermediate. The specialization of the office itself (a three–category variable) as well as the division of labor within it encourages the development of many sections. Assuming that the specialized function of an office is an antecedent of all its other characteristics, specialization cannot be influenced by any office variables, and the empirical data indicate that none of the agency characteristics exert a considerable influence on it. But Table 16.1 shows that two conditions in the community, which are manifest in six specific variables, affect the establishment of specialized offices. First, specialized employment security offices are primarily found in large cities as indicated by three variables: the community's not having fewer than 25,000 people, the size of its population, and its population density. The second set of variables influencing specialized branches refers to the heterogeneity of a city's population.

The ethnic and socioeconomic heterogeneity of the population in big cities encourages the establishment of specialized employment offices. A large proportion of blacks and of persons of foreign stock reflect ethnic heterogeneity, and the finding that high income and a large proportion of blacks exert parallel influences implies that the underlying factor is socio-

284   *The Formal Structure of Organizations*

Table 16.1 Regression Analysis of Local Office Specialization

Independent Variable	Standardized Regression Coefficient	Zero-Order Correlation
Community environment		
Town under 25,000	−.26**	−.44
Population	.10**	.28
Population density	.15**	.44
% Foreign stock	.14**	.32
% Blacks	.18**	.23
Median family income	.09**	.23

$R^2 = .31$; $n = 1,201$

** Greater than three times its standard error.

economic heterogeneity. Part of the influence of heterogeneity on specialized offices results from the fact that the populations in big cities are more
heterogeneous than those in small towns, but the three variables indicative
of heterogeneity exert some independent influence on specialization when
city size and population density are controlled. If there are many people in
a community looking for professional and other white-collar jobs as well as
many looking for unskilled work, there are good reasons to create specialized
employment offices. Yet, though the specialization of branches in heterogeneous communities is warranted on strictly rational grounds, it unquestionably brings about greater ethnic segregation in employment offices, with
mostly blacks being served in some and mostly whites in others. Specialized
offices in big heterogeneous cities are sometimes explicitly designed to provide more extensive services to underprivileged ethnic minorities, as illustrated by youth opportunity centers, but the ethnic segregation in specialized offices also opens the door to inequitable treatment, just as the segre-
gated schools that are the by-product of neighborhood segregation create
inequities in education.

The interpretation that a heterogeneous population fosters the establishment of specialized employment offices has been inferred partly from the
finding that both a high proportion of blacks and a high income level in a
community are associated with specialization of local offices. This interpretation can be tested directly, because it implies that these two independent
variables combined have an interaction effect on specialization. If the underlying factor leading to the creation of specialized offices is the heterogeneity
of the population, as the interpretation assumes, it follows that the joint
occurrence of many blacks and high incomes in a community, and not the

occurrence of either without the other, is what leads to the establishment of specialized offices. The multiple regression problem in Table 16.2 tests this interpretation by adding the product term, per cent black times median income, to the independent variables previously considered in Table 16.1. The findings clearly support the interpretation. Neither the proportion of blacks nor the income level in the community alone significantly affects the likelihood that specialized offices are found there; only the combination of both represented by the product term does. Communities with heterogeneous populations, including many blacks, most of whom are poor, and many well-off middle-class people, most of whom are white, are most likely to have specialized employment offices, which keep these groups apart.

Occupational specialization within a local office, in contrast to the specialization of the office itself, is less affected by the community environment than by the agency context. The differentiation of occupational positions in the agency relative to its size is the aspect of the agency context that most influences the subdivision of labor within local offices. The matrix of formal positions in the agency constitutes the resource of available specialties on which local offices in a sense draw in establishing their division of labor. . . .

The complex structure of urbanized communities is reflected in a more differentiated structure of employment security offices, notably a larger number of functional sections, which facilitate accommodation to the employment needs of a diverse clientele. The number of sections in an office is also greater if operations in an agency are automated than if they are not

Table 16.2 Regression Analysis of Local Office Specialization

Independent Variable	Standardized Regression Coefficient	Zero-Order Correlation	Metric Regression Coefficient
Community environment			
Town under 25,000	−.24**	−.44	−.42427**
Population	.09*	.28	.00004*
Population density	.14**	.44	.00014**
% Foreign stock	.14**	.32	.00810**
% Blacks	−.14	.23	.00884
Median family income	.04	.23	.00274
% Blacks × Median income	.33**	.33	.00044**

$R^2 = .33; n = 1,201$

* Greater than twice its standard error.
** Greater than three times its standard error.

(r = .22), mostly because the offices in automated agencies are larger (.15). But automation has a slight direct effect on number of sections too (b* = .05), which possibly also reflects the principle that organizational differentiation is an adjustment to complex external conditions. This principle is a main theme of Lawrence and Lorsch,[3] and it is supported by the findings that both the complexity of urban communities and the complexity of the agency's technology promote differentiation in local offices. . . .

The Ratio of Clerical Personnel

The ratio of clerical personnel in an office indicates how much of its work is simple enough to be performed by persons with little training and limited skills. Unemployment insurance work is simpler than furnishing employment services, which is a semiprofessional responsibility. Table 16.3 shows that the proportion of clerical jobs declines the larger the share of an office's function that is devoted to employment services (a three-category variable— whether all, some, or none of an office's responsibilities involve employment service). Two other characteristics of offices influence their clerical ratio. The extensive division of labor, by subdividing tasks among a larger number of jobs, simplifies most jobs and thus makes it possible to employ increasing proportions of clerks to fill them. The slim direct effect of size on the clerical ratio is the opposite of that of the division of labor. Although the large size of an office, by promoting the division of labor, indirectly raises the clerical ratio slightly (decomposition coefficient, .07), its direct effect is to reduce this ratio slightly again (−.06). Two interpretations of the direct effect are possible: either large size effects greater economies in clerical than in other personnel, or a large number of employees relative to the number of occupational positions (the division of labor) reduces the clerical ratio, just as a large number of positions relative to employees raises it. The second interpretation has the advantage of subsuming several findings under one principle.

The *agency's* division of labor, as indicated by the number of civil service positions, and its size exert influences on the clerical ratio in local offices that are parallel to, but much more pronounced than, the office's own division of labor and its size.[4] The larger the number of formal positions in the

---

[3] Paul R. Lawrence and Jay W. Lorsch, *Organization and Environment* (Boston: Graduate School of Business Administration, Harvard University, 1967).

[4] Interestingly enough, office division of labor mediates practically none of the influence of agency division of labor on office clerical ratio (decomposition composition, .02). Agency size directly reduces the clerical ratio (−.35) but indirectly, via agency division of labor, raises it again (.31) .Agency clerical ratio has not been included in this regression problem, although it is correlated with office clerical ratio (.59), because the two variables are tautological and including the agency clerical ratio simply reduces all other relationships.

Table 16.3   Regression Analysis of Local Office Clerical Ratio

Independent Variable	Standardized Regression Coefficient	Zero-Order Correlation
Community environment		
Western region	−.07*	−.23
Population	.08*	.24
Population density	−.05	.26
Town under 25,000	−.02	−.12
% Foreign stocks	.32**	.40
Agency context		
Size	−.35**	.08
Division of labor	.39**	.32
% Interviewers with B.A.	.12**	.30
Delegation to local managers	−.06	−.30
Local office		
Employment service function	−.27**	−.27
Size	−.06*	.06
Division of labor	.14**	.20
$R^2 = .40; n = 1,201$		

* Greater than twice its standard error.

** Greater than three times its standard error.

repertory of the agency available to local offices, the greater the chances are that several formal positions simple enough to be filled by clerks exist that are appropriate for the particular situations in most offices. By the same token, the larger the scope of the agency's entire operations, as indicated by its size, relative to the supply of different positions in the agency, the smaller is the likelihood that most offices, operating in different situations, are able to find many appropriate positions that can be filled by clerks. In parallel fashion, a pronounced division of labor in an office routinizes many jobs sufficiently for them to be performed by clerks. However, if the scope of operations of the office reflected by its size is excessively large relative to the number of differentiated occupational positions, only a comparatively small proportion of jobs can be performed by the clerks. Because the matrix of occupational positions available relative to the total scope of operations in the agency limits the development of the division of labor in local offices relative to their size, the agency's division of labor and size affect the clerical ratio much more than the office's own (see Table 16.3).

Another relationship between an agency-wide characteristic and the clerical ratio in local offices reveals a different form of the division of labor. The more college graduates there are among the interviewers in the agency, virtually all of whom work in local offices, the greater is the proportion of clerks in local offices. This finding suggests a form of the subdivision of work that differs from that expressed in the measure of division of labor, namely, the bifurcation of skills. Some agencies have more highly skilled as well as more unskilled employees in their local offices than others, which means that their personnel is more differentiated in terms of skills.

The delegation of considerable responsibilities in an agency to the managers of local offices is negatively related to the clerical ratio in these offices, and a slight negative relationship persists when other conditions are controlled (Table 16.3).[5] The clerical ratio is lower in employment than in unemployment insurance offices, and managers of employment offices probably require more autonomy. But this is unlikely to account for the negative relationship, which persists when function is roughly controlled in the regression analysis, and which moreover is observable in all five types of offices.[6] One would have expected the greater routinization of the duties in the offices of an agency to encourage rather than discourage delegation of responsibilities to office managers, just as routine duties lead to a wider span of control of first-line supervisors. The reason for the discrepancy may be that routine duties facilitate the job of supervision but their prevalence in an office is indicative of a fragmentation of responsibilities that makes the job of management more difficult. The greater internal problems with which office managers must deal as the result of the fragmentation of duties reflected in a high clerical ratio may discourage, though this is sheer conjecture, the delegation of extra responsibilities to these managers.

The employment of many clerks in an organization depends not only on its need for them but also on the supply of them in the labor market, and an ethnically mixed population with many men and women of foreign stock is an abundant source of clerks. This interpretation of the finding in Table

[5] The standardized regression coefficient is .0001 short of being twice its standard error (.0314). The inverse zero-order correlation between delegation of responsibilities to office managers and clerical ratio in the entire agency is considerably less strong (−.17) than that shown in Table 16.3 (−.30), which implies that the clerical ratio in local offices rather than at the headquarters is the important factor.

[6] But other conditions are not controlled in the cross-tabulations with type. The proportion of local offices with a high clerical ratio decreases with increased delegation of responsibilities to office managers from 42 per cent (of 399) to 34 per cent (of 233) in General LO's; from 27 per cent (97) to 13 per cent (27) in employment service LO's; from 38 per cent (91) to 8 per cent (47) in Specialized employment service LO's; from 57 per cent (130) to 28 per cent (40) in unemployment insurance LO's; and from 15 per cent (78) to 2 per cent (43) in youth opportunity centers.

16.3 that a high proportion of persons of foreign stock in the local community substantially increases the proportion of clerks in the employment security office is based on the following reasoning. Most individuals of foreign stock today are not foreign born but second generation, that is, native-born children of immigrants. These are largely men and women who have been raised in poor immigrant homes in cities. Many of them have strong ambitions to improve themselves, but their limited resources often prevent them from acquiring the educational qualifications necessary to achieve high managerial or professional positions. The assumption is that such urban young workers from lower-income homes with a strong drive to be upwardly mobile and with insufficient resources to attain a higher education provide a ready-made pool of clerical labor for government bureaus or private employers. Men and women from poor homes who are less eager to rise to white-collar levels are not likely to acquire the competence necessary for clerical positions, and persons with higher educational qualifications are not interested in clerical jobs.

But are the assumptions warranted that the second generation exhibits disproportionate strivings for upward mobility and disproportionate tendencies to occupy clerical jobs? There is empirical evidence to support these assumptions. A recent study shows that men with immigrant parents are more likely to be upwardly mobile than any other group; more than three-tenths of them achieve a substantial amount of upward mobility, as much as is achieved by only one-quarter of white native-born Northerners of native parentage, the majority group.[7] Furthermore, data from the 1960 U.S. Census indicate that the second generation is considerably overrepresented in clerical occupations.[8] Whereas 6.9 per cent of all men in the labor force are clerks, 8.2 per cent of the American-born sons of foreign-born parents are. Among all women in the labor force, similarly, fewer are clerks (29.7 per cent) than among second-generation women (35.5 per cent). If 100 signifies an equal distribution, the index for the native born of foreign parentage in clerical jobs would be 119. As a matter of fact, second-generation men are overrepresented in all nonmanual occupational groups, and they are underrepresented in all groups of farm and manual occupations except craftsmen, and the pattern for second-generation women is the same for eight of the ten major occupational groups (the two exceptions are that women are not overrepresented in the professions and not underrepresented

[7] Peter M. Blau and Otis Dudley Duncan, *The American Occupational Structure* (New York: Wiley, 1967), p. 232.

[8] U.S. Bureau of the Census, "Nativity and Parentage," Subject Report PC(2)-1A, *U.S. Census of Population: 1960* (Washington, D.C.: Government Printing Office, 1965). For data indicating the same tendency at earlier periods, see E. P. Hutchinson, *Immigrants and Their Children* (New York: Wiley, 1956), p. 202.

among operatives). However, the proportion of second-generation men and women is higher among clerks than in all but one of the nine other major occupational groups (it is still higher among managers, proprietors, and officials). These data support the interpretation that an ethnically mixed population with many persons of foreign stock increases the supply of clerks in the labor market and for this reason enables employment security offices to fill large proportions of positions with clerks.

The clerical ratio is also larger in highly urbanized places than in less urbanized ones. However, Table 16.3 indicates that the influence of urbanization on the proportion of clerks is largely indirect. An urbanized environment can increase an office's clerical ratio primarily because its ethnically mixed population increases the supply of clerks. Only one of three measures of urbanization has a weak direct effect on the clerical ratio once foreign stock is controlled. Offices in small towns cannot hire as many clerks as those in large cities, because fewer people in less urban places are candidates for clerical jobs, and the major reason for the greater availability of clerks in big cities is their ethnic heterogeneity, not simply urbanization in general. One other environmental condition affects the clerical ratio: offices in the West employ fewer clerks than those in the three other regions.

The Span of Control of Supervisors

The span of control of first-line supervisors in local offices depends mostly on the characteristics of these offices, but the agency context and the community environment exert some additional influence on it. We shall therefore first briefly review the influences of the office's own characteristics on the span of control of its supervisors. Administrative overhead depends substantially on the span of control of first-line supervisors, who constitute the bulk of the overhead personnel.

The structural complexity produced by either vertical or horizontal differentiation in local offices narrows the supervisory span of control, because problems of coordination and communication in complex structures make demands on the time of supervisors that leave them less time for direct supervision of subordinates. (See the beta weights for number of levels and number of sections in Table 16.4.) The complexity of the task also reduces the number of subordinates per first-line supervisor; the office's responsibility for employment services is one indicator of task complexity, and its low clerical ratio is another. The large size of an office indirectly increases the supervisory personnel needed for a given number of operating employees, owing to the structural complexity it produces, but it directly decreases the required supervisory component, owing to the economy of scale. Inasmuch as the

Table 16.4 Regression Analysis of Local Office Mean Span of Control of First-Line Supervisors

Independent Variable	Standardized Regression Coefficient	Zero-Order Correlation
Community environment		
Population density	− .07**	.24
Agency context		
Size	.27**	.52
Extent of personnel regulations	.03	.44
Automation	− .06	.44
Supervisory ratio	− .01	− .25
Employee-client ratio	− .06**	− .21
Local office		
Employment service function	− .10**	− .08
Size (log)	1.16**	.66
Division of labor	− .01	.32
Levels	− .44**	.25
Sections	− .36**	.25
Clerical ratio	.06**	.19
$R^2 = .71$; $n = 1,201$		

** Greater than three times its standard error.

direct effect of size widening the supervisory span of control is greater than its indirect effects narrowing it (as the simple correlation of office size shows), considerable savings in supervisory manpower are realized in large offices. All these relationships persist when agency and community conditions are controlled, but the division of labor in the office is seen to exert no direct influence on the span of control of supervisors when these external conditions are taken into account.[9] To be sure, the division of labor in the office narrows the supervisory span of control indirectly through its influence on the differentiation of levels (decomposition coefficient, − .18) and sections (− .17), though these influences are concealed in the positive zero-order correlation by the strong spurious positive association between division of labor and span of control produced by office size (.72).

Turning now to the organizational context, Table 16.4 shows that the size of an agency has a pronounced effect on the span of control of supervisors

[9] If external conditions are not controlled, the division of labor, like other aspects of differentiation, narrows the span of control (beta weight, − .11).

at the very bottom of the hierarchy in local offices. The larger an agency, the wider is the span of control of first-line supervisors. More than one-quarter of the variance in the mean span of control of first-line supervisors in 1,201 offices is accounted for by differences in the size of the fifty-one agencies to which they belong. Part of the influence of agency size on the ratio of operating employees to supervisors is indirect, mediated by the size of local offices (decomposition coefficient, .39; counteracted by levels, −.06; and sections, −.06), and part is direct (.27). Thus, the large size of an agency effects great savings in supervisory manpower not only at the headquarters, as other data show, but also in local offices, directly as well as indirectly. The reason for the indirect effect is that the larger local offices that prevail in larger agencies make it easier to establish larger work groups of employees with similar duties under each supervisor.

The direct influence of agency size, controlling office size, on the span of control of supervisors in offices may be interpreted as a structural effect. Though this concept was originally introduced to refer to the influence on individual behavior of the prevalence of individuals with a given characteristic in a social structure when the individual's own characteristic is controlled, thus revealing the external influence of the social environment on human behavior, here we have an illustration of another type of structural effect, one that is on a higher level of social system. The prevalence of *organizational* components (here, offices) with a given independent attribute (size) in a larger organization influences a dependent attribute of these components (supervisory span) when each component's own independent attribute (office size) is controlled. Since more subordinates tend to be assigned to the average first-line supervisor in large than in small offices, and since large agencies have more large offices than small agencies, a wide span of control tends to become standard in large agencies, and this standard exerts pressures in offices of all sizes to assign more subordinates to supervisors than would otherwise be the case. In the same way, *mutatis mutandis*, a narrow supervisory span of control tends to become standard in the various offices of small agencies, reflecting a structural effect of the prevalence of small offices.

The automation of operations in an agency exhibits a strong zero-order correlation with the average span of control of supervisors in local offices (.44), which decomposition shows to be the result of a variety of influences. Part of this association is spurious, produced by the effect of agency size on both automation and supervisory span of control (.23). One indirect effect of automation is to widen the span of control of supervisors because the comparatively large local offices in large automated agencies have supervisors with a disproportionately wide span of control (.38). But this positive indirect effect is diminished by the negative indirect effects owing to the complexity of these larger offices (levels, −.06; sections, −.08), and by a slight negative direct effect (−.06).[10] On the one hand, therefore, the span of control of supervisors is wider in automated than in other agencies, the reason being that automated agencies are larger and have larger local offices. On the other hand, however, automation changes the nature of the duties performed and creates new problems, primarily at the agency head-quarters, where the computer is located, but secondarily also in branch offices, where work must be adapted to the requirements of the computer. Local offices in automated agencies tend to adapt to these new problems by adding a section and thus becoming more differentiated, as we saw above, and by reducing the ratio of subordinates to supervisors, partly as the result of this differentiation and in part independently of it.

Extensive personnel regulations encourage the establishment of larger local offices, perhaps because both are manifestations of the bureaucratiza-tion of the state government. They thereby indirectly widen the span of con-trol of supervisors and thus achieve savings in the proportion of supervisory personnel needed in local offices (see the correlation in Table 16.4).[11] Another agency characteristic entered into this regression problem is the supervisory ratio at the headquarters,[12] which is inversely correlated with the supervisory span of control and directly with the supervisory ratio in local offices, in order to ascertain whether these correlations reveal that some agen-cies have a general tendency to employ higher proportions of supervisors than others. Such a tendency is not pronounced, though a slight one may exist. When other conditions are controlled, the headquarters supervisory ratio is unrelated to the span of control of *first-line* supervisors in local offices, as the table shows, but it reveals a persistent small relationship with the ratio of all supervisory personnel in offices ($b^* = .06$).[13] Most of the association between the supervisory ratio at the headquarters and that in local branches is the result of the effects of agency size and office size, and there is unex-pectedly little evidence of blanket agency policies governing the proportion of supervisors throughout the organization.

A wide span of control of first-line supervisors in local offices produces appreciable savings in the total man-hour costs of benefit operations in the

---

[10] The standardized regression coefficient falls short .0024 of being twice its standard error (.0308), but its substantive interest nevertheless makes it worthy of consideration.

[11] Decomposition shows that the zero-order correlation of .44 is mostly the result of the mediating effect of office size (.32) and the effect of agency size (.20). These figures indicate that a substantial indirect positive effect persists after agency size is controlled.

[12] Only the ratio, not the span of controls, is available for the headquarters.

[13] Using the ratio of all supervisory to total personnel in the office as a dependent variable and the same independent variables as in Table 16.4.

agency. The employee-client ratio in the agency's benefit function,[14] which is shown as an independent variable in Table 16.4, is actually assumed to be the dependent variable affected by the span of control of office supervisors. The difference between the zero-order correlation of these two variables ($-.21$) and the standardized regression coefficient ($-.06$) is largely owing to office size (decomposition coefficient, $-.13$), which indicates that most of the negative relationship is mediated by size but that part of it is direct. The supervisory ratio at the agency *headquarters* reveals no corresponding correlation with the man-hours required for benefit operations ($.03$), although a greater share of unemployment benefit than of employment service activities is carried out at the headquarters. Apparently, administrative overhead in local offices and particularly the span of control of the many first-line supervisors there have special significance for the agency's operating economy. An important means for keeping the man-hour expenditures of the organization down is to maintain a wide span of control of supervisors in the various branches, both by establishing branches large enough to facilitate the assignment of quite a few subordinates to every supervisor (as reflected in the indirect relationship), and by finding ways to extend the supervisory span of control in offices of a given size (as reflected in the direct one).

A last condition shown in Table 16.4 to influence the span of control of supervisors is the urbanization (population density) of the community in which the office is located.[15] A diverse urbanized environment makes administrative demands on employment security offices that narrow the supervisory span of control, directly and also indirectly by increasing the structural complexity of the offices, but the large size of offices in highly urbanized cities counteracts these negative effects, with the result that the zero-order correlation between population density and span of control is positive ($.24$). Decomposition reveals that the positive association between location in densely populated cities and supervisory span of control owing to the large size of the offices in these cities would be much greater ($.49$) were it not diminished by the negative influence a complex urban environment has on the number of subordinates per supervisor. The local offices in the most urbanized metropolitan centers are not only larger than others but also more differentiated—particularly into many sections, as noted earlier—and their more differentiated structure narrows the span of control of supervisors (mediated by levels, $-.08$, and by sections, $-.15$). In addition, the complexity of the urbanized environment has a direct effect narrowing this span of

[14] This is the ratio of employees to clients in the unemployment insurance function only. No such ratio is available for the employment function.

[15] The zero-order correlations of supervisor's span of control with size of the city's population ($.33$), per cent foreign stock ($.35$), and median income ($.27$) disappear when other conditions are controlled, with office size being responsible in all three cases.

control $(-.07)$. In short, the diverse needs employment security offices in highly urbanized centers must meet constrain them to develop a more differentiated structure and to free supervisors, by narrowing their span of control, to devote more time to the problems of coordination in the more complex structure and to the other problems created by the complex external environment.

Personnel Economies

The analysis of the intricate relationships in Table 16.4 makes it possible to infer some of the processes that govern the attainment of personnel economies in these government bureaus. A wide span of control of first-line supervisors in local offices creates overall manpower economies in the agency, as indicated by the empirical finding that it is inversely related to the ratio of total agency employees in the benefit function to clients served by them. Because work on employment services is more concentrated in local offices than work on unemployment benefits, it seems likely that the supervisory span of control in these local offices achieves at least as much overall savings in manpower in the employment service function, for which we have no measure. The large size of local offices plays a crucial role in widening the span of control of the supervisors in it and hence in the resulting personnel economies in operations. The chain of influence may be reconstructed in the following way: operating economy depends on low administrative overhead; a wide span of control of first-line supervisors in all the branches of an organization is a major element in low overhead; a wide span of control of supervisors depends on large branches. Ultimately, therefore, conditions in the organization that influence the size of branches are significant for improving operating economy, at least in terms of man-hours.

Office size exerts the dominant influence on the average span of control of first-line supervisors, accounting for 44 per cent of its variance. The positive effect of large-scale operations on the number of subordinates per supervisor substantially exceeds the negative effect of task complexity. Given this strong impact of office size, conditions in the agency or in the environment that exert considerable influence on the size of local offices thereby invariably widen the span of control of supervisors. This is the case regardless of whether these conditions also have a positive direct effect on the supervisory span of control, as agency size does, or no direct effect, as extensive personnel regulations do, or a negative direct effect, as automation and the urbanization of the local community do. Supervisory time is needed to adjust to the complexity imposed on local offices by automation in the agency or by a diverse urban environment, which is manifest in the negative influences of these two variables on the span of control of supervisors. Although automation has a negative, and extent of personnel regulations has no direct effect on the supervisory span of control in local offices, both widen it indirectly owing to their association with the large size of offices, which implies that automation and extensive personnel regulations improve operating economy.

The four major influences on the span of control of supervisors are all purely structural: the size of the office, its vertical differentiation into levels, its horizontal differentiation into sections, and the size of the agency. The demands on the time of supervisors made by the structural complexity large size generates diminish the savings in supervisory man-hours large size makes it possible to realize. The size of the agency exerts a stronger influence than any of its other characteristics on the supervisory span of control in its branches, indirectly by affecting the size of branches, as well as directly and thus complementing the influence of branch size. However, not only the size of branches but also their number increases with increasing agency size. The very fact that the need for supervisory personnel declines as the size of an office expands implies that this need increases as an organization becomes more subdivided into geographically dispersed branches. It appears that the extra supervisory manpower required by large roof organizations for their large number of branches virtually absorbs the savings in supervisory manpower achieved by the large size of these branches.

17. A Formal Theory of Differentiation in Organizations

The objective of this paper is to develop a deductive theory of the formal structure of work organizations, that is, organizations deliberately established for explicit purposes and composed of employees. The differentiation of a formal organization into components in terms of several dimensions—spatial, occupational, hierarchical, functional—is considered to constitute the core of its structure. The theory is limited to major antecedents and consequences of structural differentiation. It has been derived from the empirical results of a quantitative study of government bureaus. The extensive analysis of these empirical data on the interrelations between organizational characteristics, too lengthy for presentation in an article, is reported elsewhere.[1] The topic of this paper is not the analysis of the research findings but the

Originally published in 1970.

[1] Peter M. Blau and Richard A. Schoenherr, *The Structure of Organizations* (New York: Basic Books, 1971). The asistance of Sheila R. Klatzky with this research is gratefully acknowledged, and so is grant CS-553 of the National Science Foundation, the source of support of the Comparative Organization Research Program at the University of Chicago, of which this is report No. 11.

deductive theory that can be inferred from them and that therefore explains them and the parallel empirical regularities that the theory predicts to exist in other work organizations. Although the findings are not fully presented, the relevant empirical relationships observed are cited, since they are the basis of the theoretical generalizations advanced, and since they must logically follow from these generalizations to satisfy the requirements of deductive theory.

Deductive Theory

The conception of systematic theory adopted is explicated by Braithwaite.[2] An empirical proposition concerning the relationship between two or more variables is explained by subsuming it under a more general proposition from which it can be logically derived. A systematic theory is a set of such logically interrelated propositions, all of which pertain to connections between at least two variables, and the least general of which, but only those, must be empirically demonstrable. "A scientific theory is a deductive system in which observable consequences logically follow from the conjunction of observed facts with the set of fundamental hypotheses in the system."[3] The theoretical generalizations that explain the empirical findings are in turn explained by subsuming them under still more general hypotheses, so that the theoretical system may have propositions on several levels of abstraction. These principles apply not only to universal hypotheses—if A, then B—but also to the statistical ones characteristic of the social sciences—the more A, the more likely is B.

The explanatory thrust of a formal theory of this kind resides completely in the generality of the theoretical propositions and in the fact that the empirical findings can be deduced from them in strict logic. Theorizing in the social sciences usually assumes not this form of a deductive model but what Kaplan calls the pattern model, according to which "something is explained when it is so related to a set of other elements that together they constitute a unified system."[4] The psychological experience of gaining understanding by the sudden insight the theory brings of how parts fit neatly into a whole is largely missing in deductive theorizing. Instead, the theorist's aim is to discover a few theoretical generalizations from which many different em-

---

[2] Richard B. Braithwaite, *Scientific Explanation* (Cambridge: University Press, 1953); see also Carl G. Hempel and Paul Oppenheim, "The Logic of Explanation," *Philosophy of Science* 15 (1948), 135–175; and Karl R. Popper, *The Logic of Scientific Discovery* (New York: Basic Books, 1959).

[3] Braithwaite, *op cit.*, p. 22.

[4] Abraham Kaplan, *The Conduct of Inquiry* (San Francisco: Chandler, 1964), p. 333.

pirical propositions can be derived. Strange as it may seem, the higher-level hypotheses that explain the lower-level propositions are accepted as valid purely on the basis that they do explain them, in the specific sense that they logically imply them, and without independent empirical evidence; whereas acceptance of the lower-level propositions that need to be explained is contingent on empirical evidence.[5] Indeed, the reason for developing a deductive system is to empower empirical findings, confirming low-level hypotheses, indirectly to establish an abstract body of explanatory theory, and empirical evidence for any lower-level proposition strengthens confidence in all propositions.

In Braithwaite's words:

> One of the main purposes in organizing scientific hypotheses into a deductive system is in order that the direct evidence for each lower-level hypothesis may become indirect evidence for all the other lowest-level hypotheses; although no amount of empirical evidence suffices to prove any of the hypotheses in the system, yet any piece of evidence for any part of the system helps toward establishing the whole of the system.[6]

In an attempt to start building a deductive theory of the formal structure of organizations, theoretical generalizations about differentiation in the structure are inferred from a large number of empirical findings of a study of government bureaus. Several middle-level propositions are deduced from two basic generalizations, and empirical findings supporting the derived generalizations are cited. Inasmuch as the generalizations subsume many empirically demonstrated propositions, that is, logically imply them, they explain these empirical regularities. There are several crosswise connections that strengthen the interdependence in the theoretical system.

The aim, in short, is to develop a small number of interrelated general propositions that account for a considerable variety of empirical regularities about differentiation in organizations. The contribution the paper seeks to make rests not on the originality of the particular propositions, several of which have been noted in the literature, but on the attempt to derive lower-level propositions systematically from higher-level ones and thus to construct a limited body of coherent theory that is supported by numerous empirical findings. The theory is explicitly confined to inferences from the most trustworthy and pronounced empirical relationships between organizational characteristics observed in 1,500 component organizations and the 53 larger government agencies to which they belong, in the hope that these strong

[5] Braithwaite, *op cit.*, p. 303.
[6] *Ibid.*, pp. 17–18.

associations observable under a variety of conditions reflect underlying forces that would also be manifest in other types of organizations than the ones studied. A test of most propositions has been conducted in another study of 416 government bureaus of a different kind, but only future research can tell whether and to which extent the generalizations advanced are also applicable to still other types of organizations. Since the theory is restricted to the interdependence among relatively few factors, it ignores other conditions on which these factors undoubtedly are dependent as well. Thus, the theory pays no attention to the influences of the technology employed, nor to those of the organization's environment. The assumption here is that such other influences may complement but do not suppress those of the factors incorporated in the theory, because these factors are of great general importance, and the empirical data available support this assumption.[7]

Formal Structure

The formal structure of organizations is conceptualized here more narrowly than is usually the case. The term *social structure* is often used broadly, and sometimes loosely, to refer to the common value orientations of people, the traditional institutions in a society, cultural norms and role expectations, and nearly everything that pertains to life in groups. But it has a more specific meaning. The gist of a social structure is that people differ in status and social affiliation, that they occupy different positions and ranks, and that they belong to different groups and subunits of various sorts. The fact that the members of a collectivity are differentiated on the basis of several independent dimensions is the foundation of the collectivity's social structure. This differentiation into components along various lines in organizations is the object of the present analysis. The theory centers attention on the social forces that govern the interrelations among differentiated elements in a formal structure and ignores the psychological forces that govern individual behavior. Formal structures exhibit regularities that can be studied in their own right without investigating the motives of the individuals in organizations.

Formal organizations cope with the difficult problems large-scale operations create by subdividing responsibilities in numerous ways and thereby facilitating the work of any operating employee, manager, and subunit in the organization. The division of labor typifies the improvement in performance attainable through subdivision. The more completely simple tasks are

---

[7] The research of Blau and Schoenherr (*op. cit.*) presents data that show that the empirical relationships implied by the theory persist when important differences in technology and numerous variations in environmental conditions are controlled.

separated from various kinds of complex ones, the easier it is for unskilled employees to perform the routine duties and for skilled employees to acquire the specialized training and experience to perform the different complex ones. Further subdivision of responsibilities occurs among functional divisions, enabling each one to concentrate on certain kinds of work. Local branches may be established in different places to facilitate serving clients in various areas, and these branches may become functionally specialized. The management of such a differentiated structure requires that managerial responsibilities too become subdivided among managers and supervisors on different hierarchical levels.

Weber recognized the vital importance the subdivision of responsibilities has for administrative organizations and placed it first in his famous enumeration of the characteristics of modern bureaucracy.[8] His focus on a structure of differentiated responsibilities is also evident in his emphasis on the division of labor, specialized competence, and particularly the hierarchy of authority.[9] An apparent implication of this stress on structural differences is that the analysis of differentiation in the formal structure constitutes the core of the systematic study of formal organizations, but Weber himself does not pursue this line of inquiry. It is the primary concern here.

The central concept of differentiation in organizations must be clearly defined in terms that permit translation into operational measures. A dimension of differentiation is any criterion on the basis of which the members of an organization are formally divided into positions, as illustrated by the division of labor; or into ranks, notably managerial levels; or into subunits, such as local branches, headquarters divisions, or sections within branches or divisions. A structural component is either a distinct official status (for example, employment interviewer or first-line supervisor) or a subunit in the organization (for example, one branch or one division). The term *differentiation* refers specifically to the number of structural components that are formally distinguished in terms of any *one* criterion. The empirical measures used are number of branches, number of occupational positions (division of labor), number of hierarchical levels, number of divisions, and number of sections within branches or divisions.

The research from which the theory of structural differentiation has been derived is a study of the fifty-three employment security agencies in the United States, which are responsible for administering unemployment in-

---

[8] "I. There is the principle of fixed and official jurisdictional areas . . . 1. The regular activities required for the purposes of the bureaucratically governed structure are distributed in a fixed way as official duties" [Max Weber, *Essays in Sociology* (New York: Oxford University Press, 1946), p. 196].

[9] *Ibid.*, pp. 196–197; *The Theory of Social and Economic Organization* (New York: Oxford University Press, 1947), pp. 330–331.

surance and providing public employment services in the fifty states, the District of Columbia, Puerto Rico, and the Virgin Islands.[10] These are autonomous state agencies, although they operate under federal laws and are subject to some federal supervision. The empirical data were collected by a team of three research assistants who visited every agency in the country to interview key informants and obtain data from records. Most of the information about the formal structure comes from personnel lists and from elaborate organizational charts specially prepared for the research, all of which were much more detailed than the charts kept by the agencies. In addition to analyzing the formal structure of the 53 total agencies or their entire headquarters, the structure of the 1,201 local branches and that of the 354 headquarters divisions were also analyzed; these include all local branches and headquarters divisions in the country meeting minimum criteria of size (five employees) and structure (three hierarchical levels). Headquarters divisions were, moreover, divided on the basis of their function into six types, making it possible to analyze structure while controlling function. (The six types are the two basic line functions—employment services and unemployment insurance—and four staff functions—administrative services, personnel and technical, data processing, and legal services.)

First Generalization: Size and Differentiation

Increasing size generates structural differentiation in organizations along various dimensions at decelerating rates (1). This is the first fundamental generalization inferred from the empirical findings. From it can be deduced several middle-range propositions, which subsume additional empirical findings. One can consider this theoretical generalization about the structure of organizations to comprise three parts, in which case the middle-level and lower-level propositions are derived from the conjunction of the three highest-level ones. In this alternative formulation, the three highest-level propositions composing the first basic generalization about the formal structure of organizations are: (1A) large size promotes structural differentiation; (1B) large size promotes differentiation along several different lines; and (1C) the rate of differentiation declines with expanding size. The assumption is that these generalizations apply to the subunits within organizations as well as to total organiza-

---

[10] The only agency excluded is the smallest one, on Guam, which has less than a dozen employees, compared to 1,200 for the mean of the other agencies. In the four jurisdictions in which unemployment insurance and employment services are carried out by separate bureaus, they were combined for the purpose of the analysis, since it became evident that these two functions are hardly more separate there than in some other jurisdictions where they are legally in the same bureau.

tions, which can be made explicit in a fourth proposition: (1D) the subunits into which an organization is differentiated become internally differentiated in parallel manner.

A considerable number of empirical findings on employment security agencies can be accounted for by the generalization that differentiation in organizations increases at decreasing rates with increasing size, and none of the relevant evidence conflicts with this generalization. The operational definition of size is number of employees. When total state agencies are compared, increases in size are accompanied by initially rapid and subsequently more gradual increases in the number of local branches into which the agency is spatially differentiated; the number of official occupational positions expressing the division of labor; the number of levels in the hierarchy; the number of functional divisions at the headquarters; and the number of sections per division. The profound impact that agency size has upon differentiation is indicated by its correlations of .94 with number of local offices; .78 with occupational positions; .60 with hierarchical levels; and .38 with functional divisions. Logarithmic transformation of size further raises these correlations (except the one with local offices); for example, that with number of divisions becomes .54; and that with sections per division, which was before an insignificant .16, is after transformation .43. The improvements in the correlations logarithmic transformation of size achieves reflect the logarithmic shape of the regression lines of the numbers of structural components on size, and thus the declining rate of differentiation with expanding size. For an illustration of this pattern, the scatter diagram for agency size and number of hierarchical levels is presented in Figure 17.1.

The internal differentiation within the subunits that have become differentiated in the agencies assumes the same form. The larger a local branch, the greater the differentiation into occupational positions (r = .51), hierarchical levels (.68), and functional sections (.61). This differentiation occurs at declining rates with increasing size (and the correlations are somewhat raised when size is logarithmically transformed). The scatter diagram of office size and division of labor (occupational positions) in Figure 17.2 illustrates the logarithmic curve expressing this pattern.[11] Similar logarithmic curves characterize the differentiation within the functional divisions at the agency headquarters. The larger a division, the larger is the number of its occupational positions, hierarchical levels, and functional sections; and differences between very small and medium-sized divisions have again more impact on variations in these three aspects of differentiation than differences between

[11] The curves shown are rough estimates. They were drawn by dividing size into three categories for Figure 17.1 and seven categories for Figure 17.2; determining the means for both size and the y-variable (ordinate) in each category; and making a smooth curve between those points. The same procedure is used for the other figures below.

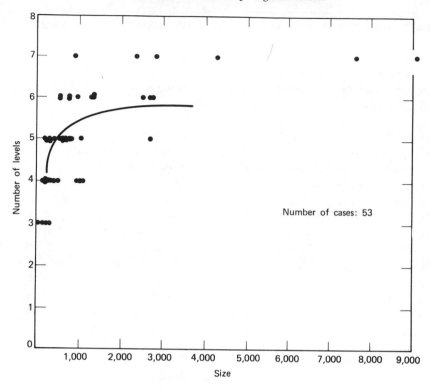

Figure 17.1. Size of agency and number of hierarchical levels at headquarters.

medium-sized and very large divisions. Moreover, this tendency for differentiation at decelerating rates to occur with increasing size is observable in six separate types of divisions with basically different functions, which suggests that it is independent of function and thus provides some support for the claim that the same tendency will be found in other organizations that have different functions from those of employment security agencies.[12]

Proposition 1.1: Marginal Influence of Size

The first proposition that can be derived from the first fundamental generalization is the following: as the size of organizations increases, its marginal

[12] This pattern is reflected in the finding that the logarithmic transformation of size improves its zero-order correlations, for all types of divisions combined, with division of labor (from .64 to .76), hierarchical levels (from .71 to .85), and functional sections (from .38 to .68). If the six functional types are analyzed separately, logarithmic transformation of size raises the corresponding correlations in fifteen of eighteen cases.

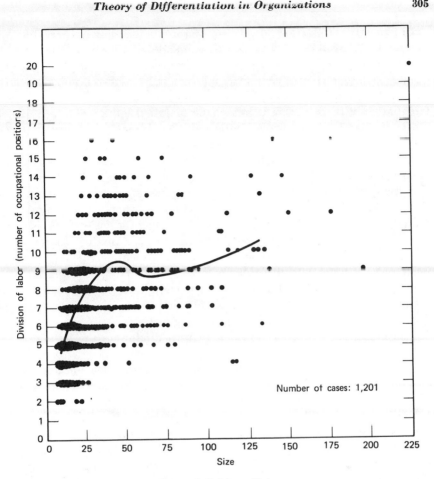

Figure 17.2. Size of local office and division of labor.

influence on differentiation decreases (1.1). As a matter of fact, this is hardly a derived proposition, since it is merely a restatement of one part of the original proposition (1C). But by translating the initial proposition into different concepts, the new proposition directs attention to a distinctive implication and an important parallel with the economic principle of diminishing returns or, in technical terms, of the eventually diminishing marginal physical productivity. In the words of Boulding: "As we increase the quantity of any one input which is combined with a fixed quantity of the other inputs, the marginal physical productivity of the variable input must eventually decline."[13]

[13] Kenneth E. Boulding, *Economic Analysis*, 3d ed. (New York: Harper, 1955), p. 589.

In a factory, production output can be raised by adding workers, but the marginal increment in output resulting from adding more and more workers without changing plant size and equipment eventually declines. In parallel fashion, a larger complement of employees in an organization makes its structure more differentiated, but as the number of employees and the differentiation of the structure increase, the marginal influence of a given increase in personnel on further differentiation declines. It seems that the differentiation produced by the expanding size of organizations stems the power of additional expansions in size to make the structure still more differentiated.

But why does the marginal influence of size on differentiation in organizations decline? If the analogy with the economic principle of diminishing returns is appropriate, it should provide some clues for answering this question. The reason for the eventually declining marginal productivity of increments in only one type of economic input is that such increments create an imbalance of inputs and the growing need for other inputs depresses productivity. For example, additional workers cannot be efficiently utilized in production without parallel increases in equipment and space. We may speculate that the influence of increasing organizational size on differentiation produces a growing need which in turn diminishes the influences of further increases in size.

The existence of differentiation in a formal organization implies a need for coordination. There are at least two inputs, using the terminology of economics, on which the development of structural differentiation in organization depends. The first is a sufficient number of employees (the measure of size) to fill the different positions and man the various subunits, and the second is an adequate administrative machinery to meet problems of coordination. The advancing differentiation to which an increasing number of employees gives rise intensifies the need for coordination in the organization, and this need restrains the further development of differentiation, which is reflected in the declining marginal influence of increasing size on differentiation. The implication of these considerations extrapolated from economic theory is that differentiation in organizations creates pressures to find ways to meet the need for coordination. We shall later return to the analysis of this problem, after discussing five other propositions that can be derived from the first basic generalization.

Proposition 1.2: Size of Structural Components

The second derived proposition is that the larger an organization is, the larger is the average size of its structural components of all kinds (1.2). This proposition logically follows from the principle of the decelerating rate of differentiation with increasing organizational size (1C), which is graphically expressed by the declining positive slopes (the downward curves) of the regression lines of the number of structural components of various kinds on size. In a diagram with total size or number of employees on the horizontal and number of structural components on the vertical axis, the average size of the structural components of an agency represented by a point is indicated by the ratio of the horizontal to the vertical coordinate of this point. As the positive slope of the regression line declines, this ratio increases, that is, it is larger for most large agencies than for most small agencies.[14] If the number of structural components increase more slowly than organizational size, the average size of these components necessarily becomes larger. Even in those cases in which the decline in the slope of the regression line is not pronounced, the average size of the structural components is strongly associated with the size of the organization. Two examples are the mean size of local branches, which variable has a zero-order correlation with agency size of .65, and the number of incumbents of the average occupational position, which is correlated .94 with agency size.

Thus, the large size of an organization raises the average size as well as the number of its structural components. Large agencies have more and larger local offices than small agencies, more and larger headquarters divisions, and the same hold true for every one of their structural components. The large size of the local offices within an agency and of its headquarters divisions, whatever their function, in turn tends to increase both the number and the average size of sections, and both the number of occupational positions and of managerial ranks and the mean number of employees occupying each position and each rank.

This double effect of organizational size has the paradoxical result that large offices and headquarters divisions constitute at the same time a more homogeneous and a more heterogeneous occupational environment for most employees than small ones. For larger offices or divisions contain comparatively many employees in nearly every occupational specialty, providing a congenial ingroup of colleagues for most employees—often not available in small organizational units—and they simultaneously contain a relatively great variety of different specialties, enhancing opportunities for stimulating contacts with people whose training and experience are unlike one's own. However, the greater opportunity for social interaction with a colleague ingroup in large offices may prove so attractive that social contacts with

---

[14] This can be readily seen by looking at the regression lines in Figures 17.1 and 17.2. For a point moving along either line from left to right, the horizontal coordinate increases more rapidly than the vertical one, indicating that the ratio of the first to the second coordinate increases.

persons from different specialties are rarer there than in small ones, despite the fact that opportunities for outgroup contacts are better in large offices too.

Proposition 1.3: Administrative Overhead

A third derived proposition is that the proportionate size of the average structural component, as distinguished from its absolute size, decreases with increases in organizational size (1.3). This follows directly from (1A): if the number of structural components, the criterion of differentiation, increases as organizational size does, the proportion of all employees who are in the average component must decrease. Hence, most groups or categories of employees in big organizations are larger in absolute numbers but constitute a smaller proportion of the total personnel than in small organizations. A consequence is that the average (*mean*) relative size of employee complements on a given dimension decreases with increasing organizational size, though not necessarily the proportion of any particular complement.

But we may reformulate this proposition (1.3) into a probability statement about groupings of employees: *ceteris paribus*, chance expectations are that the proportionate size of any personnel complement decreases with increasing organizational size. The empirical data show that this proposition applies to various kinds of administrative overhead or supportive services for the majority work force. The size of an agency is inversely related to the proportionate size of its administrative staff ($r = -.60$) and of its complement of managerial personnel ($-.45$). (The terms *manager* and *supervisor*, unless qualified, are used interchangeably to refer to all levels.) The proportion of managers is also inversely related to size in local offices ($-.64$) and in headquarters divisions regardless of function.[15]

When a certain personnel complement is singled out for attention—the staff or the managerial component—and exhibits the expected decrease in proportionate size with increasing organizational size, the remainder of the total personnel—the line or the nonsupervisory employees—must naturally reveal a complementary increase in proportionate size. This is mathematically inevitable, and it indicates that the reformulated proposition (1.3) cannot possibly apply to both parts of a dichotomy. The plausible assumption is that the residual majority actually consists of numerous personnel categories while the specialized personnel complement focused upon can be treated as a single one, which implies that the proportion of the minority

---

[15] The zero-order correlations for the six types of divisions are: $-.49$ (employment services); $-.51$ (unemployment insurance); $-.30$ (administrative services); $-.12$ (personnel and technical); $-.18$ (data processing); and $-.36$ (legal services). Size in all cases (agencies and local offices as well as divisions) has been logarithmically transformed.

complement is the one that should decrease with increasing organizational size. The data support this assumption. If employees in various organizational units are divided into clerical and professional personnel, the proportion of whichever of the two is in the minority tends to decrease as unit size does. The conclusion that may be drawn, which extends beyond what can be derived in strict logic from the premise, is that the proportionate size of any supportive service provided by a distinctive minority to the majority work force is likely to decline with increasing organizational size.

Proposition 1.4: Span of Control

Another proposition can be derived either from the last one (1.3) or from the one preceding (1.2): the larger the organization is, the wider the supervisory span of control (1.4). If chances are that the proportionate size of any organizational component declines with increasing size (1.3), and if this applies to the proportion of managers, it follows that the number of subordinates per manager, or the span of control, must expand with increasing size (1.4). Besides, if chance expectations are that the absolute average size of any structural component or grouping of employees increases with increasing (1.2), and if this applies to the various work groups assigned to supervisors, it follows that the size of the group under each supervisor, or his span of control, tends to expand with increasing size (1.4). Here again the logical implications specifying the *mean* absolute and proportionate size for *all* components have been translated into *probabilities* or statistical expectations referring to *any* component. Whether these derived propositions apply to a *particular* type of personnel component, like the managerial staff, must be empirically ascertained. If the evidence is negative, it would not falsify the theory, though it would weaken it. If the evidence is positive, it strengthens the theory, and makes it possible to extend it beyond the limits of its purely logical implications by taking into account the empirical data confirming this particular application of the merely statistical deduction from the theory.[16]

The empirical data on employment security agencies confirm the proposition that the span of control of supervisors expands with increasing organi-

---

[16] Two kinds of statistical or probability statements must be distinguished, empirical and theoretical ones. On the one hand, it is only probable that any given large agency has a lower ratio of supervisors than any given small agency, since the correlation is less than 1.00; this empirical probability is *not* what is referred to in the text. On the other hand, and this is what is discussed above, it is only probable that the ratio of supervisory personnel is inversely related to agency size, since the theory only predicts that the proportionate size of most components of the agency is inversely related to its own size and that it is probable that such an inverse relationship will be observed with respect to any particular type of component, such as the supervisory ratio.

zational size. This is the case for all levels of managers and supervisors examined in these agencies and their subunits. The larger an agency, the wider is the span of control of its director and the average span of control of its division heads. The larger a headquarters division, whatever its function, the wider is the span of control of its division heads, the average span of control of its middle managers, and the average span of control of its first-line supervisors. The larger a local office is, the wider is the span of control of the office manager and that of the average first-line supervisor.[17] Moreover, the size of the total organization has an independent effect widening the supervisory span of control in local offices when their own size is controlled.[18] Big organizations and their larger headquarters divisions and local branches tend to have more employees in any given position with similar duties than small organizations with their smaller subunits, as we have seen, thus making it possible to use supervisors more efficiently in large units by assigning more subordinates with similar duties to each supervisor.

The additional influence of the size of the total organization, independent of that of the size of the office, on the number of subordinates per supervisor, may reveal a structural effect.[19] The prevalence of a wide span of supervisory control in large organizations, owing to the large size of most of their branch offices, creates a normative standard that exerts an influence in its own right, increasing the number of subordinates assigned to supervisors; and the same is the case, *mutatis mutandis*, for the prevalence of a narrow supervisory span of control in small organizations with their smaller branches. To direct attention to the substantial influence of organizational size on the supervisory span of control is, of course, not to deny that this span is also influenced by other conditions, such as the nature of the duties.

Propositions 1.5 and 1.6: Economy of Scale

Organizations exhibit an economy of scale in management. This proposition (1.5) is implicit in the two foregoing ones. For if the proportion of managerial

[17] The zero-order correlations of size (log) of the respective organizational units and mean span of control of various managers are: agency director, .39; head of division, from .22 to .44 for the six functional types; middle managers in divisions, with one exception (.05) from .17 to .78; first-line supervisors in divisions, from .39 to .69 in the six types; managers of local offices, .40; and first-line supervisors in local offices, .66.

[18] In the multiple regression problem with the average span of control of the first-line supervisors in each of the 1,201 local offices as dependent variable, and with office size and a number of other conditions controlled, the standardized regression coefficient of the size of the agency to which the local office belongs is .27 (the simple correlation is .52).

[19] See Peter M. Blau, "Structural Effects," *American Sociological Review* 25 (1960), 178–193, which is included here as Chapter 4.

personnel declines with size (1.3) and their span of control expands with size (1.4), this means that large-scale operations reduce the proportionate size of the administrative overhead, specifically, of the complement of managers and supervisors. In fact, the relative size of administrative overhead of other kinds, such as staff and supportive personnel, also declines with increasing size, as has been noted. The question arises whether this economy of scale in administrative overhead produces overall personnel economies with an increasing scale of operations. The data on employment security agencies are equivocal on this point. The only index of personnel economy available, the ratio of all employees engaged in unemployment benefit operations to the number of clients served by them, is inversely correlated with size, but with a case base of only 53 agencies the correlation is too small ($-.14$) to place any confidence in it. Logarithmic transformation of size raises the correlation to $-.24$, which suggests that large size might reduce the man-hour costs of benefit operations slightly.

Whereas this finding is inconclusive, not inconclusive are the numerous findings that indicate that the relative size of administrative overhead declines with increasing organizational size. Large-scale operations make it possible to realize economies in managerial manpower. This can be explained in terms of the generalization that the number of structural components increases at a declining rate with increasing size (1), which implies that the *size* of work groups under a supervisor, just as that of most personnel components, increases with increasing size, and that the *proportion* of supervisors, just as that of most personnel components, decreases with increasing size, and these relationships account for the economy of scale in management.

A final derived proposition in this set is that the economy of scale in administrative overhead itself declines with increasing organizational size (1.6). This proposition follows from two parts of the basic generalization (1A and 1C) in conjunction with one derived proposition (1.3). If the number of structural components increases with increasing organizational size (1A), the statistical expectation is that the proportionate size of any particular personnel component decreases with size (1.3). The empirical data showed that the proportion of managerial personnel and that of staff personnel do in fact decrease as size increases, in accordance with these expectations. But since the increase in the number of components with expanding size occurs at a declining rate (1C), the decrease in the proportionate size of the average component, implicit in this increase in number, must also occur at a declining rate with expanding organizational size. Reformulation in terms of statistical probability yields the proposition that chance expectations are that the proportionate size of any particular personnel complement decreases at a decelerating rate as organizations become larger.

Whether this statistical proposition about most personnel components holds true for the managerial and the staff component is an empirical question, and the answer is that it does. The proportion of staff personnel decreases at a declining rate as organizational size increases (see Figure 17.3), and so does the proportion of managerial personnel at the agency headquarters as well as in local offices (see Figure 17.4). The marginal power of organizational size to produce economies in administrative overhead diminishes with growing size, just as its marginal power to generate structural differentiation does. Both of these patterns are implied by the generalization that the number of structural components in an organization increases at a declining rate with expanding size.

Transition

The structure of formal organizations seems to undergo repeated social fission with growth. In a large organization, its broad responsibilities tend to be subdivided to facilitate their performance, and it thereby becomes differentiated into a number of structural components of diverse sorts. The larger an organization, however, the larger is typically not only the number but also the average size of the components into which it is differentiated. These larger segments of larger organizations, in turn, tend to become internally differentiated along various lines. Thus, the process of social fission recurs within the differentiated units that process has produced. Differenti-

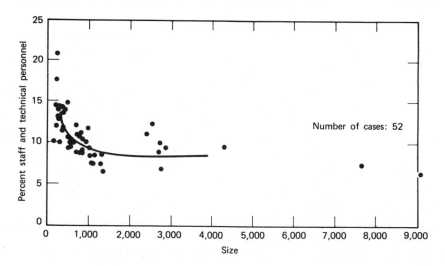

Figure 17.3. Size of agency and percent staff personnel.

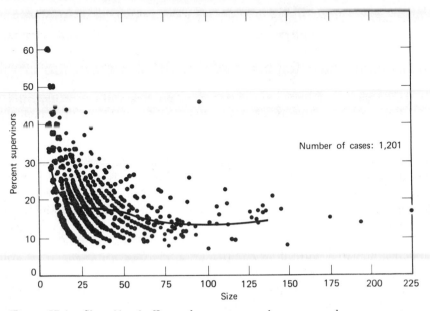

Figure 17.4. Size of local office and percent supervisory personnel.

ation lessens the difficulties the performance of duties entails by reducing the scope of the responsibilities assigned to any individual or unit, but it simultaneously enhances the complexity of the structure. Social fission makes most duties less complex at the expense of greater structural complexity.

When responsibilities become extensively subdivided, many employees will have the same duties and entire units will have similar ones, which may produce savings in supervisory manpower. At the same time, however, the greater structural complexity implicit in the pronounced subdivision of large organizations intensifies problems of communication and coordination, which make new demands on the time of managers and supervisors at all levels. In short, the very differentiation of responsibilities through which large organizations facilitate the performance of duties and reduce the need for supervision creates fresh administrative problems for supervisory personnel. The theory presented so far accounts for the effect of size on savings in supervisory manpower (1.4, 1.5) as well as for its effect on differentiation (1A), but it does not yet include an explicit proposition concerning the effect of differentiation on supervision and administration.

To be sure, the analysis of the proposition that the marginal influence of an organization's size on differentiation declines with increasing size (1.1) has already led to the inference that differentiation intensifies administrative problems. The assumption is that the problems of coordination and communication in differentiated structures have feedback effects that create resistance to further differentiation, which is the reason why the marginal influence of size on differentiation declines with increasing size. The expanding size of an organization is a social force that produces differentiation. The more differentiated an organization is, according to this interpretation, the more resistance a force must overcome to produce still more differentiation, and the more of an expansion in size it therefore takes to effect a given increment in differentiation.

This interpretation seeks to explain the decelerating rate at which increasing size generates differentiation in organizations, but it cannot be logically deduced from the propositions referring to this decelerating rate. It is important in this connection to keep in mind the distinction between inferring a higher-order generalization from a lower-order proposition, in an inductive argument, and logically deriving a lower-order from a higher-order proposition, in deductive reasoning. What is logically implied by the generalization that the rate of differentiation declines with expanding size (1C), as well as by the derived proposition that the marginal influence of increasing size on differentiation diminishes (1.1), is that differentiation gives rise to *some* problems and needs that stifle the further development of differentiation, as indicated by the decreasing power of size to effect differentiation. It does not follow, though it is a plausible inference, that these are problems of coordination and communication calling for administrative solutions. Hence, another basic generalization is postulated incorporating these ideas, which explains some of the propositions in the first set, and which in conjunction with earlier propositions yields three more derived propositions.

Second Generalization: Differentiation and Administration

Structural differentiation in organizations enlarges the administrative component (2), because the intensified problems of coordination and communication in differentiated structures demand administrative attention. In this second fundamental generalization of the deductive theory, the first part subsumes many empirical findings, whereas the second part introduces theoretical terms not independently measured in the research but inferred. The assumptions are that differentiation makes an organization more complex; that a complex structure engenders problems of communication and coordination; that these problems create resistance to further differentiation; that managers, the staff, and even first-line supervisors spend time dealing with these problems; and that consequently more supervisory and administrative manpower is needed in highly differentiated structures than in less differentiated structures. Although these assumptions of the intervening connections are not empirically tested, the implications of the conclusion are. If, in accordance with the inferred assumptions, much of the time of supervisors on all levels in the most differentiated structures is occupied with problems of communication and coordination, it follows that these supervisors have less time left for guiding and reviewing the work of subordinates.

Hence, the more differentiated the formal structure, the more administrative personnel of all kinds should be found in an organization of a given size, and the narrower the span of control of first-line supervisors as well as higher managers. This is precisely the pattern the empirical findings reveal. Vertical differentiation into levels and horizontal differentiation into divisions or sections are both positively related to the proportion of supervisors among the total personnel, controlling size, in the whole organization, in local branches, and in the six functional types of headquarters divisions. They are also positively related to the proportionate size of the staff in agencies of a given size.

Moreover, both vertical and horizontal differentiation, with size held constant, are negatively related to the span of control of managers and supervisors on different levels in local offices and in headquarters divisions, regardless of function.[20] The finding that the second generalization and its derivations discussed below are supported when the span of control of supervisors on a given level is substituted for the ratio of all supervisors is of special importance. The more levels organizations of a given size have (other conditions being equal), the larger is necessarily the proportion of their supervisors, that is, of their personnel above the lowest level. The positive relationship of number of levels with proportion of supervisors does not merely reflect this mathematical nexus, which would make it trivial, as demonstrated by its positive relationship with supervisory span of control, which is not affected by this nexus. Hence, the empirical data support the principle that hierarchical as well as horizontal differentiation, presumably by engendering problems of coordination, enlarges requirements for managerial manpower.

[20] This statement and those in the preceding paragraph are based on several multiple regression analyses with size (log) and a number of other conditions controlled; two or three measures of differentiation as the independent variables (levels, divisions, and sections per division in agencies; levels and sections in local offices and in divisions); and the following dependent variables; for agencies, managerial ratio and staff ratio; for local offices, managerial ratio, span of control of office manager, and mean span of control of first-line supervisors; for the six types of divisions, managerial ratio, span of control of division head, mean span of control of middle managers, and mean span of control of first-line supervisors.

Propositions 2.1 and 2.2: Indirect and Direct Effects of Size

One derived proposition is that the large size of an organization indirectly raises the ratio of administrative personnel through the structural differentiation it generates (2.1). If increasing organizational size generates differentiation (1A), and if differentiation increases the administrative component (2), it follows that the indirect effect of size must be to increase the administrative component. Decomposition of the zero-order correlations of size with various ratios of managerial and staff personnel in multiple regression analysis makes it possible to isolate the indirect effects of size mediated by differentiation from its direct effects. In every problem analyzed, the empirical findings confirm the prediction that the indirect effects of size mediated by both vertical differentiation into levels and horizontal differentiation into divisions or sections raise the ratio of administrative to total personnel. This is the case whether the dependent variable under consideration is the staff ratio or the managerial ratio at the agency headquarters; the ratio of supervisors on all levels; or the span of control of first-line supervisors in any of the six types of functional divisions or in local branches. In all these instances, the indirect effects of size mediated by the differentiation it generates and its direct effects are in opposite directions. The savings in administrative overhead large-scale operations make possible are counteracted by the expansion in administrative overhead the structural complexity of large organizations necessitates.

Another derived proposition is that the direct effects of large organizational size lowering the administrative ratio exceed its indirect effects raising it owing to the structural differentiation it generates (2.2). This is a logical consequence of propositions (1.5) and (2.1). If the overall effect of large size reduces management overhead (1.5), and if large size, by fostering differentiation, indirectly increases management overhead (2.1), it follows that its effect of reducing overhead must outweigh this indirect effect. All the decompositions of the zero-order correlations of size with various measures of management reflect this, as they inevitably must. For example, the direct effect of agency size on the managerial ratio at the agency headquarters, which is represented by the standardized regression coefficient when three measures of differentiation are controlled, is -1.13, whereas its overall effect, indicated by the zero-order correlation, is $-.45$, the difference being due to the strong counteracting effect mediated by differentiation.[21] For the staff ratio at the agency, with the same conditions controlled, the direct effect of size is -1.04, and its overall effect is $-.60$, revealing again a sub-

---

[21] The three aspects of differentiation controlled in this problem, as well as in the one mentioned in the next sentence, are number of (1) levels, (2) divisions, and (3) sections per division

stantial indirect counteracting effect due to structural differentiation. The direct and indirect effect of the size of a division on its managerial ratio and of the size of a local office on its managerial ratio reveal parallel differences.[22] *Ceteris paribus*, a large scale of operations would effect tremendous savings in administrative overhead, but these savings are much reduced by the structural differentiation of large organizations. Consistently, however, the economies of scale exceed the costs of differentiation, so that large organizations, despite their greater structural complexity, require proportionately less administrative manpower than small ones.

Proposition 2.3: Extent and Rate of Economy of Scale

The last proposition to be derived is that the differentiation of large organizations into subunits stems the decline in the economy of scale in management with increasing size, that is, the decline in the decrease in the proportion of managerial personnel with increasing size (2.3). The derivation of this proposition is rather complicated and must be approached in several steps. The new proposition is not as well knit into the system as the others and should be regarded as a mere conjecture.

The concept of economy of scale in administration refers to the fact that the proportion of various kinds of administrative personnel decreases with the increasing size of the organization or its subunits. The operational indication is a negative correlation between any of these proportions and size, which is represented on a graph by a negative slope of the regression line of the proportion on size. These negative correlations and slopes are evident in all empirical data on employment security agencies: size of local branch and either proportion of all managerial personnel or ratio of first-line supervisors to operating employees (the reverse of span of control); size of functional division and either ratio of all managerial personnel or ratio of supervisors to subordinates on three levels; size of total agency and either proportion of staff personnel, or proportion of managerial personnel at the headquarters, or proportion of managerial personnel in the total organization.

---

[22] In the multiple regression analysis for all divisions combined (with sections, levels, clerical ratio, division of labor, agency size, and agency managerial ratio controlled), the standardized regression coefficient indicating the direct effect of a division's size (log) on its managerial ratio is -1.32, and the zero-order correlation indicative of the overall effect is only $-.23$, with differentiation into levels (.65) and sections (.35) being responsible for most of the difference. The separate regression analyses for the six types yield parallel results. In the analysis of local offices (with levels, sections, specialization, manager's span of control, and division of labor controlled), the standardized regression coefficient of office size (log) on the managerial ratio is -1.43, but this incredibly strong direct effect is reduced to a still substantial overall effect, represented by the zero-order correlation of $-.64$, most of the reduction being due to differentiation into levels (.41) and sections (.40).

A decline in this economy of scale means that the *rate of decrease* in the ratio of managerial personnel itself *decreases* with increasing size. This is reflected on a graph by a curve in the negative slope of the regression line of the ratio on size that shows that the ratio of overhead personnel drops first sharply and then more gradually with increasing size. The per cent of supervisors in local offices illustrates a decrease at such a decreasing rate (Figure 17.4), and so does the ratio of staff personnel in the agency (Figure 17.3) and that of the supervisors at the agency headquarters (not shown), and the same pattern is observable in most other relationships mentioned in the above paragraph. The major exception is that the proportion of managerial personnel in the total agency does not reveal such a declining rate of decrease but a fairly linear decrease with increasing agency size, as Figure 17.5 shows. Although this appears to be a deviant case, the principle it expresses can be deduced from the propositions in the theory.

In local offices, the smallest organizational unit examined, the proportion of all supervisory personnel drops rapidly as size increases from ten, or fewer, to about fifty employees, but it drops much more slowly with further increases to one and two hundred employees (see Figure 17.4). From a projection of this trend, one would expect that further increases in size to several thousand employees are hardly accompanied by any decline in the proportion of supervisory personnel. As the size of the entire organization increases from about one hundred to several thousand employees, however, the total proportion of supervisory personnel decreases on the average at a constant rather than declining rate, as Figure 17.5 reveals, though there is much scatter.

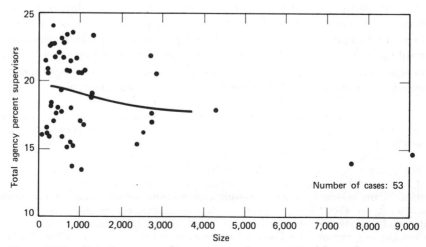

Figure 17.5. Size of agency and percent supervisory personnel in total agency.

Although this decline is not pronounced, it is by no means inconsequential; the zero-order correlation is $-.34$, which compares with a correlation of $-.46$ between size of office and its proportion of supervisors. (However, the latter correlation is raised to $-.64$ if size is logarithmically transformed. In contrast, the former correlation is reduced to $-.23$ by such a transformation, which is another indication that the regression line does not exhibit a logarithmic curve.) Why does the decrease in the proportion of managerial personnel with increasing size, which is already very small as office size expands beyond fifty employees, not become virtually zero but is again considerable as agency size expands from several hundred to several thousand? The answer suggested by the theory is that the differentiation of large organizations into many branch offices (and divisions), while raising the proportion of managers needed, simultaneously restores the economy of scale in the managerial component, that is, it recreates the decline in the proportion of managerial personnel with increasing size observed among very small organizational units.

The growing need for managerial manpower resulting from the structural differentiation engendered by expanding size (2.1) increasingly impinges upon the savings in managerial manpower that a large scale of operations realizes (1.5), which helps to explain why the economy of scale in management declines as size and differentiation increase (1.6).[23] In other words, the *rate* of savings in management overhead with increasing size is higher among comparatively small than among comparatively large organizational units, although, or perhaps because, the management overhead is bigger in small than in large organizational units. Differentiation in a large organization (1A) means that it consists of relatively many smaller rather than relatively few larger organizational subunits, such as local offices. Inasmuch as the *rate* of savings in management overhead is higher in smaller than in larger organizational units, the reduction in the size of units created by differentiation raises this rate of savings and stems the decline in the economy of scale with respect to management overhead that would be otherwise expected once organizations have grown beyond a certain size (2.3).

Conclusions

A formal theory of the formal structure of formal organizations has been presented. Its subject is formally established organizations with paid em-

---

[23] This alternative derivation of proposition (1.6) illustrates the type of crosswise connections that creates a more closely knit theoretical system. Other alternative connections are presented in the conclusions.

ployees, not emergent social systems or voluntary associations of people. It is confined to the analysis of the formal structure—specifically, its differentiation—of organizations, ignoring the informal relations and behavior of individuals within these organizations. And the endeavor has been to develop a formal theory by inferring from many empirical findings a minimum number of generalizations that can logically account for these findings. These findings come from a quantitative study of all employment security agencies and their subunits in the United States. The two basic generalizations, from which nine other propositions were deduced, are: (1) the increasing size of organizations generates structural differentiation along various dimensions at decelerating rates; and (2) structural differentiation enlarges the administrative component in organizations.

The concluding review of the theory rearranges the order of presentation of propositions to call attention to alternative connections between them and to some of the unmeasured terms assumed to underlie these connections. Organizing the work of men means subdividing it into component elements. In a formal organization, explicit procedures exist for systematically subdividing the work necessary to achieve its objectives. Different tasks are assigned to different positions; specialized functions are allocated to various divisions and sections; branches may be created in dispersed locations; administrative responsibilities are subdivided among staff personnel and managers on various hierarchical levels. The larger an organization and the scope of its responsibilities, the more pronounced is its differentiation along these lines (1A, 1B), and the same is the case for its subunits (1D). But large-scale operations—despite the greater subdivision of tasks than that in small-scale operations—involve a larger volume of most organizational tasks. Hence, large organizations tend to have larger as well as more structural components of various sorts than small organizations (1.2).

The pronounced differentiation of responsibilities in large organizations enhances simultaneously intraunit homogeneity and interunit heterogeneity. Inasmuch as duties are more differentiated and the amount of work required in most specialties is greater in large organizations than in small ones, there are comparatively many employees performing homogeneous tasks in large organizations. The large homogeneous personnel components in large organizations simplify supervision and administration, which is reflected in a wider span of control of supervisors (1.4) and a lower administrative ratio (1.3) in large than in small organizations. Consequently, organizations exhibit an economy of scale in administrative manpower (1.5). At the same time, however, the heterogeneity among organizational components produced by differentiation creates problems of coordination and pressures to expand the administrative personnel to meet these problems (2). In this formulation, the unmeasured concepts of intraunit homogeneity and interunit heterogeneity have been introduced to explain why large size has two opposite effects on administrative overhead, reducing it owing to the internal homogeneity of parts, and raising it owing to the heterogeneity among parts.

By generating differentiation, then, large size indirectly raises administrative overhead (2.1), and if its influence on differentiation were unrestrained, large organizations might well have disproportionately large administrative machineries, in accordance with the bureaucratic stereotype. However, the administrative ratio decreases with expanding organizational size, notwithstanding the increased administrative ratio resulting from the differentiation in large organizations (2.2). Two feedback effects of the administrative costs of differentiation may be inferred, which counteract the influences of size on administration and differentiation, respectively. The first of these apparently reduces the savings in administrative manpower resulting from a large scale of operations, as implied by the decline in the rate of decrease of administrative overhead with increasing organizational size (1.6). (Although differentiation into local branches may keep the rate of overhead savings with increasing size constant [2.3], it also raises the amount of overhead.) The second feedback process, probably attributable to the administrative problems engendered by differentiation, creates resistance to further differentiation, which is reflected in the diminishing marginal influence of expanding size on differentiation (1.1) and the declining rate at which size promotes differentiation (1C).

In short, feedback processes seem to keep the amount of differentiation produced by increasing organizational size below the level at which the additional administrative costs of coordination would equal the administrative savings realized by the larger scale of operations. Hence, organizations exhibit an economy of scale in administration, despite the extra administrative overhead required by the pronounced differentiation in large organizations, but this economy of scale declines with increasing size, on account of this extra overhead due to differentiation. The feedback effects inferred, though not directly observable, can explain why the influence of size on differentiation, as well as its influence on administrative economy, declines with increasing size. Figure 17.6 presents these connections graphically.

A final question to be raised is how widely applicable the theory is to organizations of different types. Since the theory was constructed by trying to formulate generalizations from which the empirical findings on employment security agencies can be derived, the fact that these data conform to the propositions advanced does not constitute a test of the theory. But it should be noted that several of the specific propositions included in the theory are supported by findings from previous empirical studies of other kinds of organizations, for example, that administrative overhead in organizations

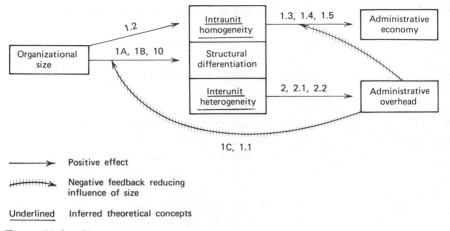

Figure 17.6. Chart of connections.

decreases with size and increases with complexity or differentiation,[24] and that its decrease with size occurs at a declining rate.[25] Moreover, an empirical test of the entire body of theory has been conducted in a study of another type of government bureau, the 416 major finance departments of American states, large cities, and large counties. This independent test confirms the propositions implied by the theory.[26] Whether the theoretical generalizations are also valid for private and other public organizations, and how they must be modified or refined to make them widely applicable, only further research can tell.

[24] See Theodore R. Anderson and Seymour Warkov, "Organizational Size and Functional Complexity," *American Sociological Review* 26 (1961), 23–28; and Louis R. Pondy, "Effects of Size, Complexity, and Ownership on Administrative Intensity," *Administrative Science Quarterly* 14 (1969), 47–60, and references therein.

[25] Bernard P. Indik, "The Relationship Between Organizational Size and Supervision Ratio," *Administrative Science Quarterly* 9 (1964), 301–312.

[26] The number of occupational positions, that of hierarchical levels, and that of functional divisions in these finance departments increases at decelerating rates with increasing size, as indicated by regression lines with positive slopes and logarithmic curves (1, 1.1, 1.2, 1.3). The span of control of first-line supervisors is positively correlated with size (1.4), which implies that the supervisory ratio decreases with size (1.5), and this relationship reveals a logarithmic curve, indicating that the economy of scale in supervisory manpower declines with size (1.6). The numbers of levels and that of divisions both raise the ratio of supervisors to nonsupervisory personnel (2), and large size indirectly does so through its influences on levels and divisions (2.1), but these indirect effects of size are exceeded by its direct effect reducing the ratio of supervisors by widening their span of control (2.2). The absence of local branches in finance departments makes it impossible to test proposition (2.3).

18. Interdependence and Hierarchy in Organizations

The two objectives of this paper are to present empirical findings from a large number of organizations of several different types and to suggest a theory to explain these findings. A previous publication advanced a theory of differentiation in organizations based on data from employment security agencies and their local branches.[1] But findings from one type of organization, even if based on quantitative data, cannot sustain a theory presumably applicable to work organizations in general. Hence the earlier analysis is replicated here with data from several very different types of organizations. Then some theoretical principles to explain the empirical findings are suggested. Whereas the previous formulation concentrated on organizing the empirically supported propositions into a deductive system, the new one focuses on underlying theoretical principles that can account for the observed regularities.

Originally published in 1972.

[1] Peter M. Blau, "A Formal Theory of differentiation in Organization," *American Sociological Review* 35 (1970), 201–218; see the preceding chapter.

Empirical Regularities

Concern is primarily with three characteristics of work organizations, that is, organizations composed of employees responsible for performing work: their size, their internal differentiation, and their administrative apparatus. Six sets of quantitative data collected in five studies of five different types of organizations are analyzed. It is impossible to discuss in detail the research procedures of these five large projects carried out over the last six years, which were concerned with many factors besides the three here considered.[2] A brief indication of procedures must suffice.

Procedures.   (1) Data on the fifty-three employment security agencies in this country (one in every state and one each in Puerto Rico, the Virgin Islands, and the District of Columbia) were obtained by three research assistants in personal visits to these agencies from informants and records. All the data under consideration, in the other studies as well as this one, consist of objective information derived from personnel records and detailed organizational charts constructed specifically for the research during the interview, which were checked against one another. (2) Data on the local branches of these agencies—1,201 of them when the smallest and simplest are excluded—were collected during the same visits from information available at the headquarters. To ensure that the measures of branch characteristics are independent of those of corresponding agency characteristics, the latter are based on the structure and the administrative personnel at the agency headquarters, excluding branches. (3) Data on the 416 government finance departments of nearly all larger American cities, counties, and states were gathered in two different ways. National Opinion Research Center interviewers visited the 256 larger and more complex ones, and self-administered mail questionnaires were returned by the rest.

In addition to these government agencies, research has been conducted on three other kinds of organizations. (4) Data on 124 department stores were obtained in visits by N.O.R.C. interviewers. These firms constitute two-thirds of the largest department stores west of the Mississippi and north of the Mason-Dixon Line. Economic considerations led to the geographical restriction, and refusals are largely responsible for the fact that not all large

[2] The research has been supported by Grants GS-553, GS-1528, GS-27073, and GS-28646X from the National Science Foundation to the Comparative Organization Research Program, which I gratefully acknowledge. This paper is C.O.R.P. report No. 16. For full discussions of research procedures, see Peter M. Blau and Richard A. Schoenherr, *The Structure of Organizations* (New York: Basic Books, 1971); Marshall W. Meyer, *Bureaucratic Structure and Authority* (New York: Harper, 1972); Paul Goldman, "The Organization of Department Stores," (Ph.D. dissertation, University of Chicago, 1974); and Peter M. Blau, *The Organization of Academic Work* (New York: Wiley, 1973).

northeastern department stores are included. (5) Data on 115 universities and colleges were collected in personal visits by research assistants. A weighting formula was applied to the analysis of this stratified sample, in which larger and higher-quality institutions are overrepresented, to make the results representative of the universe of the more than 1,000 four-year liberal arts institutions in the country. (6) Data on the 1,279 American teaching hospitals (the superior hospitals, specifically, all that have some residents, most of which have no direct university affiliation) were made available by the American Hospital Association, for which I am grateful. Although these data, secured for administrative purposes, furnish only crude indications of the organizational characteristics of interest, the large number of cases makes it tempting to use them nevertheless.

Size is conceptualized as the scope of an organization and its responsibilities; the measure is its number of employees (except in academic institutions, where it is the number of faculty members). Methodological, theoretical, and empirical considerations dictated the choice of this measure of organizational size. Whereas the number of employees can be compared among different types, this is not the case for other measures of scope, such as sales in stores and beds in hospitals. Besides, theoretical concern is with the way people—not assets or products—are organized and with the resulting structure of subgroupings of employees. Finally, there is a close empirical association between an organization's volume of responsibilities and its number of employees. The correlation between the number of insured unemployed in a state, whose needs the employment security agency is responsible to serve, and the agency's number of employees is .98; that between total sales and employees in a department store is .95; that between number of students and number of faculty in an institution of higher learning is .94.[3] As a matter of fact, an organization's personnel is quite highly correlated even with such indirect indications of its scope of operations as the population in a government finance department's jurisdiction (.62) and a hospital's total assets (.59).[4]

Organizations are differentiated in several dimensions, and the degree of differentiation in each is measured by the number of subunits. The number of hierarchical levels represents vertical differentiation. The number of major divisions under top management and of sections per division are two indicators of horizontal differentiation among subgroups with different func-

[3] If both variables are logarithmically transformed ($\log_{10}$). Without transformation their correlation is .84.

[4] No indication of the volume of operation of the local branches of employment security agencies is available. Community size does not provide a valid indirect measure of their work load, because there is more than one branch office in most larger cities.

tions.[5] The subdivision of work into occupational specialties is reflected by the number of official job titles or positions in government agencies and by the number of different departments in academic institutions and department stores. Two of the five types are geographically differentiated into branches, but since the branches of employment security agencies are analyzed separately, only those of department stores are treated as an independent measure of differentiation. The information from teaching hospitals furnished merely a single crude index of structural differentiation, the number of different types of residencies, which is indicative of the number of the major, but not of all, medical divisions in the hospitals.

The basic measure of administrative apparatus is the proportion of managerial personnel, including managers and supervisors on all levels. Inasmuch as academic and medical work is not supervised by managers in the way work in government bureaus and business concerns is, somewhat different, though conceptually analogous, variables are used for universities and colleges and for hospitals, namely, the ratio of administrators (not including clerical personnel) to faculty, and the proportion of nurses in administration, respectively. Two supplementary indicators of the ratio of administrative manpower to operating personnel are the proportion of employees in staff rather than line positions (only available for employment security agencies) and the average span of control of first-line supervisors (available for three types).

Regression analysis is used to discern direct and indirect effects of one condition in organizations on another.[6] A regression coefficient must exceed twice its standard error when other relevant factors are held constant to be considered indicative of an effect. The assumption of causal order is: size—differentiation—administration. The nature of an organization's responsibilities is roughly controlled, since each type is analyzed separately.

Effects of Size.   The larger an organization the more differentiated it is along various lines. Whether we look at hierarchical levels, functional divisions, sections per division, occupational specialties, or geographical branches, organizations become differentiated into a larger number of them with increasing size, and this is the case for very different kinds of organiza-

---

[5] Data on sections per division have been obtained only for employment security agencies and for department stores, since different sections in small organizations often are work groups performing essentially the same responsibilities. The average number of employees in these agencies (1,195) and stores (1,867) is substantially higher than the averages in the four other types.

[6] The regression coefficients for employment security agencies reported are somewhat higher than those in Blau and Schoenherr *op. cit.*, because a different computer program has been used to derive the former (SPSS).

tions. The findings from employment security agencies and their local branches are replicated, with minor variations, not only in other government bureaus and in private firms but also in universities and colleges and in teaching hospitals, as Table 18.1 indicates. Most of the correlations are high, and nearly all increase further when size is logarithmically transformed (using $\log_{10}$). On the average, size (log) accounts for more than two-fifths of the variation in hierarchical levels, nearly two-fifths of the variation in functional divisions, and more than half of the variation in occupational specialization. These findings challenge the conclusions of previous investigators that size does "not appear to affect organization as much as

Table 18.1 Zero-Order Correlations between Size and Measures of Differentiation

	ES[a]	LB[b]	FD[c]	DS[d]	U and C[e]	TH[f]
Levels						
Size	.60	.68	.55	.51	.37	
Log size	.72	.69	.66	.66	.51	
Divisions[g]						
Size	.38	.61	.50	.28	.80	.52
Log size	.54	.67	.73	.33	.82	.50
Sec./div.						
Size	.16			.43		
Log size	.43			.62		
Occupational specialties[h]						
Size	.78	.51	.81	.60	.83	
Log size	.82	.62	.80	.66	.79	
Branches						
Size	.94			.55		
Log size [i]				.62		

[a] Employment security agencies ($N = 53$).
[b] Local branches of ES agencies ($N = 1201$).
[c] Finance departments ($N = 416$).
[d] Department stores ($N = 124$).
[e] Universities and colleges ($N = 115$).
[f] Teaching hospitals ($N = 1279$).
[g] In U and C, schools and colleges; in TH, types of residencies.
[h] In DS and in U and C, departments; otherwise, job titles.
[i] Correlation with branches not available for ES.

might have been expected"[7] and that "size and organizational structure are not closely related."[8]

Increasing organizational size promotes differentiation, but it does so at a declining rate. The scatter diagrams reveal that the regression lines of size (untransformed) on the various measures of differentiation for all six sets of data have declining positive slopes. As size increases, the number of subunits into which an organization becomes differentiated in any one dimension increase at first very rapidly and then more and more gradually. It is impossible to present this score of scatter diagrams here.[9] However, some indication of this curvature of the regression lines is provided by the fact that the logarithmic transformation of size raises its correlation with measures of differentiation (in sixteen of nineteen instances), as Table 18.1 shows. Some of the curves are shallow, so that logarithmic transformation of size produces a curve in the opposite direction (an accelerating positive slope) and improves the correlation little, and in three cases the curve in the opposite direction is so pronounced that the correlation decreases slightly.[10] Thus the addition of 100 employees stimulates much differentiation in organizations with fewer than 1,000 employees, but only little in those with several thousand. While increasing size has a pronounced impact on differentiation along various lines in work organizations regardless of type, the marginal influence of a given increment in size declines with increasing size.

Contrary to the stereotype of the proliferation of bureaucratic machinery in large organizations, the administrative apparatus is proportionately smaller in large than in small organizations. Different though government bureaus and retail businesses are from universities and hospitals, the proportion of personnel responsible for administering the organization declines in all of them with increasing size, as the negative correlations in Table 18.2 indicate. These results confirm those of Melman, Anderson and Warkov, Hawley *et al.*, and Indik.[11] The span of control of supervisors is, correspond-

---

[7] Joan Woodward, *Industrial Organization* (London: Oxford University Press, 1965), p. 31.

[8] Richard H. Hall *et al.*, "Organizational Size, Complexity, and Formalization," *American Sociological Review* 32 (1967), p. 712.

[9] A number of them are shown in Blau and Schoenherr *op. cit.*, and a few are reproduced in the preceding chapter.

[10] The scatter diagram for one of these three cases is presented in Blau and Schoenherr, *op. cit.*, p. 333. It shows that the regression curve (of size on occupational specialties in finance departments) has a declining slope, even though logarithmic transformation of size reduces the correlation.

[11] Seymour Melman, "The Rise of Administrative Overhead in the Manufacturing Industries of the United States, 1899–1947," *Oxford Economic Papers* 3 (1951), 61–112; Theodore R. Anderson and Seymour Warkov, "Organizational and Size and Functional Complexity," *American Sociological Review* 26 (1961), 23–28; Amos H. Hawley *et al.*, "Population Size and Administration in Institutions of Higher Education," *American Sociological Review* 30 (1965), 252–255; and Bernard P. Indik, "The Relationship Between Organization Size and Supervisory Ratio," *Administrative Science Quarterly* 9 (1964), 301–312.

Table 18.2   Zero-Order Correlations between Size and Measures of Administration Apparatus

	ES	LB	FD	DS	U and C	TH
% Managers[a]						
Size[b]	−.42	−.46		−.24	−.17	−.30
Log size	−.45	−.64	−.28	−.53	−.28	−.48
% Staff						
Size	−.44					
Log size	−.60					

[a] Administration-faculty ratio in U and C; per cent administrative nurses in TH.
[b] Not available for FD.

ingly, wider in large than in small organizations. The correlations between size (log) and average number of subordinates per first-line supervisor are .66 for the 1,201 branches of employment security agencies, .51 for the 416 finance departments, and .34 for the 124 department stores. Despite the more complex structure of larger organizations produced by differentiation, they apparently can be administered with proportionately less manpower than small ones.

Organizations exhibit an economy of scale in administration. But this economy of scale declines with increasing organizational size. The savings in managerial and other administrative personnel that the large size of organizations seems to make possible diminish with their increasing size. Table 18.2 shows that logarithmic transformation of size increases its correlations with the measures of administration in all types of organization for which data are available. This implies that the regression line of size on administration has a declining negative slope, and the scatter diagrams confirm this inference. With increasing organizational size, the proportion of administrative personnel decreases sharply at first but less and less thereafter. The large size of organizations appears to reduce both the proportion of administrative personnel needed and the savings in administrative personnel that further increases size permit. Thus the negative marginal influence of a given increment in organizational size on administration, just as its positive marginal influence on differentiation, declines with increasing size.

Effects of Differentiation.   Although size and differentiation tend to vary together in work organizations, they have opposite implications for the administrative apparatus. Whereas large size reduces the proportion of administrative personnel, pronounced structural differentiation expands it. Interestingly enough, the division of labor among individual roles (number of occupational specialities) has no such effect,[12] only differentiation that produces a structure of interdependent subgroups does. Specifically, what enlarges the administrative apparatus are the number of levels into which the hierarchy is differentiated, the number of divisions and that of sections per division among which functions are subdivided, and the number of geographical branches. But this effect is evident only when organizational size is controlled, because size produces spurious negative associations between measures of structural differentiation and administrative apparatus, which conceal the positive direct nexus between them. Table 18.3 presents six separate regression analyses that dissect the effects of size and differentiation on administration.

The negative standardized regression coefficients in the first row of Table 18.3 reveal that large size as such, independent of differentiation, effects considerable more savings in administrative personnel than the zero-order correlations (in Table 18.2) indicate.[13] This is the case in all types of organizations examined, notwithstanding their diverse nature, though the strength of the direct relationship between size and administration varies among types (which is in part an artifact of the difference in the measures of differentiation that are controlled). But the large size of organizations is accompanied by differentiation in their structure, as we have seen, and this differentiation enlarges the administrative apparatus, as the positive regression coefficients in rows 2–5 of Table 18.3 show.[14] Hence, the indirect effect

---

[12] The regression coefficients of number of occupational specialities, with size controlled, on the percentage of the personnel in administration are insignificantly small in all types (not available for hospitals). The zero-order correlations are negative and spurious, owing to the influence of size.

[13] In department stores, managerial personnel in Table 18.3 excludes buyers, who are part-time managers, while the figure in Table 18.2 includes buyers, making the two figures not comparable. The comparable figure—the zero-order correlation for store size (log) and managers excluding buyers—is .15. If buyers were included in the regression analysis presented in Table 18.3, insignificantly small regression coefficients for levels (.10) and divisions (.07) would be observed. Thus, the effect of structural differentiation in department stores increases primarily the number of "pure" managers who are not also buyers, whereas the administrative economies of large-scale operations are only evident if these part-time managers, the buyers, are included in the measure and largely result from a reduction in the proportion of these part-time managers. (The zero-order correlation between size (log) and percentage of buyers in the store is −.79.)

[14] In universities and colleges, the regression coefficients for levels and divisions fail to exceed twice their standard error, probably because the measure of size if confined to faculty while students and other employees also effect administrative loads and structural differentiation. If number of students (log) is substituted for number of faculty (log) as the measure of size, all three standardized regression coefficients are greater than twice their standard error; they are −.75 (size), .26 (levels), and .30 (divisions).

Table 18.3 Regression Analysis of Proportion of Administrative personnel[a] on Size and Differentiation

	ES	LB	FD	DS	U and C	TH
Size (log)	−1.13	−1.47	−1.29	−.46	−.55	−.54
Levels	.47	.61	.94	.32	.25[e]	
Divisions[b]	.36	.62	.53	.21	.12[e]	.13
Sec./div.[c]	.33					
Branches				.53		
Ind. effect of size[d]	.68	.83	1.01	.61	.27	.06

[a] Percentage of managerial personnel, except: (1) excluding buyers in DS, who are included in DS in Table 18.2 (see fn. 13); (2) administration–faculty ratio in U and C; (3) percentage of administrative nurses in TH.

[b] In U and C, schools and colleges; in TH, types of residencies.

[c] Excluded from regression analysis in DS, since it has no appreciable effect ($b* = .05$).

[d] The figures in this row are not part of the regression equation but provided for supplementary information; they are the difference between the r and the $b*$ of size (log).

[e] Not twice its standard error.

of large organizational size, mediated by the greater differentiation in the structure it generates, expands the administrative apparatus, counteracting its direct effect of reducing it. Row 6 presents these indirect effects of size ($r − b*$). The pattern of influences can be represented in a simple path diagram:[15]

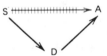

These findings raise a methodological question, however. The indicators of differentiation, particularly number of hierarchical levels, necessarily increase the number of managers in organizations of a given size. Are the observed relationships between differentiation and proportion of administrative personnel merely the result of this mathematical connection? To answer this question, regression analyses are carried out substituting a measure of

[15] The actual path diagram for each of the six sets of data can be completed with the information provided in Tables 18.3 and 18.1. Table 18.3 supplies the path coefficients between A and S (row 1) and those between A and several measures of D (rows 2–5). Table 18.1 supplies the path coefficients between these measures of D and S (rows 2, 4, 6, and 10).

**Table 18.4   Regression Analysis of Average Span of Control of
Supervisors on Size and Differentiation**

	LB	FD	DS	DS[a]
Size (log)	1.31	1.08	.44	.50
Levels	−.49	−.25	−.18[c]	−.35
Divisions	−.46	−.55	.06[c]	−.26
Ind. effect of size[b]	−.65	−.57	−.10	−.32

[a] Mean span of control of managers who supervise buyers.

[b] These figures are not part of the regression equation (see Table 18.3, fn. *d*).

[c] Not twice its standard error.

the ratio of administrative to operating personnel that is mathematically independent of the differentiation measures, namely, the average span of control of first-line supervisors, data on which are available for three types.[16] The same independent variables are, of course, expected to have the opposite effects on this ratio of operating personnel to lowest-level managers from those they have on the proportion of managers. Table 18.4 confirms this expectation in two of three cases. Large size increases, and differentiation decreases, the number of subordinates per first-line supervisor in the branches of employment security agencies and in finance departments but not in department stores, possibly because buyers there are often part-time supervisors.[17] The same pattern is observable in department stores if the span of control of middle managers instead of that of first-line supervisors is considered (column 4). Initial results are sufficiently corroborated to place some

[16] Regression analysis using the alternative measure for administrative apparatus in employment security agencies, percentage staff, yields another replication of the findings in Table 18.3. While this measure is not confounded with number of levels, it is probably affected by number of divisions and sections per division, because some of these subunits are staff units. Interestingly, however, the standardized regression coefficient for levels (.41) is greater than twice its standard error, whereas those for divisions (.28) and sections per division (.22) are not; the one for size (log) is −1.20.

[17] Branches are not used as independent variables in department stores because the mean span of control *in the main store only* is the dependent variable. (Using them alters results little.) The somewhat different findings in department stores may have several reasons: the existence of many part-time managers (the buyers); the lesser reliability of the data from this project; distinctive patterns in profit-making enterprises, of which these stores are the only representative in the research program so far. No detailed interpretation of the distinctive features of department stores is offered in this paper concerned with the similarities in different types of organizations.

confidence in the conclusion that the relationships reflect empirical forces and not the confounding of empirical measures.

In organizations established to further academic pursuits or medical treatment as well as those explicitly designed for the efficient performance of work, large size produces very great savings in administrative manpower, other conditions being equal. But other conditions are not the same in large and in small organizations. The large size of organizations is accompanied by greater differentiation in their structure, which in turn leads to the expansion of administrative manpower. The complex structure of large organizations thereby counteracts the economy of scale in administration, without completely eliminating it. It appears as if increasing organizational size gave rise to dialectical forces having opposite effects, and decomposition in regression analysis can reveal these conflicting influences. Processes seem to arise with the increasing size of organizations that lessen needs for administrative personnel, and so do processes that generate a complex structure and consequently magnify needs for administrative personnel.

The consistent empirical regularities observed in quite different types of organizations pose several questions a theory should answer. Why do large organizations have a so much more differentiated structure than small ones? Why have large organizations, despite their greater complexity, and contrary to the bureaucratic stereotype, a relatively smaller administrative apparatus than small ones? One hardly needs to ask why a differentiated complex structure increases the proportion of administrative personnel in an organization, since a plausible interpretation readily comes to mind. But can this positive effect of differentiation on administration and the negative effect of size on it be explained by the same theoretical principle? Finally, what accounts for the decline in the influence of size on both differentiation and administration with increasing size? Theoretical answers to these questions will be suggested by advancing generalizations that logically imply and thus explain the empirical findings.

Functional Differentiation

In work organizations the terms *functional differentiation* and *functional interdependence* have quite specific meanings. There are no implicit assumptions of mythical forces that create an equilibrium among diverse institutions and assure that each makes positive contributions to the others. Functional differentiation in organizations refers simply to the fact that a common enterprise has become differentiated into subunits with distinct responsibilities or functions, for example, that an automobile factory consists of a division manufacturing motors, a chassis division, a body division, and a sales division. The functions of these divisions are, of course, interdependent, and so are all functions or specialized duties that result from the subdivision of a given job, such as that for which a work organization is responsible.

Interdependence.   For large numbers of persons to be integrated in a common enterprise requires either that they share distinctive values or interests that unite them or that they perform complementary functions that make them interdependent. Reference is to Durkheim's famous distinction between mechanical and organic solidarity,[18] except that these concepts are applied, not to types of societies, but to associations within a society. The radical ideology creates the bond of solidarity among the members of a revolutionary movement. Common economic interests unify workers in a labor union. Distinctive beliefs about morality and supernatural powers make a religious sect a highly cohesive body, and as the strength of religious convictions wanes, so does the social integration in the church.

The employees of an organization have no such distinctive common values or interests. To be sure, they have in common the basic cultural values and an interest in earning a living, but both of these they share with the employees of other organizations in the society. Besides the members of most work organizations, except very small ones, do not share the more specific value orientations individuals have, such as those reflecting their ethnic subculture, religious affiliation, and political allegiance. Even when such orientations are common to all or most employees of a work organization, they are not a distinctive bond, because they are shared with many other people. Occupational interests similarly tend not to be the same for all employees of an organization, and whether or not they are, many others outside share these interests. But are not the goals of an organization those of its members, furnishing a bond of common solidarity? Not in the case of work organizations. People join social movements or clubs because they are identified with their goals. But they do not work for General Motors because they are interested in raising its profits; or for a city finance department because they are interested in the fiscal welfare of the town; or for Columbia University because they are interested in *its* ability to advance knowledge and transmit it to students. Employees join organizations and make contributions to their goals because they are interested in receiving financial rewards, utilizing occupational skills, and, particularly in the case of some occupations, enhancing their professional reputation. The goals of the organization are not goals of its employees, at least not initially, though secondary identification with them and with the organization itself often tends to develop in the course of working for it.

[18] Emile Durkheim, *The Division of Labor in Society* (New York: Macmillan, 1933).

What transforms an aggregate of individuals who happen to have the same employer into an integrated collective body is their functional interdependence produced by the subdivision of work in the organization. The employees of an organization perform complementary roles, that is, duties that have no instrumental significance unless complemented by other duties, such as those of the buyer of dresses in a department store, which require complementation by the work of saleswomen. The subdivisions of the work needed to pursue the organization's goals among subunits with different functions necessarily makes these subunits (for example, the division collecting unemployment taxes and that paying unemployment benefits), and hence their employees, instrumentally interdependent.[19]

In sum, the employees of a work organization are engaged in a common enterprise, which requires that they become an integrated social unit, but they do not have strong feelings of common solidarity, like those permeating the members of religious or political sects, for they lack the profound values shared only by the ingroup that create such firm bonds of solidarity and unite individuals in a cohesive group. The subdivision of work in organizations, however, has the result that its employees perform complementary roles and belong to subunits with complementary functions, and their consequent instrumental interdependence fuses employees into a distinctive coherent social organism. The differentiation of functions in an organization, developing for instrumental reasons, shapes its social structure and converts its employees from a collection of individuals with no distinctive common values or interests into a unified social entity.

Process of Integration.   The process of social integration of individuals in a large collectivity always involves direct social contacts in small groups. The kinship system of simple societies illustrates this. It is an institution that divides the society into small subunits that are interconnected in several ways. The intimate and frequent social interaction in small families makes it possible for individuals to be socialized, to acquire the common language and cultural values, to receive emotional support, and thereby to attain

---

[19] The degree of interdependence in work organizations varies. At one extreme, illustrated by the assembly line, the work of one individual or group cannot be performed until that of another is. At the other extreme, illustrated by different sales departments, the work of one subunit can proceed regardless of that in others, but the significance of the various functions for the organization makes them interdependent. It takes a number of different sales departments to make up a department store; heart surgery can be performed whether or not orthopedic surgery is, but both are required in a general hospital, just as instruction in both natural sciences and humanities is needed in a college. Extensive differentiation of an organization's responsibilities intensifies the degree of interdependence among the functions of subunits and makes the performance of at least some directly contingent on that of others.

social integration. These social processes make individuals integrated members not only of small families but also of larger clans and the entire society, because families are linked together in the kinship system and transmit to children the cultural and subcultural values of the larger collectivities of which they are part. Another illustration of this principle is de Tocqueville's thesis that the integration of people into the political life of a large democracy depends on widespread participation in many voluntary associations, which are relatively small and serve as mediaries between individual citizens and the state.[20] There is no direct way individuals can relate themselves to a society or any other large collectivity. Their social integration requires subunits small enough for regular personal contacts among members.

The differentiation of instrumental functions along various lines has implications for social integration in work organizations analogous to those of the kinship system in simple societies, because it too creates small interlocking subunits in which stable social relations can develop. The recurrent social interaction among colleagues in these small groups socializes newcomers to informal as well as official procedures, furnishes continuing advice on problems of the job and social support, and consequently fosters integration in the immediate work group, and in the organization as well. The groupings are interlocking, inasmuch as many employees belong to several of them—for example, with colleagues in the same specialty from different departments, with others in the same location regardless of specialty, and with fellow managers on the same level. Since these interdependent interlocking subgroups form a tight web as constituent elements of the organizations's structure, employees who become integrated in subgroups are thereby enmeshed in the larger social structure and become integral members of the organization.

The larger an organization is, the more differentiation is required to produce the small subunits in which regular personal contacts further social integration. But an explanation of the increasing differentiation with increasing organization size in these terms is subject to the criticism, often made of functional interpretations, that the existence of a social pattern is accounted for by the beneficial consequences it has for the social system, as if a benign "unseen hand" governed human existence. In work organizations, however, the existence of social patterns that make contributions to operations need not be attributed to an "unseen hand," because a specific agency exists to institute such patterns. Organizations have a management that is responsible for effective operations, rewarded for discharging this responsibility successfully, and empowered to implement its interest in efficient operations. Given the assumption that managers are interested in

[20] Alexis de Tocqueville, *Democracy in America* (New York: Knopf, 1945).

effective operations, conditions (such as large organizational size) that require certain structural arrangements for effective operations can be expected to constrain managers to institute these arrangements if possible.[21]

But does management's interest in efficient operations necessarily make it interested in the existence of highly integrated work groups? This can by no means be taken for granted, inasmuch as the social cohesion of work groups, which may strengthen the informal enforcement of output restrictions, is not consistently associated with superior performance.[22] To be sure, management has an interest in the integration of employees in the work organization, which depends on their integration in its subgroups, but it is doubtful that managers are aware of differentiation's significance for this integration, even if the conjecture that it has such significance is correct. However, the differentiation of work into specialized responsibilities also makes instrumental contributions to operations, of which management is unlikely to remain unaware, and which furnish incentives for managerial decisions that promote differentiation.

Specialization. A large volume of work requires a large number of persons to accomplish it. For many people to collaborate on common endeavors, their work must be organized. Organizing work involves subdividing it into component parts. Even a single individual organizes his work by dividing it into parts and doing one part at a time. The more complex the job, the more important it is to divide it into more homogeneous tasks that can be performed separately, because homogeneous tasks are easier than heterogeneous ones. If the volume of work is too large for an individual and requires a group, it can be subdivided among group members. Only in the most primitive collaboration of individuals, exemplified by logrolling, does everyone perform the same tasks. Work in a group is typically subdivided, with different individuals performing different tasks, which makes the job of each more homogeneous and thus simplifies it. The subdivision of work in social space, therefore, complements its subdivision by time periods in most cases of collaboration in a group.

---

[21] Another assumption is implied here: the prevailing characteristics of organizations, as distinguished from those in particular organizations, can be explained in terms of the influences of antecedent conditions in organizations (or their environment) without reference to the psychological preferences or decisions of individual managers, because these social conditions greatly restrict the options of managers who pursue an interest in efficient operations. This principle derives from Durkheim: "The determining cause of a social fact should be sought among the social facts preceding it and not among the states of individual consciousness" [*The Rules of Sociological Method* (Chicago: University of Chicago Press, 1938), p. 110].

[22] Stanley Seashore, *Group Cohesiveness in the Industrial Work Group* (Ann Arbor: University of Michigan Institute for Social Research, 1954), pp. 63–80.

If a still larger volume of work requires many persons to accomplish it and not merely a small group, it can be divided among subgroups, enabling entire subgroups to concentrate on relatively homogeneous tasks. Whereas work in small groups tends to become organized, subdivided, and coordinated in the course of direct social interaction without formalized procedures, explicit formal procedures are necessary to organize and coordinate the work of a collectivity too large for every member to have direct contacts with all others. A work organization is simply an explicit system for organizing the work of many persons in a common enterprise. A sheer increase in the volume of work, by determining whether its accomplishment requires only one person or a small group or a large collectivity, alters the principle in terms of which the work is organized (by subdivision in time, among individuals, or among subgroups).

Organizations accomplish jobs of staggering complexity as well as magnitude, jobs far too complex for an individual or any number of individuals who are not organized, because the subdivision of work facilitates that of every individual and that of every subunit by making their tasks more homogeneous. This may be illustrated by the division of labor among specialized roles of individuals. In its absence, every employee would have to perform all the tasks involved in the discharge of the organization's responsibilities and would have to have all the requisite skills. For instance, all patient care in hospitals would have to be provided by general practitioners. The division of labor segregates tasks into homogeneous jobs ranging usually from quite routine to very difficult ones. Less training suffices for the comparatively routine jobs. In the example of hospitals, nurses relieve physicians of some duties, and much patient care can be performed by aides. At the same time, greater specialized training can be required for the various difficult jobs, as exemplified by the substitution of surgeons and internists and other specialists for G.P.'s in hospitals. The division of labor consequently has a double advantage. It makes it possible to fill many positions with less trained personnel, which facilitates recruitment and achieves economies, and to fill the most difficult jobs with more highly trained experts, which improves the quality of performance. By reducing the range and enhancing the homogeneity of the tasks in any given position, the division of labor promotes specialized expertness as well as routinization. The brain surgeon's job encompasses, strictly speaking, a narrower range of more homogeneous duties than the G.P.'s, but this very fact enables the former successfully to perform tasks the latter cannot undertake.

In short, the division of labor enables an organization to perform more complex work better and with less skilled personnel. It is a mechanism that translates quantitative changes into qualitative ones. A purely quantitative increase in the volume of work, without any initial changes in the nature of responsibilities, increases the number of persons engaged in the work and the division of labor among them, and it thereby gives rise to the performance of jobs that were not originally undertaken and could not have been, that is, to a change in the nature of the work. Thus jobs are performed in large organizations that do not exist in similar small ones.

Work is subdivided in organizations not only among positions occupied by individuals but also among organizational subunits. There are the major divisions under top management with different functions, and the sections within them with varying responsibilities. Sometimes organizations have geographical branches, and these also may have specialized functions. The subdivision of work among organizational segments is the organizational form of the division of labor, and it makes important instrumental contributions to operations. An entire group can concentrate on more homogeneous tasks and gain experience and expertise in carrying them out. Consultation among colleagues engaged in similar work, which supplies advice when needed and social recognition for good advice, probably improves performance. The manager of a unit with relatively homogeneous tasks can have expert knowledge of most or all of them.

Another dimension of differentiation in work organizations is that between operations and administration. Operations involve the production of goods or the provision of services that is the organization's basic responsibility, be it furnishing services to the unemployed, retail selling, or treating the sick. Administration entails organizing the work of others and maintaining the organization, broadly conceived, including recruitment, guidance, coordination, and management. The subdivision of work in administration has the same advantages as that in operations, permitting some administrative jobs to be performed by less skilled personnel and others to be filled by specialized experts in various administrative responsibilities, including that of management. Before extending the analysis of administration, the principles of differentiation advanced should be concisely formulated.

The differentiation of instrumental functions in work organizations makes important contributions to effective operations. These exert compelling constraints on management, given its interest in effective operations, to make the administrative decisions required for the development of differentiation. But the degree of feasible differentiation in an organization is limited by its size, particularly inasmuch as differentiation occurs in several intersecting dimensions. An organization must be large for operating responsibilities to be much subdivided, and it must be still larger for administrative responsibilities to be much subdivided. Large size is a necessary condition for extensive differentiation, but not a sufficient one, and differentiation's instrumental contributions create the pressures that promote it to the degree size permits. If the increasing size of work organizations not only makes the social integration of employees dependent on extensive differentiation but also provides the opportunities for improving operations through progressive differentiation of functions, which gives management incentives to promote such differentiation, it follows that increasing organizational size is accompanied by increasing differentiation. Thus the theory can explain the first set of empirical findings. This does not prove the theory, of course.

Administrative Hierarchy

Work organizations have been briefly defined as explicit systems for organizing the work of many persons in a common enterprise. But they are specifically hierarchical control systems for doing so. An administrative hierarchy through which control over operations is exercised is a basic trait of organizations, as Weber has emphasized.[23] Whether hierarchical control is a necessary prerequisite for organizing work on a large scale is a moot question. Management has the responsibility for organizing and directing the work of other employees, has the authority that enables it to do so, and has command over resources, on which employees depend, to back up its authority. Although there is interdependence among subunits in organizations, it is asymmetrical. Functionally, every subunit is dependent on others, including management, which could not administer operations without employees to perform them. Existentially, however, the dependence of lower ranks on higher ones is unilateral, inasmuch as superiors have authority and sanctioning power over subordinates.

Economy of Scale in Administration.   The large size of an organization expands management's power, both internally, by increasing the scope of its authority, and externally, by increasing the influence of the organization in the community and thereby management's. Many employees also enlarge the volume of administrative work. The principles suggested for operations can be applied to administration. A large volume of work requires a large number of persons to perform it, in administration as elsewhere. For large numbers to work together on administering an organization, their administrative work must be organized, and organizing work entails subdividing it.

   The subdivision of administrative work takes two forms. First, administrative duties that do not depend on managerial authority, such as recruitment and bookkeeping, are separated from the rest. These staff functions are in turn subdivided among positions and organizational subunits, exemplified by personnel divisions, training sections, comptroller offices, and

---

[23] Max Weber, *Essays in Sociology* (New York: Oxford University Press, 1946), p. 197.

typing pools. The slogan that staff advises but does not command expresses that these functions are divested of official authority, though staff experts often have much influence in organizations. Second, administrative responsibilities for management and supervision are differentiated into hierarchical levels, which vary in scope of authority and hence in the nature of major duties, ranging from responsibilities for assisting with and checking on operations to those for long-range planning, fundamental policy, and the organization's viability and success. Lower managerial levels are under the authority of higher ones, and official authority is ultimately rooted entirely in the hands of top management, which has command over resources, and which delegates authority to other managers. Hierarchical differentiation crosscuts the subdivision of work in operations and that within the staff. Whereas management is merely one of many functions in purely instrumental terms, its authority distinguishes it fundamentally from the rest. The differentiation of managerial levels obscures the fundamental distinction between management and other employees without making it any less important.

In contrast to its absolute amount, the proportionate amount of administrative work decreases with increases in the volume of operations and the number of employees to be organized. The reason is that organizing work entails initial investments largely independent of the volume of work to be carried out. The time and effort spent in setting up a computer program differs little whether one tabulation is made or several hundred. Once a procedure for processing unemployment insurance checks has been designed, possibly after extensive investigation of alternatives, it can be used to issue any number of checks. The work involved in selecting the styles of dresses with most sales appeal hardly depends on the number of dresses to be bought for a store and offered for sale. To design a new procedure is a time-consuming task, whether it is applicable to the work of few employees or that of many.[24]

In short, the investment of administrative time required for organizing operations is not proportionate to their volume, increasing far less than the volume of operations increases. To be sure, not all administrative duties involve such time investments. Personnel interviews with one hundred job applicants take twice the time needed for interviews with fifty, and closely supervising and reviewing the work of subordinates requires substantially more time if there are eight than if there are six. But even such administrative efforts permit savings with increasing size, which makes more efficient utili-

[24] The time management spends in external relations—negotiating with suppliers, unions, or the I.R.S.—is also affected less than proportionately by the organization's size, but the focus here is on internal administrative responsibilities.

zation of administrative personnel possible. A personnel officer may not be fully occupied in a small organization. Fewer employees with identical than with different duties can be supervised by one person. This makes it necessary for small organizations, which have only very few employees in some job categories, to assign fewer subordinates to supervisors than can large organizations.

The principle that the time involved in organizing the work of others is independent of limited differences in the amount of work being organized, though not of extreme differences, can explain the economy of scale in administration. If the volume of administrative work increases less than proportionately as the volume of operations increases, and if the volume of work governs the number of persons needed to accomplish it, in administration as well as in operations, it follows that the number of persons in administration increases less than that in operations; and hence that the proportion of administrative personnel decreases as the total number of employees increases, which is what the data show. The great power of top management of large organizations is an extreme instance of the same principle. A small handful of persons commanding large resources and empowered to formulate basic policies and to make the basic organizing decisions is able to direct the work of hundreds of thousands of employees and to exercise tremendous influence in the society.[25]

Significance of Heterogeneity.   The complex structure of interdependent parts resulting from differentiation creates problems of coordination and communication in work organizations. The horizontal differentiation of functions among subunits produces especially problems of coordination, because interdependent responsibilities must be integrated, and the vertical differentiation of authority intensifies primarily problems of communication, because differences in authority impede the free flow of communication. The administrative attention these problems of coordination and communication demand furnish a plausible reason for the empirical finding that more differentiated organizations employ more administrative personnel than less differentiated ones of the same size.

The question arises whether the influence of structural differentiation on administration cannot be explained by a principle consistent with that advanced to explain the influence of organizational size on administration. This principle—that the administrative effort of organizing work increases much less than in proportion to increases in the volume of work—makes an

[25] The earlier statement that the structural constraints of conditions in the organization greatly restrict the options of managers referred to decisions pertaining to the way work is organized and does not imply that management lacks power in determining basic policies and courses of action.

implicit assumption, namely, that the work being organized is fairly homogeneous. For the same organizing procedures cannot be applied to entirely dissimilar responsibilities. Different problems are involved in organizing the collection of unemployment taxes from employers, the disbursement of employment benefits to those entitled to them, and the provision of employment services. A single incentive system may not be suitable for clerical and for professional workers. The same procedure cannot be used to organize the manufacture of products and their sale.

A minimum of homogeneity characterizes work organizations. Department stores only sell retail merchandise, they do not collect taxes, instruct students, or treat the sick. What is more important, the larger an organization, the larger are its subunits with relatively homogeneous responsibilities.[26] The large segments with fairly homogeneous responsibilities in large work organizations are what reduces the proportion of administrative personnel in them, because the same procedures can be used to administer a large volume of responsibilities that are homogeneous. But if homogeneity lessens needed administrative effort, heterogeneity must expand it. Since structural differentiation increases the heterogeneity of responsibilities in an organization—among managerial levels as well as functional divisions and sections—it therefore is expected to enlarge its administrative personnel, which is what the data indicate.

Large size gives a work organization two instrumental advantages: a reduction in the proportion of personnel needed for administration, and an opportunity for extensive subdivision of work along various lines which facilitates operations. The subdivision of work that develops in large organizations produces simultaneously greater homogeneity within subunits of any given kind and greater heterogeneity among them. According to the theory, the former is expected to decrease and the latter to increase the administrative apparatus. Can the prediction of such opposite effects of one factor on another be empirically tested? It can, provided one is willing to make the assumption that organizational size, with number of different subunits in several dimensions controlled, represents within-unit homogeneity (as well as larger mean size of subunits) and that number of subunits, with size controlled, represents among-unit heterogeneity. Under these assumptions the empirical findings in Tables 18.3 and 18.4 conform to the predictions implied by the theory.

Dialectical processes seem to develop in work organizations with increasing size, which effect their administration in opposite ways. The progressive

---

[26] This is the case despite the greater number of subunits in larger organizations. The positive correlations between total organizational size and average size of subunits are discussed below and presented in Table 18.5.

differentiation of functions accompanying increasing size, which makes it possible for many employees to be organized and integrated in the common enterprise, increases both the homogeneity within and the heterogeneity among subunits. Since the administrative effort needed for organizing work depends on its heterogeneity, large organizational size, by promoting differentiation and thus homogeneity in one respect and heterogeneity in another, has opposite effects on administration, one mediated by the greater homogeneity within larger subunits, and the other by the heterogeneity among subunits. Thus processes of differentiation can be considered dialectical forces through which increasing organizational size, which generates these processes, reduces the administrative apparatus proportionately, on the one hand, and expands it, on the other. The process of administration, inasmuch as it involves organizing work by differentiating responsibilities, creates new administrative problems in the course of solving others, because differentiation engenders dialectical forces. The differentiation of functions in work organizations must be kept within bounds lest the administrative problems it creates outweigh the instrumental advantages it produces.

Feedback.   The administrative problems in the complex structures to which differentiation in organizations gives rise seem to have feedback effects that modify the influence of size on differentiation and on administration. One can think of these problems, from which feedback processes engendered by the heterogeneity among organizational subunits are inferred, in economic terms—the cost of large administrative overhead—or in sociological ones— the difficulty of coordinating many diverse subgroups. The reaction to administrative problems may be either resistance to the conditions that create them or adjustment to these conditions. Both apparently occur, perhaps in different organizations, perhaps in the same ones at different times or in different parts.

If administrative problems produced by differentiation along various lines in work organizations evoke resistance against further differentiation, the pressure of increasing size promoting differentiation must overcome increasing counterpressure from this resistance, similar to the growing counterpressure the force of a piston in a cylinder compressing a gas must overcome. Given the principle that the effect of increasing organizational size on differentiation arouses increasing resistance, it follows that the influence of a unit increment in size (say 500 employees) on differentiation declines as size, and with it differentiation, increases. This is what the data show, for all measures of differentiation, in all types of organizations under examination. A further implication is deducible. If the number of subunits (the measure of differentiation in any dimension) increases less rapidly than the total size of the organization, the average size of subunits (the ratio of total size to their number) must increase with increasing size. The data reveal very high positive correlations between total size and average subunit size in all cases (Table 18.5).

Instead of resisting differentiation, because it creates administrative problems, it can be adjusted to in organizations by enlarging the administrative apparatus. Since increasing organizational size effects reductions in the proportionate size of the administrative apparatus, such adjustments to the progressive differentiation it fosters must increasingly counteract these reductions. This implies that the effect of a given increment in size on the administrative apparatus, decreasing its proportionate size, declines as size increases, and with it differentiation, which is the pattern empirically observed. Thus the declining marginal influence of organizational size on both differentiation and administration can be interpreted in terms of feedback processes assumed to result from administrative problems differentiation causes.

Resistance to differentiation in organizations, which has been inferred to explain the diminishing influence of size on differentiation, can also help explain the economy of scale in administration, the net effect of large size reducing the proportion of administrative personnel. For the strong associations between total size and mean subunit size are attributable to this resistance. The greater the size of subunits among which responsibilities are divided, the larger are the segments of employees with relatively homogeneous duties. Inasmuch as homogeneity lessens the need for administrative personnel, according to the theory, the larger subunits with comparatively homogeneous duties resulting from the resistance that keeps the differentiation in large organizations within limits can be considered to be responsible

Table 18.5   Zero-Order Correlations between Total Size and Mean Size of Certain Subunits

	ES	LB	FD	DS	U and C	TH[a]
Divisions	.96	.76	.94	.76	.32	
Sections	.95			.51		
Levels[b]	.99	.98	.94	.98	.99	
Occupational specialties[c]	.94	.85	.30	.84	.77	
Branches	.65			.74		

[a] Not available.

[b] The number of personnel per level has no concrete meaning.

[c] In DS and in U and C, departments; otherwise, job titles.

for the proportionately smaller administrative apparatus in large than in small organizations.[27]

Conclusions

The major propositions of the theory advanced are summarized in deductive form. In doing so, explications and refinements of the theoretical propositions are ignored, and so are definitions and purely tautological statements. (For example, not included are such self-evident propositions as, "if a is virtually constant and b increases substantially, $a/(a + b)$ must decrease.") Nine theoretical assumptions or axioms (which are numbered) are used to deduce seven theorems or empirical propositions (designated by numbers preceded by a T). One additional empirically supported theorem is introduced for the derivations (T-0).

> T-0.   The larger the volume of work of a certain kind, the larger is the number of persons needed to perform it.

1.   If a common enterprise, including a work organization, depends on the social integration of its members.
2.   And if social integration of employees in a work organization, who do not share distinctive basic values or interests, requires the interdependence among heterogeneous small subunits of them.
3.   And if management is interested and capable of furthering effective operations.
4.   And if effective operations are promoted by the homogeneity of tasks within subunits.
5.   And if more homogeneity within subunits, more heterogeneity and interdependence among them, and their reduced size are all results of the progressive differentiation of functions.
6.   And if the degree of differentiation is limited by the organization's size (or number of employees, many being a necessary though not sufficient condition for much differentiation).

> T-1.   It follows that increasing organizational size promotes differentiation.

[27] Problems of multicollinearity (note the very high correlations in Table 18.5)make it meaningless to perform regression analyses of size on both mean size and number of subunits, which would provide a direct test of the theoretical assumption. All zero-order correlations between mean subunit size and the index of administrative apparatus are negative, but this is simply the result of the correlation of both variables with total size.

7. If the administrative investments involved in organizing work are largely independent of the amount of similar work being organized, so that the volume of administrative work, of which these investments are a part, increases less than proportionately as the volume of operation increases.

T-0. And if the number of employees depends on the volume of work (in administration as well as in operations).

    T-2. It follows that increasing size reduces the proportion of personnel in administration.

T-0. If the number of employees needed depends on the volume of work.

8. And if the volume of administrative work depends on the heterogeneity of responsibilities (for example, the heterogeneity among subunits, other things being equal).

5. And if heterogeneity among interdependent subunits (as well as other conditions) results from differentiation.

    T-3. It follows that differentiation, independent of other conditions, expands the proportion of personnel in administration.

T-0. If the number of employees needed depends on the volume of work.

8. And if the volume of administrative work depends on the heterogeneity of responsibilities (and hence inversely on their homogeneity).

5. And if both homogeneity within and heterogeneity among interdependent subunits results from differentiation.

T-1. And if the degree of differentiation depends on organizational size.

    T-4. It follows that increasing organizational size influences the proportion of administrative personnel in opposite ways: effecting reductions in it, mediated by the greater homogeneity within (larger)[28] subunits; and effecting expansions of it, mediated by the greater heterogeneity among more subunits.

9. If differentiation creates administrative problems that arouse resistance and require adjustment to it.

T-1. And if increasing size promotes differentiation.

---

[28] The larger size of subunits in larger organizations is for the time being assumed in the deductive formulation, since it has not yet been made part of it, but this theorem will be formally derived, and empirical evidence in support of it has been presented (Table 18.5).

        T-5.   It follows that the influence of increasing size on differentiation must overcome increasing resistance and hence declines.

    9.   If differentiation creates administrative problems that arouse resistance and require adjustment to it.

T-3.   And if (adjustment to) differentiation expands administrative personnel.

T-1.   And if increasing size promotes differentiation.

T-2.   And if increasing size reduces the proportion of personnel in administration.

        T-6.   It follows that the influence of increasing size on reductions in administrative personnel is more and more counteracted by the expansion of such personnel in the increasingly differentiated structure, and hence declines.

T-5.   If the number of relatively homogeneous subunits—the indicator of differentiation in a given dimension—increases at a declining rate with increasing size.

        T-7.   It follows that the mean size of these comparatively homogeneous subunits increases as the size of the organization does (which has been previously assumed, and which is a basic reason for the economy of scale in administration).

Author Index

Subject Index

Administrative apparatus, 2, 4, 10–11, 15–
16, 29, 30, 31, 34–35, 123, 124, 125,
218, 224, 226, 227, 229–230, 232,
235–236, 238–242, 251, 306, 308,
311–312, 314–317, 320–322, 324,
326, 328–331, 333, 340, 343–346
Administrative investments, 341–343
Administrative overhead, *see* Administrative
apparatus
Advice, *see* Consultation
Alienation, 52, 69, 107, 141, 177
Allegiance, *see* Loyalty
Anonymity, 109
Anxiety, 7, 73, 106, 139, 141–143, 160,
163–165, 167–168, 177, 178–180,
183–184, 185
Approachability, 192–202
Ascription, 13
Assembly line, 59–64, 73, 125, 234, 258
Association, *see* Interaction, social
Assumptions, about administration, 340–
346
about differentiation, 333–340
causal, 11, 264, 266, 326
functional, 31, 100, 123, 132, 133, 150–
151, 155, 156, 218, 242, 333, 336–337
methodological, 245
sociological, 25, 78, 264
theoretical, 11, 13, 48, 133, 134, 194–
195, 204–206, 220–221, 249–250, 289,
300, 302–304, 314–315, 346–348
Attitude, *see* Values
Attraction, 134, 184, 188–202, 205, 277–
278
Authority, bureaucratic and professional, 33,
48–49, 128, 230–232, 246–248, 250

centralized, 115, 126, 228–235, 240–241,
249–250
hierarchy, 3, 13, 15, 30, 31, 32, 117, 123,
124, 126, 223–224, 226, 227, 230, 231,
233, 241, 243–262, 301, 340, 342
impersonal, 19, 150, 223, 258, 260–262
and performance records, 151–152
and power, 17–20, 40–41, 51
source of, 49–53, 213
structure, 5, 34–36, 120, 159–160, 244,
245
Weber's theory of, 24, 30–32, 39–54, 122
see also Managerial ratio; Span of control;
Supervision
Automation, 4, 5, 114, 115, 118, 256, 257,
258, 260, 262, 285–286, 291, 292–293,
295, 296–297

Boundaries, 118, 208

Capitalism, 39, 45–47
Career, 31, 32, 45, 113, 117, 123, 124, 125,
193, 224
Case study, 4, 5–8, 23–24, 25–26, 33–36,
99–109, 120–121, 127, 131–134, 217,
223, 244, 280
examples of, 135–186
Caseworkers, 79–94, 96, 115–116, 133, 170–
186, 195–198
Centralization, *see* Authority, centralized
Change, 39, 65, 72–75, 134, 150, 176, 213–
214, 261, 338–339; *see also* Develop-
ment; Dynamics; and Revolution
Charisma, 18, 39, 42–45, 52
Chronological order, 4
Clients, 4, 17, 65, 70, 79–94, 104, 115–116,

F